From

BENARES TO BEIJING

Essays on

BUDDHISM

and

CHINESE RELIGION

From

BENARES TO BEIJING

Essays on

BUDDHISM

and

CHINESE RELIGION

IN HONOUR OF PROF. JAN YÜN-HUA

edited by

Koichi Shinohara

and

Gregory Schopen

MOSAIC PRESS

Oakville - New York - London

CANADIAN CATALOGUING IN PUBLICATION DATA

Main entry under title:

From Benares to Beijing : essays on Buddhism and Chinese religion

Includes bibliographical references.
ISBN 0-88962-444-5 (bound) ISBN 0-88962-443-7 (pbk.)

1. Buddhism - China - History. 2. Buddhism - India - History. 3. China - Religion - History. I. Shinohara, Koichi, 1941- II. Schopen, Gregory.

BQ632.F76 1992 294.3'0951 C92-093532-X

Published by MOSAIC PRESS, P.O. Box 1032, Oakville, Ontario, L6J 5E9, Canada. Offices and warehouse at 1252 Speers Road, Units #1 & 2, Oakville, Ontario, L6L 5N9, Canada.

Mosaic Press acknowledges the assistance of the Canada Council and the Ontario Arts Council in support of its publishing programme.

Cover Illustration & Design by Marion Black
Chinese characters by Grace Wang
Photograph of Dr. Jan by Anno Kazuki
Typeset by Innovative Computer Solutions, 626 South Mitchell, Bloomington, Indiana, 47401, U.S.A.

Printed and bound in Canada

MOSAIC PRESS:
In Canada:
MOSAIC PRESS, 1252 Speers Road, Units #1 & 2, Oakville, Ontario, L6L 5N9, Canada. Box 1032, Oakville Ontario, L6J 5E9

In the United States:
Distributed to the trade in the united States by: Kampmann National Book Network, Inc., 4720-A Boston Way, Lanham, M.D., 20706 USA

In the U.K.:
John Calder (Publishers) Ltd., 18 Brewer Street, London, W1R 4A5, England.

FROM BENARES TO BEIJING: ESSAYS ON BUDDHISM AND CHINESE RELIGIONS IN HONOUR OF PROF. JAN YÜN-HUA

Table of Contents

FROM BENARES TO BEIJING; IN HONOUR OF PROF. JAN YÜN-HUA

Preface

I do not remember when the idea of honoring Dr. Jan first occurred to us. It seems like it was simply always there—a thing we wanted to do for a respected teacher, an important colleague, and a delightful friend. We—Koichi Shinohara and myself—first talked about it in concrete terms, I think, in Tokyo almost ten years ago when Koichi was spending a sabbatical there and I a year at what is now called the International Institute for Buddhist Studies. A determined plan, of course, we did not have. A book of essays seemed fittingly traditional for a man who himself embodied the best Chinese traditions of the gentleman scholar, and who taught several of us both how to read—and even write—our own books.

Over the years, although we rarely had occasion for the long talks I so much enjoyed in Tokyo, whenever Koichi and I saw each other or talked on the phone, the "Jan Volume" always came up, and as Dr. Jan's retirement from full time teaching approached, the plans for the "Volume" began to take more and more definite shape. Koichi, as the elder and more responsible partner in the enterprise, saw to that. It was he who very largely took upon himself the organizational tasks, having—I suspect—some justifiable suspicions in regard to my talents in that area. It was he who kept the project on track and moving. I licked envelopes and tried to keep up with him.

His task, in part at least, was made easier by the response of Dr. Jan's colleagues, students and friends who willingly—though often under pressures which beset academic life—agreed or volunteered to participate in the project. Our initial letter seeking contributors brought forth a warm and wide response. We received promises of papers or—when that was not possible—expressions of admiration, respect, and good wishes for Dr. Jan as a scholar and a person. And these came, quite literally, from all over the world. We were not surprised.

Typical of the initial response was a letter on stationery bearing the letterhead of the École pratique des hautes études in Paris written by Professor Guang-da Zhang, Professor of History at Peking University. It said, in part:

> "Thank you very much for your letter of January 4th, 1988, which I was so pleased to receive. I have greatly appreciated the privilege of being listed among the contributors to the volume to be presented to Dr. Jan on the occasion of his retirement. I am happy to express my deep gratitude to you for giving me the opportunity to offer my respect to a truly outstanding scholar. In view of his knowledge and experience, we have every reason to attach great importance to his academic contributions and achievements."

Professor Zhang's paper was to be an essay on the Buddhist monasteries of the region of Khotan in the fifth to tenth centuries A.D., a paper which we very much looked forward to. But—in a way that could only remind us of Professor Jan's life too—distant political events intervened. We had to go to press without professor Zhang's paper.

By early June of 1988 we had in hand a table of contents for the volume which we were able to present to Dr. Jan at a luncheon held in his honor in Ancaster, Ontario. It was a large gathering—family, colleagues, former students, and friends—and, typical of everything connected with Dr. Jan, a good deal of fun. We, again, were not surprised.

What was said on that occasion made clear to all—as we hope the present volume will as well—how much we owe to a fine scholar, a great teacher, and a very good friend.

G.S.

Professor Jan Yün-Hua: A Biographical Sketch and Bibliography of his Published Work

Dr. Jan was born on March 15, 1923 in Szuchan, China. As a young man he attended Szechwan University, graduating with a B.A. in 1948. His education continued, however, not in his native land. He, like Hsüan-tsang his famous countryman—but in very different circumstances—found himself journeying to the West, to India where he lived—and developed his unique English accent—until 1967. He completed his M.A. at Visva-Bharati University in 1955, and continued to work there, first as a Research Fellow from 1955-58, then as the Assistant Librarian in Charge of the Chinese Collection from 1958-64, all the while working as well on his Ph.D. He completed his dissertation in 1964 and was awarded the Ph.D. from the same university. For three years, then, he held the position of Lecturer in Chinese Studies at Visva-Bharati.

Dr. Jan, having finished his formal education was—this time unlike Hsüan-tsang—not able to return home. In fact his journey west was to be considerably more extensive. It would take him to Hamilton, Ontario where, in 1967, he was named an Assistant Professor in the Department of Religious Studies at McMaster University. By 1974 he was a full Professor there; by 1976, the chairman of the Department. Over the years he was also a Visiting Fellow at the Institute of Oriental Culture at the University of Tokyo (1974), and at Clare Hall, Cambridge (1981). Finally in 1987 he taught, as Visiting Professor, at Beijing University. He retired from full-time teaching at McMaster in 1988.

Like his life and travels, Dr. Jan's publications are extensive and—in several senses of the expression—cover a good deal of ground. It is interesting to note that at least two recurring themes appear in his work. The first of these themes is the connection with and experience of India by foreigners from the Far East—Dr. Jan returned again and again to work on Hui-Ch'ao's *Record*. The second concerns attempts by Chinese Buddhists to see order and system in the Buddhism they received and developed from India—his equally persistent fascination with Tsung-mi. But there is, of course, much else as well. We need do little else than append a list of his publications. They speak for themselves.

The Published Works of Dr. Jan Yün-Hua

BOOKS:

A Chronicle of Buddhism in China 581-906 A.D. Santiniketan: Visva-Bharati Research Publications, 1967.

Word-picture of a Chinese Painter, two chapters from the Autobiographical Account of Ch'i Pai-shih (1862-1957). Santiniketan: Visva-Bharati Quarterly Booklet, 1965.

Vicissitudes of Buddhism in China, (Ph.D. Thesis, Visva-Bharati University, 1963).

Buddhist Religion in the T'ang Period, with Special Reference to India, (M.A. Thesis, Visva-Bharati University, 1955).

The Hye Ch'o Diary: Memoir of the Pilgrimage to the Five Regions of India. Translated by Jan Yün-Hua and Yang Han-Sung, ed. by S. Iida (Berkeley: Asian Humanities Press, 1984). Unesco Collection of Representative Works.

Tsung-mi (in Chinese), (Taipei: Tung-da Tu-shu, 1988).

PARTS OF BOOKS:

"Ch'uan-fa-yuan, The Imperial Institute for the Translation of Buddha-Dharma in the Sung China", in *Studies in Asian History and Culture*, ed. Buddha Prakash. Meerut: Meenaksh Prakashan, 1970, 70-93.

"Dimensions of Indian Buddhism", in *Malalasekera Commemoration Volume*, ed. O.H. De A. Wijesekera, Colombo, 1976, 157-170.

"Pandita", in *Dictionary of Ming Biography 1368-1644*, ed. L.D. Goodrich, C.Y. Fang, New York: Columbia University Press, 1976, 1111-1113.

Five Articles: "Ch'i-sung", "Chih-li", "Chih-p'an", "Li P'ing-shan", "Tsan-ning", in *Sung Biographies*, ed. Herbert Franke, *Münchener Ostasiatische Studien, Band* 16, 1 Wisebaden: Franz Steinder Verlag GMBH, 1976, 185-194, 221-227, 227-230. Band 16, 2 577-582. Band 16, 3 1040-1046.

"Ch'an Buddhism as Understood by Tsung-mi" (in Chinese) in *Essays Presented to Reverend Tao-an on his 70th Birthday*, ed. Chang Man-t'ao. Taipei: Shih-tzu-hou Yueh-k'an, 1976, 109-131.

"Antagonism among the Religious Sects and Problems of Buddhist Tolerance", in *Buddhism and the Modern World*, ed. Lee, Sun Keun and Rhi, Ki Yong. Seoul: Dongguk University, 1977, 93-101.

"Tsung-mi's Theory of the Comparative Investigation (k'an-hui) of Buddhism", in *Korean and Asian Religious Tradition*, ed. A. Yu, Toronto, 1977, 11-24.

Notes on *Hsin-chin wen-chi* and on *Tsan-liao chi*, in *A Sung Bibliography*, ed. Y. Hervouet. Hong Kong: The Chinese University, 1978, 386-404.

"Li P'ing-shan and his Refutation of Neo-Confucian Criticism of Buddhism", *Developments in Buddhist Thought: Canadian Contributions to Buddhist Studies*, ed. Roy C. Amore, Waterloo: CSSR, 1979, 162-193.

"A Ninth Century Chinese Classification of Indian Mahayana", in *Studies in Pali and Buddhism: A Memorial Volume in Honour of Bhikkhu Jagdish Kashyap*, editor, A.K. Narain, assistant editor, L. Zwilling. Delhi: B.R. Publ. Corp.; New Delhi: distributed by D.K. Publishers' distributors, 1979, 171-182.

"The Bodhisattva Idea in Chinese Literature: Typology and Significance", in *The Bodhisattva Doctrine in Buddhism*, ed. L.S. Kawamura. Waterloo: Wilfrid Laurier University Press, 1981, 125-152.

"The Chinese Buddhist Wheel of Existence and Deliverance", in *Studies in Indian Philosophy* (Sukhlalji Volume), Ahmedabad, 1981, 165-180.

"Chinese Buddhism in Ta-tu: The New Situation and the New Problems", in *Yüan Thought: Chinese Thought and Religion Under the Mongols*, ed. Hok-lam Chan, Wm. T. de Bary. New York: Columbia University Press, 1982, 375-417.

"Seng-ch'ou's Method of *Dhyana*", in *Early Ch'an in China and Tibet*, ed. L. Lancaster, W. Lai. Berkeley: Asian Humanities Press, 1983, 51-63.

"Confucian Tradition and Modernity: A Dilemma on Both Sides", in *Modernity and Responsibility: Essays for George Grant*, Ed. Eugene Combs. Toronto: University of Toronto Press, 1983, 62-73.

"Rājadharma Ideal in Yogācāra Buddhism", in *Religion and Society in Ancient India: Sudhakar Chattopadhyaya Commemoration Volume*, ed. by P. Jash. Calcutta, Roy & Chowdhury, 1984, 221-234.

"Buddhist Literature", "Ch'an yü-lu", "Kao-seng chuan", in the *Indiana Companion to Traditional Chinese Literature*, ed. by William H. Nienhauser, Jr. et al. Bloomington: Indiana University Press, 1986, 1-12, 201-203, 474-476.

"The Chinese Understanding and Assimilation of Karma Doctrine", in *Karma and Rebirth: Post Classical Development*, ed. by R. W. Neufeldt. Albany: State University of New York Press, 1986, 145-167.

"The Search for the Origin of Man: A Philosophical Debate in 9th Century China", (in Chinese) in *Chung-kuo wen-hua yü chung-kuo che-hsüeh*, ed. by Tang Yijie. Beijing: Dong-Fang, 1986, 470-90.

"Fa-hsien", "I-ching" and "T'ai-hsü", in *Encyclopedia of Religion* ed. by M. Eliade. New York: Macmillan, 1987, vols. 5, 245-46; 6, 574-75; and 14, 249-50.

"Portraits and Self-portrait: A Case Study of Biographical and Autobiographical Records of Tsung-mi", in *Monks and Magicians: Religious Biographies in Asia* Ed. by P. Granoff and K. Shinohara. Oakville, Ont.: Mosaic Press, 1988, 229-246.

"Mind, Existence and Liberation: Religious Philosophy of Tsung-mi", in the *Amalā Prajñā: Aspects of Buddhist Studies*. Ed. by N. H. Samtani. Delhi: Indian Books Center, 1989, 413-418.

"Recent Chinese Research Publications on Religious Studies", contributed to the forthcoming book, the *Turning of the Tide: Religion in China Today* ed. by

Professor Julian Pas (the Royal Asiatic Society, Hong Kong Branch. 1989), pp. 25-42.

ARTICLES:

"Traces of Ancient Indian Music in China", *The Journal of the Music Academy* (Madras) XXVIII (1957) 92-99.

"The Development of Chinese Organization for the Translation of Buddhist Canons", XIX A11 Indian Oriental Conference, Delhi, 1957.

"On Chinese Translation of Avatamsakasutra", *The Orissa Historical Research Journal* (Bhubaniswar) VII (1958-59) 125-132.

"Kashmir's Contribution to the Expansion of Buddhism to the Far East", *Indian Historical Quarterly* (Calcutta) XXXVII (1961) 93-104.

"Hui-ch'ao's Record on Kashmir", *Kashmir Research Biannual* (Srinagar) II (1961) 115-124.

"Western India according to Hui-ch'ao", *Indian Historical Quarterly* (Calcutta) XXXIX (1963) 27-37.

"Fotsu T'ungchi, a Biographical and Bibliographical Study", *Oriens Extremus* (Wiesbaden) X (1963) 61-82.

"Hui-ch'ao and His Works, a Reassessment", Indo-Asian Culture (New Delhi) XII (1964) 177-190.

"Buddhist Historiography in Sung China", *Zeitschrift der Morgenländischen Gesellschaft* (München) CXIV (1964) 360-381.

"Buddhist Self-immolation in Medieval China", *History of Religions* (Chicago) IV (1965) 243-268.

"Some New Light on Kusinagara from the Memoirs of Hui-ch'ao", *Oriens Extremus* (Wiesbaden) XII (1965), 55-63.

"Pandita Sahajasri, a Forgotten Torchbearer of Indian Culture", (translated into and published in Hindi by the Editor of) *Visva-bharati Patrika* (Santiniketan) VIII/2 (1967) 93-103.

"Korean Record on Varanasi and Sarnath", *Vishveshvaranand Indological Journal* (Hoshiapur) IV (1966) 264-272.

"Buddhist Relations between India and Sung China", *History of Religions* (Chicago) VI (1966-67) 24-42, 135-168.

"Some Fresh Reflections on Yasovarma of Kanauj and Muktapāda of Kashmir", *Journal of Indian History* (Karela) XLV (1967) 161-179.

"A Sketch of Buddhist Funeral", *Concilium: Liturgy* No. 4 (Holland) (1968) 74-76. (Translated into several European languages.)

"South India in the VIII Century A.D.", *Oriens Extremus* XV/2 (1968) 169-177.

"Gandhi's Contribution to Religion", *Special Supplement in Honour of Gandhi, Centenary* (May 1969) 1-4.

"Nāgārjuna: One or More", *History of Religions* X (1970) 139-155.

"Nāgārjunakoṇḍa, Note on a New Reference from Chinese Source", *Journal of Indian History* XLVIII/2 (1970) 415-426.

"Beckettian Heroes in Buddhist Eyes", *Annual Proceedings of Canadian Society for the Study of Religion* (1971) 59ff.

"Tsung-mi, His Analysis of Ch'an Buddhism", *T'oung Pao, archives concernant l'histoire, les langues, la géographie, l'ethnographie et les arts de l'Asie orientale* (Leiden) LVIII/1 (1972) 1-54.

"Tibetans in Northwest India during the VIIIth Century A.D.", Golden Jubilee Volume, *Journal of Indian History*, 81-96.

"Le livre dans les grandes religions—Les religions chinoises", *Dossiers Parole et Mission, Nous, gens de la bible* 4 (1972) 74-77.

"The Discovery and the Identification of the Earliest Extant Printed Edition of Ch'an-yüan chu-chuan-chi Tu-hsü", (in Chinese) *The Eastern Miscellany* (Taiwan, Taipei) N.S. 8/2 (1974) 37-40.

"Gosamban and its Contribution to the Preservation of Chinese Literature", (in Chinese) *The Eastern Miscellany*, N.S. 8/4 (1974) 37-40.

"Two Problems concerning Tsung-mi's Compilation of Ch'an tsang", *Transactions of the International Conference of Orientalists in Japan* XIX (1974) 37-47.

"Problems of Tao and Tao Te Ching", *Numen* XXII (1975) 208-234.

"A Study of Hui-ch'ao's Record on Central India" (in Chinese), *Studies on Tun-huang* (Hong Kong) II (1976) 80-100.

"The Silk Manuscripts on Taoism", *T'oung Pao* LXIII (1977) 65-84.

"Conflict and Harmony of Ch'an and Buddhism", *Journal of Chinese Philosophy* IV (1977) 287-302.

"The Power of Recitation", *Studi Storico Religiosi* (Rome) I (1977) 289-299.

"Mu-sang and His Philosophy of No-thought", in the *Proceedings of the Vth International Symposium* of *The National Academy of Sciences*, Republic of Korea (Seoul, 1978) 55-86.

"The Encounter between Ch'an Buddhists and the Tibetan Lamas at Yüan Court" (A Chinese translation of the article has been published in *Fo-Kuang Hsüeh-pao*) No. 4 (Taiwan, 1979) 163-171; English Version in *Contribution of Buddhism to World Thought and Culture*, ed. W. Thakur (Bodhgaya, 1980) 3-18.

"A Biographical Study of Monk Mu-sang (694-762)", *Studies on Tun-huang* (Hong Kong) IV (1979) 47-60.

"Tsung-mi's Questions Regarding the Confucian Absolute", *Philosophy East and West* 30/4 (1980) 495-504.

"A Buddhist Critique to the Classical Chinese Philosophy", *Journal of Chinese Philosophy* 7 (1980) 301-318.

"Tao, Principle and Law: Three Key Concepts in the Yellow Emperor Taoism", *Journal of Chinese Philosophy* 7 (1980) 205-228.

"Tao Yuan or Tao the Origin", *Journal of Chinese Philosophy* 7 (1980) 195-204.

"A Study of the Questions and Answers between Master Tsung-mi and the Laymen", *The Hwakang Buddhist Journal* 4 (1980) 132-166.

"The Mind as the Buddha-nature: Concept of Absolute in Ch'an Buddhism", *Philosophy East and West* 31 (1981) 467-477.

"Master Hai-yun's Thought and Ch'an Method": (in Chinese) *The Hwakang Buddhist Journal* (Taipei) 5 (1981) 37-55.

"Tun-huang Documents on Seng-ch'ou (480-560) and his Method of Meditation" (in Chinese), *The Hwakang Buddhist Journal* 6 (1983) 73-103.

"A Study of Ch'ou-ch'an-shih i" (in Chinese), *Studies on Tun-huang* VI (1983) 69-85.

"Political Philosophy of the *Shih-liu ching* attributed to the Yellow Emperor Taoism", *Journal of Chinese Philosophy* X (1983) 205-228.

"The Change of Images: The Yellow Emperor in Ancient Chinese Literature", *Journal of Oriental Studies* (Hong Kong), vol. XIX (1981), 117-137 (Published in 1984).

"A Study of the Transmission Characteristics of Buddhist Meditation in Early China" (in Chinese), *The Hwakang Buddhist Journal* vol. 7 (1984), 63-99.

"Two Tun-huang manuscripts of the Northern Ch'an School of Buddhism", (in Chinese) *Studies in Tun-huang* vol. VIII (1984), 1-9.

"The Religious Situation and the Study of Buddhism and Taoism in China: An Incomplete and Imbalanced Picture", *Journal of Chinese Religions* vol. XII (1985), 37-64.

"The Concept of No-thought in Tun-huang manuscripts" (in Chinese) *Studies of Tun-huang* vol. IX (1985), 1-13.

"Hsüan-tsang, his Relationship with Emperor T'ang and his Political Ideals" (in Chinese) *The Hwakang Buddhist Journal* vol. VIII (1985), 135-157.

"Note on P'u-chi (651-739): The Master of the Northern School of Ch'an Buddhism", *Studies on Tun-huang* 10 (1985), 1-8.

"Cultural Borrowing and Religious Identity: A Case Study of the Taoist Religious Codes", *Chinese Studies* vol. 4 (1986), 281-295.

"A Study of *Ta-ch'eng ch'an-men yao-lu*. Its Significance and Problems", *Journal of Chinese Studies* vol. IV (1986), 533-47.

"A Reexamination of the Lineage of the Ch'an Buddhist School given by Tsung-mi" (in Chinese), *Chunghwa Buddhist Journal* (Taipei) vol. I, 43-57.

"On the Importance of *Ch'an-yüan chu-ch'uan-chi tu-hsü* to the History of Chinese Thought", (in Chinese), *Studies on Tunhuang* XII (1987), 5-12.

"Patterns of Chinese Assimilation to Buddhist Thought: A Comparative Study of No-thought (*wu-nien*) in Indian and Chinese Texts", *Journal of Oriental Studies* XXIV (1986), 21-36.

"Fa-chi and Chinul's understanding of Tsung-mi", *Pojosasang* ("Pojo's Thought"), 2 (1989), 157-184.

CHAPTERS OF BOOKS OR ARTICLES IN PRESS:

"A Biography of Hai-yun (1203-1257)" accepted for publication in the International Project of *Yüan Biographical History*, ed. I. de Rachewiltz.

"The Huang-Lao Method of Taoism", contributed to *Taoist Spirituality*, ed. Wei-ming Tu (Crossroad Press).

"The Bridge Between Man and Cosmos: The Philosophical Foundation of Music in the *T'ai-p'ing ching*", *Proceedings of the Symposium on the Studies of Taoist Ritual and Music*, Hong Kong Chinese University.

"Human Nature and Its Cosmogonic Root in the Huang-Lao Taoism", *Journal of Chinese Philosophy*.

"Taoist Silk Manuscripts and Early Legalist Thought: A Preliminary Examination of Selected Passages", contributed to the *C.C.Shih Festschrift* ed. by Julia Ching, to be published by the University of Toronto Press.

"A New Study on the Formation and Evolution of Buddhist Popular Discourse (*su-chiang*)" (in Chinese), to be published in Proceedings of the International Conference on Dunhuang and Turfan Studies, Hong Kong Chinese University.

"A Case Study of the Wall-painting: 'Mara's Assault and Temptation of the Bodhisattva' found in Dunhuang and Ajanta", contributed to the International Conference on Dunhuang Grottoes Arts held in 1987, to be published by the Dunhuang Research Institute.

"The Chinese Critique and Absorption of Vijñānavādin Ideas: A Case Study of Tsung-mi", Contributed to the volume of *Essays in Honor of Professor Jao Tsung-i* (Hong Kong, forthcoming)

"Patterns of Chinese Assimilation of the Buddhist Concept of Cessation and Insight as Presented in the Mo-ho chih-kuan", *Proceedings of the International Conference on Chinese Religions* (Beijing, forthcoming).

Buddhaghoṣa's Penance and Siddhasena's Crime: Remarks on Some Buddhist and Jain Attitudes Towards the Language of Religious Texts

Phyllis Granoff
McMaster University

I. Introduction: The Philosophical Context of Buddhist and Jain Attitudes Toward Language

Early in its history Indian philosophy developed a concept of a "sacred language", a language appropriate to matters of ritual. Eventually the concept would be extended to require that the ritually correct language should also be the only language in which serious philosophical discussion should be held. To use that language incorrectly moreover involved sin, as did any other infraction of the strict rules governing ritual. The language was Sanskrit and its correct usage was determined by the instructions on grammar given by the grammarians. The most vociferous proponents of the viewpoint that there exists only one language, the Sanskrit language, which was to be used for ritual were naturally the grammarians and after them the Mīmāṃsakas.[1]

The exact parameters of the discussion often vary; the grammarians tended to prefer the more radical view that Sanskrit must be used at all times, even outside of a ritual context, while the Mīmāṃsakas were content to restrict the necessary use of Sanskrit to the sphere of ritual. In any case, both groups were agreed in arguing that Sanskrit was the only language that was capable of making its meaning known directly; it was therefore the only "true" language capable of directly fulfilling the function that we expect of a language, to communicate meaning. In the viewpoint of the grammarians and the Mīmāṃsakas Sanskrit was the *mūlabhāṣya*, the "root language" or "primary language". Its forms, as fixed by grammar, were invariant and so could be learned by children through observation. A child hearing a Sanskrit word on a number of occasions and watching the behaviour of the speaker and listener could infer the meaning of a Sanskrit word and then understand it correctly the next time it appeared in conversation. Other languages were regarded as misusages of Sanskrit, *apabhraṃśa*, deviations from the correct form, and in fact were seen to be variable. Learning these languages was made problematic in the theory of the grammarians precisely because the individual words exhibited infinite variety; hearing a word even a few times could not insure that a child would understand it in a new context; indeed, the chances were great that the word the child heard in the learning situation would not be used in precisely that form again. The only way these other languages could make known their meaning, under this theory, was through the intermediary of a fixed and invariable Sanskrit word which a listener would call to mind on hearing the aberrant non-Sanskrit term.

While it is possible to maintain that the notion of Sanskrit as the exclusive ritual language was developed independently of the lively debates between the Mīmāṃsakas and grammarians on the one hand, and other religious groups in India on the other hand, it is not difficult to see that their insistence on the use of Sanskrit as a sacred language would affect very greatly at least two other groups who did not use Sanskrit for their religious writings, the Buddhists and the Jains.[2] Even in their canonical texts, and more elaborately in the commentaries to the various *suttas* and other post-canonical writings, the Jains emphatically assert that local languages are as valid and as direct indicators of meaning as is Sanskrit. Indeed a late text states that only a person who is conversant in many local languages should be appointed to a leading position amongst the monks.[3] The sin that accrues to a person for the misuse of language has nothing to do with the language that is being spoken, but concerns the speaker's intention and the effects his words have on another. Thus cruel speech and lies bring sin, and not the fact that the language spoken is a language other than Sanskrit.[4] The Jains also directly counter the Mīmāṃsakas and grammarians in philosophical debates, where they argue cogently that the position of the grammarians and ritualists that only Sanskrit makes known its meaning directly is not logically demonstrable. They also mockingly offer that to insist that failure to use Sanskrit entails sin and correct use of Sanskrit implies merit could have unexpected results; a Sanskrit statement to kill a Brahmin would lead to merit while a Prakrit statement to give gifts to a Brahmin would be sinful! In addition medieval Jain philosophers counter that if there is a root language that is a primary denotator of meaning, that language is not Sanskrit at all, but Prakrit.[5] The Jains would also seem to have practiced what they preached, for throughout their history they used both vernacular languages and Sanskrit for religious purposes.

The Buddhists, like the Jains, also allowed the use of languages other than Sanskrit for religious texts and rituals.[6] And like the Jains their philosophers argued against the Mīmāṃsakas and the grammarians who spoke of one single ritual language and insisted that it be Sanskrit. Dharmakīrti, in his *Vādanyāya*, argues that all languages, Sanskrit, Prakrit, Apabhraṃśa, Dravidian, Andhran, function in exactly the same way to make known their meaning. All require that there exist a common understanding that a given word has a specific meaning and that a listener be familiar with the linguistic conventions of a particular language in order to derive meaning from it. Dharmakīrti also rejects the notion that speaking any particular language is meritorious while the use of some other language is inherently sinful.[7]

Both the Jains and Buddhists, then, give evidence for their rejection of the notion of a single sacred language, of the concept that Sanskrit is especially privileged because it alone of all languages functions directly to make known its meaning, and of the theory that some language is by nature meritorious while others are by nature wicked. These assertions amount to a thorough attack on the Mīmāṃsakas and grammarians, with their emphasis on the necessary use of Sanskrit in ritual, and other orthodox schools like the Naiyāyikas who followed them on this point.

The sources for the study of Buddhist and Jain attitudes towards language are many. To date scholars on the Buddhist side seem to have concentrated on passages in the canon and its commentaries, while Jain scholarship, particularly in the editing of the relevant texts, has also examined the philosophical context for Jain attitudes towards vernaculars. There is one other source of information about Buddhist and Jain attitudes towards language that has not yet been explored in any depth in this connection. This is religious biography, particularly the biographies of Siddhasena on the Jain side and of Buddhaghoṣa on the Buddhist side. Examining these biographies in fact suggests that while a reading of the Buddhist philosopher Dharmakīrti and the Jain philosopher Prabhācandra would lead to the conclusion that the Jains and Buddhists thought very much alike on the question of language, in fact at least some members of each community would not have agreed with each other. For in the stories told of him, Siddhasena is said to have sinned for wishing to translate the Jain sacred writings into Sanskrit, the language that the dominant group in India regarded as the sacred language par excellence, and he must undergo a penance for this outrage against the Jain faith. By contrast, one of Buddhaghoṣa's most celebrated deeds is that he rendered the commentaries that existed in Śrī Laṅkā in the local vernacular into Māgadhī, which we shall see some Buddhists regarded as the root language, and above all the sacred language of Buddhism. In some versions of the biography Buddhaghoṣa even goes so far as to burn the Sinhalese books. If Dharmakīrti could argue that all languages were equal and no one language had any special status, it is nonetheless evident that the biography of Buddhaghoṣa reveals a very different attitude towards language. One language is privileged; it is no longer Sanskrit, but the attitude towards language in general revealed by Buddhaghoṣa's biography is far closer to the attitude of the orthodox Mīmāṃsaka than to anything in the Buddhist or Jain tradition. This paper will look at the biographies of Buddhaghoṣa and Siddhasena and then conclude with some remarks about Buddhist and Jain views of language and the appropriateness of the stories the two traditions told of two of their most distinguished scholars.

II. The Biographies of Siddhasena and Buddhaghoṣa

Accounts of Siddhasena may be found in a number of Śvetāmbara sources. His biography figures in all of the major *prabandhas* and in some didactic story collections. To my knowledge the earliest written source is either the didactic story collection, the commentary of Āmradevasūri to the *Ākhyānakamaṇikośa*, which was written in 1134 A.D., or Bhadreśvara's *Kahāvali*, which may be as early as the twelfth century and which is somewhere in between a biography collection and a didactic story collection. Both of these texts are in Prakrit, while the later *prabandha* collections are in Sanskrit. My comments here shall be based on the text of Rājaśekharasūri in his Sanskrit *Prabandhakośa*, which is dated 1349 A.D. The incident of Siddhasena wishing to put the Jain sacred writings into Sanskrit is a central incident in all of the extant versions of his biography and is told in much the same manner in all of these accounts.[8]

Siddhasena is introduced to the reader as an arrogant Brahmin, extremely proud of his learning, and particularly adept in speaking Sanskrit. From the beginning the biography makes the question of language its central preoccupation. Siddhasena has made the rash pronouncement that he will become the disciple of anyone who defeats him in debate. He has heard of the great prowess of the Jain monk Vṛddhavādin and he rushes to confront him. Siddhasena meets Vṛddhavādin on the road and immediately challenges him to debate. Not averse to such a contest, Vṛddhavādin nonetheless hesitates, for a debate needs learned witnesses and indeed learned judges. Siddhasena, for his part, is unperturbed. He suggests that they take the village cowherds as their audience and that they allow them to settle the question of which of them will triumph. Vṛddhavādin agrees and Siddhasena, right there in the midst of a cow-pasture, begins to discourse elegantly in Sanskrit. He goes on and on, but at last when he finally falls silent, the cowherds have a chance to vent their disapproval. "The cowherds all said, 'He doesn't know anything. All he's done is to grunt and groan and shout and scream and give us a good earache. Who needs him?'" They turn to Vṛddhavādin, who always knew what any occasion demanded. He girded-up his loins, we are told, and began to sing in a wonderfully melodious voice, with a tune that was particularly popular amongst cowherds, and of course, not in Sanskrit but in their local dialect. That Vṛddhavādin had hit the right note in more than one sense is amply clear from the text, as it says,

"The cowherds were enraptured. They said, 'Vṛddhavādin truly knows everything. Why, just see how fine he sings!' And they made fun of Siddhasena, saying, 'Siddhasena talks rubbish.'"

And so it came to be that Siddhasena converted to Jainism. In keeping with his initial vow to become the disciple of the person who could best him in debate, he becomes the disciple of Vṛddhavādin and becomes a Jain monk.

The contest between Vṛddhavādin and Siddhasena has nothing to do with the content of their statements; it is decided on the basis of how they present their remarks. Siddhasena fails because he inappropriately speaks Sanskrit to the cowherds, and Vṛddhavādin triumphs because he correctly addresses the villagers in their own idiom, in their own vernacular dialect and in a style of oral performance that is accompanied by music and dance.[9] But Siddhasena will have much to endure before he is finally completely weaned from his yearning for Sanskrit and the Sanskrit intellectual tradition. This only comes through a series of incidents.

In the service of a king, Siddhasena falls victim to the seductive charms of the courtly culture. People begin to speak ill of the monk who is so fond of secular comforts, and his old teacher Vṛddhavādin comes to know of Siddhasena's close association with the royal court and his laxity as a monk. Vṛddhavādin goes in disguise to enlighten Siddhasena and the way in which he chooses to bring his erring disciple back to his senses is again critical. He uses in effect the same tool he had first used against the arrogant Brahmin Siddhasena. He recites before him an elementary Prakrit verse. Siddhasena fails to understand the verse, which in itself is surprising, and that leads him to infer that all is not as it seems. The man he has before him is no ordinary man; it is none other than his teacher Vṛddhavādin.

The odd fact that someone who is so learned would fail to understand such a simple verse also leads the reader to infer that what is happening here is not all that it seems, either. Defeat or victory have nothing to do with the content of statements made or with intelligence; the speaker of Sanskrit simply loses out to the speaker of Prakrit as we saw was exactly the case in the initial encounter between Siddhasena and Vṛddhavādin that had led to Siddhasena's conversion to Jainism.

Once more Siddhasena is abruptly shaken from his complacency and once more he follows Vṛddhavādin, the Jain monk and Prakrit speaker, from the court of the king, who was always regarded in classical India as the champion of the elite, Sanskritic culture.

Siddhasena's conversion from Sanskrit to Prakrit, however, is far from complete. The clash between Siddhasena, the representative of Sanskrit culture, and the Jain community, the champions of vernacular learning, must openly take place one more time before the two groups can find some common ground for compromise. This will take place in an incident that is usually placed near the end of Siddhasena's biography. The incident makes explicit what the biography had implied this far, namely that Siddhasena champions Sanskrit over Prakrit and that this is his flaw.

One day Siddhasena summons the members of the Jain community and offers to put all of the Jain sacred writings into Sanskrit. His fellow monks are furious at the suggestion. The text tells us, "They said, 'Do you think that the Great and Glorious Founders of the Faith, the Tīrthaṃkaras, and the monks who led the community after them only wrote their works in Ardha Māgadhī because they were incapable of writing them in Sanskrit? In speaking like this you have committed a grave offense that demands a grave penance.'" Siddhasena then agrees to accept a severe penance; he will wander incognito, not bearing the external marks of a Jain monk, the gauze over his mouth or the broom, and disguised as a Śaiva ascetic. The completion of his penance occurs when he performs a miracle in the presence of King Vikramāditya of Ujjain. Siddhasena causes the *liṅga* of Mahākāla to split open and an image of the Jain Tīrthaṃkara Pārśvanātha to appear. The instrument of his magic is his skill in language; Siddhasena recites some verses and the *liṅga* splits. It was commonly believed that certain words, particularly the words of hymns, carry magical powers.[10] But the text that Siddhasena recites was not in fact primarily a hymn. It is indeed in Sanskrit, but the *Dvātriṃśikā* is on the whole an extremely abstruse and difficult text of philosophy. I understand that this incident in a crucial way resolves the tension that the biography has been building up between Prakrit/ Jainism on the one hand and Sanskrit/ royal court/ Brahmins on the other. Siddhasena has done his penance for wanting to put the Jain sacred writings into Sanskrit. He performs a miracle at the end of that penance, reciting a text that is in Sanskrit, but which derives its power not from its erudition and its philosophical content, which may be considered a part of the learned Sanskrit culture, but from the magical force of all sacred words. Siddhasena may use Sanskrit now that he understands it has no privileged status.[11]

The incident concludes when King Vikramāditya is converted to Jainism and Siddhasena is welcomed back by the Jain community. But lest we think that Siddhasena is once more seduced into remaining with a king and enjoying the culture of the court, the text adds an incident in which Siddhasena cleverly manipulates the king to gain a favour for the Jain community and then states that Siddhasena voluntarily welcomed death, ending his career as a pious Jain monk.

This biography of Siddhasena, then, is centered around a conflict between language that is made clear at the very outset. Siddhasena the Brahmin, the elegant speaker of Sanskrit, must humble himself before the Jain monk, Vṛddhavādin, the singer of simple rustic Prakrit verses. In this initial incident, Sanskrit as the language of debate takes second place to Prakrit as the best means of communication. This victory for Prakrit that begins the biography is then extended; a Prakrit verse again triumphs when Siddhasena is at the court of a king and has become too involved in courtly culture for a Jain monk. Vṛddhavādin awakens Siddhasena to his duties with a simple Prakrit stanza. Here Prakrit is victorious over secular Sanskrit learning. Finally, in the episode where Siddhasena desires to put the Jain canon into Sanskrit there is no contest; it is stated at once outright that this is an offense against the Jain religion. Prakrit is also the language suited for religious texts. A compromise is reached, perhaps, when after his penance Siddhasena recites his Sanskrit verses and calls forth the image of a Jain Tīrthaṃkara. Sanskrit, with the right understanding of the place of language in religion, can have a powerful effect.

When we turn to the biographies of Buddhaghoṣa, we see at once that the preoccupation with language that marked the biography of Siddhasena is also a fundamental concern of the Buddhist biographer. Sources for the life of Buddhaghoṣa are as varied as those that exist for Siddhasena; I base my comments here on the *Buddhaghosuppatti* of Mahāmaṅgala, which may have been written in the fourteenth century in Burma.[12] Buddhaghoṣa's successful translation into Māgadhī of the Sinhalese commentaries to the Buddhist canonical works may be seen in many ways as the mirror-image of Siddhasena's misguided desire to translate the Jain canonical texts into Sanskrit.

There is ample evidence that long before the extant biographies of Buddhaghoṣa were written, at least amongst some Buddhists Māgadhī had achieved something of the status of a sacred language. Some Buddhists held Māgadhī to be privileged in exactly the same terms that the grammarians and Mīmāṃsakas had argued that Sanskrit was privileged, terms which Dharmakīrti had taken such pains to refute.[13] Most telling in this connection are the statements that Buddhaghoṣa himself makes. Buddhaghoṣa has comments on the nature of language in general and on the special status of Māgadhī in a number of places in his works, including the *Sammohavinodinī* on the *Vibhaṅga*, the *Samantapāsādikā* on the *Vinaya* and the *Visuddhimagga*. I consider here the passage from the *Visuddhimagga*, which has suffered considerably at the hands of translators.[14]

Buddhaghoṣa describes the *niruttipatisaṃbhidā*, "True knowledge of the nature of language", in a paragraph that I would translate roughly as follows:[15]

> "The term '*niruttipatisaṃbhidā*', 'true knowledge of the nature of language', means knowledge in full detail of the language of Māgadhī, which is the root language of all creatures, the natural language, and is considered to be the sacred language. And such a knowledge of what is the natural language takes the following form. As soon as a person hears something being said he knows at once that what has been said is either in the natural language or is not. When we gloss the technical term 'knowledge that arises when something is spoken in the natural language of our religious texts', we gloss the word 'spoken' by the synonyms 'uttered' or 'said'. We also gloss the term 'natural language' with the words 'usage that never changes'. And when such a natural language is spoken, uttered, that is, said, with respect to the special topics covered in the scriptures, a person skilled with 'true knowledge of the nature of language' knows at once whether what has been uttered is in fact the natural language or not. For a person who has perfected his true knowledge of the nature of language, as soon as he hears words like '*phasso*' and '*vedanā*', knows that these are utterances of the 'natural language', while as soon as he hears such words as '*phassā*' and '*vedano*', on the other hand, he knows that these are not utterances of the natural language."

If we return for a moment to the Mīmāṃsakas and the grammarians, Buddhaghoṣa's statements begin to assume a recognizable contour. The Mīmāṃsakas and the grammarians had argued that Sanskrit was the natural language, the root language, and that its usage was fixed once and for all by grammar. It was unvarying, which made it possible for children to learn Sanskrit, while vernaculars were varying and thus could not possibly express their meaning directly. Buddhaghoṣa has turned the argument around. He agrees, the natural language is grammatically fixed and unvarying. But then the examples he gives of the same words, once in their correct gender for examples of natural language, and once in incorrect forms as examples of something other than natural language, indicate that what he means by this root language is Māgadhī, correctly used. He also indicates that it is this language that is to be used with respect to topics covered in scriptures, much as the orthodox Hindus had argued for the exclusive use of Sanskrit in a ritual context.

In another context, in his comments in the *Sammohavinodinī* about the monk Tissadattathera, who could preach in many languages, Buddhaghoṣa makes clear that Māgadhī is always to be preferred for religious instruction because it is the easiest of all languages to grasp and offers instantaneous understanding. He also asserts that it was the language of the Buddha, a belief that no doubt led him to promote its usage as a sacred language and elevate it to the status that Sanskrit held for the orthodox Hindu community.[16] Buddhaghoṣa also asserts in his commentary to the *Vinaya*, the *Samantapāsādikā*, that Māgadhī was the language of the Buddha and that Buddhist texts should be in Māgadhī.[17] It is necessary to keep all of this in mind as we turn to the biography of Buddhaghoṣa and see how very differently the question of translating sacred texts is handled.

Like Siddhasena, Buddhaghoṣa begins life as a Brahmin. He is learned and proud of his learning. Like Siddhasena, he converts when an heretical monk, this time a Buddhist monk, bests him in an intellectual contest. But if Siddhasena's flaw is his addiction to Sanskrit learning, Buddhaghoṣa's is a more general arrogance. One day we learn that Buddhaghoṣa was puzzling over the question of who was the more learned, himself or his teacher. Furious at this lack of respect, the teacher calls him to task. To expiate this sin Buddhaghoṣa must journey to Śrī Laṅkā and translate the sacred texts into Māgadhī. He accepts this as his penance with the added proviso that he wishes first to convert his father to Buddhism before he departs.

Buddhaghoṣa journeys to Śrī Laṅkā; by prodigious acts of memory and through his deep learning he passes tests both human and divine and is permitted to carry out the task of translating the Sinhalese commentaries into Māgadhī. The Sinhalese commentaries are then burned, and as if to prove to the world that Māgadhī indeed was the correct choice for the translation and not Sanskrit, and that he has not eschewed Sanskrit because he is not capable of writing in Sanskrit, Buddhaghoṣa publicly demonstrates his proficiency in Sanskrit by reciting some Sanskrit verses. This ends his stay in Śrī Laṅkā, and our brief look into his biography.

It is clear that there is no conflict in the text over what is the correct language for the sacred texts; whereas Siddhasena vacillated between Sanskrit and Prakrit, and the biography set up and resolved a tension between the Sanskritic culture and the vernacular culture, Buddhaghoṣa's biography knows no such conflict. It is firmly on the side of a canonical language, Māgadhī. The vernacular works are burned. It substitutes Māgadhī for Sanskrit and allows that there is indeed a hierarchy of languages, with Māgadhī at the top and the other vernaculars beneath it. In so doing it comes to the opposite conclusion of Siddhasena's biography, in which the notion of a single canonical language is denied.

III. Conclusions: The Logic of the Legends

There is about these two biographies a certain remarkable fidelity to fact. It is not the type of fact that one expects from a biography; few would wish to defend the position that Siddhasena actually proposed to put the Jain sacred writings into Sanskrit and was required therefore to undertake a penance that ended with his miraculous manifestation of the image of Pārśvanātha at Ujjain. Equally few would wish to defend the position that Buddhaghoṣa was required by his teacher to journey to Śrī Laṅkā and put the commentaries into Māgadhī because he thought he knew more than his teacher. Nonetheless the fact is that Siddhasena seems indeed to have been committed to Sanskrit and Sanskrit learning; his texts display a remarkable mastery over Brahmanical learning and over the Sanskrit language. At the same time, however, as the biography indicates, Siddhasena also knew that Prakrit was a suitable vehicle for religious instruction. After all, his major philosophical work, the *Sanmatitarka* was written in Prakrit.

As for Buddhaghoṣa, there is no question that he espoused the view that Māgadhī was the language of the Buddha, the root language that lay behind all languages, and the language best suited for teaching the Buddhist doctrine. It seems fit indeed that it is to him that the tradition ascribed the accomplishment of rendering vernacular commentaries into Māgadhī. While an assessment of the influence that Buddhaghoṣa's theories of language might have had on others is clearly beyond the scope of this paper, it is clear from the references made earlier to Dharmakīrti in the *Vādanyāya* that not all Buddhists would have shared his views. Others hotly debated the very notion of a canonical or ritual language and that any one language was privileged over others. Indeed Buddhists were engaged in translation projects and encouraged translation of texts, although the fact that some authors felt compelled to defend the practice of translation seems to indicate a resistance to changing a text from one language into another.[18]

The Jains do not seem to have developed a theory of Māgadhī as the one sacred language as Buddhaghoṣa did, although it is certainly true that they occasionally speak of Māgadhī as the base language from which other languages evolved.[19] Indeed they always wrote in a variety of languages and encouraged their monks to learn local languages. It would seem that amongst the Buddhists and Jains, who shared so much in common in their reaction to the grammarians and Mīmāṃsakas in the debate over a scriptural language, Buddhaghoṣa's was a minority opinion, though one elegantly expressed both in his own works and in the stories that grew up around him.

Notes

1. E. Frauwallner has pointed out that the Mīmāṃsakas owe much to the grammarians for their understanding of the nature of sound. In an article, "Mīmāṃsāsūtra I,1,6.23" in *Wiener Zeitschrift für die Kunde Süd und Ost-Asiens, 5, 1961, pp. 113-124*, Frauwallner proposed that the Mīmāṃsakas did not originally hold to the doctrine that sound was eternal, but that they eventually adopted this doctrine from the grammarians. I would suggest that the same is true with regard to the debate over the use of Sanskrit as the single ritual language. Patañjali in the *Mahābhāṣya* vigorously argues for the use of precisely correct Sanskrit in a ritual context, with the concomitant assertion that misuse of Sanskrit involves sin. The argument seems very much intended to establish for the grammarian a foothold amongst the orthodox scholars by asserting that their skill in analyzing language was necessary for the ritualists in order correctly to perform rituals. There is no direct evidence that the argument is directed against any particular school, Buddhist, Jain or otherwise, although Madhav Deshpande in his interesting study of Indian attitudes towards language, *Sociolinguistic Attitudes in India : An Historical Reconstruction*, Ann Arbor: Karoma Publishers, 1979, p.18 and note 50, has identified an indirect reference to a Buddhist verse in the discussion about the function of grammar and the necessity of using correct Sanskrit. The topic deserves further study. In any case, in later times as we shall see below, the necessity of using Sanskrit as a sacred language would be used as one more argument against the Buddhists and Jains. See the *Vyākaraṇamahābhāṣya*, edited with Kaiyyaṭa's *Pradīpa* and Nāgojibhaṭṭa's *Bhāṣyapradīpoddyota*, by Vedavrata Vyākaraṇācārya, Gurukul Jhajjar, Harayana Sahitya Samsthan, 1962, pp.8-23 for a sense of the grammarian's arguments.

Bhartṛhari in the *Vākyapadīya* I.139-142 argues that only Sanskrit makes its meaning known directly, while the Sanskrit-based vernaculars, which he calls Apabhraṃśas, require the intermediary of a Sanskrit word. The *Vṛtti* of Vṛṣabhadeva on verse 139 cites the maxim, *śabdaprakṛtir apabhraṃśaḥ* "The Apabhraṃśas have as their base another language", and attributes it to the *Saṃgrahakāra*, or Vyādi, who precedes Patañjali. (*Vākyapadīya of Bhartṛhari with the Commentaries Vṛtti and Paddhati of Vṛṣabhadeva*, Kāṇḍa I, edited by K. A. Subramania Iyer, Poona: Deccan College Monograph Series, 1966, p.229). This would be the earliest reference that I know to the notion that Sanskrit is the root language. While Bhartṛhari can be read as advocating the view that any failure to use precisely correct Sanskrit leads to sin, even in a context outside of ritual, (see verses I.131 and I.132), it was clear that even amongst the grammarians themselves there was no agreement as to whether the notion of a "sacred language", the use of which led to merit and the misuse of which led to sin, implied that this was the case only during ritual or always. The *Padamañjarī* commentary to the *Kāśikā* on Pāṇini notes both views but advocates the more restricted understanding of Sanskrit as a sacred language, the use of which was required only in ritual. See the *Padamañjarī*, volume 1, page 13 of the edition *Kāśikāvṛtti*, edited by Dvārikādās Śāstrī and Śrīkālikāprasādaśukla, Varanasi: Prācyabhāratīprakāśa, 1965.

The Mīmāṃsakas, who were ultimately concerned mostly with matters of ritual, advocated the view that correct Sanskrit was required only in the context of ritual. See the *Bhaṭṭadīpikā*, cited by the *Mīmāṃsākośa* of Kevālananda Sarasvatī, Satara: Prajñā Pāṭhaśālā Maṇḍala, 1952, volume 6, page 3786 and the *Tantravārttika* on I.3.18, in the edition of Pandit Gaṅgādhara Śāstrī, Benaras Sanskrit Series, 1903, numbers 5, 7, 16, 23, 27, 29, 32, 34, 36, 39, 60, 62, and 72, pages 230, 239.

On the Mīmāṃsaka side, the necessity of conducting ritual in precisely correct Sanskrit was discussed at length in every major work, most notably of course Kumārila's *Ślokavārttika* and *Tantravārttika*. The discussion in the *Tantravārttika* is particularly interesting in that it raises a question that is less often debated by the grammarians, namely what languages are to be considered as Apabhraṃśas that require the intermediary of Sanskrit in order to make known their meaning, and what languages are actually prohibited during ritual. An opponent is allowed to argue that the prohibition against using *mleccha* speech in the ritual does not in fact refer to the Sanskrit-based Apabhraṃśas, but only to the non-Sanskritic languages, explicitly the Dravidian languages. The Siddhāntin replies this is an untenable viewpoint; all but precise grammatically correct Sanskrit is prohibited during ritual. The debate in the *Tantravārttika* also makes clear that the *pūrvapakṣa* is at least at times another Mīmāṃsaka, who resists the influence of the grammarians, and not necessarily a Buddhist or Jain. Kumārila often allows the *pūrvapakṣa* to take as his main opponent the grammarians and attack the notion that one can define a proper word as opposed to one that is improper. He returns then with the orthodox Mīmāṃsaka position, which insists that the science of grammar is necessary to the ritualist. See *Tantravārttika* under I.3.18. The discussion begins in the edition cited above on page 190 and the discussion on defining the *mleccha* language is on page 198.

Any further study of the complex issues involved in the discussion about language must offer a detailed analysis of these and other passages in the *Tantravārttika*. Deshpande's book cited earlier in this note is a beginning; he has at least sketched some of the Brahmanical, Buddhist and Jain attitudes towards language. Nonetheless I would take exception with his conclusions at a number of points. Deshpande regarded the main difference between Buddhist and Jain attitudes towards language as a question of which group was most committed to the use of Sanskrit. In fact I shall develop the theory in this paper that their difference, where it occurred, concerned the more fundamental issue of whether there is any one language that has the privileged status of being the sole language suitable for use in religious ritual and writing. I shall contend that the Jains answered on the whole in the negative while a minority of Buddhists answered in the affirmative. But at least in one important case the language that they chose to privilege was not in fact Sanskrit but Māgadhī. Deshpande argues that the Buddhists, particularly the Mahāyāna community, were far more committed to Sanskrit than the Jains because they drew their teachers from the

Brahmin community while the Jains did not (p. 56). He does not substantiate this claim and in fact the stories of Jain monks told in the various Jain *prabandhas* indicate that the Jains also drew their converts largely from the most educated class of society, the Brahmins, exactly as similar Buddhist stories say the Buddhists did. Deshpande does mention in passing the tension between Prakrit and Sanskrit in the biography of the Jain monk Siddhasena, something that this paper will discuss in detail. He is silent about Buddhaghoṣa, whose attitudes towards language will be a second focus of this paper.

2. By the time of Kumārila it is undeniable that the Mīmāṃsaka argues vehemently against the Buddhists and to some extent the Jains as well in practically every context. Thus in the *Tantravārttika* Kumārila heaps scorn on the Prakrit language of the Buddhist texts and uses the fact that they are written in this poor language to argue that they therefore cannot be true. In support of my contention that the doctrine of a sacred language might well have been developed by orthodox circles independently of any debate against the Buddhists and Jains, it is worth noting that Kumārila's attacks against specifically the Jain and Buddhist texts as written in Prakrit do not occur in the section devoted to demonstrating that Sanskrit as defined by the grammarians is the sacred language, but in a section on the authority of the *kalpasūtras*. The section is part of a general discussion of the nature of valid scripture. Kumārila remarks that since it has already been proved that Buddhist and Jain scriptures cannot be valid in the same way the orthodox *smṛti* literature is valid, the next supposition might be that they have the same kind of validity as the *kalpasūtras*. He first discusses how the *kalpasūtras* are necessary aids to the Vedic ritual and then proceeds to deny that kind of validity to the Buddhist and Jain scriptures. See the *Tantravārttika*, pages 162, 168-175. The Naiyāyikas also eventually use the argument for a sacred language against the Buddhists. Jayanta Bhaṭṭa in the *Nyāyamañjarī* would seem to be presenting a Buddhist as the *pūrvapakṣa* in his discussion of Sanskrit as a ritual language. I infer this from the fact that very early in the debate he has the *pūrvapakṣa* cite verses from Dharmakīrti's *Pramāṇavārttika*, 3.318;3.319b-3.320a. The *Pramāṇavārttika*, however, does not go into a debate against the grammarians. The *Nyāyamañjarī* edition that I am using is the Vizianagaram edition. Mine lacks the title page. The relevant section is pp.372-392. The edition of the *Pramāṇavārttika* I have used is the one edited by Svami Dvārikādās Śāstrī in the Bauddha Bharati Series, volume 3, Varanasi: Bauddha Bharati, 1968 and the relevant verses are pp. 356-357.

In addition the *Tattvopaplavasiṃha*, which attacks every doctrine of orthodox philosophy, not unexpectedly also attacks the concept of a sacred language and the notion that correct usage can be ordained by rules of grammar. The text has been edited in the Gaekwad's Oriental Series, volume LXXXVII, by Pandit Sukhalalji and the passage in question is from pp. 115-125. My edition lacks the title page.

Later as Hindu religious groups also began to use vernacular languages the debate against the necessity of using Sanskrit for religious texts would expand from a Buddhist-Jain vs. Mīmāṃsaka-grammarian debate to include such groups as the Śaivas like Abhinavagupta and the Southern Tamil authors. On the use of Prakrits in the *tantras* see Navjivan Rastogi, *The Krama Tantricism of Kashmir: Historical and General Sources*, vol.1, Delhi: Motilal Banarsidass, 1979, p. 8, which cites the *Mahārthamañjarīparimala* saying that Prakrit is the language best suited to teaching its doctrines. Rastogi notes that the Tripurā *tantras* also advocate the use of Prakrit instead of Sanskrit. The extent to which these later texts are indebted to Buddhist and Jain refutations of the notion of Sanskrit as a ritual language remains to be studied.

3. See the *Kharataragacchabṛhadgurvāvali* edited by Jina Vijaya Muni, Singhi Jain Series, number 42, Bombay: Bharatiya Vidya Bhavan, 1956, page 36.

4. The Jain emphasis on the validity of local languages is clear from their concept of *bhāsāsatta*, particularly the category of "true" speech that goes under the term *janapadasatya*, "the validity of local languages", and maintains that all languages are equally capable of making known their meanings and must be seen to be equally valid in their own local contexts. The term *janavayasatta* appears in the *Ṭhānaṅga Sutta*, 10.89. The text is edited by Muni Nathmal from Ladnun, Rajasthan: Jain Vishva Bharati, 1976 and the section is on p. 922. See also the numerous references given in the *Abhidhānarājendrakośa* of Vijayarājendra Suri, Delhi: B.R. Publishing Corporation, reprinted 1985, volume IV, p.1388 and volume V, pp. 1522-1556, and those in the *Jainalakṣaṇāvali: Jaina Pāribhāṣika Śabdakośa*, of Bālcandra Siddhānta Śāstrī, Delhi: Vira Seva Mandir Prakasan, 1973, vol.2, p.455. It is clear from the many citations in these works that the Jains are arguing not only for the validity of the Sanskrit based languages, but also for the Dravidian languages as well. The concept of improper speech, either false or ill-intentioned and speech that leads to the harm of other living beings is developed in the *Ṭhānaṅga Sutta*, 10.90, the *Dasaveālia Sutta*, chapter 7 and in the *Āyāraṅga Sutta*, 2.4.1. The *Dasaveālia* is edited by Muni Shri Punyavijayaji with the *Niryukti* and *Cūrṇi* in the Prakrit Text Series, vol.XVII, Ahmedabad, 1973. The *Āyāraṅga* is edited by Muni Jambuvijayaji with the *Niryukti* and the commentary of Śīlāṅkācārya in the Lala Sundarlal Jain Āgamagranthamālā, vol.1, Delhi: Motilal Banarsidass, 1978.

There are few exceptions to the Jain respect for the use of vernacular languages in all manner of religious undertaking, ritual, transmission of sacred texts, and even the philosophical debate, and for their insistence on the fact that correct grammar has nothing to do with merit. Nonetheless they did not mean to disregard the rules of grammar, as we see in Vādi Devasūri's *Pramāṇanayatattvālokālaṇkāra*, VIII.22, where the philosopher argues that in a debate speakers must use grammatically correct expressions. The text is published with an English translation by Harisatya Bhattacharya, Bombay: Jain Sahitya Vikas Mandal, 1967, and the passage is on page 643.

5. The Jain and indeed the Buddhist refutations often occur not in the wider context of a discussion of scripture or of the nature of language, but almost as an aside in the refutation of the Nyāya flaws of debate or *nigrahasthāna*, specifically the fault known as *aprāptakāla*, where the parts of an inference are

named out of sequence. (*Nyāyasūtra* 5.11). The Naiyāyika had traditionally argued that the parts of an inference require correct sequence; when a person hears them out of sequence he must first infer the correct order and then he understands the inference. The Naiyāyika used the case of understanding Prakrit words here as a supporting example of how a listener infers an underlying correct phenomenon first and from that gains meaning. It was this statement that gave the Jain the opportunity to challenge the whole notion of the orthodox Hindu philosopher that only Sanskrit had primary denotative capacity. The peripheral position of the debate in Jain and Buddhist sources reinforces my supposition that its original context was not as an attack against the Buddhists and Jains for using Prakrit as a scriptural language. The Buddhists and Jains directly refute the Mīmāṃsaka doctrine of *apauruṣeyatva*, that valid scripture is unauthored, a doctrine which directly attacked the validity of their scriptures. In comparison to their discussion of Sanskrit as a ritual language, they devote considerable attention to the refutation of the notion that scripture is unauthored. For a cursory Jain discussion of Sanskrit as the sacred language in the context of the refutation of the Nyāya *nigrahasthānas* see Prabhācandra's *Prameyakam-alamārtaṇḍa*, edited by Mahendrakumar Sastri, Bombay: Nirnayasagara Press, 1941,p. 668. See also Vidyānandin's *Tattvārthaślokavārtika*, edited by Pandit Manoharlal, Bombay: Nirnaya Sagara Press,1918, p.290. By contrast Prabhā-candra's *Nyāyakumudacandra* stands out for the fact that it deals in detail with the issue of a sacred language in a section of the text that is devoted to a consideration of the nature of language and the nature of scripture. The text is edited by Pandit Mahendra Kumar Nyayacarya in the Manik Chandra Digambara Jaina Granthamālā, number 39, Bombay: Manik Chandra Digambara Series, 1941, and the section is in volume 2, pp.757-767. The editor has provided extensive references to relevant Jain, Buddhist and Hindu texts on the subject of a sacred language from which I have benefitted greatly in this study.

6. The attitude of the early Buddhist community towards vernacular languages and the question of the use of Sanskrit versus vernacular languages has been the subject of much writing by modern scholars. It is not my intention here to do any more than give a few of the more prominent titles in which the issue of language has been discussed. It seems clear to me, despite the muddle of much that has been written on the subject, that like the Jains, the Buddhists used many languages and allowed for the use of vernaculars in a religious context. Works that deal with this subject include the following. Étienne Lamotte, *Histoire du Bouddhisme Indien*, Louvain: Institut Orientaliste, reprinted 1967, pp. 607 ff. Heinz Bechert, *Die Sprache der ältesten buddhistischen Überlieferung: The Language of the Earliest Buddhist Tradition, Symposien zur Buddhismus-forschung, II*, Göttingen: Vandenhoeck and Ruprecht, 1980, particularly the articles "Sakāya Niruttiyā: Cauld kale het", by John Brough, pp. 35-43; "The Dialects in which the Buddha Preached", by K.R. Norman, pp. 61-78 and "Bu-ston on the Languages Used by Indian Buddhists at the Schismatic Period", by Akira Yuyama, pp. 175-182. Oskar von Hinüber, "Zur Geschichte des Sprach-namens Pāli", in *Beiträge zur Indien Forschung, Ernst Waldschmidt zum 80*

Geburtstag gewidmet, Berlin: Museum für Indische Kunst, 1977, pp. 237-247. Sylvain Lévi, "Sur la Recitation primitive des textes bouddhiques", *Journal Asiatique*, 1915, II, pp. 401-447. K.R. Norman, "The Role of Pāli in Early Sinhalese Buddhism", in Heinz Bechert, *Buddhism in Ceylon and Studies on Religious Syncretism*, Akademie der Wissenschaften in Göttingen, 1978, pp.31 ff. Lin Li-Kouang, *L'aide memoire de la vraie loi*, Paris, 1949, pp. 216 ff.

7. The text is edited in the Bauddha Bharati Series by Svami Dvārikādās Śāstrī as volume 4 from Varanasi in 1972. The relevant section is pp. 98-104. Like most of the Jain philosophy texts, this text also engages the Mīmāṃsaka and grammarian in the course of refuting the Nyāya definition of the flaw in debate known as *aprāptakāla*. The Jain and Buddhist arguments are substantially the same.

8. I have written a lengthy essay on the various biographies of Siddhasena which includes translations of the accounts in the *Ākhyānakamaṇikośa* and the *Prabandhakośa* and is entitled, "The Biographies of Siddhasena : A Study in the Texture of Allusion and the Weaving of a Group Image". Part I has been published in the *Journal of Indian Philosophy*, vol.17, 1989, pp. 329-384 and part II will appear in the same journal shortly. The *Prabandhakośa* is edited by Jina Vijayamuni in the Singhi Jain Series, volume 6, Santiniketan: Singhi Jaina Pitha, 1935 and Siddhasena's biography is pages 15-23.

9. That Vṛddhavādin sings and dances while Siddhasena discourses in Sanskrit introduces another element into their opposition. While we are not told in the *Prabandhakośa* what exactly Siddhasena says and we learn only that he rambled on and on, in the *Ākhyānakamaṇikośavṛtti* Siddhasena is directly quoted. He offers formal philosophical argument, a formal inference, in support of his contention that there is no Omniscient Being. See the *Ākhyānakamaṇikośa*, edited by Muni Śrī Puṇyavijayajī, Prakrit Text Society Series, no.5, Varanasi: Prakrit Text Society,1962, pp.171-172. It seems to me that when we consider the contrast in their presentation as well as the difference in the languages that Vṛddhavadin and Siddhasena employ, we may understand Vṛddhavādin as representing not only the vernacular culture as opposed to Sanskrit culture, but also the entire realm of orality over literacy, where orality teaches through verse and performance and literacy involves the more abstract thinking of the philosophical debate. For a discussion of oral culture as oriented around verse and performance as didactic devices and a discussion of the relationship between literacy and philosophy see the works of Eric A. Havelock. A useful introduction is his recent work *The Muse Learns to Write: Reflections on Orality and Literacy from Antiquity to the Present*, New Haven: Yale University Press, 1986, particularly chapter 8, "The General Theory of Primary Orality", pp. 62-78.

Jain biographies have much to say about the relative importance of oral transmission of teachings and book learning. I have some remarks on the primacy given to the written word among the Kharataragaccha in my paper on Siddhasena and in a paper that is soon to be published in the Festschrift for J. Deleu that is being edited by K. Watanabe.

10. See my references in the paper on Siddhasena cited above, notes 46 and 47. The belief is as ancient as speculation in religious texts in India. It was particularly prominent in medieval Jainism, where hymn-makers and hymns were given great honour. The *Bhaktāmarastotra* of Mānatuṅga, for example, gathered around itself numerous miracle tales which then were given the form of a commentary to the hymn. The text is edited by Hiralal Rasikdas Kapadia, in the Sheth Devachand Lalbhai Pustakoddhara Series, no. 79, Bombay, 1932.

11. It is also important to note that he uses Sanskrit not in the context of a philosophical debate, as he had at the outset of his career when he first encountered Vṛddhavādin, but in a type of oral performance. It is to be recalled that it was Vṛddhavādin the singer and dancer who first converted Siddhasena to Jainism, and it was suggested above in note 8 that Vṛddhavādin not only represents the Prakrit language but also the oral mode of teaching in this biography. Such an interpretation is supported by this incident in which we finally see Siddhasena emerge as the hero. For if he uses that tool of Brahmanical culture par excellence, the Sanskrit language, he does so here in a mode that is more compatible with the Jain/ vernacular culture as this biography so defines that culture than he did in his ramblings in the conversion debate. The abstract philosophical content of the *Dvātriṃśikā* is not at issue here nor is it relevant to Siddhasena's miracle; what is significant for the miracle is the mere oral recitation of his verses. Indeed all Siddhasena needs to do is utter one verse for smoke to come pouring out of the *liṅga*.

12. The text has been edited and translated by James Gray, London: Luzac and Company,1892. For information about the text see Gray's introduction and the brief comments by K.R. Norman in *Pāli Literature*, Wiesbaden: Otto Harrassowitz, in the series *History of Indian Literature*, vol. VII, page 145. On Buddhaghoṣa and other accounts of his life see Bimala Churn Law, *Buddhaghoṣa*, Bombay: Royal Asiatic Society, Monograph number 1, 1946, and Reverend Thomas Foulkes, "Buddhaghoṣa", *Indian Antiquary*, vol.19, April 1890, pp. 103-122. All of the Pāli accounts of Buddhaghoṣa, whether composed in Śrī Laṅkā or in Burma, are later than the Jain biographies of Siddhasena, which raises the question of direct influence. In addition the *Buddhaghosuppatti* weaves into the biography of Buddhaghoṣa an incident that had been associated with Śrī Harṣa in the *Prabandhakośa*. Both these remarkable men can reproduce verbatim an argument made in a langauge they cannot understand! (See chapter 5 in the *Buddhaghosuppatti* and *Prabandhakośa*, page 56; the story of Śrī Harṣa is translated in P. Granoff, ed. *The Clever Adulteress and Other Stories* (Oakville: 1990) 156-62). At this point in my research I am reluctant to argue for direct influence between the Jain *prabandhas* and the biography of Buddhaghoṣa. I prefer to see in the case of the Śrī Harṣa/Buddhaghoṣa parallel an example of a well-known and popular story that was told of many different people independently. Conceivably this story told of wise men who were gifted with language was told of many others as well; thus it is not necessary to look for direct borrowing. In the case of the rewriting of the canon into a canonical language I would also prefer to see between the Buddhists and the Jains a

similar preoccupation with the larger debate about sacred language in India rather than a direct reworking by the Buddhists of Jain material. In part I am doubtful that texts like the Jain *prabandhas* circulated much outside the Jain community, although I have no evidence to support this hypothesis.

13. K.R. Norman, "The Dialects in Which the Buddha Preached", cited above, has a number of citations from Buddhaghoṣa in which Māgadhī is said to be the root language. See pages 66ff. Oskar von Hinüber, *op.cit.*, p. 239, suggested that the earliest discussion of Māgadhī as the immutable natural language is to be found in the *Sammohavinodinī*, Buddhaghoṣa's commentary to the *Vibhaṅga*. The text is to be found in the Nalanda Pali Series, edited U.Dhammaratana, Patna: Nava Nalanda Mahavihara, 1961, pages 390-391.

14. Neither the translation of Pe Maung Tin, *The Path of Purity*, Pali Text Society 1975, reprint, page 511, nor that of Bhikku Nyayamoli, Colombo: A. Semage, 1964, p.485 correctly conveys the meaning of the passage. These are the only two translations I have had available to me. The edition of the *Visuddhimagga* that I am using is the one published in the Pali Granthamala series as volume 3, edited by Dr. Rewatadhamma, Varanasi, 1969. The passage is in volume 2, page 959.

15. I have altered slightly the order of sentences in order to unpack the tight construction and hopefully to highlight the sense of the passage. Instead of offering the technical definitions of terms such as *attha* and *dhamma*, which Buddhaghoṣa has just defined in the previous pages, I have used the loose phrase, "the special topics covered in the scriptures." I hoped thereby not to make the translation so technical or complicated that the main point would be lost.

16. *Sammohavinodinī*, pp. 390-391. The story itself is curious and seems hardly to fit Buddhaghoṣa's purpose of insisting that the object of the *nirutti-paṭisaṃbhidā* is the correct grammatical usage of Māgadhī. Nonetheless, if I understand the text correctly, the story does give Buddhaghoṣa the occasion to discuss his theory of Māgadhī as the root of all languages and as the natural language, the language that a feral child would naturally speak without being taught. Buddhaghoṣa turns the story of Tissadatta from one meant to illustrate that a monk could preach in any language to an illustration of the fact that all other languages are learnt by hard effort whereas knowledge of Māgadhī is inborn.

17. *Samantapāsādikā*, edited by Birbal Sharma, Patna: Nava Nalanda Mahavihara, 1967, volume 3, page 1297.

18. See *The Book of Zambasta*, R. Emmerick, London:Oxford University Press, London Oriental Series, volume 21, 1968, chapter 23, page 343. I am indebted to the article by Oskar von Hinüber cited earlier for this interesting reference.

19. See the *Nyāyakumudacandra*, page 764. See also the *Aupapatikasūtra* cited by K.R. Norman, "The Dialects in Which the Buddha Preached", page 66.

Taoist Thought in the *Kuan-tzu*

Kanaya Osamu
Tohoku University

The *Kuan-tzu*, which mainly deals with politics and economy, contains thoughts on a variety of topics. It is commonly known that this work exhibits a strong Taoist influence. In the present paper I will study the Taoist thought of the *Kuan-tzu* and show that it appears as a realistic and practical philosophy that has much in common with the so-called *tao-fa* thought found elsewhere. I shall also argue that this Taoist thought pervades the whole of the *Kuan tzu*.

The chapter in the *Kuan-tzu* in which the Taoist concept of *tao* appears most frequently is the "Nei-yeh p'ien". In that chapter *tao* is explained as a principle that "determines man's life and death as well as the success or failure of things"; it is also said that "though the world is replete with it, it cannot be discerned by people in general." This *tao* closely resembles the *tao* of Lao-tzu and Chuang-tzu. However, one distinctive characteristic of *tao* in the "Nei-yeh p'ien" is that it is conceived as something fluid which enters and dwells in man's mind. There is an influence of the concept of *ch'i* (ether) here. In other words, the concept of *tao* is used in the "Nei-yeh p'ien" in the same sense as are the ethereal concepts related to *ch'i*, namely, *ching*, *shên*, and *ling-ch'i*.

Tao, an objective entity existing in a fluid state on a cosmic scale, enters and abides in man's mind under certain conditions, such as when "the mind is at peace and the feelings are calm." Needless to say, this entering of the *tao* into the mind of man, as it is the indwelling of the fundamental principle, gives birth to a sage who is endowed with special abilities surpassing those of the man of ordinary mind.

Now such *tao* as described in the "Nei-yeh p'ien" is similar in nature to *shên* or *shên-ming* appearing in the "Hsin-shu shang-p'ien" in the same *Kuan-tzu*. "Hsin-shu shang-p'ien" stresses the predominance of the mind (*hsin*) over the sensory organs and teaches that *shên* or *shên-ming* comes and abides in the mind when the latter is in the state of inaction (*wu-wei*) and vacuous calmness (*hsü*-

ching); it puts the mind in an ideal state in which it can exhibit special power. This tallies with the line in the "Nei-yeh p'ien" stating that "*tao* will enter and abide in the mind when the mind is at peace and feelings are calm." Although it possible to say that *tao* and *shên* are two different concepts insofar as the terms used are different, it cannot be denied that they are at least linked through a common idea.

If we pay attention to the conceptual similarities it is clear that such statements as "if the form (*hsing*) is not right, virtue (*tê*) will never come", in the "Hsin-shu hsia-p'ien", and "Tao, when in heaven, is the sun, and when in man, it is the mind" in the "Shu-yen p'ien" are related to each other.

As it has already been pointed out, the concept of *tao* as a *ch'i*-like entity which circulates in a fluid state in the universe and enters and abides in man's mind also appears in certain parts of the "Jên-chien-shih" and "Chih-pei-yu" chapters of the *Chuang-tzu*. Those passages, however, are exceptional. *Tao* in the *Chuang-tzu* is in general conceived as ubiquitous and "to acquire *tao*" there means an "unconscious unity with *tao* in the state of self-oblivion." Aside from the above-mentioned exceptional passages, the *Chuang-tzu* does not teach that *tao* enters and abides in man's mind. The ethereal state of *tao*, therefore, may be said to be one of the distinctive aspects of the Taoist thought in the *Kuan-tzu*, as was noted by Fêng Yu-lan in his work, *Hsien-Ch'in Tao-chia san-pai ti tzu-jan-kuan ti i-t'ung* (A comparative study of the outlook of nature of the three schools of Taoism in the Pre-Ch'in period).

The linkage of *tao* and *ch'i* seen in the "Nei-yeh p'ien" and "Hsin-shu shang-p'ien" may be said to be a result of a more rationalistic way of understanding the Taoist concept of *tao*. *Ch'i* was originally thought to be an entity filling the universe in the state of a fluid and imparting life to all beings. Later, however, it came to be thought that there were two kinds of *ch'i*, good and evil, and further that there were *ching* or *ling-ch'i*, the very essence of *ch'i*. It was these concepts that were employed in the "Nei-yeh" and "Hsin-shu" chapters to give a rationalist interpretation to such conventional concepts as *shên* and *shên-ming*. It may be said that it was through such a process that the indwelling of *tao* in man's mind as the very essence of the universe or as the fundamental principle of the world came to be explained rationally.

In these sections of the *Kuan-tzu*, *tao* has hardly any religious character; nor is it based on any metaphysical system that stresses its nature as the fundamental cause of beings. It is rather conceived as a governing principle of the order penetrating the concrete movements and working of the universe and nature. This is the idea that is implied in such expressions as "*t'ien chih tao*" or "*t'ien-ti chih tao*" in other chapters of the *Kuan-tzu*. The respect for *tao* was at once respect for *t'ien* (heaven = nature). A notion of the interaction between heaven and man underlies the whole of the *Kuan-tzu*.

Now, changing the subject, let us next see the Taoist rules of life and way of government as given in the *Kuan-tzu*. Unlike the case of *tao*, descriptions regarding such topics, if we include brief fragmentary comments, are found scattered throughout the whole work. The problem here is to clarify their characteristics and how they are related to the work as a whole.

First, when we take up the "Nei-yeh p'ien" in which *tao* is discussed frequently, we find that the discussion on the rules of practical life centers on the rules for preserving health. It is quite natural, therefore, that a similar discussion is found also in the "Hsin-shu hsia-p'ien" whose descriptions overlap in many points with those in the "Nei-yeh p'ien". It is noteworthy, however, that this discussion is given far less weight in the "Hsin-shu hsia-p'ien" than in the "Nei-yeh" chapter.

The discussion about maintaining health appears also at the end of the "Pai-hsin p'ien", but its purport is avoidance of the evil effects of immoderate behaviour rather than preservation of health itself. This is all that will be said here about the positive discussion of the preservation of health in the "Nei-yeh p'ien", since it is, as shown above, quite exceptional in the whole of the *Kuan-tzu*.

What deserves more attention is the *tao-fa* thought seen in the "Hsin-shu shang-p'ien." The first half, the "Ching" section, of that chapter presents a kind of psychological view of the devices for receiving *shên* into one's mind, but the second half, the "Chieh" section, more or less features political thought. There we can find discussions on propriety (*li*) reminiscent of Hsün-tzu of the Confucian school, but there are also words giving weight to law (*fa*) and discussions of *fa* that are based on the Taoist view of *tao*. Moreover, the pursuit of the agreement between name and reality (the *ming-shih* theory) is discussed. From these facts it is surmised that the "Chieh" section of the "Hsin-shu shang-p'ien" is related also to Legalist (Fa-chia) thought. The difference, however, between the concept of *fa* in the "Hsin-shu shang-p'ien" and that of the Legalists is that the former is based on the Taoist concept of *tao*. "*Fa* based upon *tao*" here refers not to such a positive law as that propounded by Han Fei, but to a law close to the natural law which could blend with the Confucian view of morality.

The eclectic *tao-fa* thought came to draw attention for the first time when four chapters of old manuscripts including *Ching-fa* were unearthed at Ma-wang-tui. It was noted that the *tao-fa* thought in those old manuscripts was identical to the political thought that occupies an important place in the "Hsin-shu shang-p'ien": the words "*tao* gives birth to *fa*" in the *Ching-fa* tally with "*fa* derives from *ch'uan* (Perfect balance), and *ch'uan* derives from *tao*" in the "Hsin-shu shang-p'ien."

Furthermore, it gradually became clear that it is not only in the "Hsin-shu shang-p'ien" that this characteristic thought is discerned. There are words clearly expressing the *tao-fa* thought in such chapters in the *Kuan-tzu* dealing with *fa* as "Fa-fa p'ien", "Chün-ch'ên shang-hsia-p'ien", and "Pan-fa chieh p'ien". Lines expressing a similar thought, though not using the word *tao-fa*, are found in abundance in the whole work of *Kuan-tzu*.

As in the case of the Ma-wang-tui manuscripts, *tao* in the *Kuan-tzu* is conceived as a governing principle of the order of the universe and nature; the *tao-fa* thought in these works stresses the interrelations between heaven (nature) and man, regarding the former as the exemplar of the latter. In fact a stress upon the interrelations between heaven and man based upon the *tao-fa* thought is a theme that runs through all of the *Kuan-tzu*. The "Shih" and "Chiu-shou" chapters, which are closely related to the Ma-wang-tui manuscripts and to the "Hsin-shu shang-p'ien", basically conform with the *tao-fa* thought in that they teach as the way of government that one should follow the decree of heaven, earth, and nature. Words exhorting a man to follow nature are found all over the *Kuan-tzu*. Notable examples include the passage promoting agricultural production in the "Mu-min p'ien, ti-i" chapter at the outset of the *Kuan-tzu*, and the thought of "following heaven" in the "Hsing-shih p'ien, ti-êrh."

To sum up, the Taoist thought in the *Kuan-tzu* is realistic and practical, in keeping with the basic tenor of the entire *Kuan-tzu* which mainly deals with political and economic affairs. Even the concepts of "*tao*" and "*shên*" in the "Nei-yeh" and "Hsin-shu" chapters have a practical tone: *tao* and *shen* are thought to flow in the universe and, by entering and dwelling in his mind, to impart to man special powers for preserving health, conducting himself, and dealing with politics. Those chapters are not intended to give any metaphysical interpretation of *tao*.

What is most noteworthy in this context is the political thought that is based upon the eclectic *tao-fa* thought. This, together with the emphasis on the interrelation of heaven and man that underlies the *tao-fa* thought, is the distinguishing feature of the *Kuan-tzu*. The Taoist thought in the *Kuan-tzu* shows its strongest influence here. Another distinctive Taoist idea that needs to be mentioned is the concept of *tao* enveloping the universe. This idea is central to the discussion in the "Chou-hê p'ien", but a detailed discussion of this topic must be postponed to another occasion. In short, the *Kuan-tzu* mainly deals with practical matters concerning politics and economy, but underlying it is a kind of Taoist thought which provides the whole work with a philosophical background.

Reference: KANAYA Osamu, *Kanshi no kenkyū* (A study of the *Kuan-tzu*), Tokyo, Iwanami Shoten, 1987.

List of Characters

Chieh 解

Chih-pei-yo 知北遊

Ching 經

Ching-fa 經法

Chiu-shou 九守

Chou-hê p'ien 宙合篇

Chuang-tzu 莊子

Chün-chên shang-hsia-p'ien 君臣上下篇

ch'i 氣

ch'ing 精

ch'uan 權

Fêng Yu-lan 馮友蘭

fa 法

Fa-chia 法家

Fa-fa p'ien 法法篇

Han Fei 韓非

Hsien-Ch'in Tao-chia san-pai ti tzu-jan-kuan ti i-t'ung 先秦道家三派的自然觀的異同

Hsin-shu hsia-p'ien 心術下篇

Hsin-shu shang-p'ien 心術上篇

hsing 形

Hsing-shih p'ien ti-êrh 形勢篇第二

hsü-ching 虛靜

Hsün-tzu 荀子

Iwanami Shoten 岩波書店

Jên-chien-shih 人間世

Kanaya Osamu 金谷 治

Kanshi no kenkyu 管子的研究

Kuan-tzu 管子

Lao-tzu 老子

li 禮

ling-ch'i 靈氣

Ma-wang-tui 馬王堆

ming-shih 名實

Mu-min p'ien ti-i 牧民篇第一

Nei-yeh p'ien 內業篇

Pai-hsin p'ien 白心篇

Pan-fa chieh p'ien 版法解篇

Shên 神

shên-ming 神明

Shih 勢

Shu-yen p'ien 樞言篇

t'ien chih tao 天之道

t'ien-ti chih tao 天地之道

tê 德

tao-fa 道法

wu-wei 無為

Nirvikalpa-jñāna
Awareness Freed From Discrimination

Leslie S. Kawamura
The University of Calgary

This paper comprises a translation of Chapter VIII (*Adhi-prajñā*) of Asaṅga's *Mahāyāna-saṃgraha* together with Professor Gadjin M. Nagao's commentary on it.[1]

*VIII.1 [*Mahāyāna-saṃgraha-śāstra, *Asaṅga's text:]*

The superiority of [the learning of] the excellent training of mind (*adhicitta*) has been explained in the above manner. How is the superiority of [the learning of] the excellent training of wisdom (*adhiprajñā*) to be understood? That the superior quality of the excellent training of wisdom is non-discriminatory knowledge (*nirvikalpa-jñāna*) can be known through [the discussions on] its

1) essential nature (*svabhāva*),
2) basis (*āśraya*),
3) cause (*nidāna*),
4) objective-reference (*ālambana*),
5) form (*ākāra*),
6) response to criticisms (*codya-parihāra*),
7) foundation (*ādhāra, dhṛti*),
8) companion (*sahāya*),
9) maturation (*vipāka*),
10) flowing out (*niṣyanda*),
11) release (*niḥsaraṇa*),
12) reaching ultimacy (*niṣṭhā-gamana*),
13) praiseworthy qualities (*anuśaṃsa*) of [the knowledge that results from] preparatory practice (*prāyogika*), of [the knowledge] freed from discrimination (*nirvikalpa*), and of [the knowledge] obtained subsequently [after that] (*[tat-]pṛṣṭha-labdha*),

14) differentiation/distinctions (*prabheda*) [into three knowledges].

15) examples (*dṛṣṭānta*) [of the two knowledges—i.e. non-discriminatory knowledge and knowledge obtained subsequently,

16) effortlessly (*anābhoga* spontaneously) enacting (*kṛtya-anuṣṭhāna*), and

17) profundity/depth (*gāmbhīrya*).

From reflecting on the topics above, the superiority of *nirvikalpa-jñāna* should be known.

VIII.1 [NAGAO COMMENTARY:]

Among the three learnings of morality (*śīla*), meditation (*dhyāna*), and wisdom (*prajñā*), the third one, "the excellent [training of] wisdom" (*adhiprajñā*) is explicated in this text by the term *nirvikalpa-jñāna* (non-discriminatory knowledge). In this section, Asaṅga introduces 17 topics by which the nature, basis, etc. of that wisdom freed from discrimination is discussed. The 17 topics are explained in the following 25 verses that comprise the sections i.e., sections VIII.2 through VIII.18.

In topic 13 (VIII.14), *nirvikalpa-jñāna* is discussed fully in view of the three kinds of knowledges, but Vasubandhu's *Bhāṣya*[2] on this section [VIII.1] summarizes the three kinds of knowledges as follows.

The first one is called *nirvikalpa-jñāna* derived on the stage of preparatory practice (*prāyogika*); it is knowledge resulting from the investigation of non-discursiveness by means of reason. The second one is knowledge freed from discrimination; it is more commonly known as "basic non-discriminatory knowledge." The third one is knowledge that comes out of that basic knowledge; it is discriminatory and is called "knowledge acquired subsequently" (*pṛṣṭha-labdha-jñāna*). Two knowledges, the first one (which is the cause for the second one) and the third one (which is the effect of the second one), are discriminatory and function in the mundane world. Only the second one is truly non-discriminative and supra-mundane. What is ultimately aimed at is none other than the second one, "basic non-discriminatory knowledge," but insofar as the first one and the third one relate to it as its previous cause and its later effect, they are included in the knowledge freed from discrimination. In this manner, *nirvikalpa-jñāna* is discussed in view of three kinds.

The establishing of *nirvikalpa-jñāna* and, in particular, the establishing of the third knowledge acquired subsequently (although its seminal idea can be found in *Bodhisattva-bhūmi*[3]) are salient features of this text.

What is meant by the term *nirvikalpa-jñāna* is to be known through the discussions comprising this chapter. It is not an easy task to define the term, because, in spite of the fact that it refers, without doubt, to knowledge that lacks discrimination, the term "discrimination" (*vikalpa*: to construct or to divide) is understood in various ways. If one should say something about *nirvikalpa-jñāna*, it may be said that it is characterized as knowledge lacking the subject/object dichotomy; as lacking mistaken judgment; as not setting up something as a particular object; as the unity—i.e., the non-distinction between reality and wisdom; as equality and non-distinctiveness of all entities, etc.

Nirvikalpa-jñāna is explained at length in *Mahāyānasūtrālaṃkāra*. In the *Dharmadharmatāvibhāga*, it is discussed in conjunction with the "Ingress into the turn-about of the basis" (*āśraya-parāvṛtti*). It is perturbing that the idea does not appear in *Madhyāntavibhāga*. Aside from the present text, there is no other text that devotes a whole chapter to its discussion.

VIII.2 [Text: **svabhāva***]*

Among those [topics], it is said that the essential nature (*svabhāva*) of *nirvikalpa-jñāna* is rid of the five aspects [of wrong views] (*pañcākāra-vivarjita*):

1) fully rid (*parivarjana*) of [the view that *nirvikalpa-jñāna* is] a lack of attention (*amanasikāra*),

2) fully rid of transgressing (*atikrama*) the stages accompanied by reflection and investigation (*savitarka-savicāra-bhūmi*),

3) fully rid of the tranquility (*upaśānti*) gained in [the meditation on] the cessation of consciousness and sensations (*saṃjñā-vedita-nirodha*),

4) fully rid of the belief in its nature as materiality (*rūpa-svabhāva*), and

5) fully rid of delineation in mind wherein reality is taken as an object (*tattvārtha-citrikāra*).

It should be known thus that *nirvikalpa-jñāna* is fully rid of these five aspects [of wrong views].

The way in which *nirvikalpa-jñāna* is established (*vyavasthāpita*) is as explained above, and in regard to this, [there are many] verses:

For the bodhisattvas, the essential nature of non-discriminative knowledge is rid of the five
aspects [of wrong views] and is rid of the delineation of taking hold of reality variously.[4]

VIII.2 [NAGAO COMMENTARY]

Here the first topic, the "essential nature" of *nirvikalpa-jñāna* is explained. The intrinsic nature of *nirvikalpa-jñāna* cannot be explained positively; it can be explained only negatively as "not that, not that." Therefore, here five expressions that can mislead one into thinking about or that are prone to make one misunderstand *nirvikalpa-jñāna* are given and each is then negated. By means of negation, there is an attempt to captivate *nirvikalpa-jñāna*.[5]

Of the five, no. (1) the view that *nirvikalpa-jñāna* is a lack of attention (*amanasikāra*), that is a thought-less and conception-less state, is negated (*parivarjana*). If it were the case that *nirvikalpa-jñāna* meant a termination of the thinking process, then to sleep soundly or to faint would also be a case of *nirvikalpa-jñāna* and people would gain this state without effort. No (2), "transgressing (*atikrama*) the stages accompanied by reflection and investigation (*savitarka-savicāra-bhūmi*)" can be accomplished by those who have entered the second *dhyāna* or higher *dhyāna* stages. It is a possibility for even worldly and non-Buddhist people and it can be accomplished by the sages of the small-vehicle, i.e., the śrāvakas. This cannot be *nirvikalpa-jñāna*. In the same manner, no. (3) "cessation of consciousness and sensation" (*saṃjñā-vedita-nirodha*), i.e., the meditation of cessation (*nirodha-samāpatti*), is a kind of no-mind meditation in which there is neither mind nor mental activities (cf. I.52). There is no meaning of wisdom either. As for no. (4), "its nature is materiality" (*rūpa-svabhāva*), this would be no-mind in a different sense; inanimate things (*jaḍa*) like trees and boulders are motionless and senseless, but it is not possible that they be *nirvikalpa-jñāna*. Finally, no. (5) "delineation wherein reality is taken as a particular object (*tattvārtha-citrīkāra*)," one gives free reign to erroneous investigation by repeatedly questioning whether reality is like this or whether reality is like that. Delineation is truly a process of discrimination. To be freed from a process of discrimination of this kind is *nirvikalpa-jñāna*.

The above comprises an explanation of the five aspects of wrong views and the freedom from them. Vasubandhu's *Bhāṣya*[6] adds that *nirvikalpa-jñāna* is similar to visual cognition in that visual consciousness is a direct perception and accordingly the eyes perceives its object, color/form, without discriminating (*avikalpa*) or variously delineating anything concerning its object.

These five aspects indicate what *nirvikalpa-jñāna* is not because No. 1) is not knowledge just as the ignorance of stupid people is not knowledge; No. 2) has not transcended the worldly concerns; No. 3) is no-mind and thus lacks any judgment; No. 4) is without life and is emotionless; and No. 5) is the reverse of non-discrimination. In comparison to these five, *nirvikalpa-jñāna* can be said 1) to be knowledge, 2) to transcend the world, 3) to be conscious and with sensations, 4) to be alive and have emotions, and 5) to be non-discriminating.

Many verses that summarize *nirvikalpa-jñāna* follow, but it should be pointed out that the verse in this section summarizes the five aspects discussed above. The last foot is an explanation of the fifth aspect and it also defines *nirvikalpa-jñāna*, because it is rid of the delineation of reality.

VIII.3 [Text: **āśraya***]*

For the bodhisattvas, the basis for *nirvikalpa-jñāna* is not mind, yet it is mind,
because [*nirvikalpa-jñāna*] does not reflect on an object and yet is produced [from the mind].

VIII. 3 [NAGAO COMMENTARY]

The second of the 17 topics concerns the "basis" (*āśraya*) of *nirvikalpa-jñāna*. Through its discussion on whether the foundation or basis of *nirvikalpa-jñāna* is the mind (*cittam eva*) or not (*na tu cittaṃ*), this section reveals the self-contradictory position that the term *nirvikalpa-jñāna* implies. If *nirvikalpa-jñāna* is founded on the mind, since the mind is what reflects (i.e., discriminates), it would be a contradiction to claim it to be "non-discriminatory." On the other hand, if it be based upon that which is not the mind, for example some material thing, then it would be a contradiction to claim it to be knowledge. E. Lammotte read this passage, "le support (*āśraya*) du savior intuitif n'est ni pensée (*citta*) ni non-pensée (*acitta*)..."[7]

In response to this difficult problem, Asaṅga says, "is not mind, yet it is mind." Because *nirvikalpa-jñāna* "does not reflect upon an object" in the manner that the ordinary mind perceives things objectively, it does not have the mind as its basis; "and yet," because *nirvikalpa-jñāna*, gained from the long discipline of learning and practice, "is produced" from the mind, it has the mind as its basis.

VIII.4 [Text: **nidāna***]*

For the bodhisattvas, the cause of *nirvikalpa-jñāna* is the impressions gained through hearing
and [through] fundamental intense attention accompanied by [mind-]talk.

VIII.4 [NAGAO COMMENTARY]

The third of the 17 topics concerns the cause (*nidāna*). The "impressions gained by listening" (*śruta-vāsanā*) and also "fundamental intense attention" (*yoniśo-manasikāra*) accompanied by mind-talk (*sa-jalpa*) are the causes by which *nirvikalpa-jñāna* is produced. *Śruta-vāsanā* has been explained in I.45 *ff* as impressions of listening that flow out from the pure dharma-realm. Also, we have seen in III.1 *ff*, especially in III.7A, that the ingress into vijñapti-mātra is made possible when mind-talk, that is regarded as fundamental intense attention, arises with the impressions gained through listening functioning as its cause. Here we have the movement from "listening" to "fundamental intense attention" that is no other than the movement from "listening" to "reflecting" within the system of the three learnings of listening, reflecting, and practicing. This course of movement,

impressions gained by listening → mind-talk → fundamental intense attention

as the cause for ingress into *vijñapti-mātra*, has been explained in this section as the cause from which *nirvikalpa-jñāna* arises.

VIII.5 [Text: **ālambana***]*

For the Bodhisattvas, the objective-reference of *nirvikalpa-jñāna* is the inexpressibility
of the entities of reality; moreover, it is non-substantive and reality just-as-it-is.

VIII.5 [NAGAO COMMENTARY]

The fourth of the 17 topics concerns the objective-reference (*ālambana*) of *nirvikalpa-jñāna*. Because *nirvikalpa-jñāna* is a form of awareness, it must have some kind of objective-reference. Its objective-reference is summed up first as "the inexpressibility (*nirabhilāpyatā*) of the entities of reality (*dharma*)." This means that the objective-reference is of an inexpressible nature or the way of existence that is beyond expressions. Further, the meaning is augmented by the terms "non-substantive" (*nairātmya*) and "reality just-as-it-is" (*tathatā*). The first one, by referring to the non-substantiveness, the non-realness, of both the person and entities of reality, manifests the negative aspect expressed by *śūnyatā*. The latter one manifests the affirmative aspect, i.e., "reality as-it-is," revealed by the very existence of that negation. By these two aspects of negation and affirmation, the *Upanibandha* clarifies that what *nirvikalpa-jñāna* takes as its objective-reference is free of two misconceptions of (1) misconceiving what is non-existent as existent (*samāropa*) and (2) misconceiving what is really existent as non-existent (*apavāda*).

VIII.6 [Text: **ākāra***]*

For the Bodhisattvas, the modus operandi of *nirvikalpa-jñāna* is one in which there is
no acquisition of a defining-characteristic with regard to an objective-reference to be known.

VIII.6 [NAGAO COMMENTARY]

The fifth of the 17 topics concerns the modus-operandi (*ākāra*) of *nirvikalpa-jñāna*. Here the term "modus-operandi" refers to the manner in which *nirvikalpa-jñāna* perceives its object. That object is "the objective-reference (*ālambana*) which is to be known (*jñeya*)," that is, reality as-it-is as explained in VIII.5 above. However, because *nirvikalpa-jñāna* does not discern the distinction between the subject as seer and the object as the seen, the two are equal and indistinct. That is to say, the subject becomes one with the object and reality as-it-is and awareness are in total union. In other words, the manner in which reality as-it-is presents itself and the modus-operandi of *nirvikalpa-jñāna* are in harmony and there is no characteristic difference between the two. The non-characterization of the objective-reference is expressed in the verse by the words, "there is no acquisition of a defining-characteristic" (*animitta*). The non-acquisition of a defining characteristic means that there is no perception of a subject and no perception of an object. Both are in harmony and without distinction; consequently, the awareness called, "*nirvikalpa-jñāna*" is a knowing in which there is no perception of a defining-characteristics of any kind. Therefore, to see without perceiving a defining-characteristic—i.e., the non-acquisition of a defining-characteristic—is the modus-operandi of *nirvikalpa-jñāna*.

VIII.7 [Text: **codya-parihāra***]*

That which has the nature of origination from being a composite is discriminated; there is no other [object].

When letters are mutually combined together, they constitute a [meaningful] object. This refers to origination from being a composite. [1]

When expressions [of conceptual knowledge] do not exist, there is no knowledge regarding what is expressed.

Because [expression and the expressed] are contrary, there is no [knowledge of the expressed] in the expression; therefore, all things are beyond words. [2]

VIII.7 [NAGAO COMMENTARY]

The sixth of the 17 topics concerns response to criticisms (*codya-parihāra*). In this section, it is assumed that criticisms regarding the topics above are stated by the outsiders i.e., non-Buddhists, and it sets out to respond to them. The verses contain only the responses and not the criticisms. According to *Bhāṣya*[8], the criticisms concern the ideas expressed in VIII.5 above—i.e., if it is the case (as explained in VIII.5 above) that entities of reality are beyond expressions and cannot be perceived, then what is the objective-reference of discrimination, judgement, or perception? In what manner is the object of perception beyond expression? Verse [1] is a response to the first question and verse [2] is a response to the second.

Verse [1]: When words come together, concepts are established and our discriminative perception takes those concepts as its object of perception. The opening statement, "from being a composite (*sāṃyogika*)"—i.e., what is aggregated—refers to the statement, "letters are mutually combined together" of the third line, and when letters (*vyañjana*) mutually come together (*anyonya-saṃyoga*), the concepts of nouns and verbs are established as verbal expressions. A thing the nature (*svabhāva*) of which is an aggregation becomes the "meaningful object" (*sārthakatva*) of perception; therefore, to the question, "What is the objective-reference of our discrimination, judgement, and perception?" the response is "a composite is discriminated" and "there is no other (*anyathā*) [object]." In other words, it is not the case that some substantive existence is the object of perception.

And how is it that "all things are beyond words (*anabhilāpya, avācya*)?" Verse [2] responds to this question by using the two technical terms "expressions" (*abhidhāna*) and "what is expressed" (*abhidheya*). "Abhidhāna" refers to language and concepts, that is, name. "Abhidheya" refers to sense, that is, the meaningful object of perception. Our daily perceptions are based upon concepts, that is, upon expressions. Consequently, "when expressions [of conceptual knowledge] (*abhidhāna*) do not exist, there is no knowledge (*jñāna*) regarding what is expressed (*abhidheya*)." What does this mean? If the object of our perception was something that had substantive existence, then we should be able to comprehend an object without "expressions." However, if we lack the knowledge of expression by concepts, even if an object should exist substantively, knowledge with respect to that object would not arise. It follows that an object of perception is not something that exists substantively, but it is what is expressed through words (Verse [2]).

Now, if it should be asked whether the knowledge of an object is already included in the "expressions [of conceptual knowledge]" the response is that it is not the case. "Expression and the expressed are contrary (*viruddhatva*)," because they have different defining-characteristics (*lakṣaṇa*). They are contrary because the processes of expressing by means of concepts and of perceiving what is expressed by concepts as its objective-reference are operationally different from each other, one being "active" and the other "passive." The active "expression" cannot be the same as the passive "what is expressed." This is totally different from the fact that *nirvikalpa-jñāna* and *tathatā* are of one substance, because there is no discrimination between the "active" and the "passive." Consequently, "there is no knowledge regarding what is expressed."

The expression and the expressed constitute what we understand as our everyday, conventional perceptions and discriminations; however, no knowledge is found in them and therefore, viewed from the standpoint of ultimate reality, it is said that "all things are beyond words."

VIII.8 [Text: **ādhāra/dhṛti]**

Nirvikalpa-jñāna is a foundation of the bodhisattva's practice
that is obtained after that, because it strengthen [the practice].

VIII.8 [NAGAO COMMENTARY]

The seventh topic refers to the foundation (*ādhāra/dhṛti*). The so-called "knowledge obtained subsequently" arises on the foundation (*ādhāra, dhṛti*) of *nirvikalpa-jñāna*. According to the commentary, the statement, "the bodhisattva's practice that is obtained after that (*tat-pṛṣṭha-labdha*)" in the verse, means that a bodhisattva's practice is a practice guided by the knowledge that follows after *nirvikalpa-jñāna*. Because *nirvikalpa-jñāna* "strengthens" that practice, it is "a foundation of the bodhisattva's practice." The word *ch'ih* affixed to all four Chinese translations—Buddha śānta, Paramārtha, Dharmagupta, and Hsüan-tsang, has the meanings "to support," "to uphold," "to sustain" and so on.

VIII.9 [Text: **sahāya]**

For the bodhisattva, the companion of *nirvikalpa-jñāna* is expressed
in terms of the two paths comprised of the five perfections.

VIII.9 [NAGAO COMMENTARY]

The eighth of the 17 topics concerns the companion (*sahāya*). Here the relationship between the six perfections (*pāramitā*) and *nirvikalpa-jñāna* is explained. The word *sahāya* is used in the sense of a friend when in need, an attendant, a companion. *Nirvikalpa-jñāna* is treated as the sixth perfection (*prajñā*) and the other "five perfections" (*pañca-pāramitā-maya*) beginning with the perfection of giving (*dāna-pāramitā*) are considered to be its companion. This companion is said to be comprised (*maya*) of "two paths" (*mārga-dvaya*) to which the *Bhāṣya* (Vasubandhu's commentary) refers as the path of preparatory equipment (*saṃbhāra-mārga*) and the path of resource (*niśraya-mārga*). The first one is called "path of preparatory equipment," because one accumulates "roots of merits" by practicing the four perfections from the perfection of giving to the perfection of energy (*vīrya*). The second one is called "path of resource," because on the basis of the four former perfections, the perfection of wisdom (*prajñā-pāramitā*)—i.e., *nirvikalpa-jñ āna* is attained with the perfection of meditative absorption (*dhyāna*) as its resource.[9]

VIII.10 [Text: **vipāka]**

For the bodhisattvas, the ripening of the fruit of *nirvikalpa-jñāna* takes
place in
the two assemblies of the Buddha through practice and attainment.

VIII.10 [NAGAO COMMENTARY]

The ninth of 17 topics concerns the ripening of the fruit (*vipāka*). The next four verses (VIII.10-VIII.13) explain how *nirvikalpa-jñāna* functions in the steps from saṃsāra to liberation. That this and the following verse belong to the stage of saṃsāra is clearly indicated at the beginning of *Bhāṣya* when it states, "when the fruition of Buddhahood has not yet been attained"[10] (*Paramārtha-Bhāṣya* does not make this clear). This is also evidenced by the fact that the function, or cause and effect of *nirvikalpa-jñāna* is explained by using conventional worldly terms regarding cause and effect, such as, the "ripening of the fruit" (*vipāka*) used here and the "issuance of the fruit" (*niṣyanda*) discussed in the next verse.

Now, the term "ripening" refers to no other than the saṃsāric world—that is, emotions (*kleśa*) and actions (*karman*) of one's present moment of existence ripen into their respective fruits in the next moment of existence. However, insofar as the discussion is on the fruition of the function of *nirvikalpa-jñāna*, the term "ripening" cannot refer to saṃsāric existence; consequently, "the ripening of the fruit ... takes place in the two assemblies of the Buddha (*buddha-maṇḍala*)." The "two assemblies" refer to Buddha assembly of the transformation-body (*nairmāṇika-kāya*) and the Buddha assembly of the enjoyment-body (*sāṃbhogika-kāya*). When in one's effort to attain *nirvikalpa-jñāna* (that is, the first of the three non-discriminative knowledges discussed in VIII.19 below) "through practice" (*prayoga*), one gains the fruit of birth into the Buddha assembly of the transformation-body wherein one listens to the teachings of the Enlightened One. Or if one has already realized the "attainment" (*adhigama*) of *nirvikalpa-jñāna* (the second, basic knowledge discussed in VIII.19 below), then one is born into the Buddha assembly of the enjoyment-body. It should be noted that "attainment" has its various depth; thus, this indicates one form of Enlightenment, because as stated previously, this attainment takes place while one has not yet attained the full fruit of Buddhahood. In this manner, one can meet the Buddha in the next moment of existence by means of *nirvikalpa-jñāna* and one can join the two Buddha assemblies. This is the meaning of the passage, "the ripening of the fruit."

VIII.11 [Text: **niṣyanda***]*

For the bodhisattvas, the issuance [as the fruit] of *nirvikalpa-jñāna*
is thought to become more excellent (superior) as life goes on from moment to moment.

VIII.11 [NAGAO COMMENTARY]

The tenth of the 17 topics concerns "issuance" (*niṣyanda*). The term "issuance" refers to the cause/effect relationship that obtains when the wholesome, unwholesome, or indifferent qualities flow out naturally and effect a similar wholesome, unwholesome, or indifferent quality. This form of causal relationship is different from that of the "cause/effect relation-ship of ripening." With regard to *nirvikalpa-jñāna* also, there is the idea of "issuance;" consequently, through one's birth in the Buddha assembly "as life goes on from moment to moment (*uttarottara-janman*)" or as one flows through from the first bodhisattva stage to the second, or from the tenth bodhisattva stage to Buddhahood, that *nirvikalpa-jñāna* "becomes more excellent (superior) (*viśeṣa-gamana*)." This is what is meant by the statement, "the issuance [as the fruit] of *nirvikalpa-jñāna*."

VIII.12 [Text: **niḥsaraṇa / niryāna***]*

For the bodhisattvas, release [from saṃsāra] by means of *nirvikalpa-jñāna* is [actualized] on the ten stages because of achievement and consummation.

VIII.12 [NAGAO COMMENTARY]

The eleventh of the 17 topics concerns release (*niḥsaraṇa / niryāna*). "Release" means that one is liberated from worldly concerns and attains final nirvāṇa and this "is actualized on the ten stages" (*daśa-bhūmi*) of the bodhisattva's practice. After eons of practice, there is the highest "achievement" (*prāpti*) of *nirvikalpa-jñāna* on the first stage of insight, but during the course of practice from the second through the tenth stages, that *nirvikalpa-jñāna* which had been attained is gradually brought to "consummation" (*niṣpatti*).

VIII.13 [Text: **niṣṭhā-gamana***]*

For the bodhisattva, *nirvikalpa-jñāna* reaches ultimacy
because the three pure bodies are attained and because unbounded power is attained.

VIII.13 [NAGAO COMMENTARY]

The twelfth of the 17 topics concerns "reaching ultimacy" (*niṣṭhāna*). That "*nirvikalpa-jñāna* reaches ultimacy," is explained by the two reasons of "because the three pure bodies (*śuddha-tri-kāya*) are attained (*lambhana*)" and "because unbounded power (*vaśitā-uttama*) is attained." Although the three bodies of the Buddha—*svabhāvika-kāya*, *sāṃbhogika-kāya*, and *nairmaṇika-kāya*—are attained on the first stage of the path, there still remains something impure there. Because the impurities are gradually removed as one progresses through the stages and *nirvikalpa-jñāna* becomes completely purified on the tenth stage, the verse states, "the three pure bodies are attained." Furthermore, even though the three bodies are there on the first stage, when the three bodies reach the tenth stage, "unbounded power is attained." The three bodies are explained in detail in Chapter X of this text. In that discussion, ten kinds of "unbounded powers" are explicated in view of explaining the highest, unbounded power.[11]

VIII.14 [Text: **anuśaṃsa***]*

Just like open-space [is not defiled by clouds etc.,] that *nirvikalpa-jñāna* is undefiled
by the various powerful evils owing to devotion and conviction. [1]
The undefiled state of that *nirvikalpa-jñāna*, like open-space, is freed from all obstructions
insofar as it is endowed with Achievement and consummation. [2]

The undefiled state of that *nirvikalpa-jñāna* like open-space, is free of all afflictions.
Even though it functions within the ordinary world, it is never defiled by worldly things. [3]

VIII.14 [NAGAO COMMENTARY]

The thirteenth of the 17 topic concerns the blessings (*anuśaṃsa*) of the three knowledges. The term "blessings" refers to blessings as derived from virtuous actions. From this section on, *nirvikalpa-jñāna* is divided into three kinds (the one resulting from practice, the one freed from discrimination, and the one obtained after the one freed from discrimination) and its virtues are explained from various aspects by means of examples. This division of *nirvikalpa-jñāna* into the three kinds of knowledges is introduced for the first time here in this section, but the text does not clearly indicate their respective names. The text simply uses the term *nirvikalpa-jñāna* in most instances, the three knowledges being grouped into one with the basic *nirvikalpa-jñāna* at their center. Only the *Bhāṣya* (see note 2) gives the division of the three knowledges and summarizes them in VIII.1. Here, in this section, a similar statement is repeated again.

The "blessings," that is, the virtues of *nirvikalpa-jñāna*, are that "it is like open-space" (*ākāśa*) and "it is undefiled" (*nirlipta*). Space has many qualities; its infinite expanse is used to exemplify the infinite expanse of *śūnyatā* and *dharma-dhātu*, and its fundamental purity is often used as a comparison for the purity of mind. Here, purity is used as an example for *nirvikalpa-jñāna*.

Verse one explains the undefiled state of the knowledge derived on the path of preparatory practice. It is said that *nirvikalpa-jñāna* "is undefiled by the various powerful evils" (*tīrva-pāpa*). Furthermore, it is stated that this is "owing to devotion and conviction." Although this first knowledge is knowledge gained through the religious practices of ordinary beings that take place before the "path of insight," insofar as it is knowledge that seeks after *nirvikalpa-jñāna*, it is not defiled by the evils of the past. The use of the words "devotion only (*śraddha-mātra*) and conviction (*adhimukti*)" in this context is worthy of notice. The fact that these two words are used probably indicates that this knowledge belongs to the level of the ordinary people; however, to link this knowledge directly with the practice of religion based on faith of the ordinary people is problematic, because it refers to *nirvikalpa-jñāna* and confidence-trust is spoken about in regard to that knowledge.

Verse two refers to the undefiled state of the fundamental *nirvikalpa-jñāna* which is "free of (*mukta*) all obstructions (*āvaraṇa*)." In regard to the statement, "endowed with (*upeta*) achievement (*prāpti*) and consummation (*niṣpatti*)," *nirvikalpa-jñāna* is achieved on the first bodhisattva stage and consummated on the tenth, as explained in section VIII.11 (release) previously.

Verse three explains the knowledge obtained after that *nirvikalpa-jñāna*. The knowledge obtained subsequently is knowledge that, departing from enlightenment, re-enters into the ordinary world after enlightenment is attained. Owing to great compassion, a bodhisattva takes on a new birth and always "functions (*vicaran*) in the ordinary world (*loka*)" and yet, like the lotus flower that blooms and is untouched by the murky water, the bodhisattva "is never defiled by worldly things (*loka-dharma*)" such as praise and blame, etc.

VIII.15 [Text: **prabheda***]*

Just as a deaf-mute wishes to experience a thing; [just as] a deaf-mute has already experienced a
thing; [just as] a non-deaf-mute experiences a thing, just so are the three kinds of knowledges explained. [1]
Just as the dull-witted wishes to experience a thing; [just as] the dull-witted has experienced a thing;
[just as] the dull-witted experiences a thing, just so are the three kinds of knowledges explained. [2]
Just as the five [sensory organs] wish to experience a thing; [just as] the five have experienced a thing;
[just as] the mind experiences a thing, just so are the three kinds of knowledges explained. [3]
Just as one who is in the dark regarding treatises but wishes [to know] them and one who has experienced the
contents and meaning [of the treatises], just so are the three kinds of knowledges beginning with the one resulting from practice to be known in order. [4]

VIII.15 [NAGAO COMMENTARY]

The fourteenth of the 17 topics concerns the differentiation/distinction (*prabheda*) into three knowledges (*jñāna-traya*). In VIII.1, we encountered only the name, "*prabheda*" (differentiation according to distinction), but here the distinction of *nirvikalpa-jñāna* is clarified through the use of four examples. The words, "to experience a thing" means to take hold of some external thing; it simply means to perceive and refers to our world of ordinary perceptions and experiences. Perceptions and experiences are followed by the verbal expressions of the contents of those experiences. Thus the examples illustrated in verses one and two are stated in a manner of incorporating the two elements of the experience of a thing and the expression of the experience in words.

The "deaf-mute (*mūka*)" in verse one cannot speak, but "wishes (*iccha*) to experience a thing (*arthānubhāva*)." This illustrates the knowledge to be acquired on the stage of preparatory practice and is to be called the first *nirvikalpa-jñāna*. Another deaf-mute, though unable to speak, "has already experienced (*anubhūta*) a thing;" this illustrates the second *nirvikalpa-jñāna* as the basic non-discriminatory knowledge. The "non-deaf-mute," that is, one who is not a deaf-mute (*a-mūka*), can express in words what has been experienced fully; this illustrates the third *nirvikalpa-jñāna*, the one attained subsequently. In short, in knowledge derived on the stage of preparatory practice, one has not experienced anything and cannot express anything in words; in basic non-discriminating knowledge, one experiences all things but does not express them in words; in the knowledge that follows, one has already experienced things fully and expresses them in words.

The dull-witted (*mūḍha*), mentioned in verse two, is not versed in words and cannot create concepts; consequently, the dull-witted is unable to express anything in words. The rest is to be understood in the same manner as verse one above.

The "five [sensory organs] (*pañca-indriya*)," mentioned in verse three, refer to the five sensory organs of seeing (eyes), of hearing (ears), of smelling (nose), of tasting (tongue), and of touching (skin covering of the body) together with "the first five cognitions." In contrast to this, the "mind" (*manas*) mentioned in the verse refers to the sixth cognition (mental cognition, *mano-vijñāna*) or the organ (*manas*) for this cognition. Instead of the words, "to express" what has been experienced, here we find the words "to discriminate" things experienced. As the first five cognitions are direct perceptions, they are non-discriminative; that is, they are without intervention of thinking that is discriminative. In contrast, the "mind" (*manas*) or mental cognition (the sixth cognition) is no other than that which thinks and discriminates. Consequently, the five cognitions are contrasted with the mind respectively in view of the non-existence and existence of discrimination. Thus, the three knowledges are illustrated as follows. The first is the five cognitions that neither experience nor discriminate an external world; the second is the five cognitions that experience an external world but dare not (or cannot) discriminate it; the third is the mind that both experiences and discriminates an external world. Verse four contrasts the dull-witted one "who is in the dark (*avidita*) regarding treatises (*śāstra*)" and the learned one "who has experienced the contents and meaning (*dharmārtha-anubhūta/vid*)." According to the *Bhāṣya*, the word "contents" (*dharma*) means "only the words."[12] In contrast, "meaning" (*artha*) refers to the function of words. In this manner, *nirvikalpa-jñāna* of the stage of preparatory practice (*prāyogika*) is illustrated by the dull-witted who is in the dark regarding treatises but who seeks after them; the basic *nirvikalpa-jñāna* is illustrated by the learned one who has a thorough knowledge of words that comprise the contents of the treatises; knowledge obtained after that is illustrated by the learned one who not only is thoroughly versed in the contents of the treatises, but also is able to explain their meanings in all ways.

VIII.16 [Text: **dṛṣṭanta***]*

Nirvikalpa-jñāna is just like when one closes one's eyes;
knowledge obtained subsequently is just like when one opens one's eyes. [1]
Nirvikalpa-jñāna is to be known to be like open-space.
Just as the appearance of color/form [is infinite], therein, knowledge obtained subsequently is the same. [2]

VIII.16 [NAGAO COMMENTARY]

The fifteenth of the 17 topics concerns examples (*dṛṣṭānta*) of the two kinds of knowledges—*nirvikalpa-jñ āna* and [*tat-*]*pṛṣṭha-labdha*. Unlike the previous sections that aligned and compared the three knowledges, here only the "basic non-discriminatory knowledge" and "the knowledge obtained subsequently" are considered.

Verse one explains their distinctions and in verse [2] examples are explained. In other words, verse [1] distinguishes the two knowledges by comparing them to "when one closes ones eyes (*nimiñjita*)" and "when one opens ones eyes (*unmiñjita*);" verse two illustrates basic non-discriminatory knowledge "to be like open-space" and the knowledge obtained subsequently as "just like [the appearance of color/form (*rūpa-pratibhāsa*) [is infinite] therein."

In VIII.14, "open-space" was used in the sense of purity, but the *Bhāṣya* here gives four meanings for the term regarding which *Hsüan tsang* and Tibetan translations are closely aligned. The four meanings given for "open-space" are: 1) expansive (*sphuraṇa*), 2) stainless (*nirlepa*), 3) not self-contriving (*avikalpana*), and 4) not to be discerned by others (*avikalpya*).[13] *Gupta's* translation corresponds closely to these, but *Paramārtha's* translation is quite different.

"Knowledge obtained subsequently" refers to the situation in which all entities manifest their form in open-space (that is compared to basic *nirvikalpa-jñāna*). In other words, being developed from *śūnyatā*, their form exist *śūnyatā*. This knowledge obtained subsequently differs from basic non-discriminatory knowledge in that it discerns (discriminates) and is discerned (discriminated) by others. Basic non-discriminating knowledge is negative and transcendental. Knowledge obtained subsequently is affirmative and re-appears in the world of existence.

VIII.17 [Text: **kṛtyānuṣṭhāna***]*

Just as the maṇi-jewel and the [heavenly] drums perform their own respective acts [spontaneously] without discriminating,
So too Buddha activities occur always [spontaneously] in various ways without distinguishing.

VIII.17 [NAGAO COMMENTARY]

The sixteenth of the 17 topics refer to 'effortlessly (*anābhogena*) enacting various acts (*kṛtyānuṣṭhāna*).' If *nirvikalpa-jñāna* that has been explained in the sections above is the fundamental essence of a Buddha, then it would be without discrimination (*vinā kalpam*) and therefore would not distinguish sentient beings. That being so, how could it benefit sentient beings? Such a question is assumed here, and this section is a response to it. If this question is to be related to the idea expressed in the statement, "Just like the appearance of color/form [is infinite] therein" of the previous section, it would take the following form. From a negative non-discriminatory knowledge (*nirvikalpa-jñāna*), how does the affirmative discrimination of existence called "color/form" arise in the knowledge obtained subsequently? The response to that is: 'naturally,' 'spontaneously,' or 'on its own accord.' Here the examples of the maṇi-jewel (*maṇi*) and heavenly drums or cymbals (*tūrya*) are given. The word "maṇi" refers to a wish-fulfilling gem (*cintā-maṇi*) that fulfills a person's wish spontaneously without distinguishing. The word "tūrya" refers to heavenly musical instruments of the (various) gods. Even when there is no one to strike the drums or cymbals, the sounds of music flow out of them spontaneously. The analogy of the maṇi-jewel and the heavenly instruments in regard to fact that the Buddhas and Bodhisattvas have no self-interest in their act of salvation is used to show that the activity of the Buddha (*buddha-kriyā*) and Bodhisattvas arises spontaneously on its own accord. Knowledge obtained after that *nirvikalpa-jñāna* is understood as an act of compassion towards sentient beings that arises spontaneously from *śūnyatā* (emptiness) and the negation of *nirvikalpa-jñāna*. In short, "knowledge obtained after *nirvikalpa-jñāna*" is śūnyatā enacting spontaneously.

VIII.18 [Text: **gāmbhirya***]*

[*Nirvikalpa-jñāna*] exists neither wherein [there is discrimination] nor in some other; it is neither
knowledge nor not knowledge. A knowing which is not distinct from what is known is non-discriminating. [1]
Because there is no entity [whatsoever] that is discriminated, it is taught [by the Buddha] that all Entities are by nature free of discrimination.
Therefore, knowing in such a manner is non-discriminative [knowledge]. [2]

VIII.18 [NAGAO COMMENTARY]

The seventeenth, i.e., the last of the 17 topics concerns profundity (*gāmbhīrya*). Being named "profundity," this section is naturally full of paradoxical expressions, and there are many points that are difficult to explain.

The *Bhāṣya*[14] gives two interpretations of the first verse:

(1) The perceptual-object of unreal imagination (*abhūta-parikalpa*) or of cognition (*vijñāna*) in general is of the other-dependent (*paratantra*) nature. This is testified, for instance, by the statement (II.16) that other dependent nature is taken as what is discerned (*parikalpya*), that is, as the object of discerning (*parikalpa*). Does *nirvikalpa-jñāna* also occur with such an existence as its object of perception or does it have something other? In response, the verse says that such an existence that is discriminated (*vikalpya*) is not the object of its perception, but there is no other object apart from it. The statement, "[*Nirvikalpa-jñāna*] exists neither wherein [there is discrimination] (*nāsti tasmin*)" means that because *nirvikalpa-jñāna* is non-discursive (*nirvikalpa*), it does not occur wherein there is discursive thought. However, *nirvikalpa-jñāna* is a knowledge that perceives the reality or suchness (*tathatā*) of all beings, that is, dharmatā (reality per-se) of all entities (*dharma*). Since *dharmatā* is not perceived separately from *dharma* and relates to it as 'neither one nor different,' when *nirvikalpa-jñāna* realizes reality per-se (*dharmatā*), its object is nothing

but *dharma*. This is the meaning of the statement, "nor in some other (*na cānyasmin*)."

Now another question is raised concerning the relationship between *nirvikalpa-jñāna* and knowledge (*jñāna*). If *nirvikalpa-jñāna* is knowledge, then how can it be said to be non-discriminatory (*nirvikalpa*)? If it is not knowledge, then *nirvikalpa* should not form a compound with *jñāna* as its last member. The response in the verse is the paradoxical statement, "it is neither knowledge (*na jñānaṃ*) nor not knowledge (*na cājñānaṃ*)." This means that since the basic *nirvikalpa-jñāna* is different from the other two knowledges, the knowledge on the stage of preparatory practice and the knowledge obtained subsequently, it is said to be "neither knowledge," but since it is an effect of the knowledge on the stage of preparatory practice and the cause for the knowledge obtained subsequently, is said to be "nor not knowledge."

(2) The second interpretation combines the two items above into one. It is expressed in the verse by the statement, "[*Nirvikalpa-jñāna*] exists neither wherein [there is discrimination], nor in some other." Because *nirvikalpa-jñāna* does not exist wherein there is discrimination, the verse states "It is neither knowledge" and because suchness (*tathatā*) or reality per-se (*dharmatā*) is not found "in some other" apart from wherein there is discrimination, the verse states "nor not knowledge."

Thus, *nirvikalpa-jñāna* is an 'equality-knowledge' in which there is no distinction between the seeing-subject and the object-seen. The verse concludes: "a knowing which is not distinct (*na viśiṣṭa*) from what is known (*jñeya*)," that is, knowledge which is of one substance with the object, "is non-discriminating (*nirvikalpaka*)." Asvabhāva's *Upanibandhana* adds: "A knowing that is not distinct from what is to be known" is compared to the relationship that obtains between open-space and color/form that appears therein[15] (cf. VIII.16, Verse 2).

Now, with regard to the second verse, there is a problem in interpreting the fourth line, but the first three lines give no problem. A certain sūtra quoted here in the verse explains that the Buddha "taught that all entities (*sarva-dharma*) are by nature (*prakṛtyā*) free of discrimination (*avikalpatva*)." And why is it that all entities are free of discrimination? The response is given in the first line thus, "Because there is no entity that can be discriminated (*vikalpya*)." The words "that can be discriminated" is contextually the same as the words 'an existence that is discriminated' (*vikalpya*) explained in the discussion on interpretation (1) above. Because what is discerned and conceptualized in the cognitive process is nothing other than what has been created through discrimination, it does not exist in reality. Whatever is established through discrimination or through the thought process cannot be said to have real or actual existence. In contrast, the entities truly existent are found only in knowledge (*jñāna*) that is non-discriminating (*nirvikalpa*). This is what the Buddha meant in the statement, "all entities are by nature free of discrimination."

However, if all entities are by nature free of discrimination, then people should not need to put forth the effort of going through religious practices in order to attain *nirvikalpa-jñāna*; they should be liberated just as they are. The response to this criticism is given in the fourth line, but it is interpreted differently by the different translators. According to the three translations by Paramārtha, Gupta, and Hsüan-tsang, the reason that people are not liberated just as they are is that they lack *nirvikalpa-jñāna* or that their knowledge is not *nirvikalpa* (both with the double negation, 'no nirvikalpa' and 'not nirvikalpa'). In contrast to this, the Tibetan translation, that has only one negative particle, states "therefore, knowing in such a manner is non-discriminative [knowledge]." Buddhaśānta's translation is very close to this in that it has only one negative particle. Thus the translations differ from each other.

The statement "knowing in such a manner" in the Tibetan translation means to know all entities in the manner that the Buddha explicated them and that is said to be *nirvikalpa-jñāna*. If we interpret this Tibetan translation to imply that people lack *nirvikalpa-jñāna* and thus cannot be liberated just-as-they-are, then it has the same intention as the other three Chinese translations. Consequently, after explicating that meaning, the *Bhāṣya* explains that only when one is awakened (enlightened) to *nirvikalpa-jñāna* there is liberation, but so long as it is not realized, there is no liberation.[16] The present translation has followed tentatively the Tibetan text, because it seems to be most conducive to keeping the verse form.

VIII.19 [Text: Three kinds of **Prāyogika-jñāna, Mūla-jñāna** *and Five kinds of* **tat-pṛṣṭha-labdha-jñāna***]*

Here, *nirvikalpa-jñāna* that results from practice (*prayogika-nirvikalpa-jñāna*) [on the stage of preparatory practice] is three-fold, on account of its divisions according to whether it arises (1) from a cause (*hetu*), (2) from being drawn out (*ākṣepa*), or (3) from repeated praxis (*abhyāsa*).

[The basic] *nirvikalpa-jñāna* is also three-fold, because it is *nirvikalpa-jñāna* by virtue of being (1) satisfaction (*saṃtuṣṭi*), (2) unperverted (*aviparyāsa*), and (3) without conceptual fabrication (*niṣprapañca*).

[The knowledge] obtained subsequently (*tat-pṛṣṭha-labdha*) to *nirvikalpa-jñāna*] is five-fold, because of its distinctions of careful observation (*vicāra*), (1) thorough penetration (*prativedha*), (2) repeated recollection (*anusmaraṇa*), (3) establishing [what is recalled as a teaching] (*vyavasthāna*), (4) integrating [all teachings] (*sambhinna[-ālambana]*), and 5) perfecting as one wishes (*samṛddhi*).

VIII.19 [NAGAO COMMENTARY]

The three knowledges—*nirvikalpa-jñāna* that results from practice on the stage of preparatory practice, basic *nirvikalpa-jñāna*, and knowledge acquired subsequently to the basic *nirvikalpa-jñāna*—are divided further into three or five kinds. The basis for these divisions differs in each case.

Nirvikalpa-jñāna that results from practice is distinguished according to the cause from which it arises (Parmārtha's *Bhāṣya* says 'with regard to cause'[17]).

(1) The first, "cause" (*hetu*), means the family line or lineage (*gotra*) into which one is born. Family lineage means, with respect to the mundane world, that one is endowed with a particular physical body and belongs to a special genealogy, and that this has been going on since time immemorial. In the same way, one who belongs to the bodhisattva family is one who has the qualification of being a receptacle to receive Buddhahood and this is understood to be the "cause." According to the *Upanibandha*,[18] *nirvikalpa-jñāna* that results on the stage of preparatory practice will arise in one who possesses this cause by virtue of meeting 'powerful condition.' (Here 'condition' is contrasted with 'cause;' by virtue of realizing that it is a powerful condition, it is ascertained that one has been in the Buddha-family.) (2) The second, "being drawn out" (*ākṣepa*), means that, in some case, knowledge resulting from practice is "drawn out" in the present life owing to the repeated praxis of the former life functioning as its cause. (3) The third, "repeated praxis" (*abhyāsa*), means that, in some case, knowledge resulting from praxis arises owing to the repeated praxis in the prsent life by each individual.

Basic *nirvikalpa-jñāna* is distinguished into three according to the kind of person who possesses it (Paramārtha's *Bhāṣya:* 'with regard to person'[19]). The first one is *nirvikalpa-jñāna* of the worldly or ordinary person. The second one is of the śrāvakas and others. The third one is of the bodhisattvas, and it is needless to say that only this one is the true *nirvikalpa-jñāna.*

(1) The first one is "non-discriminatory" in that an ordinary person gains "satisfaction" with a low level enlightenment and does not try to attain a higher state. Or the ordinary person, by means of the ordinary wisdom of hearing, thinking, and practice, attains the highest worldly state (*bhavāgra*), mistakes it for nirvāṇa, and, being satisfied, does not try to attain anything higher. (2) The second one is "non-discriminatory" in that the śrāvaka and other sages, who have already awakened to the "unperverted" suchness by realizing the impermanence, suffering, and so on of the world, do not fall again into erroneous discrimination of permanence, and so on. (3) The third one is "non-discriminatory" in that the bodhisattvas envisage all entities "without conceptual fabrication," fabrication being nothing more than an activity belonging to the world of conventional language.

Knowledge obtained subsequently is a discriminatory knowledge that is attained after the negation implicit in "basic *nirvikalpa-jñāna*" is realized. Its discriminatory process of careful observation (*vicāra*) is distinguished into five kinds according to its content (Paramārtha's *Bhāṣya*: 'with regard to events'[20]).

(1) As for the first, "careful observation of thorough penetration," thorough penetration (*prativedha*) refers to intuitive realization of truth (*abhisamaya*). Having arisen from the samādhi of *nirvikalpa-jñāna*, an awareness that 'I thoroughly penetrated such and such' occurs to the bodhisattva and he carefully

observes it. (2) The second, "its recollection (*anusmaraṇa*)" means not to forget what has been penetrated by recollecting it later. (3) The third, "establishing (*vyavasthāna*) [what is recalled as a teaching]" means to establish what was penetrated as a teaching and explain it to others. (4) The fourth, "the intergrating [all teachings]" (*sambhinna[-ālambana]*) means to comprehend the teachings by (synthesizing and) integrating all of them into one. This enables one to attain the turn-about of the basis (see III.12). (5) The fifth, "perfecting as one wishes" (*samṛddhi*) is so translated because Buddhaśānta translates the text here by the term *ch'êng-chiu* (perfection) and all the other three Chinese translations by the term *ju-i* (fulfilling as one wishes) and thus, it includes the meaning "mastery" (*vibhutva*). Mastery, in this context means, for example, if one so wishes one can change a piece of dirt into gold (refer to verse [4] in the following section) and this is the working of supernatural power (*ṛddhi*) that operates in the knowledge obtained subsequently after *nirvikalpa-jñāna*. The words "carefully observing" qualifies all of five topics, but in regard to the fifth, the *Bhāṣya* gives two possible interpretations: (1) carefully observing the fulfilling according to one's wishes and (2) carefully observing in order to fulfill according to one's wishes.[21]

VIII.20 [Text: Demonstration/proof of nirvikalpa-jñāna*]*

There are separate verses to demonstrate (prove *sādhaka*) *nirvikalpa-jñāna*:[22]

(1) Hellish beings, animals, man, heavenly beings—each according to one's ability thinks differently
about a single same thing; therefore, it is claimed that an object is not something effected.
preta-tiryaṅ-manuṣyāṇāṃ devānāṃ ca yathā-arhataḥ /
tulyavastu-manobhedād artha-aniṣpattir iṣyate / 1 /

(2) In regard to the past etc., also in a dream or two images, because objects of perception do not exist and because
[in such a case,] that [cognition itself] is taken as the objective referent [a world external does not exist].
atīta-ādau tathā svapne pratibimba-dvaye 'pi ca /
asann-ālambanatvāc ca tad-ālambana-yogataḥ / 2 /

(3) If an object of perception were effected as an object, then non-discriminating knowledge could not exist.
And on account of the non-existence of that, the attainment of Buddhahood also could not occur.
arthasya arthatva-niṣpattau jñānaṃ na syād akalpakaṃ /
tad-abhāvāc ca buddhatva-prāptir naiva-upapadyate / 3 /

(4a) Because when a bodhisattva attains [mental] mastery, earth and so on are perceived as existing [just as
one wishes] owing to the strength of zealous application, and [so also] for a meditation practitioner,
bodhisattve vaśi-prāpte 'dhimukti-vaśād yataḥ /

tathā-bhāvaḥ pṛthivy-ādau dhyāyināṃ ca-upalabhyate / 4a /

(4b) and here because to a knowledgeable one who has attained calm and who has fulfilled his investigation
all dharmas become manifest just-as-they-are [as objects] when he is intensely attentive to them,
niṣpanna-vicayasya-iha dhīmataḥ śama-lābhinaḥ /
sarva-dharma-manaskāre tathā-artha-khyānato 'pi ca / 4b /

(4c) and again because, when the activity of knowing is non-discriminating, all objects do not become manifest;
therefore, you should know things [as such] do not exist! when it does not exist, its representation [also does not exist].
jñāna-cāre 'vikalpe hi sarvārtha-akhyānato 'pi ca /
artha-abhāva-upagantavyo vijñaptes tad-abhāvataḥ / 4c /

VIII.20 [NAGAO COMMENTARY]

The text opens with the statement, "to demonstrate (prove *sādhaka*) *nirvikalpa-jñāna*." The *Bhāṣya* also states that the explanation regarding *nirvikalpa-jñāna* ended with the last section; thus, from this section onward the text attempts to demonstrate *nirvikalpa-jñāna*. The sanskrit version of these verses can be found in *Abhidharmasamuccayabhāṣya* (see note 22); however, from where these verses originate cannot be established accurately.[23] As pointed out in II.14B, in the Tibetan translation these six verses appear both there in II.14B as well as here in this section; however, as attested to by the Chinese translations, these verses were found in the original text, in all probabilities, in this section only.

The ideas explained in these six verses have been discussed already in prose in II.14A (the section preceding II.14B). In that section, the knowledge by which the non-existent quality of the external world is known was divided into four. In order to parallel the discussion of the four in section II.14A, here, they have been indicated by the numbers in parentheses (1)-(4), the fourth one (4) being divided further into three, indicated by (a)-(c). It should be noticed, however, that whereas sections II.14A and 14B were devoted to the explication of *vijñapti-mātra* (hence, the non-substantial quality of the external world), here the six verses are used to demonstrate *nirvikalpa-jñāna*. Therefore, although an outline of the four knowledges has been presented in the previous sections from the viewpoint of *vijñapti-mātra*, here the four will be investigated especially in regard to how they demonstrate *nirvikalpa-jñāna*.

(1) The statement, "an object is not something effected" (verse 1, line 4), suggests the conclusion that what is perceived as the external world is non-substantive. Hellish beings see water as a plateau; animals see as pure water what man sees as filth; what man sees as pure water is seen by heavenly beings as impure. In this manner, the fact that "each according to one's ability thinks differently about a single same thing" demonstrates (proves) that what is perceived as the external world lacks determinate substantive qualities.

(2) Even though "the past" and "the future" do not exist substantively just as the Sautrāntikas claim, they are still cognized as real. Even though we are sleeping in a small room, we enjoy the wide expanse of the mountains and rivers "in a dream." We have "two images," the image we see in a mirror or the image we see in meditation. In such cases, "those objects of perception do not exist" substantively. Instead, cognition "itself," that is, what has been constructed as an object (of cognition) within the cognitive process becomes the "objective referent." In other words, "the past" and so on "possess that [cognition itself] as the objective referent." This means that the mind sees mind itself. In other words, the mind perceives the image that it has itself constructed. It is in this sense that cognition-only is established and what is perceived substantively as an external object does not exist.

(3) *Nirvikalpa-jñāna* is knowledge that arises in the negation of the substantive quality of an object. "If an object of perception were effected as an object," then the knowledge that discerns the reality of that object could not be a "non-discriminating knowledge." If non-discriminating knowledge did not exist and there was only discriminating knowledge, then "the attainment of Buddhahood" would become meaningless, because the claim for discriminating knowledge simply rejects the fundamental meaning underlying "wisdom" and "enlightenment" of Buddhahood.

(4) Here in (4a) to (4c) also, the manner in which the external world or the object appears is discussed. Division (4a) clarifies that "when a bodhisattva attains masteries, earth and so on are perceived as existing [as one wishes]," for example, as gold "owing to the strength of zealous application." When the knowledge obtained subsequently was discussed in the previous section (VIII.19), the fifth point, "perfecting," was interpreted to include the meaning of supernatural power of 'mastery' in terms of '*ju-i*' (fulfilling one's wishes). Here, in this context, the same super-natural power is at work.

The term "meditation practitioners" refers to the śrāvaka and others who have attained meditative practices fully; by virtue of this, the same supernatural power is obtained by them and the manner in which the external object appears is the same for them.

Division (4b) explains that when a bodhisattva "is intensively attentive to [the dharmas taught in the sūtras]," the meaning of the sūtras and the images of the buddhas "become manifest just-as-they-are."

In contrast to divisions (4a) and (4b) above that explain that objects become manifested, division (4c) explains that *nirvikalpa-jñāna* means that an object is not manifested. In all these cases, "the non-existent quality of the world" is exemplified and the statement found in the fourth foot of the first verse is simply highlighted.

The discussion up to this point can be considered to be a re-statement of a sūtra (on this point see II.14A). Finally, in (4c), pāda c and d, a conclusion is given. Although the statement, 'cognition-only exists, objects do not exist,' a statement fundamental to the Yogācāra Vijñānavāda school, can be established through the realization of "the non-existence of thing [as such]," it is further concluded that when a thing [as such] does not exist, "representation" of cognition also is non-existent. When the world that is to be represented by cognition (as its object) does not exist, "representation" itself loses its meaning and cannot be an object of cognition. This means that when an outer object does not exist, cognition-only also cannot be established (in *nirvikalpa-jñāna*).

VIII.21 [Text: nirvikalpa-jñāna/prajñā*]*

The perfection of wisdom (*prajñā-pāramitā*) and *nirvikalpa-jñāna* are not different (*nirviśiṣṭa*). It is, for example, as stated [in a sūtra]: "A bodhisattva dwells (*tiṣṭhati*) in the perfection of wisdom according to non-dwelling (*asthāna-yogena*) and then he fulfills (*paripūri*) the other [five] perfections (*pāramitā*) by means of intense practice (*bhāvanā*)."

How does the bodhisattva fulfill (*paripūri*) according to non-dwelling? By rejection (*parityāga*) of the five kinds of dwelling (*pañca-vidha-sthāna*). (1) Rejection of dwelling in the conceit of "I" (*ahaṃkāra-sthāna*) as held by the non-Buddhists (*tīrthika*). (2) Rejection of dwelling in the discriminating thought (*vikalpa-sthāna*) held by a bodhisattva who has not yet seen truth (*adṛṣṭa-tattva-bodhisattva*). (3) Rejection of dwelling in either of the two extreme views (*anta-dvaya-sthāna*) of saṃsāra and nirvāṇa. (4) Rejection of dwelling in the contentment (*saṃtuṣṭi-sthāna*) that the mere removal of the obstruction of afflictions (*kleśa-āvaraṇa-prahāṇa-mātra*) is sufficient. (5) Rejection of dwelling in a world of nirvāṇa without [afflictional] remainder (*nirupadhiśeṣa-nirvāṇa-dhātu-sthāna*) where the benefitting of sentient beings is disregarded (*sattva-artha-nirapekṣa*).

VIII.21 [Nagao Commentary]

Here it is made clear that *nirvikalpa-jñāna* is not different from the perfection of wisdom (*prajñā-pāramitā*) expounded in the Prajñāpāramitā Sūtras. It is also evident that the Yogācāra school considered the Prajñāpāramitā Sūtras as the most superior texts on which to base one's tenets. The statement, "dwells according to non-dwelling," in the passage quoted above reflects a convention found in the Prajñāpāramitā Sūtras—that is, the statement is paradoxical and contradictory. The term *nirvikalpa-jñāna* does not appear there, but the paradoxical statement, "dwelling according to non-dwelling," demonstrates what *nirvikalpa-jñāna* means. Accordingly, it reminds one of the modus operandi of *nirvikalpa-jñāna* which is to discriminate without discriminating.

Here, however, in order to dissolve the contradiction of dwelling without dwelling, the author explains in what a bodhisattva should not dwell, so that he can dwell properly—that is, the author explains what kind of dwelling is to be rejected. Dwelling in this context can mean 'dwelling happily in trust,' hence it can refer to one's own conviction or standpoint. There are five kinds of dwellings that belong to five kinds of persons and that are to be rejected. (1) The non-Buddhists dwell happily in the attachment to a belief in ātman. (2) A bodhisattva who has not understood reality as-it-is dwells in the thought in which he discriminates wisdom to be such and such. (3) Worldly people dwell happily in saṃsāra while the śrāvakas dwell happily in the thought of escaping from it and of aiming for nothing but nirvāṇa. (4) The śrāvakas dwell in the thought of removing the obstacles of afflictions without showing any interest in the removing of the obstacle of the knowlables. (5) Again, the śrāvakas, without placing importance on the practice of benefitting other fellow beings, dwell in the ultimate nirvāṇa, the nirvāṇa without remainder, in which afflictions are totally removed. Because these five dwellings are to be rejected, it is said that the bodhisattva dwells according to not dwelling.

VIII.22 [Text: śrāvaka's and bodhisattva's wisdom: distinctions]

What distinctions (*viśeṣa*) are there between the wisdom (*jñāna*) of a śrāvaka and that of a bodhisattva? It should be known that there are distinctions in view of five aspects (*ākāra*). (1) Distinction in view of non-discrimination (*nirvikalpa*): [unlike the śrāvaka,] the doctrines of psycho-physical constituents and others (*skandha-ādi-dharma*) are viewed without discrimination [by a bodhisattva]. (2) Distinction in view of not being restricted to small portions (*a-prādeśika*): [a bodhisattva, unlike the śrāvaka,] not being limited to small portions, pursues completely [the three matters of] penetrating into truth (*tattva-prativedha*), entering all modes of the knowables (*sarvākāra-jñeya-praveśa*), and performing for the sake of (*adhikṛtya*) [benefitting] all sentient beings. (3) Distinction in view of not residing (*anavasthita*): [a śrāvaka resides in nirvāṇa, but for a bodhisattva] nirvāṇa is not dwelt in (*apratiṣṭhita-nirvāṇa*). (4) Distinction in view of the infinite (*ātyantika*): [the virtues of a bodhisattva, unlike those of the śrāvaka are] inexhaustive (*a-kṣaya*) [and are working infinitely] even when a bodhisattva enters the nirvāṇa-domain (*nirvāṇa-dhātu*). (5) Distinction in view of having nothing higher (*niruttara*): there is not separately another particularly superior (*viśiṣṭa-tara*) vehicle (*yāna*) beyond that [bodhisattva-yāna, that is, the mahāyāna]. Here there is a verse:

> Those [bodhisattvas] who have acquired wisdom (*jñāna*), the nature of which is compassion and is sublime owing to the five kinds of distinctions,
> are said to acquire (*saṃpad*) quickly (*adūra*) [fortunes] worldly (*laukika*) and transworldly (*lokottara*).

VIII.22 [Nagao Commentary]

The distinction of the śrāvaka's and the bodhisattva's intuitive realization (*abhisamaya*) has been discussed already in III.15. The distinction of wisdom discussed in this section is closely aligned with those distinctions and the meanings overlap. Moreover, the five distinct aspects of wisdom has many points in common with the five rejections of dwelling discussed in the previous section.

(1) Unlike the śrāvakas who doctrinally systematize the teachings of the five psycho-physical constituents and others through intellectual analysis, the bodhisattvas observe the same teachings through the wisdom of *nirvikalpa-jñāna* that surpasses the common intellect. This characterizes the distinctive quality of

this wisdom. (2) In contrast to the śrāvaka whose understanding is fractional, that of the bodhisattvas is "not limited to a small portion." The reason for this is that a śrāvaka's "penetration into truth" consists of an understanding of the non-substantiality of the personality (*pudgala-nairātmya*) only while that of the bodhisattvas consists of the non-substantiality of both the personality and the entities (*pudgala-dharma-nairātmya*; cf. VII.8 §7). Among the "three matters" discussed above, the latter two are understood to be varieties of the first one, "penetration into truth." (3) As for nirvāṇa, the śrāvakas dwell in and cling to nirvāṇa, but the bodhisattvas do not. Therefore, the nirvāṇa of the bodhisattvas is called "nirvāṇa not dwelt in" (*apratiṣṭhita-nirvāṇa*) which is discussed in the next chapter (chapter IX) of this text. (4) The nirvāṇa of the śrāvakas is none other than an ultimate cessation, wherein wisdom comes to an end; but in the nirvāṇa of the bodhisattvas, the activity of dharmakāya is endless (according to *Upanibandha*[24]), and this means that on the basis of dharmakāya, enjoyment body (sambhoga-kāya) and transformed body (nirmaṇa-kāya) are active constantly and without limit. (5) The spiritual path of the śrāvakas has something higher above it insofar as the pratyekabuddha and bodhisattva vehicles are beyond it, but the bodhisattva vehicle, that is, the Mahāyāna, is without superior and there is nothing higher than that. Here the word "vehicle" is used in the meaning of "wisdom." The wisdom of the bodhisattva is distinguished from that of the śrāvaka owing to these five reasons and it is admirably superior.

In the verse, a bodhisattva's wisdom is said to be established on the basis of compassion and is superior by virtue of five aspects. Accordingly, a bodhisattva is able to completely accomplish the mundane and supermundane bliss.

VIII.23 [Text: The outcome/result]

When the bodhisattvas , having acquired the virtues (*guṇa-saṃpad*) of the excellent training of discipline (*adhiśīla*), the excellent training of mind (*adhicitta*), and the excellent training of wisdom (*adhiprajñā*), have attained masteries (*vibhutva*) over all fortunes (*dhana*) and others, why is it that [when, without doubt, the bodhisattvas generously share these fortunes and so on] sentient beings who suffer the pains of poverty (*upakaraṇa-vyasana[?]*) appear? The reason for this are:

(1) Sentient beings are seen to possess karma that hinder (*vibaṃdha-karma*) [the bodhisattva's act to bestow fortune, status, and so on upon them by means of his supernatural powers].

(2) If enjoyment is brought forth (*bhoga-upasaṃbhāra*) upon them, it is thought that this proves to be something that hinders (*antarāya*) the occurrence of the wholesome (*kuśala-dharma-utpāda*).

(3) If [on the other hand, enjoyment is not brought upon them and they suffer from poverty,] it is thought that they experience face to face (*abhimukha*) disgust (*saṃvega*) of this world.

(4) If enjoyment is brought upon them, this is thought to prove to be the cause (*hetutva*) for increasing the unwholesome (*akuśala-dharma-upacaya*).

(5) It is also thought that enjoyment brought upon them becomes the cause for harming (*ghātana*) other sentient beings much more than themselves (*bahutara-sattva*).

Here, there is a verse:

Acts (*karman*), hindrances (*pratibandha*) [to the wholesome], face to face experience (*abhimukhatva*) [of disgust], accumulation (*caya*) [of the unwholesome], and injury (*pīḍana*) [to others] are seen;

therefore, people are unable to acknowledge enjoyment [of fortunes and so on that are brought forth] by a bodhisattva.

VIII.23 [Nagao Commentary]

This section comprises the conclusion for chapters VI through VIII in which excellent training in the three learnings were discussed. As a result of the excellent training in the three learnings, a bodhisattva becomes a liberated person who "has mastery over all fortunes and so on." However, in spite of that, this section points out several cases in which sentient beings are not able to enjoy the benefits bestowed upon them by the bodhisattvas (cf. X.19A verse). If the bodhisattvas bestow all of the fortunes amassed by them upon sentient beings, then "why is it that the sentient beings suffer the pains of poverty?" The fact that sentient beings cannot enjoy the fortunes bestowed upon them is not the fault of the bodhisattva but is the fault of the sentient beings (cf. X.28A [7]) who are like a cracked dish that cannot be filled with water and house the reflection of the moon. When there is a flaw like a crack inherent in the sentient beings, the bodhisattva is unable to do anything. The fault of the sentient beings are explained as fivefold. Sentient beings possess "karma that hinder" the bestowing of fortune (reason no. 1 discussed in text above). So long as sentient beings possess these acts, even though a bodhisattva may have the supernatural power of bestowing fortunes, he cannot exercise that power positively. The *Upanibandha* quotes a verse which describes a mother who attempts to breast feed her child, but even though milk is plentiful and the mother wishes to feed her child, if the child's throat is clogged, there is nothing that the mother can do.[25] The *Bhāṣya* exemplifies this by the example of a man's ability to drink water from a river, but the hungry ghost's (preta's) inability to drink the water owing to its own karma.[26] Moreover, among the reasons why the Bodhisattva is unable to bestow fortunes is the fact that the bestowing of fortune becomes "hinderance to the wholesome" (reason no. 2) for the sentient beings, because it functions as "a cause for increasing the unwholesome" (reason no.4), and because it function as "a cause to harm others" (reason no. 5). These are all faults possessed by the sentient beings. If, on the other hand, fortune is not bestowed upon them, then they will "experience face to face the disgust of the world" (reason no. 3), and this leads people towards the wholesome. These four exemplify that "not to bestow" represents the bodhisattva's great compassion and the act of benefitting others. For these five reasons, it is said that there are "sentient beings who suffer the pains of poverty." Finally, the meanings are summarized in a single verse.

I would like to acknowledge the Sabbatical Leave Research Grant from the University of Calgary that made it possible to work personally with Professor Nagao in preparing this paper. I also wish to express my gratitude to Professor Nagao without whose guidance this English translation would not have been accomplished.

Notes

1. Professor Nagao's research into all aspects of Buddhism in India, China, and Tibet has been, in a sense, for the sake of accomplishing a definitive Japanese translation of Asaṅga's work. Consequently, it seems most appropriate that a small segment of his work appear as a contribution to Professor Yün-hua Jan's retirement volume as these two scholars have been life long colleagues. The translation of Asaṅga's text is marked by the roman numeral VIII to indicate the chapter; the arabic numbers that follow indicate the sub-divisions as devised by Professor Étienne Lamotte in his monumental work, *La Somme du Grand Véhicle d'Asaṅga (Mahāyāna-saṃgraha), Tome I and II* (Louvain: Bureaux du Muséon, 1938). Professor Nagao's study is indicated by the words "Nagao Commentary." It should be mentioned that the end notes appearing here have been added for the sake of this paper by me and that they are totally different from the extensive footnotes appearing in Professor Nagao's Japanese translation for which see note 11 below.

2. See, *Theg pa chen po bsdus pa'i 'grel pa* in *Sde Dge Tibetan Tripiṭaka*, hereafter *SDTT*, Tokyo: Sekai Seiten Kankō Kyōkai, 1980. Sems tsam 12. p 88, 175a.

3. See Unrai Wogihara ed. *Bonbun Bosatsuji-kyō (Bodhisattvabhūmi)*. Tokyo: Sankibo Buddhist Book Store, 1971. p. 38.

4. svabhāvo bodhisattvānāṃ pañcākāravivarjitaḥ /
jñānasya nirvikalpasya na bhūta-artha-vicitrakaḥ /
(The reconstucted sanskrit verse is by G.M. Nagao)

5. *SDTT*, Sems tsam 12. p 133, 266a-b.

6. *SDTT*, Sems Tsam 12, p. 88, 175b.

7. Ét. Lamotte, ibid. Tome II. p. 234.

8. *SDTT*, Sems tsam 12, p.88, 176a.

9. For a complete discussion, see *SDTT*, Sems Tsam 12, p. 88, 176b: lam gnyis ni tshogs lam dang / rten gyi lam mo // de la tshogs kyi lam ni sbyin pa dang / tshul khrims dang / bzod pa dang / brtson 'grus kyi pha rol tu phyin pa'o // rten gyi lam ni bsam gtan kyi pha rol tu phyin pa ste / gang gi phyir sngar bstan pa'i pha rol tu phyin pa las yang dag par byung ba'i dge ba'i rtsa ba dang / bsam gtan la brten nas rnam par mi rtog pa'i ye shes shes rab kyi pha rol tu phyin pa zhes bya ba de 'byung bar 'gyur bas so //

10. ibid. p. 88, 176b: sangs rgyas nyid ma thob kyi bar du .../

11. G.M. Nagao, *Shodaijōron—Wayaku to Chūkai*. Tokyo: Kōdansha Inc. 1982 (vol 1), 1987 (vol. 2). See vol. 2, Chapter X, section 3B, p. 322-325.

12. *SDTT*, Sems tsam 12, p. 89, 178a: 'dir chos ni ye ge tsam du bzhed do //

13. ibid., p. 89, 178b: nam mkha' bzhin du zhes bya ba ni / ji ltar nam mkha' khyab pa dang / ma gos pa dang / mi rtog pa dang / brtag par bya ba ma yin pa de bzhin du rnam par mi rtog pa'i ye shes kyang chos thams cad la ro gcig pa stong pa nyid kyis khyab pas na khyab pa'o // chos thams cad kyis ma gos pas na gos pa med pa'o // rang nyid kyis rnam par mi rtog pas na rnam par med pa'o // gzhan gyis brtags par bya ba ma yin pa nyid kyis rnam par brtag par

bya ba ma yin pa ste / rnam par mi rtog pa'i ye shes ni de ltar blta bar bya'o //

14. ibid., p. 89-90; 178b-179b.

15. *SDTT*, Sems tsam 12, p. 135, 269b-270a: shes bya dang ni khyad med pa'i // shes gang de nyid mi rtog nyid / ces bya ba ni gzung ba dang 'dzin par rnam par dbye bar yongs su chad pa med pa'i phyir 'di ni shes pa'o // 'di ni shes bya'o zhes khyad par med pa gang yin pa de ye shes de'i rnam par mi rtog pa nyid de / gang shes bya dang tha dad pa [270a] ma yin pa de ni nam mkha' dang snang ba bzhin no //

16. See *SDTT*, Sems tsam 12, p. 90, 179b.

17. *Taishō* (hereafter *T.*), vol. XXXI, p. 243c.

18. *SDTT*, Sems tsams 12, p. 135, 270a.

19. *T.* vol. XXXI. p. 243c.

20. *T.* vol. XXXI, p. 244a.

21. *SDTT*, Sems tsam 12, p. 90, 180b.

22. The following six sanskrit verses can be found in the *Abhidharma-samuccaya-bhāṣya*, N. Tatia, ed. Patna: Kashi Prasad Jayaswal Research Institute, 1976. p. 42, Section 41C(2)iii.

23. Refer to G.M. Nagao, op.cit., vol 1, II.14B note 1.

24. *SDTT*, Sems tsam 12, p. 136, 272b.

25. *SDTT*, Sems tsam 12, p. 137, 273a: / ma ni byis pa'i bu rnams la // nu zho blug par nus mod kyi // kha yi bu ga thums pa yi // bu la mas ni ji ltar bya /

26. This example of the hungry ghost is found in the Chinese version of the *Bhāṣya*. The Tibetan text has interpolated comments on three kinds of *rten-gnas* (= āśraya?) and on ten definitions with respect to whether a buddha comes or does not come into the world—ideas not related to topics in this chapter. The interpolation is from line 7, fol. 181b to line 3, fol. 182b in *SDTT*, Sems tsam 12, p. 91 and is from line 5, fol. 221a to line 5, fol. 222a in the Peking edition, vol.112, p. 304-305. Following this interpolation, the commentary resumes with comments on ideas found in chapter X section 28A[2]; consequently, this example cannot be found, at least in this section of the Tibetan text.

ART CRITICISM AND SOCIAL STATUS IN NORTHERN SONG CHINA: LIU DAOCHUN'S "GENRE THEORY" OF ART[1]

Charles H. Lachman
Dartmouth College

> ...nothing can be a reason why a painting is good or bad unless it is concerned with what can be looked at in the painting, unless it is concerned with what can, in some sense, be seen.[2]

(i) Introduction

The *Songchao minghua ping* ("Evaluations of Song Dynasty Painters of Renown"; hereafter SCMHP),[3] compiled before 1059 by Liu Daochun, has been rightly described as one of the "most important histories of tenth and early eleventh-century [Chinese] painting".[4] The work comprises a collection of biographies and critical comments for some ninety-one painters active between roughly 950 and 1050 C.E., although there are actually one hundred and ten entries in all, as some artists appear more than once.[5] These notices are divided into six categories as follows:

1. Figure painting (40 entries)
2. Landscape (18 entries)
3. Domestic and Wild Animals (19 entries)
4. Birds and Flowers (22 entries)
5. Demons and Spirits (4 entries)
6. Architecture (7 entries)

Each of these six subject categories is further divided into three "classes" (*pin*): the Inspired (*shen*), the Subtle (*miao*), and the Talented (*neng*); and in the case of Figure painters, each of these classes is then subdivided into "upper" (*shang*), "middle" (*zhong*), and "lower" (*xia*) grades. For painters of the Inspired classes, each entry is followed by an individual Evaluation (*ping*), while those who are ranked Subtle or Talented are evaluated in groups.

In terms of its basic structure, the SCMHP interweaves several strands from earlier critical systems. For instance, the practice of "grading" painters goes back at least as far as Xie He's (fl. 500-535) *Gu huapin lu* ("Old Record of Gradings of Painters"), one of China's earliest extant art-critical texts, while the tripartite Inspired-Subtle-Talented scheme can be traced back to the eight-century critic Zhang Huaiguan.[6] There are no known antecedents, however, for the subject-matter categories which Liu employs to organize his text, and one of the main points to be considered here is that an appreciation of the implications of this unique arrangement is crucial to an understanding of Liu's evaluative system and its place in the development of Chinese art theory. That is, whereas Western art criticism since the time of Alberti has usually concentrated on the formal properties of the art object itself, a review of early textual sources shows that Chinese criticism generally tends to view the work as an extension of its maker; accordingly, to evaluate the artifact is to evaluate the artist, and *vice versa*. A close analysis of the SCMHP, however, reveals that Liu Daochun's "genre theory" approach to evaluation implicitly challenged traditional assumptions about the relationship between social status and artistic quality, and suggests that some long-held opinions about the status of painters during the Five Dynasties (906-960)/ Northern Song (960-1127) period should perhaps be reconsidered.

(ii) The Position of the Artist in pre-Song Texts

Attaching names to specific works of art is far from a universal practice; indeed, the great bulk of the world's art production has been anonymous, and often remains so even within those "rare art traditions" where the assignation of authorship has evolved.[7] In China, for instance, the voluminous extant historical records yield fewer than one thousand names—and many of those are only names—of artists active during the entire Song period (960-1279),[8] while the SCMHP reports that over three thousand painters responded to the Emperor's summons when it came time to decorate the Taoist Palace of the Pristine Realm of Jade Clarity (*yuqing zhaoying gong*) in 1008.[9]

According to Kris and Kurz, the custom of linking the creator's name to his creation depends "not upon the greatness and perfection of his artistic achievement—even if this were objectively ascertainable—but upon the significance attached to the work of art".[10] In turn, once the work of art has been accorded such significance, a natural consequence is that a greater interest in the artist is thus generated, and it is precisely this interest in art and its makers that allows that artist's biography, as a literary category, to come into being.[11]

In comparison with the West, such interest was relatively slow to develop in China. In the fifth century C.E., for instance, the painter Wang Wei (415-443) lamented the fact that there was "no general appreciation of fine painting"—and by extension, no general appreciation for fine painters, either—among his contemporaries, whereas calligraphy was universally admired.[12] In part, this situation would soon change, however, inasmuch as "fine painting" did in fact come to be more generally appreciated; and although this heightened awareness was accompanied by a grater interest in (if not appreciation of) painters, as well, it is instructive to note the specific shape that this interest assumed for pre-Song writers, particularly with regard to their concern for the social status of the artist.

One of the first texts to speak to this point is not an art-historical or art-critical work, but belongs to the category of "family instructions" (*jiaxun*).[13] Among the earliest surviving examples of this genre, Yan Zhitui's (ca. 531-595) *Yanshi jiaxun*, or "Family Instructions of the Yan Clan", describes the position of the artists of the day in no uncertain terms:

> To find amusement in looking at the art objects of all times is particularly valuable and enjoyable. But, if your official position is not high enough, you are frequently ordered to paint for the government or for private friends, and this is a disgusting kind of service.[14]

Yan goes on to discuss the cases of three contemporary officials, and cites examples of the "shameful" treatment they received because of their artistic inclinations and talents. He asks, "If these three scholars had been ignorant of painting, simply engaging themselves in their original professions, would they have met such humiliation"?[15]

Moreover, such disdain was apparently not limited to painters, but extended to calligraphers (see above, Note 12) and to musicians, as well. Apropos playing the *pipa* (lute"), Yan cautions that:

> you should not allow yourself to have a reputation in this art, for then you will have to entertain nobles, sitting in a humble place and taking the insult of drinking the dregs and eating the cold remains.[16]

Zhang Yanyuan's *Lidai minghuaji* ("A Record of Famous Painters of all Ages"; hereafter LDMHJ),[17] China's earliest (847) full-fledged history of art (and a work that, as one scholar claims, "easily surpasses Vasari's *Lives*, written seven centuries later, in scope and sophistication")[18] also addresses itself to the issue of the artist's status. Zhang's earliest notices go back to Shi Huang (ca. 2400 B.C.E.), who is himself said to have served as a Minister at the Court of the Yellow Emperor (*Huangdi*);[19] and while such figures must be consigned to the realm of legend, beginning with the accounts for the Later Han period (25-220 C.E.) we are on somewhat firmer ground. Of the six painters listed for this period in the LDMHJ, Zhang mentions that one was Director of the Board of Sacrificial Worship,[20] one was a Prefect,[21] one became the Vice-president of a Board,[22] one rose to the rank of Minister,[23] and two served as Painters-in-Attendance (*daizhao*) at the Imperial Workshops.[24]

This emphasis on non-artistic achievement is not limited to Zhang's entries for the earlier periods, but persists up to, and through, his notices of "the present day", and virtually without exception. Nor among ninth-century writers is this emphasis unique to Zhang Yanyuan: Zhu Jingxuan's *Tanghchao minghua lu* ("A Record of Tang Dynasty Painters of Renown"), for example, written shortly before the LDMHJ, reflects a similar concern, as Zhu writes of Presidents and Vice-presidents of Boards, members of State Councils, and even a provincial Governor.[25] Concealed by all of this interest in prestigious ranks and titles, however, is the desire to make a sharp distinction between "artists"—that is, great men who happen also to paint—and mere "artisans", and also to illustrate what may result when the dividing line is blurred.

The classic illustration of this point is made in the following well-known story about Yan Liben (610-670):

> [Once] when Taizong was paying a visit to the Xuanwu Lake and saw some mandarin ducks at play, he summoned Liben to depict them. The attendants were so tactless as to shout, "Summon the master painter!" Liben was so deeply chagrined by this that he finally gave up painting, and warned the junior members of his family against making any study of the art.[26]

Referring to the vice-president of the Board of Justice as a "master painter" (*huashi*) was clearly construed as a slur of the highest order, which underscores the importance that was attached to distinguishing sharply between artist and artisan. Still, if Yan Liben had been summoned politely, he would have been summoned none the less. Thus, as texts such as the TCMHL and the LDMHJ make clear, artists in the Tang (even those with resounding titles) were still essentially at someone's beck and call; even the "incomparable" Wu Daozi (active ca, 710-760) was not permitted to execute a painting "unless there was an edict".[27] Though socially superior to artisans, even the greatest artists seem not to have enjoyed a significantly greater degree of artistic autonomy than their fifth-, sixth-, and seventh-century forerunners.

Several early anecdotes detail another aspect of the artist's circumscribed freedom; namely, the desire to please the public. Zhang Yanyuan, for instance, records the following about Dai Kuei (d. 396 C.E.):

> Since Kuei was inventive in the mechanical arts, he was also good at the casting of Buddha images, and also at the carving of them. Once he was working on a wooden image of Wuliangshou (Amitayus) which was sixteen feet tall, and the accompanying Bodhisattvas. Kuei considered that the ancient rules for making Buddhist images were primitive and clumsy, and that when this work was opened for public worship it would not move men's hearts. So, he would sit hidden behind a curtain and secretly listen to the discussions of the crowds who came to see it. Whatever praise or blame he heard he would immediately subject to detailed analysis, and after three years of intensive thought he finally completed the carving of the image.[28]

In a similar vein, Zhu Jingxuan relates that Zhou Fang (d. ca. 800) was once commissioned by the Emperor Dezong (r. 780-805) to execute a work at a monastery in Chang'an:

> When he brought down his brush, the populace of the capital came jostling each other to see, pushing their way to the garden of the temple. Among them were both wise men and simpletons; some talked of the excellence of the work, while others pointed out its flaws. The artist made revisions to suit their ideas, and in little more than a month, all criticism ceased.[29]

Such concern for the opinions of the public at large—and the corollary notion that the artist should conform to it—would have been unthinkable to the later artists who painted, so they claimed, to please themselves alone.

There are, to be sure, a few exceptions to the generalized portrait of the pre-Song artist that emerges from the foregoing, but they do indeed stand out as exceptions: Han Gan (d. after 781), for example, is recorded as having been ordered by the Tang emperor Xuanzong (r. 712-756) to use Chen Hong (active ca. 735-760) as his model for painting horses. When the Emperor found out that he had not done as told, and inquired why, Han Gan replied: "His Majesty's servant has taken his own models; namely all the horses in the Imperial stables."[30] Han's fortunate blend of flattery and artistic skill may have spared him the Emperor's wrath, but that this story is preserved at all testifies to the fact that while being commanded to paint a specific subject in a specific way was a common occurrence, asserting one's individuality and doing otherwise was certainly not.

There are other instances in the LDMHJ, mostly involving pre-Tang painters, where the artist appears at first glance to be more "assertive" and less concerned with status than most of the men discussed thus far. Dai Kuei, for example, "was summoned to take official positions at intervals throughout his life, but he never accepted any of them:,[31] nor did his son or grandson consent to serve in an official capacity.[32] Zong Ping (375-443), too, was offered several positions, but chose instead to spend his time among the mountains.[33] As a last example, there is Tao Hongjing (ca. 452-536), who resigned from office and took to the hills, calling himself the Hermit of Huayang. As Zhang reports:

> The Emperor Wu Di (r. 502-550) once wished to summon him for employment in the government, but the Hermit made a painting of two oxen, one being pulled along by a golden halter, and the other meandering off in search of water and grass. Wu Di understood his meaning, and did not pester him further with office or rank ... and gave him the unofficial title of Prime Minister in the Mountains.[34]

The first thing to note about the artists in the above examples is that they all come from "noble families", and that—for each of them—painting is but one among several accomplishments. A further common feature is that the "assertiveness" of the artist does not arise directly in conjunction with his art, as it did in the case of Han Gan, but arises, rather, in connection with his reluctance to take on an official governmental position. In these respects, all of these cases fit very neatly into the pattern that has been described as the "one socially acceptable form of escape" for the man who "found it impossible to meet the demands of Confucian conformity";[35] namely, withdrawing from society to live as a recluse.

But as the literary historian Li Chi has pointed out:

> ...as early as the time of Confucius the concept of the recluse had begun to change from a man who had renounced the world and had hidden himself in the wilderness to one who kept himself apart from the world of affairs and yet was anxious to make himself heard.[36]

Moreover, a great deal of prestige was accorded these high-minded souls who lived in "retirement", to the point that a ruler would often be "inclined to pay more heed to a recluse whom he had summoned to court than to ordinary officials".[37] Thus, the "refusal to serve" witnessed in the above examples was part and parcel of the behaviour expected of the recluse;[38] it cannot be taken as necessarily signifying lack of interest in status, nor should it be viewed as attesting to the artist's independence or individualism: as will be suggested below, it was not until the Song that these features would be indelibly added to the artist's portrait.

In short, Tang and pre-Tang textual sources indicate a growing public interest in both painting and painters, and manifest a particular concern for the question of the social status of the artist, as this alone, it would seem, could redeem the fact that a Gentleman was a painter at all. In general, even artists of rank were liable to be treated as artisans, and they themselves were much concerned with keeping a sharp line of demarcation between the two. Though there are instances that suggest that some artists displayed no lack of confidence in their social position, this was clearly not a common attitude among painters, and seems not be have been shared by the public at large.

Finally, it is interesting to note the parallels that can be discerned in Hans Frankel's analysis of the way in which writers of poetry and prose were viewed in the Tang. In his study of the biographical sections of the *Jiutangshu* ("Old History of the Tang Dynasty"), Frankel points out that one hundred and one writers are given biographies in a special "Garden of Letters" (*wenyuan*) section—a category that is ranked fairly low—and that the basis for inclusion in this group was not governed by literary criteria, as one might expect that it would have been.[39] He writes,

> To be sure, some of the best known poets and prose writers are included—men like Chen Zi 'ang, Li Hua, Wang Wei, [and] Li Bo ... but one misses others of equal stature, such as Zhang Yueh, Bo Juyi, and Li Deyu. The explanation ... [is that] the latter were prominent statesmen, whereas the "Garden of Letters" is reserved for those who were famous only as literati, and this, in the view of the Confucian historiographer, is a shortcoming.[40]

Though brilliant and successful as writers, those who did not couple this with a high-ranking government position were thus consigned to a special category "reserved for those who fall short of the Confucian ideal of the well-rounded gentleman".[41] Being "only" a brilliant poet was certainly more acceptable than being "only" a brilliant painter, reflecting the relative worth accorded these two talents in the Tang, but neither accomplishment was highly enough regarded that it could stand completely on its own.

[iii] The Rise of the "Independent Artist"

Liu Daochun's entry for the Inspired landscapist Li Cheng (919-967) contains the following anecdote:

> During the Kaibao reign era (968-976),[42] a certain Sun Sihao extended invitations to masters from the four corners of the land. Although he was aware of the fact that a skilled artist like Li Cheng would not be easily persuaded, he still sent him a letter of invitation. Cheng replied: "I am a scholar by birth and have always known whom to avoid. By nature, I love mountains and rivers, but I wield a brush only for my own satisfaction. How could I go galloping off to the home a rich and powerful family to mingle with mere artisans?"[43]

This was not to be the end of the matter, however, as the tenacious Mr. Sun contrived to bribe an official in Li's hometown and thereby managed to procure several of his paintings. Sometime later, Li was in the capital and acceded to Sun's request that he at least pay a visit; upon his arrival, though, when he saw his paintings on display, he was "taken aback and thus departed in anger".[44]

Looking back on this account from a modern vantage point, there is a tendency, perhaps, to see it simply as providing more examples of the "persistent collector" and the "temperamental artist"—frequently encountered *topoi* for which countless citations, from both East and West, could be adduced.[45] And while these associations can never be completely left behind, it may be fruitful, nonetheless, to attempt to approach the text from the other side; that is to say, to come upon it from the point of view of the works that preceded it, such as those touched on above.

When looked at from this angle, a rather different picture emerges, though many of its components are familiar. (For instance, echoes of Yan Liben's umbrage at having been called a "master painter" may be heard clearly in Li's reply to Mr. Sun, confirming that the artist's sensitivity to being treated as an artisan had not been dulled.) But while a demonstration of the artist's self-confidence may not be totally without precedent, that this confidence is ultimately rooted in his view of himself as an artist, independent of any accomplishments outside of the realm of painting, is indeed a new note. Moreover, that other artists in the texts are frequently presented as sharing a similar attitude, and the Liu Daochun endorses their stance—Li Cheng, after all, is ranked as the "most Inspired" landscape painter in the SCMHP—seem particularly novel features when compared with the views that prevailed in the Tang period and earlier.

Also, and again in marked contrast to the situation presented in pre-Song texts, it is clear from the Li Cheng anecdote, and from many others, as well, that the nature of the artist/patron relationship has changed. Painters are now persistently courted by ardent admirers:

> —as soon as they heard that Sun Mengqing (act. mid 10th c.) desired to undertake a commission, the wealthy "would flock to his door and compete to be the first to secure a purchase";[46]
>
> —"people of wealth and rank would come to [Wu Zongyuan 's] door daily";[47]
>
> —"Yuan Ai (act. late 10th c.) "earned a resounding reputation, and ministers and nobles competed for his brushwork";[48]

—"it reached the point where there was vying in the nobles ' residences for portraits" by Yin Shi (act. ca. 1025-1050);[49]

—A wealthy southern merchant offered one hundred thousand cash to Gao Keming (act. 1st half 11th c.) to "commission a picture of 'A Spring Dragon Emerging from Hibernation'".[50]

Among other things, examples such as these indicate something of the degree to which both artists and artworks had generally increased in public esteem, a contention supported by much other evidence from the SCMHP. Not only are collectors shown going to great lengths in their attempts to secure certain paintings, but one also receives the impression that collecting is itself a more common activity than it had been in the past. In part, this last may be due to the fact that the gradual eclipse of figure painting by the landscape and bird-and-flower genres resulted in the greater availability of works that were more "portable" than those executed on large screens, or on monastery and temple walls. At the same time, burgeoning interest in painting no doubt stimulated the production of these more collectable formats (though which is cause and which effect is a moot point).

Other evidence from the SCMHP suggests that, to some extent, the motivation behind the urge to collect is connected to the issue of status—a phenomenon not infrequently associated with acquiring and commissioning works of art—and in several instances here, the "status" accrues not so much from the painting itself as from the fact that it was painted by the "right" artist. For example, Liu reports that the works of Wang You (act. late 10th c.) were so similar to those of the better known Zhao Chang (ca. 960-ca 1016) that they could hardly be distinguished one from the other; yet, whenever a family got hold of a work by Wang, "they would often regard it as if it were by Zhao",[51] with the implication being that some may not have been above conscious deception. And might this not account for the fact that the *Xuanhe huapu* catalogue lists one hundred and fifty-four pictures by Zhao Chang as belonging to the Emperor Huizong's (r. 1101-1126) Imperial collection—even though concurring with Liu 's report that Zhao's works were very difficult to obtain, as the artist himself had tried to buy them back—while not a single Wang You is mentioned?[52]

In some respects, then, as the foregoing suggests, artist (and their works) were treated differently in the early years of the Song than they had been previously.[53] At the same time, of course, artists also *acted* differently, and themselves took new views of their creations. Corroboration for both of these points is amply provided in the SCMHP.

This new behaviour, as it were, manifests itself most clearly as a marked independence, already hinted at in the Li Cheng-Mr. Sun story. And if the pre-Song artist was necessarily compliant, his successor was increasingly willful: thus, although Wu Zongyuan was besieged with commissions, he was "rarely willing to accede" to these requests;[54] and even though Gao Keming was offered a large sum of money for a work, "he was not a common practitioner and resolutely would not yield" to such entreaties.[55]

Private collectors and patrons were not the only ones, however, to be confronted by such recalcitrance on the part of the artist, as there are instances in the SCMHP when even Imperial commands are greeted with defiance. Zhao Guangfu (act. late 10th c.), for instance, was appointed to the Imperial Academy but secretly fled;[56] as did Chen Yongzhi (act. early-mid 11th c.) when he became dissatisfied with the assignments he was given.[57] Likewise, Li Xiong (cat. ca 975-1000) refused to paint a silk fan on order from the Emperor, claiming that he could only paint on a large-scale.[58]

In terms of the artist's attitude toward his own paintings, there are indications in the SCMHP of a growing personal "attachment" for which there is little precedent in earlier sources. Something of this has already been seen in those cases above where a painter is reluctant to part with one of his works, and in the somewhat extreme example of Zhao Chang, who did not part lightly with his works to begin with, and then in his later years went so far as to try to buy back as many of them as he could.[59] This same sort of protective attitude can be seen in the entry for Yin Zhi: although he began a commissioned portrait, he never returned to finish it, much to the agitation of the family by whom he had been hired. When he learned that someone else had finally been asked to complete his rough sketch, he responded by saying, "To copy my sketches is alright, but having the colours applied [by someone else] is not something that I am willing to permit!"[60] Now, while a detailed investigation of the psychological roots of this phenomenon of the artist's attachment to his work would go far beyond the bounds of the present inquiry, it seems reasonable to surmise that it is the artist's new pride, spurred by public recognition of his accomplishments, that occasions this proprietary attitude toward his creations.

In all, if Tang and pre-Tang texts stress that the artist worked "on command", the SCMHP allows that the early Song painter worked "at will"; and if the former was "ordered" to execute commissions, the latter was frequently "begged": an oversimplification, to be sure, yet there can be little doubt that the "independent" artist of the SCMHP was both a social reality and a post-Tang creation. As will be seen below, however, this new artist existed side by side with more traditional practitioners, Liu Daochun's attitude towards whom will now be considered.

[iv] The Academy

> "Academy, Academic, Academism (Or Academicism)—the words mean 'bad' in the conversations of the art community, much worse than 'pretty' or 'decorative' or even 'sentimental'—they are about as dirty as polysyllables can get".[61]

Although the author of these words is referring to modern western attitudes towards the European tradition of Academies of art, they aptly characterise the stance that the Chinese literati would come to adopt toward their own tradition of the *tuhuayuan*. "By the end of the Ming dynasty", as Joseph Levenson writes, "...[p]ainters by *profession* [i.e. "academics"] were disparaged".[62]

Ironically, and in contrast to later developments, when the first European academies of art were founded in Renaissance Italy they were set up in opposition to the medieval Guild workshops and viewed as the vanguard of a new humanist sensibility. Though the contrast in China was certainly less marked, the earliest academies there, too, were viewed in a comparatively better light than were their later counterparts, even if they may never have been accused of standing at the forefront of new directions in art. Still, that so many of the various sovereigns during the Five Dynasties/Northern Song period took such an active interest in painting—manifest in their creation of these court-linked academies—was no doubt a contributing factor in the general rise in esteem that painting enjoyed in this period.

Some scholars have claimed that the Academy may have been an important historical factor in another sense, as well. As Wai-kam Ho writes:

> One cannot but be convinced that the rise of scholar-official painting was directly caused, stimulated, and conditioned by the conspicuous presence of the Academy. It was an inevitable antithesis in such a dialectical historical development.[63]

While the "inevitability" to which he refers may be questioned, his conclusion that scholar-official painting [*shidafu hua*] would have followed a different course of development had the Academy not existed is well warranted. For our purposes here, however, the central question that needs to be considered is that of the value which Liu Daochun attributed to Academic success; or to rephrase it, what is the correlation between Liu's evaluations and a painter's "official" rank?[64]

In the SCMHP, certainly, the presence of the Academy is pervasive. Of the ninety-one biographical entrants, more than a third (31)—including five who served the Southern Tang (937-974), Later Liang (907-923), and Shu (929-966) kingdoms—are mentioned as having received appointments. Of these, four later left the organization, and two declined to serve from the start. Moreover, of the thirty-six painters known to have entered the Academy during the reigns of Taizu (r. 960-976), Taizong, Zhenzong (r. 998-1023), and Renzong (r. 1023-1064), Liu devotes entries to twenty-six of them.[65]

Not surprisingly, far and away the greatest number of painters whom Liu connects with the Academy were known primarily as figure painters, while the rest are spread fairly evenly over the other five genres. This distribution may be tabulated as follows:

From a simple numerical point of view, then, Liu does not (on the surface at least) exhibit any traces of the anti-academic sentiments that later were common. But if he recognized that many painters connected with the Academies were well-deserving of notice, a closer look at the text reveals that they are nonetheless consistently denied his highest accolades. For example, two of the six Inspired academy members who appear in Table I are among the painters, mentioned above, who left the Academy, and if they are removed from the chart, four of the six subject-matter categories are left without a single Inspired painter to represent them. Moreover, of the four who remain (two painters of

	Inspired	Subtle	Talented	Totals
Figures	2	7	5	14
Landscapes	-	1	2	3
Animals	1	1	3	5
Birds/Flowers	2	1	1	4
Demons	1	-	-	1
Architecture	-	2	2	4
Totals	6	12	13	31

Table I

figures, and two of birds and flowers), not one is at the top of his class. Conversely, of the thirteen painters associated with the Academy who fall into Liu's lowest ranking, at least six were Painters-In-Attendance (*daizhao*)—the *highest* office a painter could hold.

This statistical reading of the place of the Academy in the SCMHP is bolstered by a number of factors. For one, and as will be discussed in more detail below, those artists who are presented as at odds with the strictures of Academic life are portrayed in a generally sympathetic manner and are certainly not criticized by Liu—if anything, their behavior is lauded. Also, Liu is not above the occasional veiled barb: for example, he reports that the Emperor Taizong was so taken with Xu Xi's (act. 3rd. quarter 10th c.) bird-and-flower paintings that all the official painters had to take them as a standard, though Xu himself, of course, is not reported to have had anything to do with the *tuhuayuan*.[66]

Liu's attitude toward the Academy, then, seems ambivalent at best. While he obviously does not ignore its members, nor fail to heap much praise on many of them, there is certainly no indication that the status of membership was in a painter's favor *vis-à-vis* Liu's evaluations. In fact, at the highest levels of evaluation at any rate, a happy association with the Academy may have affected one's ranking adversely.

[v] Status and Evaluation

While the foregoing indicates a certain antipathy toward Academic painters on the part of Liu Daochun, this does not, in and of itself, indicate his alignment with the traditional opposition: namely, the proponents of *shidafu hua*, or "scholar-official art". In the first place, the lines of combat had probably not yet been drawn in quite such terms at the time when Liu was writing. Moreover, an examination of his characterizations of the highest-ranked painters in each subject-matter divisions reveals that they do not appear to constitute any easily identifiable group:

FIGURES: Wang Guan (act. ca. 963-975) was from a poor family that could not afford to finance his studies; no mention is made of his ever having held an official position, or of any other scholarly accomplishments;[67]

LANDSCAPE: Li Cheng was descended from a long line of scholar-officials, and though he is reported to have taken the *jinshi* ("Doctor of letters") examination, he is not reported to have passed it, nor is it mentioned that he ever held an official post;[68]

ANIMALS: Very little is reported concerning the background of Zhao Guangfu, except that he was appointed to the painting Academy as an Apprentice (*xueshi*); but "he had no desire to accept this post and thus fled in secret";[69]

BIRDS AND FLOWERS: Xu Xi came from an honorable family of Jiangnan, but there is no mention of office or other such achievement;[70]

DEMONS AND SPIRITS: Li Xiong was "barely literate and disliked following conventions"; though he was appointed to the Academy, he disobeyed an imperial command and had to flee in secrecy to his native village;[71]

ARCHITECTURE: Guo Zhongshu (ca 930-977) was a Scholar of Broad Learning (*boshi*), and held a fairly high rank in the government of the Later Zhou (951-960) state; however, after Taizong came to power, he, too, disobeyed an Imperial command and was consequently banished to a remote outpost.[72]

In reading through these six accounts in the SCMHP, one of the most striking features is precisely the fact that the social standing of the artist enters the discussion obliquely, if at all; further, the same feature is discernible throughout the text. By contrast, comparable entries in earlier texts such as the TCMHL and the LDMHJ are much concerned with offices and titles; indeed, many entries in both of these texts consist of little more than the artist's name and rank. It is this, in fact, that defines the "artist" (a man of rank who also paints), as opposed to the "artisan" (one who only paints). As Zhang Yanyuan writes:

> From ancient times, those who have excelled at painting have all been men robed and capped and of noble descent, rare scholars and lofty-minded men who awakened the wonder of their own time and left behind them a fragrance that shall last a thousand years. This is not a thing that humble rustics from village lanes could ever do.[73]

In this context, it is interesting to note one modern art historian's claim that there was never any "sudden amelioration in the social status" of Chinese artists, since "[c]alligraphers and painters always enjoyed the highest possible social distinction, by virtue of the major accomplishment of literacy. It was inside the scholar caste, in the ranks of the civil administration, that the twin arts developed and reached maturity".[74] But if the artist is defined in terms of his social standing and official position to begin with, then the conclusion that artists always "enjoyed the highest possible social distinction" is obviously tautological. Moreover, as late as the Tang period, as has been seen in the case of Yan Liben, even artists of rank were not necessarily held in high esteem—as artists.

In addition, it has been seen above that there was a striking volte-face in the artist/patron relationship from the Tang to the Song, and that this can be taken as confirmation of the fact that public esteem for artists was on the rise. Thus, while the change was not, perhaps, so "sudden"—nor the cause so immediately apparent—as in the West, when the breakdown of the Guild system in the fifteenth century turned "artisans" into "artists", there was nonetheless a general amelioration in the social status of Chinese artists over the course of the tenth and eleventh centuries.[75]

In a certain sense, the culmination of this trend was sparked by Su Shi (1037-1101) and his circle who, in part through the equation of painting with poetry, took the last step in securing for painting a legitimate place among the pursuits of the scholar-official.[76] Such artists (i.e., scholar-officials), certainly, were in little danger of being subjected to the "humiliating" treatment that caused such grief for their Tang counterparts. Still, "social standing" remained a fundamental aspect of the definition of the artist for these theorists, and those who practiced the art under other circumstances (that is, other than as officials "lodging their interest" [*yuxing*] in painting in their leisure time) continued to be viewed with scorn.

This continued concern with the status of the artist can be detected in Guo Ruoxu's remarks that,

> the rare works of the past were mainly those by talented worthies of high position or by superior gentlemen in retirement...and their lofty and refined emotions were all lodged in painting. If a man's condition is high, his spirit-consonance [*qiyun*] cannot be but lofty.[77]

A similar sentiment is echoed by Deng Chun (act. mid 12th c.). In the Preface to his *Huaji* ("Painting Continued") he writes that, following Guo Ruoxu, he has "in a similar fashion specifically established the two categories of High Officials and Retired Scholars".[78] As he explains elsewhere in the same work,

> When Guo Ruoxu deeply despised common artisans, saying (of their work) 'although called "painting" it will not be painting', it was because they were only able to transmit the form and could not transmit the spirit. Therefore, 'animation through spirit consonance' is the first of the laws of painting, and Ruoxu was right when he only attributed it to those in high position or in retirement.[79]

While numerous other examples could be presented here, they would merely serve to underscore this same basic point; namely, that the late Northern Song spokesmen for scholar-officials' art were, *mutatis mutandis*, fundamentally in agreement with the earlier view that *only* men of a certain social standing could truly be artists, and with the corollary notion that being *only* an artist—or better, "painter"—excluded one from the start from membership in this élite group. Indeed, anyone who was only a painter was thus an "artisan" by definition.

It is against this background that the unorthodoxy of the stance adopted in the SCMHP can be viewed most clearly, inasmuch as Liu Daochun takes strong exception to both of these cardinal points of scholar-official art theory. To be sure, a number of "High Officials and Retired Scholars" do appear in the SCMHP, some of whom are graded very high in Liu's system, but throughout the text—and at the highest levels—are entries for painters whose only accomplishments are connected to their painting. Thus, while "rank" need not work against someone, neither is it alone sufficient to warrant high praise for him—as an artist.

Ultimately, for Liu Daochun, social standing alone, whether high or low, neither defines the "artist", nor determines his worth as an artist. (This latter, rather, is primarily based on the quality of the work itself.) In sum, espousing a view that departed radically from those of earlier theorists, and that would be rejected wholesale by those who were to follow him, Liu Daochun turned tradition on its head by boldly asserting that being a great artist made one, in some fundamental sense, a "great man".

[vi] Liu Daochun's "Genre Theory" of Art

To summarize briefly: From a broad historical point of view, evaluation in Chinese art criticism, like evaluation in Chinese literary criticism, was to a significant degree based on social factors. In early art-critical writings, this is manifested by a great concern for the official position and rank of the artist (who is opposed to the mere artisan); in later writings, the terms would change—to "amateur" and "professional"—but the concern for status would remain. Indeed, even the formal qualities of the work of art were seen through a social filter by literati theorists such as Guo Ruoxu: in their view, what matters in a painting is that it expresses *qiyun*; but *qiyun* is an innate characteristic of High Officials, Nobles, and recluses, and only their works, therefore, can be imbued with this quality.

In the SCMHP, however, evaluation is approached from an altogether different direction. In the first place, Liu Daochun shows himself to be essentially indifferent to the social background of the artist. While his biographical entries usually mention if someone held a particular office or title, and so on, there is no obvious correlation between these and the grade that a painter is assigned in the SCMHP, and it could be argued, in fact, that Liu includes such information merely to conform to the expected requirements of the "artist's biography" as a literary form. In any case, such data are confined to the biographical portions of the text, and do not appear in the discrete Evaluations, nor is such information ever called upon to account for artistic greatness.

Coupled with this indifference to the personal attributes of the artist is a correspondingly greater interest in, and emphasis upon, the formal qualities of the work of art. Thus, for Liu Daochun, the criteria appropriate to the valuation are those that are ultimately based in art. Lacking a large corpus of indubitably authentic works, it is impossible, of course, to be very precise about these standards of quality, but a constant factor in Liu's discussions is that no one feature of the work of art is treated as necessarily "decisive"; rather, his final arbitrations are based on the consideration of a complex web of factors. This general principle is further complicated by the fact that Liu establishes different criteria for different genres of painting; that is, since the various types of painting (based on subject matter) are postulated as having dissimilar ends, it follows that these cannot be achieved by identical means. Accordingly, neither can they be judged by constant standards.

The underlying premise of this approach to evaluation is that art is a fully legitimate and worthwhile pursuit, and that it is perfectly acceptable to be "only" a great artist. This theme is illustrated not only by the content of the SCMHP, but is revealed through and reinforced by the form of the text, as well. This contention is perhaps best illustrated by contrast: In the THJWZ, for instance, Guo Ruoxu adopts subject-matter divisions for his biographical entries for painters from the Five Dynasties on; however, within these groupings he also employs certain special categories for "princes, nobles, and scholar-officials", and for several "lofty-minded recluses". (Buddhist monks and Taoist masters also have a special place: the very end of each section.) In other words, despite the use of these divisions, the artist and his social status remain a central feature of Guo's accounts.

But for Liu Daochun, this division of material into subject-matter groups serves a very different function: by disregarding all social categories and by including separate Evaluations, the genre arrangement thus implicitly helps to assert the primacy of the work of art. This is further underscored by the fact that painters can appear in more than one grouping and with different rankings in each. Thus, the very structure of the SCMHP is itself a carrier of meaning, and the form and content of the text complement each other at every turn.

In conclusion, though the specific stylistic features upon which Liu bases his standards of quality must of necessity remain somewhat vague, it is nonetheless very clear that his general approach to the evaluation of painting was a dramatic departure from tradition; indeed, it is not too much to say that Liu's new "genre theory" of art, as embodied in the SCMHP, represents a radical moment in the history of Chinese art theory and art criticism. In light of this, it can be seen that the late Northern Song formulation of the relationship between social status and evaluation (which might be summed up by the phrase, "Only a great man can become a great artist") was not simply a benign refinement of Tang and pre-Tang views, but seems rather to have been a conscious rejection of the theories put forward by earlier Northern Song critics such as Liu Daochun.

Notes

1. For the sake of consistency, pinyin romanization is used throughout this essay, even within citations from works which originally used another system; all bibliographic references, however, retain their original orthography.
2. Paul Ziff, "Reasons in Art Criticism", in Joseph Margolis (ed.), *Philosophy Looks at the Arts* (New York: Scribner's, 1962), p. 162.
3. All references are to the translation in C. Lachman, *Evaluations of Sung Dynasty Painters of Renown: Liu Tao-ch'un's "Sung-ch'ao ming-hua p'ing"* (Leiden: E.J. Brill, 1989 [T'oung Pao monograph 16]).
4. Richard Barnhart, *The Marriage of the Lord of the River: A Lost Landscape by Tung Yüan* (Ascona: Artibus Asiae, 1970), p. 22 (note 38).
5. Hin Cheung Lovell erroneously writes that there are entries in the SCMHP for 110 painters, but this count overlooks the fact that 10 painters are given multiple entries; see her *An Annotated Bibliography of Chinese Painting Catalogues and Related Texts* (Ann Arbor: Center for Chinese Studies, 1973), p. 3. The recently published *Early Chinese Texts on Painting*, edited by Susan Bush and Hsio-yen Shih (Cambridge MA: Harvard-Yenching Institute, 1985), p. 367, states that there are 120 entries in the SCMHP, but there is no explanation for how this figure was derived.
6. Bush and Shih, *Early Chinese Texts*, p. 47. See W.R.B. Acker, *Some T'ang and pre-T'ang Texts on Chinese Painting*, vol. I (Leiden: E.J. Brill, 1954) for a translation and discussion of the *Gu huapin lu*.
7. See Joseph Alsop, *The Rare Art Traditions* (London: Thames and Hudson, 1982), pp. 181-183.
8. Yu Jianhua, *Zhongguo huihua shi* ["A History of Chinese Painting"], 2 vols., (Shanghai: Shang-wu, 1937), vol I, p. 168.
9. SCMHP, p. 26. A description of the construction of this shrine is provided by Suzanne Cahill, "Taoism at the Sung Court: The Heavenly Text Affair of 1008", *Bulletin of Sung and Yüan Studies* 16 (1980), p. 32.
10. Ernst Kris and Otto Kurz, *Legend, Myth, and Magic in the Image of the Artist: A Historical Experiment* [based on *Die Legend vom Künstler*, 1934] (New Haven: Yale University Press, 1979), p. 3. According to their analysis, this "urge to name the creator" generally indicates that "the work of art no longer serves exclusively a religious, ritual, or, in a wide sense, magic function", and that "its valuation has at least to some extent become independent of such connections" (p.4).
11. See Ernst Kris, *Psychoanalytic Explorations in Art* (New York: Schocken Books, 1964), p. 66.
12. Quoted in Max Loehr, "The Question of Individualism in Chinese Art", *Journal of the History of Ideas* 22.2 (April-June 1961), p. 147. That admiration for calligraphers was still perhaps less than universal, even a century or more later, is suggested in a passage from the late sixth-century *Yanshi Jiaxun* ["Family Instructions for the Yan Clan"] (discussed below):

> Wang Bao was a man of eminent family background, brilliant talent and excellent knowledge...Because he was a master of calligraphy, he had a rough road among stone tablets and pillars, and toiled at service with brush and ink. Frequently he regretted this, saying, "If I were not a master of calligraphy, I should not be so harassed as I am today". (Quoted from Ssu-yü Teng, *Family Instructions for the Yen Clan* [Leiden: E.J. Brill, 1968], p. 99 [slightly revised]).

13. For a historical summary of this genre see Teng, *Family Instructions*, pp. ix-xiv.
14. Translation from *ibid.*, p. 201 (slightly revised).
15. *Ibid.*, p. 202.
16. *Ibid.*, pp. 205-206.
17. Translated in W.R.B. Acker, *Some T'ang and pre-T'ang Texts on Chinese Painting*, 2 vols. (Leiden: E.J. Brill, 1954 and 1974); hereafter cited as *Tang Texts* 1 and II.
18. James F. Cahill, *Parting At the Shore* (Berkeley: University of California Press, 1982), p. 6.
19. *Tang Texts* II, p. 1.
20. *Tang Texts* II, p. 7.
21. *Tang Texts* II, p. 10.
22. *Tang Texts* II, p. 11.
23. *Tang Texts* II, p. 13.
24. *Tang Texts* II, p. 14.
25. See A.C. Soper (trans.), "T'ang Ch'ao Ming Hua Lu: Celebrated Painters of the T'ang Dynasty by Chu Ching-hsüan of T'ang", *Artibus Asiae* 21.3/4 (1958): 204-230; hereafter cited as TCMHL.
26. Translation from *ibid.*, p. 213 (slightly revised).
27. *Tang Texts* II, p. 232.
28. *Tang Texts* II, p. 95. For an earlier version of this story, see A.C. Soper, *Literary Evidence for Early Buddhist Art in China* (Ascona: Artibus Asiae, 1959), pp. 19-21.
29. Translation from TCMHL, p. 211.
30. *Ibid.*, p. 215.
31. *Tang Texts* II, p. 95.
32. *Tang Texts* II, p. 100.
33. *Tang Texts* II, p. 115.
34. *Tang Texts* II, p. 173.
35. James R. Hightower, "The Question of Individualism in Chinese Literature", *Journal of the History of Ideas* 22.2 (April-June 1961), p. 159.
36. Li Chi, "The Changing Concept of the Recluse in Chinese Literature", *Harvard Journal of Asiatic Studies* 24 (1963), p. 237.
37. *Ibid.*, p. 240.
38. As Frederick Mote writes in "Confucian Eremitism in the Yüan Period", in A. Wright (ed.), *The Confucian Persuasion* (Stanford: Stanford University Press,

1960), the renunciation of public life was "the keystone of Chinese eremitism" (p. 204).

39. Hans Frankel, "T'ang Literati: A Composite Biography", in A. Wright and D. Twitchett (eds.), *Confucian Personalities* (Stanford: Stanford University Press, 1962), p. 67.

40. *Ibid.*

41. *Ibid.*

42. In his *Tuhua jianwen zhi* ("Experiences in Painting"; hereafter THJWZ), completed ca. 1080, Guo Ruoxu records the year of Li's death as 967—a date that is generally accepted as accurate—which would indicate that the text here is in error. Oddly enough, Guo himself repeats the mistaken reign era elsewhere in the same passage noted here. See A.C. Soper (trans.), *Kuo Jo-hsü's "Experiences in Painting" (T'u-hua chien-wen chih)*, (Washington, D.C.: American Council of Learned Societies, 1951), p. 46.

43. SCMHP, p. 56.

44. SCMHP, *ibid.*

45. See Kris and Kurz, *Legend, Myth, and Magic*, for numerous examples.

46. SCMHP, p. 21.

47. SCMHP, p. 27.

48. SCMHP, p. 47.

49. SCMHP, p. 49.

50. SCMHP, p. 60.

51. SCMHP, p. 87.

52. *Xuanhe huapu* ("Painting Catalogue of the Xuanhe Era"; hereafter (XHHP), preface dated to 1120, (Taibei: Shijie, 1974), p. 502.

53. This is not to suggest that this "different" treatment is manifested in every entry in the SCMHP, as there are many instances where painters are "commanded" to execute certain works; what I mean to call attention to, rather, is a general trend.

54. SCMHP, p. 27

55. SCMHP, p. 60.

56. SCMHP, p. 22.

57. SCMHP, p. 39.

58. SCMHP, p. 90.

59. SCMHP, p. 83.

60. SCMHP, p. 49.

61. Thomas Hess, "Some Academic Questions", in Thomas Hess and John Ashberry (eds.), *The Academy: Five Centuries of Grandeur and Misery, from the Caracci to Mao Tse-tung* (New York: Macmillan, 1967 [Artnews Annual 33]), p. 8.

62. Joseph R. Levenson, "The Amateur Ideal in Early Ch'ing Society: Evidence from Painting", in John Fairbank (ed.), *Chinese Thought and Institutions* (Chicago: University of Chicago Press, 1957), p. 323. Levenson's overall discussion of the "amateur ideal" should be read in light of James Cahill, "Style as Idea in Ming-Ch'ing Painting", in Maurice Meisner and Rhoads

Murphy (eds.), *The Mozartian Historian* (Berkeley: University of California Press, 1976), where exception is taken to many of its arguments.

63. Wai-kam Ho, "Aspects of Chinese Painting from 1100 to 1350", in *Eight Dynasties of Chinese Painting* (Cleveland: Cleveland Museum of Art, 1980 [exh. cat.], p. xxv.

64. Prior to the reign of Huizong, the "offices" held by Academy members were outside of the regular governmental ranks; see *ibid.*

65. These figures are based on information contained in the SCMHP, and on statistical tables compiled by Yu Jianhua; see his *Zhongguo huihua shi*, vol. 1, pp. 168-170.

66. SCMHP, pp. 78-79.

67. SCMHP, pp. 16-18.,

68. SCMHP, pp. 56-58.

69. SCMHP, p. 22.

70. SCMHP, pp. 78-79.

71. SCMHP, p. 90.

72. SCMHP, p. 93.

73. *Tang Texts* I, p. 153.

74. William Willetts, *Chinese Arts*, 2 vols. (Harmondsworth: Penguin Books, 1958), vol. 2, p. 514.

75. For a discussion of the artist/patron relationship in the West, and of how it was affected by the breakdown of the Guild system, see Rudolf and Margot Wittkower, *Born Under Saturn: The Character and Conduct of Artists* (London: Weidenfield and Nicholson, 1963), Chapter 2. In *The Rise of the Artist in the Middle Ages and the Early Renaissance* (London: Thames and Hudson, 1972), especially pp. 97-106, Andrew Martindale argues that too much has been made of the differences between Medieval and Renaissance artists, and claims that it is a lack of sources concerning Medieval painters that makes the contrast appear so sharp; however, what he seems to overlook is that it is precisely this lack of sources which demonstrates the low esteem in which artists were held in this period.

76. See Susan Bush, *The Chinese Literati on Painting: Su Shih (1037-1101) to Tung Ch'i-ch'ang (1555-1636)*, rev. ed., (Cambridge MA: Harvard University Press, 1978 [Harvard-Yenching Institute Studies 27]), pp. 22-28, for a succinct and trenchant analysis of this equation as it came to be made in the Northern Song period.

77. Quoted in Bush and Shih, *Early Chinese Texts*, pp. 95-96.

78. *Ibid.*, p. 131.

79. *Ibid.*, p. 132.

List of Characters

boshi 博士

Chen Hong 陳宏

Chen Yongzhi 陳用之

Dai Kuei 戴逵

daizhao 待詔

Deng Chun 鄧椿

Dezong 德宗

Gao Keming 高克明

Gu huapin lu 古畫品錄

Guo Ruoxu 郭若虛

Guo Zhongshu 郭忠恕

Han Gan 韓幹

Huangdi 黃帝

huashi 畫師

Huaji 畫繼

Huizong 徽宗

jiaxun 家訓

jinshi 進士

Jiutangshu 舊唐書

Kaibao 開寶

Li Cheng 李成

Li Xiong 李雄

Lidai mingghuaji 歷代名畫記

Liang 梁

Liu Daochun 劉道醇

miao 妙

neng 能

pin 品

ping 評

pipa 琵琶

qiyun 氣韻

Renzong 仁宗

shang 上

shen 神

Shi Huang 史皇

shidafu hua 士大夫畫

Shu 蜀

Siku quanshu zhenben 四庫全書珍本

Su Shi 蘇軾

Sun Mengqing 孫夢卿

Sun Sihao 孫四浩

Songchao minghua ping 宋朝名畫評

Taizong 太宗

Taizu 太祖

Tangchao minghua lu 唐朝名畫錄

Tao Hongjing 陶弘景

Tuhua jianwen zhi 圖畫見聞志
tuhuayuan 圖畫院
Wang Guan 王瓘
Wang Wei 王微
Wang You 王友
wenyuan 文苑
Wu Daozi 吳道子
Wu Di 武帝
Wu Zongyuan 武宗元
xia 下
Xie He 謝赫
Xu Xi 徐熙
Xuanhe huapu 宣和畫譜
Xuanzong 玄宗
xueshi 學士
Yan Liben 閻立本
Yan Zhitui 顏之推
Yanshi jiaxun 顏氏家訓
Yin Zhi 尹質
Yu Jianhua 俞劍華
Yuqing zhaoying gong 玉清昭應宮
yuxing 寓興
Yuan Ai 袁靄
Zhang Huaiguan 張懷瓘
Zhang Yanyuan 張彥遠
Zhao Chang 趙昌
Zhao Guangfu 趙光輔
Zhenzong 真宗
zhong 中
Zhongguo huihua shi 中國繪畫史
Zhou 周
Zhou Fang 周方
Zhu Jingxuan 朱景玄
Zong Ping 宗炳

Women in Chinese Religions: Submission, Struggle, Transcendence

Daniel L. Overmyer
University of British Columbia

"We women (*wo nü tzu*) are despised for troubling our mothers' bodies. Our parents must bring us up, but when a girl grows up she abandons her parents and is married to another."

"When a woman is married to a husband for her whole life she is controlled by him. All her joys and sorrows derive from him. After they are married she necessarily suffers the pains of childbirth, and cannot avoid the sin of offending the sun, moon, and starts with a flow of blood. Now I will speak to you in more detail about the sufferings women endure in childbirth."

Old nun's sermon, *Liu Hsiang pao chüan* (18th century),
(*chüan* 1, pp. 4b-5a, 6b-7a)

"What's the use of reading books [for the civil service examinations]? It is better to study the Way; profit lies therein... To be an official for one life is to gain enemies for 10,000 lifetimes. Every wrong [you do] will be avenged without ceasing. I am pointing out to you the path to the Western Land. I urge you, husband, to take the earliest opportunity to practice spiritual discipline."

Liu Hsiang to her husband, *Liu Hsiang pao-chüan*,
(*chüan* 1, pp. 41b-42a)

Introduction

The history of women in Chinese religions is long and complex, but a few facts are clear. As has been true in every traditional civilization, women in China were kept in an inferior social position. They were controlled by their fathers and husbands, denied status until they had male children, expected to do menial work, forced to welcome concubines, and in desperate situations sold for cash. In the process, however, many women became social entrepreneurs who established a degree of status and power for themselves, both within the family and in the marketplace. Chinese religions in general supported the established social hierarchy, with women near the bottom. Nonetheless, religious activities offered alterative consolation and status to women, outside the home, so that to this day many religious participants are women. Through ritual, scripture study, and moral acts women had access to a world of meaning partly their own, a world that provided support for most, and social transcendence for a few.

This paper is intended as an introduction to some of the roles women played in Chinese religions, as household ritualists, lay devotees of a deity, shamans, nuns, and sectarian teachers. In all of this the quantitative social and economic background should be kept in mind. In traditional China the overwhelming majority of women were poor, illiterate, and had to work hard every day to survive. This was true for men too, but women had the additional burdens of inferior status and the dangers of childbirth. The religious activities of most women were confined to worshipping their husband's ancestors and occasionally visiting a local temple to pray for healing or sons. For them such rituals were at best a temporary consolation with no social implications other than making it easier to stay where they were. Even if a woman were a pious lay Buddhist the values in sermons she might hear would emphasize frugality, obedience, chastity, acceptance of her lot, hope for paradise after death. For all but a few religion was socially conservative. The more active religious roles for women discussed in this paper should be understood against this background. They represented theoretical possibilities that were realizable only by a few, and even most of those had to define themselves over against men. If this ground theme is understood it will not need to be repeated in what follows.

The focus of this paper is on the participation of living women in Chinese religious activities. It is not directly concerned with related issues such as theories of a "feminine" principle in Taoist philosophy or the development of female deities. There is no doubt that women have been actively involved in a variety of cults and rituals throughout Chinese history, but records concerning them are few and scattered. It is important to distinguish what women actually did from theories composed by men that indicate a sexually balanced view of cosmic forces, such as *ch'ien* and *k'un* in the *I-ching* and *yang* and *yin* in Han thought. The *Tao-te ching* contains many statements praising non-interference, yielding, lowliness, and the virtues of water, all of them conventionally regarded as showing appreciation for the "feminine" side of existence, but of course all these virtues are simply expressions of what men would like women to be. Praising the Tao as mother of the world does not mean that one thinks highly of women, and indeed there is no hint of such appreciation in the *Tao-te ching*. The same is true of other philosophical Taoist books such as the *Chuang-tzu* or the *Huai-nan tzu*; they contain no consideration or appreciation of the role of living women. Other early philosophical texts are the same; it is assumed that women are necessary as wives, concubines, and mothers, but otherwise they are ignored. Their ritual roles are limited to assisting at sacrifices to their husband's ancestors. When Mencius states that all men have the potential for goodness, that's what he means: all men. The potential of women for moral self-cultivation is not denied, it is just not considered. The goal of such self-cultivation is better management of family and state, a role not open to women. Though there are some positive statements about mothers and wives, Chinese philosophy is almost entirely a discussion by and for men in their controlling intellectual, moral, and social roles. If women are mentioned at all it is to note the obedience they owe to parents, husband, and adult sons as part of the hierarchical order of society. Beyond that the spirit of philosophical discussion was set by a famous passage in *Analects 17:25:*

> The Master said, "In one's household, it is the women and the small men that are most difficult to deal with. If you let them get too close, they become insolent. If you keep them at a distance, they complain.[1]

One must maintain a critical perspective as well on the relationship of female deities to women participants in their cults. There have been three great national goddesses in the history of Chinese religions, the Queen Mother of the West (Hsi Wang-mu), Kuan-yin, and Ma-tsu (T'ien Hou). In addition, there have been a large number of lesser deities with more specific functions, such as healing and the bringing of (male) children. Women have been active worshippers of these deities, but their role as formulators and organizers is not clear. I know of no evidence that women wrote texts about these deities or established temples for them; indeed the role assigned to women in society at large would have prevented such activities. There is some evidence that princesses, courtesans, and prostitutes worshipped the Queen Mother of the West during the T'ang dynasty, but for the most part the Taoist tradition of this goddess was maintained by men. This is largely the case with other Taoist female deities and immortals as well; their beauty and power were praised by men; they are what men wanted to believe in and worship, but there is no necessary connection between their cults and attitudes toward living women. In China as elsewhere, that goddesses are worshipped does not mean that women are honored. On the contrary, goddesses can be projections of male desires and needs to a cosmic level, by-passing women on the way. Hence, this paper will concentrate on evidence for what women actually did in Chinese religions, both in general descriptions and in texts in which women are given active roles. This paper attempts a preliminary survey of its whole topic, to bring together what I know so far, and to clarify where further reading and research are needed. It will proceed by first discussing the evidence for women's religious activities in rough historical order, culminating in the most independent role women had, as teachers and leaders in early modern religious sects. Once the evidence is before us we can analyze, compare, suggest areas for further research, and attempt to draw lessons for today. This is a large task that I approach with diffidence but also with a conviction that it needs to be done.

The Shang and Mid-Chou Periods (c 1500-600 B.C.E.)

The first archaeologically verified kingdom in Chinese history was the Shang (c 1500-1050 B.C.E.), which arose due to technological innovation such as bronze casting, and the development of new forms of social and administrative control. The great majority of the population continued to live in semi-subterranean houses in small villages, employing stone tools in subsistence agriculture, as had been the case in the prehistoric period. The emergence of a hereditary royal clan made possible a new concentration of the surplus resources of this neolithic agricultural base. The specialized rulers, administrators, priests, and technicians who relied on these resources developed bronze metallurgy, writing, new techniques of divination, military weaponry and organization, and more elaborate architecture. Social stratification became much more pronounced, with political and economic power concentrated in the hands of a small hereditary elite.

Most of our records of Shang religion describe the activities of men, but in some cases aristocratic women are referred to as well. The wives or consorts of kings occasionally participated in rituals intended to exorcise harmful spirits. They also made formal announcements to ancestors of such events as a successful harvest or a plague of locusts. A third kind of ritual carried out by women was that of invocation to ancestral spirits to aid in childbirth, and to petition for male children, a theme oft repeated in later centuries. There are many references to palace ladies in oracle bone (divination) texts. Prayers are offered for their health and safe childbirth, and after death some were worshipped as ancestors themselves. The wives of subject rulers sometimes came to offer tribute to the Shang court. Fu Hao, a consort of King Wu Ting in the 13th century B.C.E., is described as a military leader who led attacks on neighboring tribes. Thus there is evidence that at least a few Shang women had active religious and social roles, perhaps more so than in later periods.

There is also a bit of evidence for female deities in the Shang, particularly an Eastern Mother (Tung-mu) and a Western Mother (Hsi-mu) who seem to have been deities in charge of directions. Oxen were sacrificed to them as they were to ancestors.[2]

The Chou succeeded the Shang in the eleventh century B.C.E. Early Chou society was dominated by hereditary aristocratic lineages who controlled land, taxation, military force, literacy, and ritual access to their own ancestors and deities. The agricultural population worked the land as serfs, bound to their lords by obligations to provide food, other material needs, and labor service.

The religious activities of the early Chou aristocracy were focussed on their ancestors, who were believed to reside in a celestial court presided over by T'ien, "heaven," the Chou high god. These ancestors had power to influence the prosperity of their descendants, their fertility, health, and longevity. Through ritual equation with deities of natural forces the ancestors could also influence the productivity of clan lands. In addition, royal ancestors served as intermediaries between their descendants and T'ien.

There are very few references to women as active participants in Chou religion; to get any sense at all of what they might have done I have turned to late Chou or Han (202 B.C.E.-220 C.E.) sources such as the *Li-chi* (Record of Rites), which was edited in the Han but includes earlier material. From such material it appears that Chou women could have three religious roles, as assistants in ancestor worship, as ritualists for a silk-worm cult, and as shamans or spirit-mediums.

There are several passages in the *Li-chi* that mention the role of the ruler's wife in assisting at ancestral sacrifices. Wives are described as bringing in the stands for sacrificial dishes, serving as representatives of their husbands' female ancestors, and supervising the raising of silkworms and the making of silk robes worn at sacrifices. Before ancestral rituals both the ruler and his wife were expected to purify themselves in a ten-day period of abstinence and mental concentration, to facilitate communion with the spirits. The cooperation expected of the wife in these rituals is well summed up in such passages as the following:

> In sacrificing, husband and wife had their several duties which they personally attended to... When the victim was introduced the ruler held it by the rope... the wives of the ruler's surname followed the wife with basins; she presented the purified liquid; the ruler held in his hand the knife with the bells; he prepared the lungs (to be offered to the personator [ritual representatives of the ancestor]), and his wife put them on the dishes and presented them. All this shows what is meant in saying that husband and wife had their parts which they personally performed.[3]

Shamanism in China most commonly took the form of deities and spirits possessing receptive human beings. Spirit mediums both female and male are mentioned in discussions of early Chou religion as participants in court rituals, responsible for invoking the descent of the gods, praying and dancing for rain, and for ceremonial sweeping to exorcise harmful forces. They were a subordinate level of officially accepted ritual performers, mostly women, who spoke on behalf of the gods to arrange for sacrifices. In conditions of extreme drought they could be exposed to the sun as an inducement to rain. Female mediums were called *wu*; a word etymologically related to that for dancing; male mediums were called *hsi*. In the state of Ch'u south of the center of Chou culture there were shamans believed able to practice "magic flight," that is, to send their souls on journeys to distant realms of deities and immortals.

Han historical sources indicate that by the third century B.C.E. there were shamans all over China, many of whom were invited by emperors to set up shrines in the capital. This was done in part to consolidate imperial control, but also to make available fresh sources of sacred power to support the state and heal illness. So, for example, in 201 B.C.E. Kao-tsu (r. 202-195 B.C.E.), the founding emperor of the Han, invited female spirit mediums from four important regions of the realm to sacrifice regularly in the palace; Emperor Wu (r. 141-87 B.C.E.) summoned shamans when he was ill, while one of his sons invoked such aid to determine his succession to the throne.

One of the most detailed discussions of early Chinese shamanism is by J.J.M. de Groot, who provides a variety of Chinese primary texts in his citations. One, from the *Kuo Yü* (Conversations of the States), compiled in the third century B.C.E., notes that some particularly upright and intelligent persons could be possessed by spirits (*shen*), and continues:

> When an intelligent spirit descends into them, in the case of men they are called *hsi*, while women are called *wu*. As functionaries they regulated the places for the position of the gods [at sacrifices], the order of their tablets, the [proper] sacrificial victims and implements [to be used], and the ceremonial dress to be worn in accord with the seasons.[4]

De Groot notes that, "As the Wu-ist priesthood consisted largely, probably, even principally, of women, we cannot wonder that its influence was prevalent to a great extent among the female sex." He goes on to cite a statement by the late Han scholar Wang Fu,

> The *Book of Poetry* criticizes a woman who did not twist her hemp, but sauntered in the marketplace, yet even now there are many who do not occupy themselves with providing food at home, or raising silkworms or weaving, but give priority to studying the occupations of shaman and invocator. Dancing to the sound of drums, they serve the spirits and thereby cheat the people and mislead women of the common folk.[5]

De Groot's subsequent discussion cites several other passages referring to female shamans, and includes a chapter on their activities in the Fujian province of his day, emphasizing their particular role of summoning deceased ancestors to ask about their well-being, and to petition their aid for descendants. This role is emphasized by Jack Potter as well in his article on Cantonese shamanism in the twentieth century, where he describes the mediums as "old ladies who speak to spirits." He summarizes their activities by saying that they,

> ...act as intermediaries between the villagers and the supernatural worlds of heaven and hell. Assisted by their familiar spirits, the [mediums] send their souls to the supernatural world, where they communicate with deceased members of village families. They also know how to recapture the souls of sick village children, and they can predict the future. They take care of the souls of girls who die before marriage, and protect the life and health of village children by serving as... fictive mothers [to take advantage of the shaman's authority over spirits].

Potter notes that several of the women he interviewed became shamans after some of their children had died. The spirits of these children were among their helpers.[6]

Though women continue to have a role in Chinese shamanism, it is clear that over the centuries this role has been reduced to the more limited and specialized function of intermediary for family spirits. It is male shamans who are possessed by the more important gods, and who carry out dramatic public exorcism rituals.[7]

Women in Taoism

Taoism is China's own "indigenous higher religion," characterized by the fifth century C.E. by a literate and self-perpetuating priesthood, a pantheon of celestial deities, complex rituals, and revealed scriptures in classical Chinese.

Most branches of Taoism eventually traced their origin to a new revelation from the Most High Lord Lao to Chang Tao-ling in 142 C.E., establishing him as "Celestial Master." He was empowered to perform rituals and write talismans that distributed this new manifestation of the Tao for the salvation of humankind. Salvation was available to those who repented of their sins, believed in the Tao, and pledged allegiance to their Taoist master. The master in turn established an alliance between the gods and the devotee, who then wore at the waist a list (register) of the names of the gods to be called on for protection. The register also served as a passport to heaven at death. Taoist ritual consists essentially of the periodic renewal of these alliances by confession, visualization, petition, and the offering of incense and sacred documents. Taoists texts are concerned throughout for moral discipline and orderly ritual and organization.

Though men still dominated the tradition, women had a more important role in the first centuries of Taoism than in any previous form of Chinese religion. Early Taoist texts are addressed to households, not just to men, unlike the male orientation of classical philosophy. To be sure, Taoist householders are assumed to be men, but women are included and sometimes specifically mentioned as participants. One fifth century text praises both the Celestial Masters and their wives as founders of the tradition. Another devotes several pages to instructing women in various stage of life. Writing of the Celestial Master tradition, Henri Maspero comments:

> Beginners were called the Sons and Daughters of the Tao: *tao-nan*, *tao-nü*. The higher rank was that of Man or Woman Wearing the Cap, *nan-kuan* or *nü-kuan*, and this was sometimes written with a character of the same pronunciation which signified Mandarin. Further progress gave the right to the title of Father or Mother of the Tao, *tao-fu* or *tao-mu*. As we see, all these ranks were accessible to women as well as to men; there seems to have been no difference between them, and religious life was open equally to the two sexes. However, for the title which seems to have been the highest, that of Divine Lord, *shen-chün*, no feminine equivalent has been found.[8]

There was also a Taoist tradition of sexual rituals that it was believed could bring immortality to women as well as men. There is evidence that during the T'ang dynasty (618-907 C.E.) some aristocratic women became Taoist nuns renowned for their piety. From this period as well there are also a number of biographies of women who became immortals.

However, the later Taoist texts I have read seem to be addressed more particularly to men. There are occasional references to Taoist families, but if women are mentioned at all it is to urge that they be avoided if they have recently given birth, or that they not be allowed to observe a male practitioner mixing alchemical potions. The chief exception to this that I know of is in the early Ch'üan-chen tradition in which several women attained positions of leadership.

Some of the more important references to women in early Taoist texts I have read are as follows:

1. *Cheng-i fa-wen T'ien-shih chiao chieh k'e ching* (The correct and unified ritual text, the scripture of the teachings, precepts and regulations of the Celestial Masters) (Harvard-Yenching index (HY) 788; 3rd. cen. C.E.).

> If you do not remember the Tao, the Tao will not remember you. Therefore common people and [Taoist] officers, male and female, you should all put your affairs in order, cultivate your character, purify yourselves, think on your masters and uphold the Tao [the term here includes both the cosmic Tao and the teachings of the sect]. The customs of the world are shallow, so you husbands and wives, fathers and sons in your households should together be devoted to and preserve [the Way]... You should be pure, upright and filial, obey the Tao, reverence your master, pay ritual homage to the souls of the dead, and accord with the gods. (pp. 14b-15a)

There are also injunctions in this text that, "each household should transform itself," so as to practice all the principles of morality (p. 18a), and that prohibit male and female sect officials from appointing themselves to office (p.16b). This whole text is directed to women as well as men as a matter of course, and hence all of its teachings apply to the roles and responsibilities of women.

2. *San-t'ien nei-chieh ching* (Scriptures of the inner explanation of the three heavens (HY 1196, 5th cen.).

A passage describing the first Celestial Master Chang (2nd cen. C.E.) says:

> He set up twenty-four parish districts [in the area of present Sichuan province], and put in office male and female officials and libationers to be in charge of the correct laws and rituals of the Three Heavens [the new dispensation revealed by the Most High Lord Lao]. In transforming the people and receiving households [the work of conversion] they used five pecks of rice as a pledge of sincerity. They converted 10,000 households in 100 days; people came in clouds. For administration they made regulations and documents that were complete and effective in every way, and handed them over to their descendants to transmit through the generations as national preceptors [intended as religious advisers to emperors]. When laws and rituals were established, then humans and spirits were in security and peace. [Master] Chang subsequently ascended to heaven in broad daylight and personally received the office of Celestial Master. The son of the Celestial Master Chang Heng and his grandson Chang Lu, with their wives, were released from the corpse and ascended to heaven. So, there were three [Celestial] Masters and their wives. Since the three Masters ascended, libationers of the various parishes have transmitted the laws and rituals of the Tao. (1:6a)

Here we see women involved in founding the Taoist tradition.

3. *Cheng-i fa-wen T'ai-shang wai-lu i* (Text of the correct and unified ritual teachings, protocol for the exterior registers of the Most High) HY 1233 (5th cen.).

This text begins: "Male and female Masters all establish parish districts. Being of honored or humble position, worshipping and showing reverence, advancing and stopping, [all] depend on the regulations..."

Then follows a section titled, "Important registers received by five types of women." Registers are lists of the titles of gods who protect devotees, written on talismans worn at the waist. The five types of women are:

a) Unmarried daughters dwelling at home. Here they are to obey the instructions of their parents and receive ritual teaching from [Taoist] mistresses/masters. When taking leave of their parents they are to inform the [Taoist] official of their district responsible for the livelihood of the people, male and female. [They are to say],

"Grateful for the weighty kindness of the Tao from which I obtained life, I, an unmarried daughter, in such and such a year, with a devoted mind take pleasure in the Tao. Although I am ignorant I embolden myself to advance, and now take refuge at the master's gate [among his or her disciples]. I beg you to bestow success upon [my quest]; relying on the ritual teaching, I maintain belief and sincerity, and offer these phrases to be heard. I request to receive such and such a register and to devote myself to religious practice according to the ritual teaching. Bowing down I desire that [you] enlightened master/mistress, will deign to give me permission. Respectfully uttered."

All those who receive the ritual teaching while living at home, when they are about to be married should announce it to their master/mistress. If their master is not home, they should report it in memorial form to one of high virtue of the same Tao. If the woman must go to the family of her husband she should submit another report.

In all cases when she enters her husband's household she should tell her husband what register she has received. Her husband announces this to his parents, and goes to his master to inform him. The woman should only change her surname, and is not allowed to change the writing of it (?) (*wen*; could this be a misprint for *ming*, "given name"?). When she is at home she is called by her father's surname, when she meets others [marries] she is called by her husband's surname.

b) Daughters who leave home. Daughters who put forward their own destiny (*t'ing-ming*) and do not wish to meet others [marry] should announce to their parents that they are going to leave home to study the Way. Some establish another cloister [of their own]; some join the disciples of a master. Male masters who live alone are not permitted to accept female disciples. If a master is married she is called Mistress (*shih-mu*). When female disciples come they are to rely on a mistress. If there is no mistress they can turn to an unmarried woman master (*nü-shih*). An unmarried woman master leaves home, is devoted to her task, makes her thoughts harmonious, and follows a master to receive a register...

There follows the text of the vow taken by such an unmarried woman master, announced to the local Taoist officer:

"[I], daughter so and so, was born at such and such a time and date. The sins of my previous karma being weighty, when I was born I received a female body. I am weak and ignorant and do not wish to marry. In my parents home there is no way for me to study. Now I vow to devote my life and take refuge at the master's gate. I will exhaust my strength in sincerity and devotion, and will exert myself in sprinkling and sweeping [a standard phrase for entering disciples, male and female]. For my whole life I will continue the light, [offering] incense morning and evening. I will not dare to feel regret halfway through, and will not backslide. I will carry out this pledge in accord with the regulations. I offer up these phrases, hoping only that [you], enlightened master, will deign to bestow upon me a successful result. Respectfully uttered."

c) Married women. There are many reasons why women marry. Some do not wish to marry, but in obedience to superiors [parents] are compelled to do so. Some are taken by force by aristocratic and powerful secular households. Some attend on and uphold the ritual teaching. Some have nothing to worship. [Registers] previously received should be immediately returned to their master/mistress. The master should instruct them that if their husband upholds the Tao they should give up and change their original surname. If [the woman] has not yet received a register she should follow (accord with) her husband in receiving one. When husband and wife have the same master and the master goes some distance away, she can go to one of high virtue and give him or her allegiance according to the regulations, saying,

"[I], the wife of a local man named so and so, born at such and such a date and time, fortunately due to my past karma have been able to uphold the great Tao. Although I have been given the weakness of a woman, I have been able to rely on the people of the Tao. Just now I am expressing to the utmost my sincere devotion [to the Tao] while I attend to holding the basket and broom [work as a housewife]. I look up to the Tao to extend my life, praising its marvelous transformations; overcome with gratitude for its profound blessings, may I forever fill the role of a 'seed person' [a member of the elect, waiting for Lord Lao to return], diligently rely on the ritual teaching, and offer pledges of my sincerity and faith. I offer up these phrases, requesting to receive such and such a register. I hope that [you], enlightened master/mistress, will deign to grant permission. Respectfully stated."

Here we see that a married Taoist woman could have a complete religious status of her own.

d) Single women. This category refers to several kinds of women: widows who have vowed not to remarry, those of advanced years who have not married, those who are old with no sons, those who are wealthy and not willing to go [out to marry], and those who are poor and no one has asked for, or too sick to go. Such women can enroll with a master or mistress. Here again the text of a vow is supplied, similar in tone to those translated above, confessing sin, and petitioning to join with a master and receive a register.

e) Daughters who return to live at home. This category refers to women whose husbands have died, who have transgressed one of the seven grounds for divorce, or whose horoscopes are incompatible with those of their husbands, to the point that they are forced to live apart. Such women who cannot support themselves return to their original families, and, "...bound about with anxieties and afflictions, take refuge at a master's gate," Their vow of allegiance is similar to that of unmarried daughters living at home. (pp. 1-3a)

There are other references in this text as well to male and female masters, and all the rituals in it appear to be intended for devotees of both sexes.

There are scattered references to women in other early Taoist texts, concerning such matters as taking vows, exchanging registers with husbands at marriage, and wearing ritual robes. In general in these texts women are assumed to be an integral part of the Taoist ritual system.

Another interesting but less direct source for understanding the role of Taoist women is biographies of female immortals; living women who attain sainthood through piety and good works. There is a collection of sixteen such biographies, all short, in the *Yün-chi ch'i-ch'ien* (HY 1026), an 11th century collection of Taoist texts compiled for the emperor. Though these stories are presented in what for us is legendary form, they do give some indication of what was understood as possible for exceptional Taoist women. Most of these stories are set in the Eastern Chin dynasty (317-420 C.E.). This is not the place for a detailed discussion of this material, but one can note that the women involved were both commoners and the wives or daughters of officials who studied the Tao with such devotion that they attracted the aid of immortals. One is described as a childless widow who became an innkeeper. She made her guests feel at home, and cared for the sick. As a result she was visited by an immortal.

One woman attained the Tao because of her compassion for birds and animals, for which she put out grain on the snow in winter. Of another we are told that she,

> ...had compassion and love for others, constantly did good deeds in secret, and even loved and protected mantises and other small creatures. Through studying the Tao she became an immortal, and now lives in a cave on Mt. Sung. (p. 1608)

One woman began as a pious Buddhist who

> ...daily sprinkled and swept the floor before Buddha images, and frequently vowed her deep desire for the Tao of immortality. After she had attained it she sang so beautifully that wild birds gathered in front of her to hover and dance, moved by her profound sincerity. (p. 1609)

We also read of a female Taoist priest, of a woman who was good at exorcism, who though several hundred years old still looked twenty-five, of women hermits who regularly communed with immortals, and of a married woman who lived alone because of illness, daily reciting the *Yellow Court Scripture* (an important text of internal visualization and meditation) three times. As a result female immortals descended to visit and instruct her. Most of these women lived alone and were aided by female immortals. (*chüan* 115, pp. 1607-1616 in Vol. III of the Taipei Tzu-yu Publishing Co. edition (1978).)

In a recent article Suzanne Cahill describes the Mother Queen of the West as the patron deity of aristocratic women during the T'ang dynasty (618-907). The literary evidence for this is poems, most written by men, but a few written by women themselves, including a prostitute who became a Taoist nun. These poems are in high literary style, with much comparison of court women with the Queen Mother's divine attendants, but there are references as well to women who go to the Mother's paradise at death, to palace ladies who take religious vows and become nuns, and to women performers of Taoist ritual music. The Queen Mother is referred to as the chief guide to immortality for women, who refer to her intimately as "Amah." There are few details, but enough to indicate a cult of the Queen Mother of the West available specifically to women.[9]

There is evidence in later Taoist history of women who were leaders, teachers, and nuns. One was Tsu Shu (fl. 889-904), who was one of the formulators of the Ch'ing-wei (Clarified Tenuity) Taoist tradition. Scriptures and teachings attributed to her were transmitted through several generations of female leaders.

A woman named Sun Pu-erh was one of the "Seven Perfected" (Immortals) of the Ch'üan-chen Taoist tradition in the 12th century. She was the wife of Ma Yü, who in turn was a close disciple of Wang Che (1112-1170), the founder of the Ch'üan-chen school. After she and her husband both became disciples they separated. Sun acquired a following of her own, and became a model for other Taoist women ascetics. There are records of many other Ch'üan-chen Taoist nuns as well.[10]

By the early fifth century, if not before, some Taoists had developed methods for nourishing the body's vital force, *ch'i*, through ritual sexual intercourse. For the most part this was a matter of stimulating and purifying the *yang ch'i* of the male through successive intercourse with a number of women without ejaculating semen. At the point of climax the man was supposed to press the base of the penis with his hand, grinding his teeth in great determination, thus diverting the semen up a conduit in the back to the head, which was a receptacle for storing refined vital essence, the liquid of immortality. This ritual could be carried out only on certain days of the year, after a period of purification. It was to be practiced with young women in the household, preferably between the ages of fourteen and nineteen, changing partners as frequently as possible. For a time there was also a communal sexual ritual called *ho-ch'i* "the blending of vital breath" in which members of Taoist congregations exchanged partners.

Though the emphasis is on the attaining of immortality by men, some texts indicate that women too could benefit from these practices. It appears that all adult members could join in the communal rituals, and all of those who did were promised healing, forgiveness of sins, and protection from hostile forces. In some texts discussing private sexual rituals it is noted that women who know their secrets can also benefit; indeed, men are enjoined to avoid such women! In one detailed description it is clear that both partners can gain immortality:

> After they have concentrated and purified their thoughts, then a man and woman may practice together the art that leads to longevity. This method must be kept secret, it must be transmitted only to adepts. It allows a man and a woman together to activate their *ch'i* and the man to nurture his semen and the woman her "blood." This is not a heterodox method; it concentrates on activating *yin* and strengthening *yang*. If this discipline is practised in the correct manner, then the *ch'i* fluid shall spread like clouds throughout the body, the seed will solidify and become harmonious, and soon all those who practise it, whether young or old, shall become [vigorous] like adolescents.
>
> ...
>
> The elixir thus formed [in the bodies of the two participants] if nurtured for a hundred days, will become transcendental. And if this discipline is continued over a very long period, then it will become a natural habit, the method for living long and attaining Immortality.[11]

In sum, during its first several centuries the Taoist tradition gave a relatively high level of support to the religious role of women. Their role in later Taoism appears to have been reduced, though future research may modify that judgment. In later centuries the women religious leaders that I know of were almost all from the realm of popular religion, to be discussed below.

Women in Chinese Buddhism

Buddhism has always included lay members of both sexes, and, according to early accounts, an order of nuns began in the Buddha's lifetime, but the defining core of the tradition has always been controlled by celibate male monks. The religious goal of these monks is to escape the emotional and social bonds of ordinary life in order to attain a supreme state of detachment, freedom and inner peace. To further this goal, monks are expected to leave the household life as fathers, husbands, and sons and join an all male community designed to minimize competition, temptation, and sexual stimulation. In such a community women are perceived as a threat because they represent the social and sexual life the monks are trying to deny. Because of this tension, early Buddhist texts portray women as emotional temptresses with powerful sexual desires, though the desires of men are strongly criticized as well.

Male monastics continued to control the Mahāyāna Buddhist tradition that became dominant in China after the second century C.E., but Mahāyāna theory is non-dualistic and egalitarian. An enlightened perspective sees all things as fundamentally one because of their shared emptiness, that is, their lack of independent being and permanent distinguishing characteristics. In this perspective, eventually all dualities disappear, including that between male and female. Unfortunately, however, despite this generous theory, Mahāyāna

Buddhist monks continued to be influenced by the old attitudes toward women, who were still seen as sensual threats to the quest for Nirvāṇa. For the most part Mahāyāna texts maintain that before women can attain the status of bodhisattvas or Buddhas they must change their sex.

The varied images of women in Mahāyāna literature have been admirably discussed by Diana Paul, so there is no need for detailed treatment here. Her own perspective is summed up in the introduction:

> Like Judaism and Christianity, Buddhism is an overwhelmingly male-created institution dominated by a patriarchal power structure. As a consequence of this male dominance, the feminine is frequently associated with the secular, powerless, profane, and imperfect. Male Buddhists, like male religious leaders in other cultures, established normative behavior for women by creating certain ideals of femininity. At the same time, men's opportunities for interaction with women were minimized by the restrictions of devout practice. In early Buddhist monastic communities, interaction with laywomen was necessary for economic support but otherwise avoided. When we find texts in which the sacred is represented as masculine while the profane or imperfect is represented as feminine, we have a polarization that suggests both internal psychological conflicts and external social barriers between the sexes.[12]

Diana Paul's *Women in Buddhism* is essentially a translation of texts with introduction and commentary, thematically arranged, beginning with depictions of women as evil temptresses, coupled with sharp criticisms of men as weak sensualists easily led astray. There follow sections on women as mothers, nuns, and pious daughters. The succeeding chapters are on a women who became bodhisattvas with and without sexual transformation, on the celestial bodhisattva Kuan-yin, and on queen Śrīmālā who becomes a Buddha in her own right. The images discussed move from negative to positive, and leave one with the conclusion that despite its faults the Mahāyāna perspective on women is more affirmative than that of many other religious traditions.

The issue before us here, however, is not literary images of women but their actual participation in religious activities. Mahāyāna texts are addressed to all beings in the universe, including lay men and women, described in Chinese translation as "good men" and "believing women" (*shan-nan*, *hsin-nü*, Sanskrit *upāsaka*, *upāsikā*), so it is clear that female piety is assumed and encouraged. For most Chinese women such piety involved offering prayers and incense to Buddha images, reciting the names of Buddhas and bodhisattvas to invoke their aid, and participating in such temple festivals as the one marking the Buddha's birthday on the eighth day of the fourth lunar month. Women also joined in pilgrimages to famous monastery temples. Women make up the majority of lay Buddhist devotees in China today, as can easily be seen in any visit to a living temple. The recent study of the Kuan-yin cult on P'u-t'o shan off the Zhejiang coast by Chün-fang Yü of Rutgers University has demonstrated anew the central importance of women in Chinese Buddhism.[13]

There is no doubt that lay women have been active supporters of Chinese Buddhism for centuries, but they are not often mentioned in the sources. However, Buddhist scriptures composed in China from the fifth to eight centuries emphasize that their message is for all, men and women alike, a spirit well summed up in the *Life Protecting Sūtra* (*Hu shen-ming ching*, *Taishō* 2866):

> The Buddhist Way must be studied, and the dharma of the scriptures must be read. That I am now a Buddha is due only to accumulated studies. As for the wonderful dharma of the Mahāyāna, without regard to sex or status, those who hear this scripture will be protected by all the Buddhas, and will obtain all they desire. (85:1327a)

The *Hsiao fa-mieh chin ching* (*The Smaller Sūtra on the Complete Extinction of the Dharma*, *Taishō* 2874) promises that in the turmoil at the end of the age, "Girls and married women will all attain the Way, diligently progress as one, and so can avoid these calamities" (85:1358c). A similar indigenous text from the same time (fifth century) notes that,

> When the dharma is about to be extinguished women will be zealous, constantly doing meritorious deeds, [while] men will be lazy and indifferent, will not engage in religious discourses, will look on monks as manure, and will not have believing minds.[14]

In the fifth century many Chinese Buddhists believed that the age of the decline of the dharma had begun, so comments like these may reflect actual situations of the time.

There is some evidence for women disciples of Ch'an masters, while Buddhist women were active in lay societies of the Sung dynasty (960-1279), led by monks. These societies ranged in membership from a few score to several thousands, including both men and women, gentry and commoners. They were devoted to reciting the names of the Buddhas, reciting and copying scriptures, carving images, and providing vegetarian feasts for monks and laity. Records of these societies mention women members as a matter of course, and we know of at least one group composed of fifteen women, "devoted to the promotion of friendship among women."[15]

Women's activities in these Sung Buddhist societies were important antecedents of their activities in popular religious sects later on.

In addition to these references to ordinary women there are many royal ladies who patronized Chinese Buddhism as early as the fourth century. Two empresses of the Eastern Chin dynasty founded nunneries in Jiankang (modern Nanjing); later empresses did the same, and also invited famous monks to preach and perform rituals in the palace. The most famous empress to actively support Buddhism was Wu Tse-t'ien (625-705) who interrupted the T'ang dynasty and founded her own, the Chou, from 690-705. Empress Wu had monasteries built all over China, rock images carved, and scriptures printed and distributed. Her efforts were anticipated by the wife of Emperor Wen of the preceding Sui dynasty (581-618) who actively encourage her husband's support of the T'ien-t'ai school. Thomas Shiyu Li and Susan Naquin have recently published an article that describes in detail the support of royal women for a Buddhist temple outside Beijing in the Ch'ing period. To discuss this topic further would take us too far afield, but it is one that deserves attention, and for which references should be relatively easy to find because of the prominence of the women involved.[16]

The first Chinese nun was ordained in 317 C.E., beginning a tradition which has continued to exist until today. In the fifth century two delegations of Singhalese nuns came to China and helped establish a truly orthodox lineage through ordination by Indian masters in the presence of other nuns. A text edited in 516, the *Pi-ch'iu-ni chuan* (*Lives of Nuns*) provides information about nuns from upper-class and educated families in the region of Jiankang. Most of these exceptional women were literate in Buddhist texts and active preachers and organizers. A few were renowned for their mastery of certain scriptures, their devotion to meditation, and their ability to visualize Buddhist paradises while in trance states. Their reasons for becoming nuns are given as devotion to Buddhism in early life, refusal to marry, illness, and grief at the loss of a parent. Convents were also a refuge for women who had been abandoned or orphaned during the destructive civil wars of the fourth and fifth centuries. Chinese nuns can still be observed in Taiwan and the mainland, living in small convents and carrying out daily rituals of recitation.[17]

Women in Family and Village Popular Religion

A major tradition that took its early modern shape during the Sung period was popular religion in the family and village, the religion of the whole population except those who specifically opted out of it, such as orthodox Taoist priests, Buddhist monks, and Confucian scholars and state officials in their public roles. (Indeed, this might better be called "common religion.")

While popular religion came to include deities, concepts, and values from Taoism, Buddhism, and Confucianism, where it is still active it is above all a local religion that provides a focus for community life and hope in the face of difficulties. It can be defined by its location in the midst of ordinary social life, its pantheon of personified deities, views of afterlife, demonology, and characteristic specialists and rituals.

This popular tradition is based on ancestor veneration and the cult of household gods. Beyond the household its rituals are performed at shrines for locality gods and at village temples. Temples are residences of the gods, where they are most easily available and ready to accept petitions and offerings of food and incense.

Women have always been an integral part of popular religion as performers of household rituals, worshippers at village temples, participants in pilgrimages, and spirit-mediums. Hence, to a large extent to discuss the role of women in this tradition is to discuss the tradition itself. Most participants in modern popular religion are women, and one suspects this has long been the case.

Married women with male children are considered full members of their family and lineage and as such have primary responsibility for offering incense and food to family ancestors and household deities. They also participate in annual festivals, as mourners at funerals, and as worshippers and preparers of food at rituals of community renewal (*chiao*). Such women can become ancestors worshipped by their descendants.

Within the larger religious realm there are cults of female deities of particular concern to women, particularly those deities involved with bringing children. In addition, there is some evidence that women have their own understandings of what they are doing in ritual, different from that of men.

In a recent article on the social contexts of the goddess T'ien Hou (Empress of Heaven = Ma Tsu) in the Hongkong New Territories, James Watson emphasizes her role as a symbol of territorial control and lineage power. He adds, however, that this understanding is that of men, and continues:

> Women, as indicated earlier, have a very different vision of T'ien Hou from that held by any category of men—so different, in fact, that one begins to wonder if we are dealing with the same deity. Women play no role whatsoever in the formal organization of the temple cults, not even to the extent of forming a women's auxiliary to complement the activities of their husbands and fathers. For women the worship of T'ien Hou is usually defined in personal or family terms. Wives appear at the annual festivals with individual sets of offerings, which they present to the goddess on behalf of their households. Men never make these presentations, as they are said to be "too busy" attending to the collective rituals associated with the cult.[18]

In addition to this difference of perspective, the role of women in family and village popular religion is restricted in two ways. First, they do not usually found or manage village temples, or serve on councils of local elders that decide on temple leadership, repairs, and special festivals. However, a woman spirit-medium can be in charge of the shrine to her helper deity, either in her home or by the roadside. In the Macao village of Tai-pa, for example, there is a small temple to Kuan-yin run by an elderly woman; perhaps it is a remnant of what was once more common elsewhere as well.

A second restriction on the religious activities of women is based on their supposed pollution due to menstrual flow and the blood of childbirth. Menstruating women and those who have recently given birth are not allowed to enter temples, because their blood is believed to offend the gods. Though children are demanded by the family, and a woman must give birth in order to become a full member of society, the act of giving birth is considered a polluting sin that automatically condemns a woman to a bloody pool in purgatory! After she dies a son must arrange for a special ritual to symbolically release her suffering soul.[19]

Francis Hsü notes that the birth of a child calls for special rituals performed by women. A pregnant woman must observe several taboos, such as not looking at images of deities with animal heads, or at the sun and moon in eclipse. She consults a diviner before giving the baby a name chosen to ward off evil influences. A difficult labor may be due to a local ghost who is struggling to replace the baby's soul with its own and thus obtain a new body. In such a case, women in some areas propitiate the ghost with food, incense, and paper money offered at a spot it is believed to haunt.

The birth of a healthy child is celebrated with offerings to the ancestors, the kitchen god, and the deities on the family altar, and to the locality god (T'u-ti kung). The offerings are to report the birth and express gratitude for it. In west China the offering to the locality god is usually made by the baby's grandmother. Francis Hsü has described this ritual in some detail.[20]

In Cantonese families a diviner is asked to cast a horoscope for the baby; if it clashes with that of its mother, it may become ill or die young. In such a situation one remedy is to bond the child to someone else—a relative, a spirit-medium, a god, a sacred stone or tree; anything that will deflect bad fortune from the child. The mother is responsible for arranging this ritual adoption, and for making regular offerings to the deity involved, or visits and gifts if the protector is a person. This is again the kind of religious activity particularly carried out by women.[21] At the Wong Tai Sin temple in Kowloon one can see many women making offerings for this purpose, and confirming the results with divination sticks.

Women in Popular Religious Sects

By the early fourteenth century another form of popular religion appeared, the voluntary association or sect that could be joined by individuals from different families and villages. These sects developed out of lay Buddhist societies in the twelfth century, but their structure owed much to late Han religious associations and their popular Taoist successors, Buddhist eschatological movements from the fifth century on, and Manichaeism. By the sixteenth century the sects were characterised by predominantly lay membership and leadership, hierarchical organization, active proselytism, congregational rituals, possession of their own scripture texts, and mutual economic support. For the most part the sects simply provided a congregational alternative to village popular religion, an alternative that offered mutual support and assurance, an additional path to religious merit, and a means of going directly to paradise at death, without passing through purgatory.

In these popular religious sects women had higher relative status than anywhere else in traditional Chinese society and religion. They were not only active members from the beginnings of the sectarian tradition, but could also be congregational leaders and teachers, or even the founders of new groups. This role was facilitated by a mythology based on a supreme goddess, the creator and mother of all, in which male and female children have equal religious status. This Eternal Mother is superior to all other deities, including the Buddhas and the Jade Emperor. She waits in her paradise, sending messages to her lost children to return home. Some women sect leaders were believed to be her incarnations. The positive role of women in the popular sects was also supported by a series of scriptures related to them in which determined religious women are the chief protagonists. Born to auspicious signs, these women at an early age are attracted to Buddhist piety, maintain vegetarian diets, and vow to become nuns. They resist all family pressures to marry, and leave home in apparent disgrace, but go on to become heroic religious figures. In the end they convert their stubborn families, and are revealed to have become gods or bodhisattvas. In areas of south China there were groups of pious lay women who recited and transmitted these scriptures, women who had resisted marriage and now lived a communal life together. Similar "lay nuns" may be found in residential temples in Zhejiang province today, and no doubt elsewhere as well. Recent research by David Jordan and myself has revealed that women continue to have an important role in popular religious sects in Taiwan, as congregation leaders, spirit-writers, members of scripture chanting groups, altar women, and active worshippers. Some of them have their own distinctive interpretations of sect teaching and ritual, as do the T'ien Hou devotees observed by James Watson.

From the beginning the sources note that sect membership included women, in part because male devotees married and sometimes brought along their families when they joined. The presence of women scandalized orthodox Confucian scholars and celibate Buddhist monks, who repeatedly mention it as evidence for the vulgarity and heresy of the sects. An early fourteenth century source written by an orthodox Buddhist monk notes that in White Lotus congregations, "men and women mix together in confusion, thus disrupting proper human relationships," and that, "Though commoners, they presume to call themselves 'living Buddha Tathāgatas', with women given the title of 'Buddha mother great beings'."[22]

In a 1981 article I summarized the evidence for women with important positions in popular religious sects, including leaders of armed uprisings, congregation heads, teachers with both men and women as their pupils, and a sixteenth century nun who wrote five vernacular scripture texts of her own.[23] More detailed comments can be found in Susan Naquin's excellent study of a sectarian uprising in north China in 1813. She notes that there were no restrictions concerning who could join a sect, and that women as well as men could transmit its teachings.[24]

Women in Sectarian Scriptures (pao-chüan)

Of the many different types of Chinese vernacular literature one was developed primarily in the popular religious sects, a form of scripture text called *pao-chüan* "precious volumes." The first dateable sectarian *pao-chüan* appeared in the early 16th century, drawn from a variety of earlier resources, but written in relatively simple language promising aid and deliverance for all men and women of whatever status. These books are egalitarian and non-sexist in tone throughout.

There are several types of *pao-chüan* content, ranging from straightforward religious and moral teaching to stories that express the same values, but in more dramatic form. The doctrinal texts are addressed to "good men" and "pious women" as a matter of course, while many of the stories include women characters and are clearly addressed to all those willing to listen. In some of the story *pao-chüan* heroic religious women are the major actors. The earliest book of this type is the *Hsiang-shan pao-chüan* (Fragrant mountain *pao-chüan*), the first form of which appeared in the twelfth century, with antecedents going back to the seventh. This text opens with an introduction describing its origin and purpose, and then proceeds to the story of a young princess named Miao-shan, who, after a long struggle, becomes enlightened and discovers that in fact she is Kuan-yin. This story in effect provides mythic background for the cult of Kuan-yin of 1000 eyes and arms, who sees and aids all.[25]

The story of Miao-shan became a model for later accounts of similar heroic women, such as that in the *Liu Hsiang pao-chüan* (*The pao-chüan* of Fragrance Liu), which is discussed at length in my article on "Values in Chinese Sectarian Literature," cited above. The earliest edition of this book known to me was published in the late eighteenth century. It concerns a pious young woman who refuses to consummate her marriage and goes off on her own as a religious teacher. In the end she saves her husband's evil family, and convinces him and his second wife (forced on him by his mother) to join her in a life of celibate meditation. At death they go the Western Pure Land, where the Buddha Amitābha predicts they will become gods.

In the *Liu Hsiang pao-chüan* there is a long sermon by the old nun who converts Fragrance to Buddhism, and this sermon in turn includes a short *pao-chüan* called the "Pregnancy *pao-chüan*." Both sermon and text show a keen awareness of the situation of women in late traditional China and give strong support to refusing marriage. The nun notes that:

> ...when a boy is born, his mother is joyous, the neighbors all congratulate her, the relatives are happy, and father and mother love the child as if he were a precious jewel. When he grows up he studies, and perhaps becomes wealthy, honored, and famous throughout the world. When he goes out he is honored; when he returns home his wife and concubines diligently look after him. As a husband he fulfills his aims and honors his ancestors.
>
> ...

However, when a girl is born, everyone hates her, and no on in the household rejoices. "We women (*wo nü tzu*) are despised for troubling our mothers' bodies. Our parents must bring us up, but when a girl grows up she abandons her parents and is married to another" (*chüan* 1, pp. 4b-5a).

...

> By giving birth to children she befouls the heaven and earth,
> and offends the river god by washing bloody skirts.
>
> ...
>
> If she is on good terms with her mother-in-law she can visit her mother
> every year or so.
> But if she is not in accord with her other-in-law's wishes,
> she is never able to return to her mother's home.
> She thinks of the pain in the hearts of her parents, and of when she will be
> able to repay their kindness.

> No matter how many plans you might have, women have always submitted to others and served them.
> This is because of serious sins in their former existences. (*chüan* 1, p. 6a)
>
> ...
>
> When a woman is married to a husband for her whole life she is controlled by him. All her joys and sorrows derive from him. After they are married she necessarily suffers the pains of childbirth, and cannot avoid the sin of offending the sun, moon, and stars with a flow of blood. Now I will speak with you in more detail about the sufferings women endure in childbirth. (*chüan* 1, pp. 6b-7a)

Then follows a description of ten different forms of childbirth brought on as retribution for past sins, including several forms of birth in which the hands or feet come out first, or which involve entanglement in the mother's viscera, stillbirth, and so on. The theme is repeated that menstrual blood and the blood of childbirth offend the gods. The nun continues:

> Now the suffering of giving birth which I have discussed, the suffering of ten months of pregnancy and of three years of nursing, and after birth, the bitter toil day and night of exchanging dry and wet [clothing], these are what is called, "in loving a child, there is nothing parents won't do." (*chüan* 1, p. 9a)

The nun then recites the *Pregnancy Pao-Chüan* (*Huai-t'ai pao-chüan*), which is a detailed month-by-month account of the pains and anxieties of pregnancy. (*chüan* 1, pp. 9a-12b)

The explicit conclusion of this text is that children should repay the suffering and pain their parents have gone through by maintaining a vegetarian diet and reciting the Buddhas' names. (*chüan* 1, p. 12a) It seems reasonable to suggest, however, that such material might have led some women to question marriage itself, as did those described by Marjorie Topley in her "Marriage Resistance in Rural Kwangtung." Topley writes,

> Aimed expressly at women was the "precious volume" (*pao-chüan*) which contained biographies of model women.... Many of my informants had "precious volumes"... which further emphasize that refusing to marry is not morally wrong...

These books were read by women who lived in "girls' houses" or joined religious sects that "stressed sexual equality." Most of these women were involved in making silk, and hence had independent means of support. Thus, there was a specific social context in which books such as the *Liu Hsiang pao-chüan* made sense, that of religious voluntary associations in which unmarried women played an important or dominant role.[26]

Though the explicit ethical values supported in the *Liu Hsiang pao-chüan* are quite conventional, the chief implicit value is not, because at a basic level this text is devoted to the courage, freedom and salvation of women. Hsiang nü (Fragrance) is a full-scale religious heroine with great strength of conviction and powers of persuasion, just as Miao-shan was. She firmly remonstrates with her social superiors, and eventually brings them all around to her side. She endures the worst insults and beatings and yet remains ready to forgive. She breaks social custom by insisting on her own betrothal agreement, without an intermediary. She opposes that most established of traditional values, obtaining office through the civil service examination system. When she is eventually driven out of her husband's home, she develops her own vocation as a religious preacher and leader. And in the end she succeeds, and all the rest depend on her for deliverance.

From the social point of view, perhaps what is most important is that Hsiang nü never really has a normal marriage. The text does not say that she didn't sleep with her husband in their few days together, but she certainly remained celibate thereafter. What she values is meditation, not sex and children. There is in this text, then, a strong implicit resistance to marriage and all the toil and submission it requires. This is made abundantly clear in the sermon preached by the old nun, which contains a long section on the suffering and dangers of pregnancy and childbirth and other difficulties a wife must endure. To be sure, the point is made that these are all grounds for being filial to one's own mother, and that a woman should be especially pious so as to be reborn a man. But the resentment is strong, and the implication not far off that it is better not to marry at all, as the nun herself had not.[27]

Another *pao-chüan* in my collection is based on a similar story, the *Hsiu-nü pao-chüan* (The *pao-chüan* of daughter Elegance) (19th cen.). This is a lively tale about another heroic girl, pious from an early age, who is abducted and forced to become a concubine. She refuses to sleep with her husband, despite repeated beatings by her mother-in-law. She converts a maid in the family to Buddhism, and they meditate and worship every night. For this both are beaten unconscious with a club. Elegance then helps the maid escape, for which she herself is again beaten unconscious. When she recovers she is tied to a pillar, where boiling water is poured over her until she dies. Her soul goes to purgatory, but because of her piety is soon released, and a female Taoist immortal is sent to earth to resurrect her body. She returns to her husband's home, greeted by gods and ancestral spirits along the way. She releases all of her husband's ancestors from purgatory. When she reaches home she tells her mother-in-law the whole story, but when the older woman asks what the form of her own next life will be, Elegance tells her it will be as a domestic animal (a karmic punishment for her sins). At this the mother-in-law flies into a rage and beats her again, but now the blows have no effect. Elegance finally orders disease-causing demons to attack her husband and his mother, and then leaves. When she returns two weeks later her husband begs her to heal him; she says she will, on three conditions: first, that he stop charging a doubled rate of interest on loans; and second, that he maintain a vegetarian diet, be a good person, provide food for monks, repair bridges, roads, and rest houses, aid the poor and be compassionate. The third condition is that she be allowed to go home to her parents. She makes her mother-in-law agree to the same conditions, then heals them both by ordering the demons to leave. In the end, all the evil people in the story are either rehabilitated or punished.

When she returns home, Elegance preaches a sermon exhorting Buddhist piety and good works. It begins:

> [Since] I am a woman I don't read books and am not thoroughly versed in the scriptures, so what I say will not be literary and polished. I simply urge people to do good, maintain a vegetarian diet, recite the names of the Buddhas, and explain the Way. Now I will first preach about the glorious rewards of those in the thirty-three heavens, and the bitter sufferings of those in the eighteen [courts of] purgatory... (p. 58b)

In the end she and her parents are reborn in Amitābha's paradise.

Texts such as this are the high point of feminist thought in traditional China. Nowhere else do we find such a clear affirmation that women can attain superior status and power.

The end result of the long sectarian tradition of affirming the religious role of women may be seen in contemporary popular congregations in Taiwan, where women serve as leaders, spirit-mediums, and ritualists, and make up a substantial portion of active members. Since a description of all this is readily available in a recent book by David Jordan and me, I see no reason to discuss it at length here. Suffice it to note that in this book there are discussions of women in the early spirit-writing tradition (pp. 38-39), of Eternal Mother mythology (pp. 57-63, 123), the *Earth Mother Scripture* (pp. 72-74), the calling and work of a woman spirit-writer (pp. 149-165), and of dreams and visions of women sect members (pp. 174-212). The material on dreams and visions includes a discussion of two women who developed a sub-cult of their own, based on revelations made available only to them.[28]

Concluding Comments

This paper is intended as a preliminary inventory of what one historian of Chinese religions has learned so far about the activities of women in that history.[29]

Sources for learning about the roles of women are few and far between, but at least we know enough to suggest topics for further research, including all those noted in this paper. The most important single step is to become aware of the issue, to look for references to women, and be conscious of how much their role has been ignored. It is astounding that the lives and activities of half the Chinese population are so little mentioned in the sources. One must literally go through piles of notes and texts to find just a few nuggets here or there. To ignore actors in history is to deny them of what little immortality they might have, but in the Chinese case as in most others, such immortality has been limited almost entirely to men. Though the lives of all depended on them, it is as if women were not there. There are profound ethical issues at stake here for contemporary scholars.

The study of women in Chinese religions is also a study of their place in the culture as a whole, so continued research in this area can contribute to a more balanced understanding of the realities of China, past and present. There is also ample material for comparing Chinese women with women in other traditional cultures, a comparison I have begun to make in the case of the popular religious sects discussed above.[30]

From the material presented here one can see that in the history of Chinese religions most women had a subordinate role, but a few struggled to establish their own perspective and vocation. Through our research we can try to help them find their voices again.

Notes

1. The translation of *Analects* 17: 25 is taken from that of D.C.Lau, *The Analects of Confucius* (Harmondsworth: Penguin Books Ltd., 1979), p. 148. For discussions of the Queen Mother of the West see Michael Loewe, *Ways to Paradise: The Chinese Quest for Immortality* (London: George Allen and Unwin, 1979), pp. 86-126. See also Suzanne Cahill, "Performers and Female Taoist Adepts: Hsi Wang Mu as the Patron Deity of Women in Medieval China," *Journal of the American Oriental Society* 106.1: 155-168 (January-March, 1986). On other Taoist female deities, see Edward H. Schafer, *The Divine Woman* (Berkeley: University of California Press, 1973). For good recent summaries of Confucian attitudes toward women see Richard W. Guisso, "Thunder Over the Lake: The Five Classics and the Perception of Women in Early China," in Richard W. Guisso and Stanley Johannesen, eds.; *Women in China: Current Directions in Historical Scholarship* (Youngstown, New York: Philo Press, 1981), pp. 47-61, and Theresa Kelleher, "Confucianism," in Arvind Sharma, ed., *Women in World Religions* (Albany: State University of New York Press, 1987), pp. 135-159.

For a more positive assessment of the attitude of some Neo-Confucian scholars toward women, see Tu Wei-ming, "On Neo-Confucianism and Human Relatedness," in George A. De Vos and Takao Sofue, eds., *Religion and the Family in East Asia* (Berkeley: University of California Press, 1984), pp. 111-125.

2. Professor Ken'ichi Takashima, University of British Columbia, personal communication, June 23, 1988; Chou Hung-hsiang, "Fu-x Ladies of the Shang Dynasty," *Monumenta Serica* XXIX: 346-390, and K.C. Chang, ed., *Studies of Shang Archaeology* (New Haven: Yale University Press, 1986), pp. 103-140 (articles by Chang Cheng-lang and Chang Ping-ch'üan). I am grateful to Prof. Takashima for these references.

3. *Li-Ki*, tr. James Legge, in Max Müller, ed., *Sacred Books of the East* (London: The Clarendon Press, 1885), xxviii: 33, 74-75, 238-241. This material is discussed in Lester James Bilsky, *The State Religion of Ancient China* (Taipei: The Chinese Association for Folklore, 1975), I: 76-83. For the silkworm cult, see Dieter Kuhn, "Tracing a Chinese Legend: In Search of the Identity of the 'First Sericulturalist'," *T'oung Pao* LXX: 213-245 (1984).

4. J.J. m. de Groot, *The Religious System of China* (Leiden, E.J. Brill, 1892-1910), VI: 1191, citing *Kuo Yü* 18, *Ch'u Yü, hsia*, pp. 559-560 in the 1978 Shanghai Guji chubanshe edition. Translation modified by D.O. Introductory material here is drawn from Daniel L.Overmyer, "Chinese Religion: An Overview," in *The Encyclopedia of Religion* (New York: Macmillan Publishing Co., 1987), 3:257-289. For the activities of female shamans at the Han court see Ssu-ma Ch'ien, *Records of the Grand Historian of China* trans. Burton Watson, (New York, Columbia University Press, 1961), II: 32, 42-43.

5. Groot, *Religious System*, VI: 1209-1210, citing Wang Fu, *Chien fu lun, chüan* 3, number 12, pp. 143-144 in the 1978 Shanghai Guji chubanshe edition.

6. Jack M. Potter, "Cantonese Shamanism," in Arthur P. Wolf, ed., *Religion and Ritual in Chinese Society* (Stanford: Stanford University Press, 1974), pp. 207-231. This article is very much worth reading for its detailed transcriptions of seance conversations.
7. The most comprehensive discussion of modern Chinese shamanism is by Alan J.A. Elliott, *Chinese Spirit-medium Cults in Singapore* (London: University of London Press, 1955).
8. Henri Maspero, *Taoism and Chinese Religion*. Trans. by Frank A. Kierman, Jr., (Amherst, University of Massachusetts Press, 1981), p. 378. Originally published in French in 1971.
9. See the reference to Professor Cahill's article in note 1 above.
10. Judith Boltz, *A Survey of Taoist Literature, Tenth to Seventeenth Centuries* (Berkeley: Institute of East Asian Studies, 1987), pp. 38, 69-70, 155. See also Chen Yüan, *Nan Sung ch'u Hopei hsin Tao-chiao k'ao* (The New Taoism in the Northern Provinces at the Beginning of the Southern Sung), Beijing, 1958), pp. 42-49. Professors Julian Pas and Man Kam Leung of the University of Saskatchewan are translating this book into English: I am grateful to Prof. Pas for this reference.
11. Maspero, *Taoism and Chinese Religion*, pp. 517-541. R.H. van Gulik, *Sexual Life in Ancient China* (Leiden: E.J. Brill, 1961), pp. 197-200. The quoted passage may be found on p. 199. Its source is the *Yun-chi ch'i-ch'ien*, Vol. 27, *chüan* 105; p. 1435 in Vol. III of the 1978 Taipei reprint.
12. Diana Paul, *Women in Buddhism: Images of the Feminine in Mahayana Tradition* (Berkeley: Asian Humanities Press, 1979), pp. xiii-xiv.
13. Chung-fang Yü, oral report and video tape, Harvard workshop on Chinese religions, April, 1988. The film of pilgrimage women prostrating themselves every few steps is most moving.
14. *Fa-mieh chin ching* (*Sūtra on the Complete Extinction of the Dharma*), *Taishō* 396 12: 1119a. For a discussion of these Chinese indigenous scriptures see Daniel L. Overmyer, "Buddhism in the Trenches: Attitudes Toward Popular Religion in Chinese Scriptures Found at Tun-huang," *Harvard Journal of Asiatic Studies* 50.1:197-222 (June 1990).
15. Kenneth K.S. Ch'en, *The Chinese Transformation of Buddhism* (Princeton: Princeton University Press, 1973), p. 288.

See also the discussion of these societies in Daniel L. Overmyer, *Folk Buddhist Religion: Dissenting Sects in Late Traditional China* (Cambridge, MA: Harvard University Press, 1976), pp. 85-89. On Ch'an women, see Miriam L. Levering, "Lin-chi (Rinzai) Ch'an and Gender: The Rhetoric of Equality and the Rhetoric of Heroism" (unpublished paper, 1988), and her article "The Dragon Girl and the Abbess of Mo-shan: Gender and Status in the Ch'an Buddhist Tradition," in *The Journal of the International Association of Buddhist Studies* 5.1.19-35 (1982).
16. For the Empress Wu see C.P. Fitzgerald, *The Empress Wu* (London: Cresset Press, 1968); Antonino Forte, *Political Propaganda and Ideology in*

China at the End of the Seventh Century (Naples: Instituto Universitario Orientale, 1976), and Diana Paul, "Empress Wu and the Historians: A Tyrant and Saint of Classical China," in Nancy Auer Falk and Rita M. Gross, eds., *Unspoken Worlds: Women's Religious Lives in Non-Western Cultures* (San Francisco: Harper and Row, Publishers, 1980), pp. 191-206.

On imperial support of Buddhism during the Sui see Arthur F. Wright, *The Sui Dynasty: the Unification of China, AD 581-617* (New York: Alfred A. Knopf, 1978).

The article by Li Shiyu and Susan Naquin is, "The Baoming Temple: Religion and the Throne in Ming and Qing China," *Harvard Journal of Asiatic Studies*, 48: 1.131-188 (June 1988).

17. On Chinese Buddhist nuns see Kathryn A. Tsai, "The Chinese Buddhist Monastic Order for Women: The First Two Centuries," in Guisso and Johannesen, eds., *Women in China*, pp. 1-20; and Nancy Schuster, "Striking a Balance: Women and Images of Women in Early Chinese Buddhism," in Yvonne Yazbeck Haddad and Ellison Banks Findly, *Women, Religion and Social Change* (Albany, NY: State University of New York Press, 1985), pp. 87-111.

18. James L. Watson, "Standardizing the Gods: The Promotion of T'ien Hou ('Empress of Heaven') Along the South China Coast," in David Johnson, Andrew J. Nathan and Evelyn S. Rawski, eds., *Popular Culture in Late Imperial China* (Berkeley: University of California Press, 1985), pp. 320-321. On this point see also Margery Wolf, "China and Gendered Anthropology: Some Notes Toward Integration," (Durham, NC: Department of Anthropology, Duke University, 1985), pp. 14-15.

19. On women as a source of ritual pollution see Marjorie Topley, "Cosmic Antagonisms: A Mother-Child Syndrome," in Arthur P. Wolf, ed., *Religion and Ritual in Chinese Society* (Stanford, CA: Stanford University Press, 1974), pp. 233-249; Emily M. Ahern, "The Power and Pollution of Chinese Women," in Margery Wolf and Roxane Witke, *Women in Chinese Society* (Stanford, CA: Stanford University Press, 1975), pp. 193-214; Cordia Chu, "Menstrual Beliefs and Practices of Chinese Women" (unpublished paper, 1977); and Gary Seaman, "The Sexual Politics of Karmic Retribution," in Emily Martin Ahern and Hill Gates, eds., *The Anthropology of Taiwan Society* (Stanford, CA: Stanford University Press, 1981), pp. 381-396. See also the film by Gary Seaman of the ritual for releasing a mother's soul from the pool of blood, "Breaking the Blood Bowl" (Far Eastern Audio Visuals, 1974).

20. Francis L.K. Hsü, *Under the Ancestors' Shadow: Kinship, Personality and Social Mobility in Village China*. Revised and expanded edition (Garden City, NY: Doubleday and Co. Ltd., 1967, pp. 200-203. First published in 1948.

21. Topley, "Cosmic Antagonisms," pp. 241-245.

22. For this passage and a discussion of other sources for early White Lotus history, see Daniel L. Overmyer, "Alternatives: Popular Religious Sects in Chinese Society," *Modern China* 7.2:169-184 (April 1981).

23. Overmyer, "Alternatives"; for the scripture writing nun see Li and Naquin, "The Baoming Temple."

24. Susan Naquin, *Millenarian Rebellion in China: The Eight Trigrams Uprising of 1813* (New Haven and London: Yale University Press, 1976), pp. 38-42. For a good summary of women in popular religious sects see Yu Songqing, *Ming Qing Bai-lian jiao yan-jiu* (A study of Ming and Qing White Lotus sects), (Chengdu, Sichuan ren-min chubanshe, 1987), pp. 295-311.
25. Daniel L. Overmyer, "*Pao-chüan*: Types and Transformations" (unpublished paper, 1978), pp. 7-14; Glen Dudbridge, *The Legend of Miao-shan* (London: Ithaca Press, 1978). See also Daniel L. Overmyer, "Values in Chinese Sectarian Literature: Ming and Ch'ing *Pao-chüan*," in Johnson, Nathan, and Rawski, eds., *Popular Culture*, pp. 219-254.
26. Overmyer, "Values," pp. 245-253. From the third paragraph of 110 to the middle of 111 this material is quoted from the "Values" article. For associations of unmarried women see, Marjorie Topley, "Marriage Resistance in Rural Kwangtung," in Wolf and Witke, eds., *Women in Chinese Society*, pp. 71-76. For other discussions by Dr. Topley of these and similar groups see her "Chinese Women's Vegetarian Houses in Singapore," *Journal of the Malayan Branch of the Royal Asiatic Society* 27.1:51-67 (1954); Topley, "The Great Way of Former Heaven: A Group of Chinese Secret Religious Sects," *Bulletin of the School of Oriental and African Studies*, 26.2:362-392 (June 1963); and Topley and James Hayes, "Notes on Some Vegetarian Halls in Hong Kong Belonging to the Sect of the Hsien-t'ien tao: The Way of Former Heaven," *Journal of the Hong Kong Branch of the Royal Asiatic Society* 8: 135-148 (1968).
27. This paragraph is quoted from Overmyer, "Values," pp. 250-251
28. David K. Jordan and Daniel L. Overmyer, *The Flying Phoenix: Aspects of Chinese Sectarianism in Taiwan* (Princeton: Princeton University Press, 1986).
29. For further information, see for example an interesting account of a charismatic woman religious leader who was the daughter of a Ming official, in Ann Waltner, "T'an-yang-tzu and Wang Shih-chen: Visionary and Bureaucrat in the Late Ming," *Late Imperial China* 8.1:105-133 (June 1987).
30. On this see Overmyer, "Values," pp. 228-229.

Research for this article concluded in the summer of 1988.

List of Characters

Chang Tao-ling
張道陵
chen-hsing pu-huai
真性不壞
Chên Yuan, Nan Jung ch'u Hopei Hsin Tao-chiao Kiao
陳垣，南宋初河北新道教考
Cheng-i fa-wen T'ai-shang wai-lu i
正一法文太上外籙儀
Cheng-i fa-wen T'ien-shih chiao chieh k'e ching
正一法文天師教戒科經
ch'i
氣
chiao
醮
Ch'ien-fu lun
潛夫論
Chin-tan tao
金丹道
Ch'ing-wei
清微
Chüan
卷
Ch'üan-chen
全真
fen
分
Fu Hao
婦好
ho-ch'i
和氣
hsi
覡
Hsi-mu
西母
Hsiang-shan pao-chüan
香山寶卷
Hsiao fa-mieh chin ching
小法滅盡經
Hsing-lin
興林
Hsiu-nü pao-chüan
秀女寶卷
Hu shen-ming ching
護身命經
Huai-t'ai pao-chüan
懷胎寶卷
Kuan-shih-yin
觀世音
Kuo Yü
國語
li (Chinese mile)
里
Li-chi
禮記
Ling-kuang sheng-mu
靈光聖母
Liu Hsiang pao-chüan
劉香寶卷
Liu Kung
劉龔
Lo Ch'ing
羅清
Ma-tsu
媽祖
Ma Yü
馬鈺
Mao Tzu-yüan
茅子元
Mi-le fo
彌勒佛
Miao-shan
妙善
Miao-chuang
妙莊
Miao-shu
妙書
ming
名
Miao-yin
妙音
Nan Pi-tao
南畢道
ni-huan
泥丸(洹)
nü-shih
女師
pao-chüan
寶卷
Pi-ch'iu-ni chuan
比丘尼傳

p'in 品

Pu-ning 不佞

San-t'ien nei-chieh ching 三天内戒經

shan-nan, hsin-nü 善男信女

Shang-ch'ing 上清

Shang-ti 上帝

shen 神

shih-mu 師母

Sun Pu-erh 孫不二

T'an-yang-tzu 曇陽子

Tao-tsang 道藏

Ti-tsang 地藏

T'ien 天

T'ien Hou 天后

T'ien Hou Niang-niang 天后娘娘

T'ien-t'ai 天台

t'ing-ming 挺命

T'u-ti kung 土地公

Tsu Shu 祖舒

Tung-mu 東母

Wang Che 王嚞

Wang Fu 王符

Wang Shih-chen 王世貞

Wong Taai Sin 黃大仙

wen 文

wo nü-tzu 我女子

wu 巫

Wu-sheng lao-mu 無生老母

Wu Ting 武丁

Wu Tse-t'ien 武則天

Yu Songqing, *Ming Qing Bai-lian jiao yan-jiu* 喻松青 明清白蓮教研究

Yün-chi ch'i-chien 雲笈七籤

An Enquiry Into the Sino-Indian Buddhist Debate in Tibet

W. Pachow
University of Iowa

It appears to be a natural phenomenon that our opinions differ from one another. This is exemplified in the polls and in elections. In an election, if the winner achieves a majority of 50.5 per cent of the votes, and the loser's percentage is 49.5, it may mean the former is lucky enough to be successful. But it does not necessarily mean that he is absolutely right and the other absolutely wrong. By this yardstick one may trace the source of debates, disputes, conflicts and wars. They share a common concern of trying to express something, but differ in intensity and the manner in which it is expressed. If war should break out between two groups of people, the consequences would be terrible. If it is a debate, it may mean an exhibition of eloquence, and its outcome could not be very serious or harmful. Based on this consideration we may say that debate is a healthy way of expression. It is preferable to an act of violence.

In Buddhist literature we find that Gautama Buddha on many occasions held discourses or discussions with contemporary religious leaders. He exhibited great wisdom and winning eloquence to gain victory over his opponents, and many of them eventually became his disciples. The *Dīgha-Nikāya* contains many sūtras of this nature.[1] His discussions with other people may be termed "conversation of the wise", in that one will never get angry over whether or not one is victorious or being defeated by the argument of one's opponents. When King Milinda expressed the wish to discuss matters with Nāgasena, the latter insisted that it should be in the style of "conversation of the wise," but not that of "conversation of the kings."[2] Over the centuries there are instances concerning debates between the Buddhists and other Indian religious sects. Among the Buddhists Nāgārjuna and Ārya Deva were great experts who defeated many of their opponents in public debates.[3] This tradition continued in later times.

Of special interest to us is the fact that when Hsüan-tsang was studying at the Nālanda University in India, he encountered philosophical confrontation with Buddhist scholars like Siṁhaprabhāsa and Chandrasiṁha. Later, at the request of King Śīlāditya, he represented that university and was ready to discuss the subtlety of Mahāyāna Buddhism with Prajñāgupta, a Hīnayāna teacher of the Saṁmitīya sect. It was about this time that a pundit of the Lokāyatika sect challenged the scholars of the Nālanda University, saying that he would forfeit his head if anyone could defeat him on his forty tenets. Hsüan-tsang accepted the challenge, and in the presence of Śīlabhadra, president of the Nālanda University and other scholars, he methodically disarmed his opponent's argument. The loser acknowledged defeat and was about to carry out his promise of forfeiting his own head. However, Hsüan-tsang accepted him as his personal attendant instead. His "*Hui-tsung-lun*" (A Treatise on the Conference of Doctrines) and "*P'o ê-chien lun*" (A Treatise on Destroying Evil Views) were composed in this connection.[4]

The foregoing instances, from the time of the Buddha to the seventh century, indicate that friendly discussions or debates among the Buddhists themselves or in relation to other religious groups were a normal phenomenon. Indeed, there were many debates over the centuries, and only the important ones were recorded. This assumption could be applicable to the Sino-Indian Buddhist debate which took place in Tibet in the eighth century. Being a rare occasion in Tibetan history, it was recorded in both Tibetan and Chinese documents. We shall examine the authenticity of the event in the following sections.

1. Was there a Sino-Indian Buddhist debate?

We assume that most of us know something about the Buddhist debate that took place either in Lhasa or at bSam Yas in the second half of the eighth century. The confronting parties were Mo-ho-yen (Mahāyāna) or Hva-san from China and Kamalaśīla, a disciple of Śāntarakshita from India. The focus of the dispute was that the Chinese Ch'an practice was not in accordance with the traditional Buddhism from India. Scholars such as Paul Demiéville, G. Tucci, David Snellgrove, A.K. Warder, R.A. Stein and Ueyama Daishun and others made careful investigations of this topic,[5] and the Tibetan and Chinese works such as *A History of Buddhism*[6], *The Genealogy of Kings of Tibet*[7] and *Chêng-li chüeh* (A Ratification of Suddenly Realizing the Right Principles of Mahāyāna).[8] The last name in the list was discovered from the Tun-huang caves and it was attributed to Mo-ho-yen. The authors of these documents assert that there was a Buddhist debate between the Chinese and Indian teachers. However, there are other scholars who hold a different view saying "that the Indian Kamalaśīla and the Chinese Hva-shang Mahāyāna never met, and that their confrontation is an invention of the later Tibetan historians." This view was attributed to Yoshirō Imaeda and supported by H. Guenther in his book review.[9] Thus we face an important issue; namely, was there really a Sino-Indian Buddhist debate held in Tibet? If so, when? Before we attempt to answer the question, we would like to trace the possibilities which might have led to the event in question.

The introduction of Buddhism to Tibet from both India and China took place in the seventh century during the reign of King Srong-brtsan-sgam-po. The Chinese teachers who went there were mostly Ch'an masters, and they emphasized the doctrine of sudden enlightenment. On the other hand, the Indian teachers promoted the traditional Buddhism based on analytic wisdom. Because of these differences, the former was known as the sect of Sudden Enlightenment (Tun-mên p'ai, Tibetan: Ston-min pa) and the latter the sect of Gradual Realization (Chien-mên p'ai, Tibetan: Rtsen-min pa). During the reign of King Khri-srong-lde-brtsan (died in 797) there occurred great activities for the development of Buddhism. For instance, Indian teachers such as Śāntarakshita, Padmasaṃbhava, Kamalaśīla and others were invited to Tibet, Buddhist Sanskrit texts were translated into Tibetan, Buddhist ordination was officially performed, the bSam Yas monastery was constructed (ca. 763-775), stūpas were built and students were sent to India to study Sanskrit, linguistics and other sciences.[10] In the course of time, Buddhism was firmly established in Tibet. But owing to the different traditions coming from India and China there appeared uneasiness among the Tibetan followers. Eventually there emerged noticeable friction between them which in turn brought about the official debate between the Indian and Chinese teachers under the sponsorship of King Khri-srong-lde-brtsan. The *History of Buddhism* by Bu-ston describes this event in great depth. The outcome of the debate was that the Chinese party headed by Mo-ho-yen was defeated and he was deported from Tibet.[11]

In addition to the Tibetan sources, we have the *Chêng-li chüeh* of Mo-ho-yen from Tun-huang. It gives us a different account of the story. It states the date of his visit to Tibet, a brief description of the opponent and the result of the debate. We regard this text to be of great historical significance, in that it confirms the Tibetan tradition regarding the debate; and it gives us a definite date of the said event.

In regard to the date of the debate, there is strong evidence to indicate that it took place in 781, or between 780-782, rather than 792-794, as suggested by Demiéville. This is substantiated by the statements found in the introduction to the *Chêng-li-chüeh.*[12] The author of this text says that when Sha-chou (including Tun-huang) was captured by the Tibetans, the Tsan-po (King of Tibet) extended his invitation to the Śramaṇa Mahāyāna to go there and preach the teaching of Ch'an (or dhyāna). When he arrived at Lhasa many people inquired about the method of Ch'an. The date for the fall of Sha-chou, according to Chinese documents such as *Yüan-ho-Chün-hsien chih* and *Hsi-yo-sui-tao chi*, was "the second year of Chien-chung"[13] (781). It is possible that the debate did not take place in the early months of 781, although both Indian pundits and Mahāyāna, the Chinese teacher (or Mahāyāna Hva san), were invited to Tibet. However, the smothered fire of disharmony may have been planted for a very long time. It exploded only at this juncture. The prophesy[14] made by Śāntarakshita years ago was an unmistakable indication. The introduction[15] to the *Chêng-li chüeh* informs us that at the beginning of the year of the monkey (780) Mahāyāna was informed of the complaint made by Indian monks that 'Sudden Enlightenment' taught by the Chinese teachers was not the teaching of the Buddha; therefore, it should be prohibited. The message was conveyed to Mahāyāna by the King himself. Consequently, he proposed to the King that a debate with the Hīnayāna teachers in the form of written questions might be arranged. The Indian teachers took a long time to prepare a lengthy list of queries with the intention of exposing the blemish spots of their opponents. Later, the two parties confronted each other. Mahāyāna Hva-san was able to defend his position in making suitable responses. The monks from India were defeated in the discussion. However, they incited the ministers to form a faction in order to discredit and slander the practice of Ch'an. Some Tibetan disciples of Mahāyāna committed suicide by burning, killing or letting themselves fall from a lofty cliff as a means of protest against such action. As a sequel, on the 15th day of the first month in the year of the dog (782) the King issued a decree saying, "The doctrine of Ch'an preached by Mahāyāna is fully in accord with the Canonical texts and free from any errors. From now on, members of the Order and laity may study and practice it."

The above-noted outline is the Chinese version of the debate. It has shown one side of the story, but it may not be the whole truth. One may suspect the suicidal action of the disciples of Mahāyāna. If their party was rally victorious, then that action was unnecessary. The significance of this account lies in the fact that there was indeed a debate between the Chinese and Indian parties in Tibet in 781. Probably, the Ch'an sect was defeated and temporarily suspended in that year. At the beginning of 782 the ban was officially lifted.

On the basis of both Tibetan and Chinese documents we are inclined to think that there was a Sino-Indian Buddhist debate, or even debates in Tibet on the differences of Buddhist doctrines. The date for the event seems to be 781 or during 780-82, or 792-94 as suggested by other scholars.

2. The place of the debate

If we accept the proposition that the Sino-Indian Buddhist debate was an authentic event which took place in the fourth quarter of the eighth century, our next question is related to the location in which it was held. There are two possibilities. One was Lhasa. It was stated in the *Chêng-li chüeh* that Mo-ho-yen travelled to that city to teach the method of dhyāna practices.[16] Paul Demiéville supported this site as the title of his work *Le Concile de Lhasa* indicates. The other place mentioned was bSam Yas. G. Tucci was a strong advocate for this location. His rationale was that the cultural and religious centers of Tibet in the eighth and ninth centuries were "at Yar Klun, where the old palaces, and the tombs of kings were located, or in Bragmar (dmar), a little to the north of bSam Yas."[17] Based on this observation, probably bSam Yas was the spot where the debate took place. Moreover, bSam Yas was famed for its grand monastery bearing that name. We are informed that it took more than twelve years to get the construction completed. Possibly the debate was held within the monastery.

3. The main topics of the debate

Our next enquiry would be the subject matter which was debated by the participating parties. Of course, the main concern was related to the differences between the sudden enlightenment theory represented by Mo-ho-yen, and the traditional Buddhist doctrines of gradual realization represented by Kamalaśīla. Bu-ston in his *History of Buddhism* recorded the views of both parties.[18] Given below is a condensed outline.

1. The propositions of the Chinese Mo-ho-yen:

a) Good or evil deeds may result in blissful or evil births respectively.

b) These deeds (whether good or evil) will not help anyone to gain deliverance from Saṁsāra.

c) Anyone who observes the practices of no-thought or inclinations can be delivered from Saṁsāra.

d) The absence of thought will bring about the non-perception of the reality of separate entities.

e) Being in a state of non-perception of the reality one is able to attain Buddhahood instantaneously.

f) A Bodhisattva has attained the 10th stage.

2. The objections from Kamalaśīla's party:

a) The theory of absence of thought means the rejection of the highest analytic wisdom. It is non-constructive, similar to a person in a swoon or at the time of intoxication. Such being the case, one will not possess the cognition of non-substantiality, nor will he be able to remove the obscurations. Also, he will not extirpate the passions.

b) One may attain to Buddhahood by possessing the Highest Wisdom—That means one reflects and discriminates.

c) It is impossible to attain to Buddhahood at once, just as one walks step by step when one ascends a mountain.

d) When passing through gradual training on the ten stages, one attains to Buddhahood by means of the ten virtues, and

e) For a long time after the passing away of the Buddha, there was no dissenting points in the teaching.

The essence of Mo-ho-yen's thesis as noted above is that the effect of karma would operate in normal existence, but it would not enable one to be liberated from saṁsāra. On the other hand, the practice of thoughtlessness would help one achieve that goal. Besides, it would bring about non-perception of phenomena, reality, and thereby one may suddenly attain to Buddhahood. Undoubtedly, this theory could be easily traced to the *Platform Scripture* of Hui-nêng, the sixth patriarch of the Ch'an school.[19] In brief, it is concerned with karma, saṁsāra, absence of thought and sudden enlightenment. In the *Chêng-li chüeh* there are many questions and answers concerning concepts such as "not to attain to any dharma is the highest bodhi," "not to speak means to preach the dharma," "to be freed from all characteristics means the identity of the Buddhas," the nature of the conventional and transcendental truths and differences between the Buddha-nature and ātman and so forth.[20] It is a sizable composition of about 11,000

Chinese words. It cites many Mahāyāna sūtras such as *Vajracchedikā*, *The Lotus*, *The Laṅkāvatāra*, *The Hua-yen*, *The Nirvāṇa*, and others. Most of the questions and answers in this text did not appear in Bu-ston's account. Perhaps, he merely recorded the barest outline of the debate.

The main objections from Kamalaśīla's party focused on the irrationality of thoughtlessness and sudden enlightenment. They emphasized that without analytic wisdom one could no longer recognize evil from good, and thus it could hinder the progress of religious cultivation. They also stressed the importance of gradual realization, taking one step at a time, and the practice of the ten virtues.

Reviewing the arguments of the two parties based on Tibetan and Chinese sources, we notice that they confirm the principles of the Ch'an school and the traditional Indian Buddhist teachings. There is no evidence to indicate that the said debate was "an invention of the later Tibetan historians." Even if that claim is substantiated, how could one account for the fact that in the *Chêng-li chüeh* the Chinese party was said to be victorious? That claim could not arise if there were no debate. Further, one could not say that the Chinese document from Tun-huang was fabricated by the Tibetan historians!

In conclusion, we are inclined to think that there was a debate, or a series of written questions and answers being communicated between the Indian teachers and Mo-ho-yen from China. It took place around 781, although 792-94 has been suggested by others. The purpose of the debate was to decide which of the two schools taught the correct teachings of the Buddha. The result was that the Indian party was the winner, and Mo-ho-yen the loser; hence the promotion of Ch'an was temporarily suspended. But the ban was lifted at the beginning of 782. Moreover, the manner in which the debate was conducted appeared to be fair and friendly. The rule being prescribed for the occasion was that the loser should offer a wreath of flowers to the winner and be deported from Tibet.[21] Such being the case, it does not appear that there was a need for anyone to invent a story. Therefore, we believe that there was a Sino-Indian Buddhist debate.

Notes

1. T.W. & C.A.F. Rhys Davids, trans., *The Dialogues of the Buddha* (London: H. Frowde, 1899-1921), in three volumes.
2. H.C. Warren, trans., *Buddhism in Translation* (Cambridge, Mass: Harvard University, 1896), p. 128.
3. See *Life of Nāgārjuna* in *Taishō* T. 2047, vol. 50, p. 184c-185a; *Life of Ārya Deva*, Ibid., T. 2048, pp. 186-87. However, these biographies are blended with lengendary accounts.
4. See *Life of Hsüan-tsang*, in *Taisho* T. 2053, vol. 50, pp. 244b-45b.
5. Paul Demiéville, *Le Concile de Lhasa* (Paris: Imprimerie Nationale de France, 1952); Giuseppe Tucci, *Minor Buddhist Texts* (Rome: Instituto Italiano per Il Medio ed Estremo Orient, 1958), part 2, pp. 26,32, 36, 40, 41, 52, 65 and 82; David Snellgrove, *A Cultural History of Tibet* (New York: Frederick A. Praeger, 1968), pp. 73, 77, and 275; A.K. Warder, *Indian Buddhism* (Delhi: Motilal Banarsidass, 1970), pp. 476-77; R.A. Stein, *Tibetan Civilization* (Stanford: Stanford University Press, 1972), p. 67; Ueyama Daishun, "Donkō to Tonko bukkyōgaku" (T'an-k'uang and Buddhist Studies at Tun-huang), in *Tōhōgakuho* (1964) XXXV, p. 151.
6. Bu-ston, *A History of Buddhism*, trans. by E.E. Obermiller (Heidelberg: 1931), in 2 parts, pp. 192-96.
7. Wang I-luan, trans. *Hsi-tsang wang-t'ung chi* (Shanghai: The Commercial Press, 1955), pp. 62-63.
8. See Pelliot Collection, p. 4646 or the photo copy attached to Demiéville's *Le Concile de Lhasa*.
9. See Herbert V. Guenther's book-review of *Tibet: A Handbook* in *Journal of Asian Studies* XXXVII (1978), p. 503.
10. Wang I-luan, op. cit. pp. 64-76; W. Pachow, *A Study of the Twenty-two Dialogues on Mahāyāna Buddhism* (Taipei: Chinese Culture, 1979), pp. 34-38.
11. Bu-ston, op. cit. p. 193.
12. Pelliot and Demiéville, op. cit., f. 154A-154B.
13. Su Yin-hui, *Tun-huang lun chi* (A Collection of Essays on Tun-huang) (Taipei: The Student Book Co., 1967), pp. 218, 215-230.
14. Bu-ston, op. cit., p. 191.
15. Demiéville, op. cit., f. 127b, 128a.
16. Ibid., f. 154a-b.
17. Tucci, op. cit., p. 177.
18. Bu-ston, op. cit., pp. 193-95.
19. Wing-tsit Chan, trans., *The Platform Scripture* (New York: St. John University Press, 1963), pp. 49, 51-53, 85, 87, 89.
20. Demiéville, op. cit., f. 131a-b, 132b, 136b, 142a.
21. Bu-ston, op. cit., p. 193.

Bragmar 郎瑪

Chien-men p'ai 漸門派

Chen-li chüeh 頓悟大乘正理決

Hsi-you-sui-tao chi 西域水道記

Hsüan-tsang 玄奘

Hua-yen 華嚴

Hui-nêng 慧能

Hva-san 和尚

Hui-tsang-lun 會宗論

Kamalaśīla 蓮華戒

Mo-ho-yen 摩訶衍

Platform Scripture 六祖法寶壇經

P'o e-chien lun 破惡見論

Padmasambhava 蓮華生

Santarakshita 寂護

Śīlabhadra 戒賢

Tun-men p'ai 頓門派

Tun-huang 敦煌

Tsan-po 贊普

Ueyama 上 山大峻

The Human Gods of China
New Perspectives on the Chinese Pantheon

J.F. Pas
University of Saskatchewan

Introduction

How very human are the deities of the Chinese people! Their origin and rise to prominence are often shrouded in mystery; their yielding of spiritual power is often as shaky and transitory as that of political leaders. Occasionally, like some political leaders, they make a comeback: in the People's Republic of China, gods and goddesses and Buddhas have regained some of their ancient prestige since the late seventies.

Looking at the various Chinese pantheons, one is overwhelmed by their complexity. They reflect the complexity of Chinese religion itself. Again the plural, "religions", is more adequate, since more than one religious tradition has shaped the religious consciousness of the Chinese people. Even admitting that some mutual absorption and borrowing have occurred, one must yet recognize an independent, autonomous status for the Taoist and Buddhist pantheons, and a less clearly defined, yet real autonomy for the pantheon of the Popular Religion, and perhaps of Confucianism.

The common worshipper is not always clearly aware of these differences, and is not even able to identify many of the statues of deities enthroned in the temples. The major ones they would be able to recognize, but all the lower ranking gods and goddesses are just there to receive incense and offerings of fruit and to bestow favours on the devotees, even if they do not know their names.

The purpose of this essay is not to enumerate and describe all the deities worshiped in China. Some studies made by western scholars can still be consulted effectively in this regard. (I think especially of Maspero's long article in *Asiatic Mythology*.) Several Chinese monographs have been published in recent years. My objective is rather to discuss certain aspects of the Chinese pantheons, which have been more or less neglected and to emphasize new perspectives that have to be looked at more carefully in the light of recent developments in the study of Chinese religion. The "human" character of the Chinese deities is a very fascinating dimension in such a study: like human beings, the gods have birthdays, families, careers, titles, temperaments, and authority. They fit into some kind of hierarchical structure, on which their precise function and special appeal very often depend.

First of all, what is the meaning of "pantheon"?

The word *pantheon* (from the Greek *pan*, "all" and *theos*, "a god") originally indicated a specific temple built in Rome in 27 B.C., dedicated to all the gods worshipped by the Romans. Derived from this, the word can also mean "the gods of a people taken collectively".[1] The term "gods" is sometimes used loosely, so that a pantheon can very well be a set of deities or holy beings of a transcendent nature, who serve as symbols and objects of worship of a particular group of people. Whereas the Greek and Roman pantheons were closely associated with particular peoples, the Chinese pantheons only partially do so. In China we face a very complex situation. The Greek and Roman gods are almost entirely mythical creations, but the Chinese deities or spirits are not always; many of them are deified historical personages.

It has been a western concern to "arrange" these pantheons into some kind of structured hierarchy: it is a desire for classification and order. Otherwise one is faced with a sense of great confusion, easily leading toward contempt, as when Maspero refers to this "unheard-of swarm of gods and spirits of every kind, an innumerable rabble".[2] (*Asiatic Mythology*, p. 263) Numerous as the Chinese deities are, with some effort it is quite possible to create some order among them, or to classify them into some categories. As I said, this is perhaps only a concern of western scholars. The Chinese worshipper does not care too much for classification: his only expectation is to receive help in a particular situation. Rank and hierarchy do not matter, as long as the deity possesses enough *ling* ("spiritual potency") and is willing to bestow it on the worshipper.

In recent years several Chinese scholars have made new contributions to the study of their pantheons and in an effort to create order in the chaos, they have proposed new categories of classification. Three works were published in Taiwan, one in the People's Republic of China.

The first model is proposed by Ch'i Te-tsai in *Taiwan miao-shen chuan* (*TMSC*) [Biographies and Legends of Deities (worshipped) in Taiwan Temples], 1979. The author divides the pantheon into seven categories:

(i) sage philosophers and culture heroes (*sheng-che ying-lieh*): 89 personalities.

(ii) holy worthies of Buddhism (*Fo-men sheng-chün*): 33 personalities

(iii) deities of nature worship (*tzu-jan shu-wu*)[3]: 31 personalities

(iv) deities of the folk religion (*t'ung-su hsin-yang*): 54 personalities

(v) spirits of the earth (or spirits of heaven and earth?): (*hsiang-t'u shen-shih*): 79 personalities
(vi) oppressive ghosts, not receiving sacrifices [from their descendants] (*wu-szu kui-li*): 29 personalities
(vii) anonymous spirits, enshrined in temples, but whose origin is unknown (*tai-k'ao miao-shen*): 55 listings.

The second categorization is found in Fan P'ing-shan's *Chung-kuo sheng-ming kai-lun* (*SMKL*) [A General Discussion of the Gods of China], 1979. He divides the pantheon into six groups:

(i) gods of the origins (*yüan-shih shen-ming*): 9 personalities: P'an-ku, the Taoist Triad of Three T'ien-tsün, Wu-Lao (Tung-wang kung, Hsi-wang mu, Huang-Lao, Shui-ching, Ch'ih-ching).
(ii) gods of heaven and spirits of earth (*t'ien-shen ti-shih*): 18 names, of which some may be collective deities.
(iii) gods of the human realm (*jen-ching shen-ming*): 15 names, including gods of the household.
(iv) saints (sages) and immortals (*shen-hsien*): 21 names.
(v) legendary deities (*ch'uan-chi shen-ming*): 19 names.
(vi) Holy Ones of Buddhism (*Fo-shen*): 8 names.

The third Taiwan publication is of a different nature. Chui Yün-yen. *Taiwan min-chien hsin-yang chu-shen chuan.* (*TMHC*) [Biographies of the Deities of Taiwan Folk Religion], 1984. It does not categorize but lists 413 deities arranged according to their birthdays within the twelve months of the lunar calendar.

The mainland publication is the most recent one. Authored by Lü Dzongli and Liu Qun, *Zhongguo minjian zhushen* (*MJZS*) [The Popular Deities of China] (1986), it is 924 pages long and divided into ten parts. Unfortunately, it does not have chapter headings, which would indicate the author's rationale of categorization. It is up to the reader to try and discover for himself the standards used for making up the ten groups. The following is then, tentatively, my own interpretation:

(i) The Supreme deities: Three Pure Ones of Taoism, Yü-huang Ta-ti; the Buddha(s).
(ii) Ancient deities, gods of heaven, star deities.
(iii) Fertility and household deities (Hou-t'u, Ch'eng-huang, T'u-ti, door gods, kitchen god).
(iv) Nature deities: Five mountains, especially Tung-yüeh, River deities, Dragon kings.
(v) Minor nature spirits.
(vi) More nature spirits.
(vii) Deities to assist in daily life and in the after-life: gods of epidemics, gods of healing, spirits in the netherworld (Yen-lo-wang, Ti-tsang wang), some apotheosized heroes (like Kuan-shen Ta-ti).
(viii) Gods of daily life: wealth, happiness, professions.
(ix) Taoist deities, such as Heavenly Master Chang, the Eight Immortals.

(x) Buddhist Saints: Kuan-yin, Mi-lo-fo, Buddha Amita, the Arhats (*lohan*).

Although this encyclopedic volume contains a mass of useful information about many deities, its system of categorization is not well thought out. It shows, however, that a fully logical, consistent way of grouping the Chinese pantheons is probably inconceivable.

To compare and contrast the above three Chinese models with just one example of western scholarship, we can look at Henri Maspero's classification in "Mythology of Modern China":[4] he does not divide the pantheon into a clear number of categories, but just lists the following groupings: supreme gods; gods of nature; gods of heavenly ministries or boards; gods of administrative districts; household gods; gods in Buddhist temples; gods of trades and professions; gods charged with watching over mankind individually; and gods of other worlds (hells and paradises).

These models each have their own relative justification, but the criteria used or implied are not totally convincing, and the categories are not always clearly differentiated.

In an attempt to arrive at a better type of categorization, one can be inspired by two guidelines: one either follows the total historical development of Chinese religion through the ages and then discusses the pantheons of each major historic period (horizontal); or one studies one by one the various religious traditions: the ancient religion, Confucianism, Taoism, Buddhism, Folk Religion (vertical). Since the growth of the pantheons is intimately linked with the development of their respective religion, the second method seems to be preferable. Each method has its advantages and shortcomings.

Therefore, taking into account as much as possible the data provided by previous researchers, and partially reflected in the above cited modern works, I'll propose the following categorization:

a) The gods of ancient times (prehistoric and early historic)
b) The gods of later times: the "Three Teachings": Confucianism, Taoism, Buddhism
c) The deities of the Popular Religion
d) A discussion of ancestors and ghosts.

Once again, my purpose is not to provide complete lists of the gods and goddesses, sages and saints, nor to provide a complete profile for each member of the pantheon (the best I can do is to refer to relevant literature), but to build a solid framework through which categorization of the Chinese pantheons becomes internally consistent and externally intelligible.

Categorization of the Pantheons

1. *The Gods of Ancient Times*

Supreme Deities: *Ti* (*Shang-ti*) of the Shang period; *T'ien* or *Huang-t'ien* (August Heaven) of the Chou dynasty. In early writings the two are sometimes combined and seen as functional synonyms: *Huang-t'ien Shang-ti*;

Nature Gods: thunder, lightning, rain (dragon-kings), wind, sun, moon, stars (perhaps Shang period, but certainly of Chou times);

Earth Gods: fertility spirits: soil, grain, sovereign Earth, rivers, mountains (probably Shang period or even from prehistoric times; certainly Chou);

Ancestral spirits (Shang and Chou): possibly evil spirits or *kui* (since Chou?); *Ti* or *Shang-ti* of Shang period may have started as first royal ancestor of the clan.

Animal Spirits: very likely rooted in totemism and/or shamanism.

Many of these deities or spirits continue to exist in later times' myths, legends and theories about them are amplified; their importance and worship are susceptible to changes, even to decline.

2. *The Gods of Later Times*

Although the traditional concept of *san chiao* ("three teachings", rather than "three religions") has been strongly criticized as perhaps too elitist, old-fashioned, irrelevant, or even as an abstraction, yet it must be reaffirmed that each of these three has had an autonomous existence. All three are clearly distinct, and even if one can point out some similarities between them, it does not mean identity. Their existence and recognition of their existence does not diminish the great importance of the Folk Religion as another autonomous system. It is not the place here to discuss the thorny problem of *san-chiao* versus popular religion.

a) *Confucianism and Imperial (or State) Cult*

These two are certainly not one and the same, but their objects of worship do occasionally overlap. Confucian writings extol the virtues of culture heroes and sage kings and praise them as models of virtue and ideal political leadership. In general, however, they are not deified.

TMSC lists here: Confucius, Kuan-kung, P'an-ku, Nü-kua, Shen-nung, Huang-ti, San-kuan, Chang T'ien-shih, Pao-kung, P'eng-tsu and many others. The majority of the remaining ones do not belong here.

SMKL has: Fu-hsi, Shen-nung, Huang-ti, San-kuan (also identified with Yao, Shun and Yü), K'ung-tzu, Kuan-ti, Lu-pan, and some famous pioneers and generals.

MJZS shows some interesting changes: whereas San-Kuan and Kuan-ti have been retained, a host of famous mythical figures are missing: no more culture heroes, no more K'ung-tzu. Cult figures like Kuan-ti are examples of the bridge between Confucianism and the State cult. Although Kuan-ti is not a Confucian personality, the state and the state bureaucracy promoted his cult for its ethical symbolism. Kuan-ti was seen as a model of loyalty and overall civic virtue and his cult was used as a powerful instrument to encourage these virtues amongst the people.

b) *Taoism*

Early Taoism adopted many of the traditional nature deities, but also created a set of their own: Szu-ming, god of alchemy and master of destiny, is one of the earliest Taoist creations. Then Lao-tzu and the Yellow Emperor were deified as Huang-Lao. Followed some Taoist triads: T'ai-I, T'ien-I, and Ti-I, and 36,000 spirits within the human body who also control the macrocosm. A new triad eventually replaced the former one: the Three Heavenly Worthies (*T'ien-tsun*): Yüan-shih, Ling-pao and Tao-te (the third one is the apotheosis of Lao-tzu). The second trinity was followed (but not fully replaced) by a new one: the Three Pure Ones (San-ch'ing), who are certainly different from the Three rulers (San-Kuan) of religious Taoism.

Within the growth of inner alchemy, the Taoist gods were multiplied on a grandiose scale, "mass-production", as H. Welch humorously remarks.[5] Many of them appear in some basic Taoist scriptures and play an important role in Taoist meditation techniques, especially those advocated by Mao-shan Taoism.[6]

c) *Buddhism*

Here is a case of worshipping transcendent beings who are not technically "gods", but rather like "incarnations" of the ultimate Buddha-nature in the form of Buddhas and bodhisattvas. The latter also assume a place of high eminence in the folk religion.

The Buddhist cult objects are not that numerous. Although hundreds of mythical Buddhas and bodhisattvas appear in some of the sutras, those who gained popularity among Buddhist devotees are only a handful. Among the Buddhas figure Shakyamuni, the historical founder of Buddhism, and mythical creations such as Buddha Amita, residing in the Western Land of Happiness, and the Buddha of Healing. These three are often seen as a trinity in temples.

Among the bodhisattvas, only a few well-known figures are seen over and over again: Kuan-yin, or Kuan-shih-yin, Mi-lo-fo (Maitreya), P'u-hsien, Wen-shu and Titsang wang.

Among the Buddhist saints some are outstanding; Chi-kung (the "crazy" monk), always an attractive figure because of his humour;[7] and Bodhidharma, usually called Ta-mo (or "dharma") have penetrated into the folk religion. The Buddhist saints, prototypes of the Taoist Immortals, have been grouped into sets of 16 or 18 (seen in many temples), or even larger sets of 500, which can still be seen in some monasteries in China.

3. *Deities of the Popular Religion*

The pantheon of the folk religion displays the greatest variety, and also causes the greatest confusion. The deities do apparently not like to be regimented and organized into neat rows. Leaving aside, for the time being, ghosts and ancestors, who together with the real deities populate the spiritual universe of the Chinese, we must try to find some criteria of classification. The results of former scholars must be taken into account.

Assuming the validity of what appears to be a general consensus amongst scholars, namely that there is a hierarchical structure in the heavenly bureaucracy, we must examine how such a hierarchy can be worked out in practical terms. Hierarchy implies a supreme authority at the top, some intermediate levels, and a whole gamut of lower levels. On which level one should place individual deities is not per se clear but both popular practice, field observation, and specialized studies are helpful guides to formulate a workable hypothesis.

a) *At the top*, we must of course place *T'ien* (Heaven). Although his formal worship was strictly reserved to the emperors, the common people privately worshipped Heaven as *T'ien-kung* (Lord Heaven) or *T'ien Lao-yeh* (Granddad Heaven, Venerable Old Man Heaven). Sometimes one meets the combination *Huang-t'ien Hou-t'u* (August Heaven and Queen Earth) as the primordial divine pair. It is often stated that *T'ien-kung* has been assimilated with *Yü-huang Ta-ti*, the Jade Emperor, who is Heaven in a more concrete and personalized form. Whatever the case may be, the Jade Emperor is ranked as the supreme deity of the Folk Religion, but he has also strong links with Taoism.

In most Chinese temples one sees a large bronze incense burner placed in the outer courtyard near the entrance gate of the major hall: this is where the worshippers put their first incense stick, as an act of homage to *T'ien-kung*. But otherwise, in the minds of the devotees, there is quite a distance between this superior deity and the daily concerns of the people.

b) *At the intermediate level* one finds a great number of deities of varying majesty and power, which are more often approached by the people. Their ranks are not all the same, and one can easily divide them into three sub-levels. This reflects what I believe to be the people's own mind, who do see some hierarchical differentiation among their gods.

It is very difficult, however, to be accurate, and one has to be very cautious. For instance, extreme popularity of a particular deity does not necessarily prove its higher ranking. Consideration of career making and of the local, regional, and national spread of a cult must also be taken into account.

With these cautions in mind, we may then proceed and group a large number of deities in one of the three sub-levels: higher, middle and lower.

(i) *higher middle level*: here I like to place deities of heavenly boards or ministries and some personified gods of nature, including star gods and dragon-kings. Individual deities like the Three Rulers (*San-kuan*): Sun and Moon (Yin and Yang, seen as deities); the god of the Eastern Peak (*Tung-yüeh* or T'ai-shan) and Yen-lo Wang, who is the Ruler of the netherworld; Hsüan-t'ien Ta-ti or god of the Pole Star (also called Chen-wu Ta-ti, Pei-chi Ta-ti or Shang-ti Kung); and Tou-mu (Earth Mother), would be included here. Most of these gods are of a mythical nature or are personified natural forces. In the human world they can be compared with high government officials, directors of boards, or even provincial governors.

(ii) *middle middle level*: here could be listed deified human beings of great achievement and special miraculous power whose cults have become very popular. Although most were originally historical figures, their cults are overgrown with later legends. Examples are: Queen of Heaven (Ma-tsu), Kuan-ti or Kuan-kung, Pao-sheng Ta-ti (although of regional importance only). Parallel with them we could list here some of the mythical emperors or culture heroes.

(iii) *lower middle level*: this category includes the greatest number of deities, many of them very close to the people: city gods, gods of trades and professions, patrons of business, protectors of health, childbirth, and gods of healing or protection against epidemics, patrons of the literary and military arts, and gods of general human happiness (*san-fu*). Many of these deities are apotheosized human beings, but some are rather mythical in origin. The city god indicates a rank or office rather than one individual: this position is in fact occupied simultaneously by many individuals of great reputation in different locations.

In the human world, their counterparts can be seen in the various local officials.

c) *at the lowest level*: we find the mass of humble gods or rather 'spirits' which are closest to daily life: the household gods, the gods of the kitchen (stove), of the bedroom, of wealth, of the privy and the extremely popular spirits of the local soil (*T'u-ti-kung*), as well as the door gods, guardians of the house. Some of these have a historical base, and reflect human personalities of some real, but lower achievement, whereas others are rather mythical. The spirits of the soil, similar to the city gods, are a function or office, rather than one individual. Within this group also fall minor nature spirits, viz. some animal or tree-spirits, or spirits of "strange" phenomena such as rock-spirits.

Many questions can be raised when looking at this arrangement. The importance of one particular deity is subject to fluctuations, not only due to imperial decrees, but also depending upon individual or group interest. For example, Ma-tsu can be considered as a deity of higher middle category, whereas for some present-day temple organizations, Kuan-ti, called *Kuan-shen Ti-chün*, would certainly be placed on the top level.

Since the deities included in this three-level scheme are, by definition, only those belonging to the popular religion, others have been omitted: the Taoist deities, Buddhas and bodhisattvas (and perhaps the Immortals) would fall within the middle group. Buddhist and Taoist saints (arhats, and ordinary immortals) seem to belong to the lower level, and are technically not "deities" but "saints" or "sages" (see below).

The above categorization reflects what I believe to be the view of the majority of worshippers; it is open to questioning and challenge: gods are still being promoted and demoted today (at least in the minds of worshippers ... and scholars), and individuals may put the spirit of the earth on a higher level than many a famous culture hero. Some Christians would have a greater devotion to the Virgin Mary than to her divine Son, or some would prefer going to mass on Tuesdays to honour St. Anthony rather than on Sundays. Leaving this flexibility, the above categorization has its definite usefulness in ordering the chaos of the supernatural world.

4. *A Discussion of Ancestors and Ghosts*

These two groups, although very important in the total world view of the Chinese believer, do not strictly belong to the pantheons. They are not divine beings. As in the human bureaucracy again, there are government officials, and there are private citizens. Amongst the latter, the ghosts are on the boundaries of normal society, or even downright outcasts. They have been compared to beggars. Ancestors belong to the spirit-world but are only venerated by their own descendants. A funeral is a family affair; it takes place in or near the home of the deceased (or in a funeral hall today), never in a community temple. Moreover, ancestor spirits are not strictly immortal: they will be offered sacrifices, as long as the descendants remember them. At some point in time, their tablets will be removed from the home shrine and placed in a common clan ancestral temple. Therefore, ancestors belong to the family religion, rather than to the community religion as such. They cannot be called gods in the strict sense.

Ghosts qualify even less to be considered deities. They are closer to ancestral spirits but with the understanding that they are lonely spirits: they do not have descendants to carry on sacrifices, or they have died a premature or violent death and bear a grudge against the living. These ghosts or *kui*, have been identified with the *preta* or hungry ghosts of the Buddhist tradition, and since medieval times, have received lavish banquets at least once a year.[8]

The attitude of most Chinese people is one of fear and uneasiness rather than positive respect. Ghosts are the beggars of the spirit-world and must be appeased lest they come back and harm the living. Again, it is clear that one cannot put them on the same level as the deities. It is ironical that people seem to spend more ritual time in propitiating ghosts and cancel their evil influences than worshipping and praying to the gods proper.

Human Characteristics

The Chinese people have created their gods and goddesses in their own (idealized) images and likenesses, and have endowed them with quasi-human, but slightly idealized, powers and attributes. They are the mandarins and ministers of the spirit-world.

Except for the "supreme beings", the ancient gods of nature and fertility, and the Buddhas and bodhisattvas, most of the gods and goddesses, and what one should call "saints" rather than deities, have been created by man in historic times. The processes of deification or canonization have not been uniform (see below) but include euhemerization and legend building in many instances.

Some mythical beings and truly historical personages of exceptional significance have been exalted to the rank of divine hierarchy. But in doing so, the Chinese have often provided them with purely human paraphernalia: they have birthdays; they enjoy family life with wives and children; they live in sumptuous residences, sometimes palaces; they possess wealth and influence over other spirits, especially over evil spirits, as well as over human beings; they have body guards and servants, sometimes even armies of spirit-soldiers, and are carried around in sedan chairs. When a divine image is paraded around a city or village to inspect his/her territory, it is a procession similar to that of a great mandarin on the move. Finally, the deities have temperaments and even tempers.

This detail is extremely important when it comes to dealing with them (see below, under relationships).

That the deities (and saints) of the Chinese pantheon imitate many features of human career-making and bureaucracy is very well known. However, generalities are easily stated, but specific details are often missing. The pantheon is not an exact replica of the imperial hierarchy. For instance, the traditional ranking of officials into nine categories does not seem to apply to the divine hierarchy. On earth, appointments were made by the imperial government usually after candidates had successfully passed civil or military examinations. Appointments in the supernatural administration are not so uniform. Sometimes one reads that every year, at the occasion of the (lunar) New Year, the Supreme Lord Yü-huang or Jade Emperor reviews his administrative personnel: gods are then promoted or demoted according to their demonstrated merits or demerits. There are, however, cases in literature and history where gods are appointed by the earthly emperors, by religious leaders, or even by popular acclamation. Emperors may also bestow special honours and titles on gods of unusual merit. One can thus see that the record is not clear and that generalizing statements tend to be misleading.

A close examination of the titles given to many deities is very revealing: it shows that there is some hierarchical structure, but also that it is not too rigorous, quite different from the imperial hierarchy.

In this examination, the "supreme beings" will be left out: they are often identified with the creative energies of the cosmos and are beyond human manipulation. As for the lower ranking deities, the many titles given to them reflect somehow their divine status and enforce the common view that they are conceived of in a pattern similar to that of the imperial hierarchy.

General terms used to refer to divine spirits are *shen* and *shen-ming*: "spirits" and "bright spirits" (compare with Hindu *devas*: "shining ones"). More rarely one encounters *shen-ch'i*, "spirits or gods of heaven and earth". Among the common people one also hears *Fo* (literally "Buddha") and *p'u-sa* ("bodhisattva") not just to refer to the Buddhist cult figures, but even to the gods of the folk religion. Especially *p'u-sa* is frequently used as a practical synonym of *shen*.

In temple worship, the major deity enthroned on the central altar, and usually the patron deity of the community, is called *chu-shen*, "master-deity", in contrast with the *p'ei-ou shen*, the "auxiliary or accompanying deities", installed on side altars (Compare with "master-guest" and "accompanying guests" at a Chinese banquet.)

Among the higher ranks in the celestial hierarchy, one finds titles like *Ta-ti*, "Great Lord", or perhaps "Great Emperor", "Great Ruler"; *Ti*, "Lord"; *Sheng-ti*, "Holy Lord.

Parallel with those, and probably of similar status are:

T'ien-chün	Heavenly Monarch
Ti-chün	Lord Monarch
Hsing-chün	Star Monarch

Chen-chün	True Monarch
Lang-chün	Master Monarch
Chün	Monarch
T'ien-tsun	Heavenly Honourable
T'ien-fu Ti-mu	Father Heaven and Mother Earth

Among the family members of those high ranking celestial officials are listed divine spouses, princes, and princesses:

T'ien-shang Sheng-mu	Holy Mother in Heaven (commonly named *Ma-tsu*, ancestral aunt)
Mu	Mother
Lao-mu	Old Mother
T'ien-Fei	Heavenly Concubine (= Holy Mother)
T'ien Hou	Heavenly Queen (= Holy Mother)
Niang-niang	Lady
T'ai-tzu	Prince
Kung-chu	Princess

The following series of titles seem to be of a slightly lower rank but exceptions are possible. The titles are parallel to human titles of nobility and relate to *wang* (king), *chu* (lord), *kung* (duke), *hou* (marquis), and *po* (earl):

Wang	King, Prince, Lord
Sheng-wang	Holy King
Ta-wang	Great King
Tsun-wang	Honourable King
Ta-wang-kung	Great Lordly King
En-wang	King-Benefactor
T'ien-wang	Heavenly King
Lung-wang	Dragon King
Wang-yeh	Royal Master, Respected Master
Chu	Lord
En-chu	Lord-Benefactor
Chiao-chu	Lord-Founder, Religious Founder, Master of the Doctrine
Kung	Duke
Wen-kung	Literary Duke
Kung-yeh	Respected Duke
Hou-kung	Duke-Marquis
Kung-tsu	Duke-Ancestor
Hou	Marquis
Sheng-hou	Holy Marquis
Tsun-hou	Honorable Marquis
Po	Earl
Ch'ien-sui	(literally: 'thousand years') His Highness

Another series of titles do not refer to any rank of rulership or nobility but seem to be given to famous teachers (perhaps honorary, like 'Doctor honoris causa'), and to other meritorious persons, familiarly called *yeh*, 'uncle, old man, ...'. Added to these two which occur most frequently, are a few other titles.

Shih	Teacher
Tsu-shih	Ancestral Teacher, Founder
Ming-shih	Bright Teacher
T'ai-shih	Great Teacher
Hsien-shih	First Teacher
T'ien-shih	Heavenly Teacher (refers to Chang Tao-ling and successors: 'Heavenly Master sect' of Taoism)
Tsu	Ancestor (cf. *Fo-tsu*, Buddhist ancestor or ancestral Buddha, title of Kuan-yin in the popular religion)
Lao-tsu	Old Ancestor
Hsien-tsu	Ancestor-Immortal (see also above *Kung-tsu*)
Yeh	Respected (old man)
Shen-yeh	Respected Spirit
Shih-yeh	Respected Scholar
Shih-yeh	Respected Ambassador
Ti-yeh	Respected Lord (see above) see also above *wang-yeh*; and below *chiang-yeh*
Ta-sheng	Great Saint
Ta-hsien	Great Immortal
Ta-shih	Great Ambassador
Hsien-sheng	"First-Born", Sir

Among the military officials, the most remarkable and numerous are the generals and marshals:

Chiang-chun	General
Ta chiang-chun	Great General
Chiang-chun wang	King-General, or General King
Yüan-shuai	Marshall
Ju-shuai	Lord-marshall

Among the female deities of lower rank, are the following titles:

Fu or *Fu-jen*	Lady, Spouse
Fei	Consort
Niang	Lady, Aunt
Hsüan-nü	Mysterious Female
Hsien-ku	Female Immortal, Fairy
Ma	Mother
Wang-ma	Royal Mother
Chen-chieh-ma	Faithful (chaste) Widow
Chieh	Elder Sister

Although we have left Buddhist objects of worship out of our discussion, for reasons of comparisons it is important to note the variety of titles used in this context.

Fo	Buddha
Ku-fo	Old (ancient) Buddha
P'u-sa	Bodhisattva
Fo-tsu	(see above) literally Ancestral Buddha, in fact it is an epithet for Kuan-yin
Wang	King, Prince, applied to Bodhisattva Ti-tsang
Sheng	Saint
Ming-wang	Bright King
Tsu-shih	Ancestral Teacher
Ho-shang	Monk
Lo-han	Arhat, Saint
Kung	Duke or Honorary Title "Uncle"
Tsun-wang	Honourable King
T'ien-nü	Heavenly Maiden
T'ung-tzu	(Heavenly) Youth

For reasons to be mentioned later (see the discussion about "ghosts becoming gods"), we must include the terminology used in the folk religion when referring to several groups of "ghosts", *kui*. The following titles point to different types of rationalization:

You-ying-kung	Duke Responding to Prayers
You-ying-ma	Goddess Responding to Prayers
Ta-chung-yeh	Public Old Man?
Ta-chung-ma	Public Mother?
I-min-yeh	
Pai-hsing-kung	

Besides these titles, there are several others given to ghosts for reasons of 'spiritual diplomacy' (see below), such as "duke, great king, marshall", etc. The more common titles given to ghosts are the following:

kui	Ghost, Evil Spirit
Mo	Evil ghost (also combined, *mo-kui)*
kui-shen	Spirits (in general, includes both good and evil spirits
erh-kui	Hungry Ghosts
hao hsiung-ti	Literally "Good Brothers", euphemism for "Hungry ghosts"
k'u-hun	Lonely Spirit, Orphan Spirit
hsieh-shen	"Demonic Spirit", evil ghosts manifesting themselves as good spirits
yao-kuai	Evil Fairy
yao-ching	Evil Fairy
hsiao-shen	"Little God"
hsiao-niang	"Little Maid"
nü-hun	Female Spirit
shui-kui	Water Ghost

The great variety of these titles and appellations is amazing and testifies to the great imagination of the Chinese worshippers. But one conclusion is quite obvious: there is a hierarchy of authority implied in the nomenclature. Yet, one should be careful: the distinctions of functions and levels of official positions are not so clearcut as is often believed. In that respect, the divine hierarchy is not totally similar to its human counterpart. Some authors have greatly overstated the case, as for example:

> The different gods are positive bureaucrats with a strict hierarchy of rank and with clearly defined powers. They keep registers, make reports, issue directives, with a regard to formalities and a superabundance of papers which the most pedantic administration on earth might well envy.[9]

The overstatement refers to the "strict hierarchy" and "clearly defined powers". The belief system and the terminology used within it do not warrant this conclusion. For instance, *wang*, king or prince, seems to be a higher position in the human realm than *kung*, duke. Yet Kuan Kung is for all practical purposes, a higher deity than many others called *wang*. Powers are not always clearly defined and frequently overlap: several deities are responsible for health; some deities once had particular functions but these gradually extended so as to make them "general purpose" protectors. Examples are Ma-tsu and even Kuan Kung.

The variety of titles does however point to the fact that there is a divine hierarchy, that the gods and goddesses or divine spirits all obey the highest ranking god (in the popular religion), the Jade Emperor. But the clear distinction of offices and responsibilities does not literally copy the human administration. There is probably room left for the imagination of the worshipper and for the use of "spiritual diplomacy".

Since these titles do not often indicate the precise status of a particular deity compared to others, one needs other criteria to supplement them. Without going into detail, I'd list the following: origin, popularity and spiritual power (*ling*); number and size of temples, extent and type of worship (for example the type of spirit-money offered); iconography; function; official patronage. Used in combination, sometimes with caution, one can gain a fairly accurate idea of the rank of a particular deity in the heavenly administration. Most of these criteria have been implicitly used in establishing the various levels described above.

What is perhaps a more decisive characteristic of the 'human' aspect of China's deities, is the way relationships between human beings and their gods are portrayed in literature or take place in the realities of daily life. Toward the deities of the highest level, an attitude of respect and worship prevails: they receive lavish sacrifices, are approached with humble prayers of supplication, forgiveness and thanksgiving. This is exemplified in the traditional imperial sacrifices to Heaven, and, in a different but parallel way, in the great sacrificial rites of renewal performed by Taoist priests to honour the Three Heavenly Honoured Ones. The deities (and spirits or saints) of the lower levels are approached in quite different ways by the common people. People's attitudes toward them reflect, or rather imitate, their ways of behaving toward various categories of their fellow-men. When a person approaches a deity he/she usually has a very concrete motive in mind: the obtaining of some material favour. The way in which this favour is requested depends very much on the relationship between the two principals involved. In human society parents usually give orders to their young children. Social equals may request favours in a polite way, sometimes with insistence, up to the point of insolence. At other times they may use flattery, promises, and, if that does not work, threats which can include feelings of bitterness and anger. In extreme cases, and especially toward inferiors or enemies, one might use violence or torture. Toward one's superiors one is more cautious and polite, but flattery, gifts, and even bribery often accompany the request for a favour.

It appears that most of these human social relationships also apply to man's attitude toward his gods. The efficacy of a particular god's response to human prayers constitutes his/her *ling* or spiritual potency and reputation. In daily worship, people burn incense to their gods, offer fruit and other kinds of food and wine, and present 'paper' money to accompany their prayers and make them more effective.

Examples abound in the literature of cases in which gods are not only requested to help, but are sometimes threatened, coerced, or at least exhorted with reason and arguments. A few cases should suffice to illustrate the general principle:

(i) Many worshippers ask divine favours and make vows in return for a prayer granted.

(ii) Sometimes the god's statue is exposed to the heat of the sun in the marketplace in order to force him to send rain in cases of protracted drought.[10]

(iii) There is a hilarious example in the biography of the Sung Poet-statesman Su Tung-po who went to pray for rain in a mountain temple:

> On the south of the Wei River there is a high mountain range, generally known as the Tsinling Mountains, and in this range the highest and best-known peak is the majestic Taipo. On top of the Taipo Mountain, in front of a Taoist temple, there was a little pool where lived the God of Rain, a "dragon" who could disguise himself in the form of any small fish. Su tung-po went up to this temple and prayed. He pleaded for the farmers, but, like a good lawyer, he tried to make the Dragon God see that a drought or famine was not to the god's own interests. After flattering the god a little, he said in the official prayer, "there has been no rain or snow since last winter. Thou knowest well that the people's lives depend upon their crops. If it doesn't rain now, there will be a famine; the people will starve and be forced to become bandits. This is not only my personal duty as a magistrate to prevent; as a spirit, thou shouldst not stand quietly by and do nothing about it. His Imperial Majesty has conferred upon thee the different honours, and we have kept up the sacrifices, all for this day when we may need thee. Wilt thou please listen and fulfil thy obligation to His Majesty?"[11]

(iv) The god's displeasure and human promises to mend evil ways is the sequel to the above story. After Su's prayer, there was still no rain. He eventually discovered that a Sung dynasty emperor had declared the god a count, whereas during the earlier T'ang period, he had been a duke. This was equivalent to degradation and had caused the god's anger. After Su wrote to the court for reconsideration, the rain finally came.[12] Many more examples like this can be found in literary sources.

People's attitudes toward ghosts and ancestors are somewhat different. Ghosts are certainly not cherished or respected, rather they are feared, but because of their powers, they are still treated with caution. People often treat them in ways that resemble the treatment of beggars and bandits (and in some societies, policemen) in the human world. Rather than merely chasing them away, they are offered some food and drink (bandits and policemen are bribed) in the hope that they will leave people in peace. Even rituals of exorcism are sometimes conceived of in this way. Rather than displaying only a simple show of spiritual power that results in expelling the evil spirit, Chinese exorcists usually also give the spirit a meal and some (pocket) money. In the case of some higher-placed but potentially obnoxious spirits, they are even feasted (wined and dined) before being finally chased away. It is, once again, a "humane" way of dealing with the spiritual forces, in which some concessions are made. (The Gospel has a similar story: Jesus cast out a horde of devils, but allowed them to enter into a herd of swine.)

Towards their ancestors, the Chinese are both respectful and pragmatic. They cherish the memory of their deceased kin, but do not shrink back from "using" their ancestors' bones to their own advantage. This is certainly a way of manipulating the supernatural for one's own worldly benefits.

One final application of the general principle of human/spiritual interaction can be seen in the powers of Taoist priests. While it is common experience that human beings in a position of authority are able to manipulate and control those below them, it is similarly believed that Taoist priests are able to control various divine spirits and summon them to the world of men in order to bestow spiritual blessings. The hierarchical rank of a priest increases as the number of deities under his control expands. This is also a general principle in exorcism: evil spirits, and even benevolent deities are expelled through the supernatural help of higher spirits. The more spirits a priest controls, the more effective he will be as an exorcist. There is a report of a Taoist master who chased away from the temple a lower ranking but popular deity, Third Prince, who had entered the premises during a ceremony without the priest's permission.[13]

Origin or "Birth of the gods"

In most general terms, one can state that the Chinese deities were born in the minds of the Chinese people. Some of them had a factual or historical base to start with, but legend builders, religionists and worshippers embroidered the historical facts so that in the end, history and myth are imperceptibly interwoven.

The details of these various processes are very complicated. First, one has to take into account the "three teachings" (*san chiao*) each with its own pantheon; next, one cannot treat all the deities or spirits in an identical way: there is, it appears, although this impression has to be verified, a variety of ways in which individual deities or spirits are "born"; the proportion of history and legend may greatly vary. In the third place, the categorization of deities, which was discussed above, is not at all clear, otherwise one would have neat groups of deities whose origins would be very similar, if not identical. Therefore, instead of helping, those lists are often an obstacle creating more confusion.

It is not my intention to discuss the origin of religion in general, nor of Chinese religions in particular. The only objective here is to discover and analyze the various ways in which Chinese deities or spirits, more in particular those of the folk religion, have probably come into subjective existence. ("Subjective" here means that one must leave out their objective existence, or "true" existence. This question cannot even be asked in our present context.) The origins of belief in Heaven (*T'ien*) or *Shang-ti* belong to prehistory; so do the origins of belief in most nature deities, including the gods of fertility and the origin of the ancestor cult. One may speculate here about animistic, totemistic, and shamanistic beginnings, but it remains pure speculation.

The gods of Taoism and Buddhism, on the other hand, can be more closely examined. There are historical clues about their creation, and, in general terms, one can propose the mythologizing tendency (instinct?) of the respective religious communities as the creative force behind the Buddhas, bodhisattvas, Taoist deities and immortals. Many of the mythical sage-rulers are probably culture heroes, who were later endowed with true human personalities: this is the opposite of the euhemeristic phenomenon, a characteristic of the more rationally oriented Confucian scholars.[14] Of course, one single factor does not usually explain the origin and later evolution of one cult figure. For example, *Huang-ti* or the Yellow Emperor is a complex figure: the achievements attributed to him make him appear as a culture hero; later on he was apotheosized together with Lao-tzu into a divine being (he still is an important Taoist deity today), but perhaps his origins can be found in a localized clan figure, that outgrew its limited boundaries and gradually became more universal.[15] Separate studies should be undertaken about each of the sage kings and mythical beings to unravel the various influences and factors involved in their final *Gestalten*: Shen-nung, Fu-hsi, Nü-kua, Yao, Shun, Yü, etc. Their genesis and final configurations may have a lot in common, but there certainly are also individual characteristics assigned to each of them.

When we come to our more important and most interesting target, the gods and goddesses of the folk religion, we are faced with a phenomenon that is rightly called euhemerism or mythologizing, but this latter term is rather ambiguous. It is the phenomenon that many of the deities of the Chinese popular pantheon were historical personages to begin with, but have later on, for a variety of reasons, been elevated to super-human status or become deified. (This is one reason why I keep talking about the "human" gods of China.) Once again, each deity or cult figure deserves a separate study since, besides similarities in their genesis, there are also many differences.

Rather than discussing abstract principles, we should examine some concrete examples. Only then can inductive rules be established. If one looks at the divine objects of worship most popular in Taiwan today, one has a good starting point. According to Lin Heng-tao,[16] the popularity of a particular deity can be evaluated by means of the number of temples dedicated to this deity. Once the popularity level is established, one can further investigate the origin of the cult. Here follows a list of the fifteen most popular cult figures in modern Taiwan (list established in 1960); they all have at least 50 temples dedicated to them. Altogether they "own" 3,303 out of 4,220 temples.

	Name of Deity	*Number of Temples*
1.	Wang Yeh (Royal Master)	717
2.	Kuan-yin	441
3.	Ma-tsu	383
4.	T'u-ti-kung (Local Spirit of the Soil)	327
5.	Shakyamuni (Historical Buddha)	306
6.	Hsüan-t'ien Ta-ti (Lord of Pole Star)	266
7.	Kuan Kung or Kuan-ti	192
8.	Pao-sheng Ta-ti (God of Healing)	140
9.	San-shan-kuo wang (Three Mountain Gods)	124
10.	Third Prince, or Na-ch'o	94
11.	Shen-nung Ta-ti (Culture Hero, Agriculture)	80
12.	Ch'ing-shui Tsu-shih (Fukien Buddhist Monk)	63
13.	San-kuan Ta-ti (Lords of Three Realms)	60
14.	K'ai-t'ai Sheng-wang (Koxinga, Pioneer Settler of Taiwan)	57
15.	K'ai-chang Sheng-wang (Pioneer god of Changchou in Fukien province)	53
		3,300

We are not discussing here the popularity level of particular deities, but the origin of their cults. Therefore, (2) and (5) can be left out since they are Buddhist cult objects. The remaining 13 belong essentially to the folk religion, although they have definite connections with either Taoism (6,13), Buddhism (12), or Confucianism-State cult (7). Moreover, the cult of T'u-ti-kung (4) and Shen-nung (11) can also be ignored here: their cults have roots in prehistoric times as one type of fertility cults or culture heroes.

The remaining deities are thus open for discussion: Wang-yeh, Ma-tsu, Kuan-ti, Pao-sheng Ta-ti, San-shan-kuo wang, Third Prince, Ch'ing-shui Tsu-shih, K'ai-t'ai sheng-wang and K'ai-chang Sheng-wang. But let us keep the series intact for a moment and briefly indicate the nature of their origins:

1.	Wang-yeh	historic roots plus legend
2.	Kuan-yin	mythological

3.	Ma-tsu	historic roots plus legend
4.	T'u-ti-kung	mythic (fertility cult)
5.	Shakyamuni	historic roots plus myth
6.	Hsüan-t'ien Ta-ti	mythic (stellar deity)
7.	Kuan-ti	historic roots plus legend
8.	Pao-sheng Ta-ti	historic roots plus legend
9.	San-shan-kuo wang	(not certain, probably nature deities)
10.	Third Prince	mythic
11.	Shen-nung Ta-ti	culture hero, mythic
12.	Ch'ing-shui tsu-shi	historic roots plus legend
13.	San-kuan Ta-ti	mythic (deities of Three Worlds)
14.	K'ai-t'ai	historic roots plus legend
15.	K'ai-chang	historic roots plus legend

Summarizing the above table, it is easy to see that there are (at least) four processes of deification at work in the Chinese religion (probably more):

1. "created" mythology-deities born from literary fiction: Third Prince.
2. culture hero and mythology: Shen-nung
3. historic roots plus mythology: Shakyamuni
4. historic roots plus legend: Wang-yeh, Ma-tsu, Kuan-ti

Focussing on the fourth group, which most directly relates to the folk religion, one can easily notice their human origins. These deities were originally true historical personages, whose biographies can be studied, although later legendary accretions make it sometimes extremely difficult to separate historical facts from legends. Among the clearest examples figure deities such as Kuan-ti or Kuan Kung; from a popular warrior during the Three Kingdoms period, he became a legendary hero, glorified in literature and opera. Having become a model of loyalty to his king, he became the patron saint of the military (not the "god of war" as many authors have called him), and even of businessmen. Today he is a major cult figure among spirit-writing associations; one group has even elevated him to the highest top of the pantheon: the successor of Yü-huang Ta-ti, and renamed him Kuan-sheng Ti-chün. In the course of time, emperors bestowed special titles upon him, from "Duke" Kung (Kuan Kung), he became Kuan-ti, "Lord Kuan" (or "Emperor" Kuan).[17]

One of the most intriguing groups of deities are the *wang-yeh* ("Royal Princes"), especially worshipped in southern Taiwan, but who originated on the southeast coast of China (Fukien and Kwangtung) where they used to be called *wen-wang* ("Lords of pestilence"). The number of temples dedicated to them hits the top of the list: 717. This is however, somehow misleading. The *wang-yeh* group consists of 132 individual deities (98 of them are found in Taiwan worship)[18] each with their own family name, which betray their original human roots. They are worshipped especially as protectors against epidemics. In Taiwan, the most popular ones are worshipped together in groups of five (surnamed Li, Ch'ih, Wu, Chu, and Fan) or three (surnamed Chu, Ch'ih and Li). As individual deities, Su-fu *wang-yeh* seems to be the most popular one, especially among the medium cults.[19] According to some legends, they would have been 360 loyal officers of the Han or T'ang dynasty,[20] but that is probably purely legendary.

Each case of "deified human being" has to be carefully investigated to discover the many possible variations on the same theme. Some cases have already been mentioned in earlier studies of Chinese religion; I'd like to refer to the works of C.K. Yang and D.C. Graham. The latter states:

> Many of the gods whose images are worshipped are noted national heroes, such as Kuan-ti, Yo-fei, and Chu-ko Liang, commemoration being actually a motive for deification. Of course there is the idea that they have supernatural power and that if worshipped they will use this superhuman potency for the benefit of the worshippers.
>
> Many of the gods who are deified men are patron deities of the occupations pursued by these men when living.[21] The deification of men has gone on until very recent years. (Several cases are mentioned.)[22]

All the examples cited by Graham refer to persons deified by the local people on account of their good government or of their generosity; moreover three of the four had been deified during their lifetimes.

When C.K. Yang discusses the "cults of deified men", he divides them into two categories: "cults of nationally prominent personalities who were worshipped throughout the country, and local cults of figures whose temples were found only in certain localities".[23]

Both types of temples, Yang goes on, are found in every community, but the number of temples devoted to deceased local figures (more rarely to living men) was the higher. An example of a national cult figure is Kuan Yü,[24] others cited are Ma Yüan of Han times and Yo Fei of the Sung Dynasty. We already know about Kuan Yü or Kuan-ti; more interesting are the cults of local deified persons:

> ...every Chinese community had a number of cults dedicated to local leaders and officials who in their lifetime had prominently served the public interest, sometimes by sacrificing their lives and fortunes. These were the men (and occasionally women, as pointed out by Shryock) who served as virtuous examples for later generations because of their great deeds, and who acquired a sacred character in the eyes of the public by being enshrined in a temple.[25]

Yang further mentions the example of "two military commanders who died" in Chekiang during the opium war of 1841-42 and whose influence continued throughout the French invasion of 1881-82. This case presents a well-documented and modern example of how a cult arises and develops "through the building of sanctuaries, public sacrifices, bestowing of imperial honours, and a whole set of mythological lore woven around the two military figures..."[26]

The reason why I felt it necessary to discuss this particular process of deification in greater detail is to set the stage for the discussion of one more type of cult formation, which has been proposed in recent years as an alternative type of deification in China: the transformation of a ghost into a god. Philip

Baity appears to be one of the pioneers of this theory, but he was followed by Steven Harrell, and more cautiously, by Alvin Cohen.[27]

Baity is the most outspoken of the three when he states that "Gods begin as 'hungry ghosts' and are gradually transformed by sacrifices into deities ...".[28] He seems to say that this is the normal process of deification, since ghosts are seen as childless, with no descendants to sacrifice to them, and are, as a result, free to serve and protect the whole community rather than just their own family. Ancestor cult is thus seen as an obstacle to a more widely spread cult.

There are several problems with this theory, some of them implied in contradictory statements of Baity himself; for instance:

> The fact that most gods were created by the worship of the dead was not only repellent to the maxims of Confucian orthodoxy, but in addition would have been repugnant to the sensibilities of the villagers and the folk tradition and their insistence on the separation of the dead ghosts and the living gods.[29]

The wide gulf between deities and ghosts has been already mentioned above and makes it unlikely that transformation of ghosts into deities would be the normal process. As I commented in a review article on Baity's book:

> None of [the gods studied by the author in his research area], can be proven to have developed from a 'withered corpse'; on the contrary, several of them were historical personages of much fame, who had been great leaders in their life-time and almost certainly led a normal life within a family. If a deceased person of great merit to the community cannot become a cult object because he has posterity, then by the same token, a great official cannot serve the community at large during his lifetime either. Family ties are not necessarily an obstacle either for government service or for cult formation. When the people start worshipping a great person after his death, they do not worship him as an ancestor but as a great person who transcends the limitation of his family.[30]

One can add that when historical human beings become deified, it often happens quite some time after their death, so that the ancestral ties may have become very loose or even forgotten. In other cases, a person continues to receive ancestral sacrifices in the clan temple, but because his role has outgrown the family framework, he is also worshipped by a wider community. Confucius certainly is such a case.

That ghosts in exceptional cases are elevated to higher ranks of worship cannot be denied. But much more historical study is needed to verify and refine such a thesis.[31]. One crucial issue at stake here is who the 'ghosts' of Baity are. In China, there are several types; first, the mass of so-called 'hungry ghosts' (assimilation of ancient *kui* with the Buddhist inspired *preta*): they are anonymous ghosts and feasted regularly during the ghost festival and on other special occasions. These are not eligible to the status of deity. Rather, after being freed from their ghostly condition, they will be reincarnated as sentient beings.

Besides these, and in the mind of the Chinese people very distinct from them, are ghosts like *yu-ying-kung* or *ta-chung ma* ("public mother"?) who receive roadside offerings after their bones have been accidentally found and buried by farmers.[32] They also are anonymous ghosts, who are given adulatory names for reasons of spiritual diplomacy. Small, local cults may arise near those shrines. But do they ever rise to the status of real deities?

Then there is another category of ghosts, who were known to the community during their lifetime. They may be individuals or groups,[33] who may have died a violent, unnatural or premature death and are believed to seek revenge on society. They may be individuals who had a long life but lived on the verge of society as loners, semi-outcasts, yet feared as powerful. I would believe that only such ghosts have a change to become deities, after sacrifices to them, made mostly out of fear, prove to be effective. In such a case, *ling* is the best guarantee of cult-formation; like saints in Christianity become saints if they could perform miracles. Perhaps such ghosts are making a point: those who were outcasts during their life, were perhaps already during their life persons of great power; a developing cult may then be seen as a rectification of an injustice. In other words, spiritual value does not always coincide with socially acceptable norms.

My conclusion in this particular matter is that much more study is necessary: Baity did some field work research, but his historical foundation was too weak. The two aspects have to be more fully investigated.

Conclusions

One firm conclusion to be drawn from the above study is that to determine "who is who?" and "who is where?" in the spirit world of the Chinese people is a most difficult enterprise. Yet it is not hopeless. Maspero's outcry is an exaggeration, and if he had looked more closely to the pantheon of the Catholic Church, he would have also been perplexed and astonished by the parallels. Besides the Three Persons of the Trinity who constitute the supreme deity, there is also Jesus Christ, god-and-man. Then there is Mary, Jesus' Mother, and the twelve or thirteen, or perhaps fourteen apostles, the four evangelists (not including the apocrypha), then the saints of all kinds, martyrs, confessors, abbots, Church fathers, holy virgins, great and small, famous or obscure, universal or local. Many are real historical figures, others only legendary. But do not forget the Old Testament: patriarchs, judges, kings, prophets, and other holy persons. Then there are all the nine choruses of angelic beings: angels, archangels, (Michael, Gabriel, Raphael, Uriel, ...) and the seven other ranks of angelic figures. There are also the guardian angels, one for each human being living on earth. Alas! there are also *kui*, the devils like Lucifer, Beelzebub and his innumerable host of minor devils, frightening and powerful. There is also a hierarchy and also, surprisingly, a process of promotion (and demotion). Saints used to be acclaimed by the faithful, now they are "processed" by the Vatican, going through a painful and long procedure of beatification and canonization. Although saints are made by God's divine grace, the Church on earth decides who has really been godlike, who has reached the ideal of Christian perfection. The Church of Rome would never canonize a Protestant or a Moslem!

The confusion about the Chinese pantheon is just a bit worse than that concerning the Roman Catholic pantheon. Incidentally, one finds movements of iconoclasm in both religions. Much could be clarified about the Chinese pantheon if the distinctions of Supreme Being versus subordinate spirits (nature spirits) and versus canonized human "saints" were clear and consistent. If such principles prevailed, things would be simplified. Looking at the pantheon from a comparative viewpoint, there is not much difference in essence, only in the details and in quantity. The Chinese pantheon is much more elaborate, partly because more than one religion has contributed to its divine personnel, and partly because Chinese religion did not have a central religious authority to curb the popular fantasy. That is what perhaps best explains the so-called confusion: the popular imagination, unbridled, uncontrolled by a higher religious authority, followed its own instincts and created new "idols" or "ideals" to worship and to ask favours from in the people's harsh struggle for survival. Possibly the people's access to those many supernatural helpers, contributed to their mental and physical survival: the gods were more benign than the government officials!

Another parallel with the Christian pantheon comes to mind: in the Middle Ages, many saints were invoked to help in specific situations: St. Anthony, in order to find lost property; St. Barbara, to obtain a good death; St. Christopher (now demoted, since he was not historical!), for protection during travel; St. Rochus, against pestilence, etc. We can see parallel functions exercised by Chinese saints—each has his/her own competence and is worshipped for particular needs.

Moreover, another analogy between Chinese and Christian pantheons is their use of stereotyped iconography making it possible to recognize the identity of a saint or a deity.

As mentioned above, both the Christian Church and Chinese religion have known periods of iconoclasm. In Catholicism, the latest but not too violent wave of reformation concerning the saints took place around Vatican Council II. The saints had become irrelevant to religious life and were also seen as obstacles to ecumenical dialogue with protestant Churches (as if saints were greater obstacles than infallible popes!). In China, the wave of hatred against religion in the 1960's resulted in the destruction of many religious artifacts and books, and many deities have probably been sent into oblivion. Yet the cult of deities continues, not only in Taiwan and other areas of large Chinese settlements, but even on the Chinese mainland.[34] The flourishing of religious life in Taiwan and the vigourous temple building within the last twenty years seems to be an eloquent refutation of the Marxist thesis that religion would die out spontaneously once people's economic problems have been solved. Moreover, growing affluence perhaps creates stronger religious aspirations: there is more material well-being, but new frustrations arise with it and that may create the need for stronger supernatural protection. As communities in Taiwan and everywhere in the developing and developed world are being divided, there is a new need for unifying symbols: the "old" gods and goddesses who can demonstrate their *ling* will remain popular as symbols of community cohesion.

In this whole process of change, perhaps many small, local spirits will fall along the roadside, but the overall cult of deities and the extreme caution to appease the malevolent ghosts will remain as strong as ever, if not stronger.

Buddhist Monk Chi-Kung
(Sung Dynasty)

Buddhist Monk Bodhidharma
Founder of Ch'an Buddhism
in China (6th C.A.D.).

Sage Emperor Yao
(2357-2255 B.C.?)

Sage Emperor Shun
(2255-2205 B.C.)

Sage Emperor Yü, Founder
of HSIA Dynasty
(2205-2197 B.C.?)

T'ang, Founder of Shang
Dynasty

Duke of Chou, Solidified the Chou Dynasty

K'ung-fu-tzu: Great Master K'ung (551-479 B.C.)

King Wen of the Chou Dynasty. Rearranged the 8 Diagrams of I-Ching.

King Wu, of the Chou, Founder of the Dynasty.

Notes

1. Webster's *New 20th Century Dictionary.*
2. *Asiatic Mythology*, p. 263.
3. Literally all kinds of nature creatures.
4. *Asiatic Mythology*, pp. 252-384.
5. H. Welch. *Taoism. The Parting of the Way*, p. 107.
6. See Isabelle Robinet. *Méditation Taoiste.*
7. Recently Chi-kung has become extremely popular among lottery-gamblers in Taiwan. He reveals the lucky lottery numbers.
8. S. Teiser. *The Ghost Festival.*
9. Ou-I-Tai, "Chinese Mythology", p. 380.
10. See Eberhard. *Folk Tales of China*, pp. 113-116; and A. Cohen, "Coercing the Rain Deities in Ancient China:, *History of Religions* 17 (1978), 244-265.
11. Lin Yutang. *The Gay Genius*, p. 61.
12. Lin Yutang. *The Gay Genius*, pp. 61-62.
13. M. Saso. *The Teachings of Taoist Master Chuang*, pp. 120-121.
14. "Euhemerism" is the "theory that the gods of mythology were deified human beings", and "that myths are based on traditional accounts of real people and events" (Webster's *New World Dictionary.*) The theory was proposed by Euhemeros in 4th century B.C. Greece.
15. Jan Yün-hua. "The Change of Images: The Yellow Emperor in Ancient Chinese Literature".
16. *TSM*, pp. 36-37.
17. See P. Duara. "Superscribing Symbols".
18. Lin Heng-tao. *Taiwan Min-su lun-chi*, p. 69.
19. Liu Chih-wan. "The Temple of the Gods of Epidemics in Taiwan".
20. Lin, p. 69.
21. D.C. Graham. *Folk Religion in Southwest China*, p. 176. He mentions Tu-k'ang, Shen-nung, Lu-pan, Chang-yeh, Chang-huang, Wen-ch'ang, Confucius, Ts'ang-chih; Hua-t'o.
22. *Ibid.*, pp. 176-177.
23. C.K. Yang. *Religion in Chinese Society*, p. 159.
24. Yang, pp. 159-161.
25. Yang, p. 161.
26. Yang, p. 171. (For more detailed discussion, see pp. 168-173.
27. P. Baity. *Religion in a Chinese Town*, Ch. 6, "The Genesis of Gods", pp. 238-269. S. Harrell, "When a Ghost Becomes a God". A. Cohen, "Coercing the Rain Deities".
28. Baity. *Religion*, p. 249.
29. *Ibid.*, p. 248.
30. J. Pas. "Chinese Religion Rediscussed", p. 172.
31. A. Cohen. "Coercing the Rain Deities".
32. L. Thompson. "Yu-ying-kung".

33. I remember a mass grave erected by the local people near Kaohsiung: buried here were several scores of young working girls, drowned when their ferry sank near the Kaohsiung harbour. The grave was built to pacify their spirits and protect the community against retaliation.
34. See J.P. Pas, Editor. *The Turning of the Tide*. Hong Kong; Royal Asiatic Society & Hong Kong University Press, 1989.

Bibliography

Baity, Philip C. "The Genesis of Gods in Taiwanese Folk Religion: A Preliminary Analysis", *Proceedings of the American Academy of Religion*, 1974, pp. 33-47.

Baity, Philip C. *Religion in a Chinese Town*. Taipei, 1975.

Baity, Philip C. "The Ranking of Gods in Chinese Folk Religion", *Asian Folklore Studies* 36 (1977), 75-84.

Bredon, Juliet and Igor Mitrophanow. *The Moon Year. A Record of Chinese Customs and Festivals*. New York: Paragon Book Reprint Corp., 1966 (1st Edition: Shanghai, 1927).

Burckhardt, V.R. *Chinese Creeds and Customs* (3 Vols.). Hong Kong: South China Morning Post Ltd., 1953-58, Taipei Reprint: 1969.

Chamberlain, Jonathan. *Chinese Gods*. Hong Kong: Long Island Publishers, 1983.

Cohen, Alvin. "Coercing the Rain Deities in Ancient China", *History of Religions* 17 (1978), 244-265.

Day, Clarence B. *Chinese Peasant Cults, Being a Study of Chinese Paper Gods*. Shanghai: Kelly & Walsh Ltd., 1940. Reprint: Taipei: Ch'eng Wen Publishing Co., 1969.

Doré, Henri. *Researches into Chinese Superstitions* (Vol. 6). Taipei Reprint, 1966.

Duara, Prasenjit. "Superscribing Symbols: The Myth of Guandi, Chinese God of War". *JAS* 47 (1988), 778-795.

Eberhard, Wolfram. Tr. & Ed. *Folktales of China*. Chicago: University of Chicago Press, 1965 (1st Edition: London: Kegan Paul, 1937).

Goodrich, Anne Swann. *The Peking Temple of the Eastern Peak*. Nagoya (Japan): Monumenta Serica, 1964.

Graham, D.C. *Folk Religion in Southwest China*. Washington D.C., 1961.

Grube, Wilhelm. Tr. *Feng-shen-yen-i, Die Metamorphosen der Götter*, (Ch. 1-46, & Summary of Ch. 47-100 by Herbert Mueller), 2 vols. Taipei: Ch'eng Wen Co. Reprint, 1970.

de Harlez, Charles. *Le Livre des Esprits et des Immortels. Essai de Mythologie Chinoise* (Mémoires de l'Académie Royale des Sciences, des Lettres et des Beaux-Arts de Belgique, Tome 51). Brussels, 1893.

Harrell, Steven. "When a Ghost Becomes a God", pp. 193-206 in A.P. Wolf, Ed., *Religion and Ritual in Chinese Society*. Stanford University Press, 1974.

Hodous, Lewis. *Folkways in China*. London: A. Probsthain, 1929.

Jan Yün-hua. "The Change of Images: The Yellow Emperor in Ancient Chinese Literature". *JOS* 19 (1981), 117-137.

Lin, Yutang. *The Gay Genius. The Life and Times of Su Tungpo*. New York: The John Day Co., 1947.

Maspero, Henri. "The Mythology of Ancient China", pp. 252-384 in J. Hackin, *et al, Asiatic Mythology*. New York: T.Y. Crowell Co., n.d.; Reprinted in 1963.

Ou-I-Tai. "Chinese Mythology", pp. 379-402 in *New Larousse Encyclopaedia of Mythology*. London, 1968 (1st Edition, 1959).

Pas, J.F. "Chinese Religion Rediscussed" (Review Article of Baity. *Religion in a Chinese Town*. Taipei, 1975). *JRAS*, Hong Kong Branch, 19 (1979), 149-175.

Robinet, Isabelle. *Méditation Taoiste*. Collection "Mystiques et Religions". Paris: Dervy Livres, 1979.

Saso, Michael. *The Teachings of Taoist Master Chuang*. New Haven: Yale University Press, 1978.

Teiser, Stephen F. *The Ghost Festival in Medieval China*. Princeton: Princeton University Press, 1988.

Thompson, Laurence G. *Chinese Religion: An Introduction*. Encino & Belmont, California: Dickenson Publishing Co., 1978 (4th Edition) (1st Edition: 1969, 2nd Edition: 1975).

Thompson, Laurence G. *Chinese Religion in Western Languages: A Comprehensive and Classified Bibliography of Publications in English, French and German Through 1980*. Tucson, Arizona: University of Arizona Press, 1985 (published for the Association for Asian Studies).

Thompson, L. "Yu-ying-kung: The Cult of Bereaved Spirits in Taiwan". pp. 267-277 in L. Thompson, ed. *Studia Asiatica. Essays in Felicitation of Professor Ch'en Shou-yi*. San Francisco, 1975.

Welch, Holmes. *Taoism: The Parting of the Way*. Boston: Beacon Press, 1957 & 1966.

Yang, C.K. *Religion in Chinese Society*. Berkeley & Los Angeles: University of California Press, 1961.

Chinese Sources

Ch'i, Te-tsai. *Taiwan miao-shen chuan* (*TMSC*) ["Biographies and Legends of Spirits (Worshipped) in Taiwan Temples"]. Toulin, Yünlin County (Taiwan): Hsin-t'ung Bookstore, 1979.

Chui Yün-yen. *Taiwan min-chien hsin-yang chu-shen chuan*. [Biographies of the Deities of Taiwan Folk Religion], Taipei, 1984.

Fang, P'ing-shan. *Chung-kuo shen-ming kai-lun* (*SMKL*) ["Introduction to the Deities of China"]. Taipei: Hsin wen feng Publishing Co., 1979.

Ling, Heng-tao. "Taiwan min-chien hsin-yang te shen-ming" ["Deities of Taiwan Folk Belief"], pp. 67-89. In: *Taiwan min-su lun-chi* (*TMSL*) ["Essays on Popular Customs of Taiwan"]. Taiwan-sheng wen-hsien, 1977.

Lin, Heng-tao. *Taiwan Szu-miao Ta-ch'üan* (*TSM*) ["Complete List of Taiwan Temples"], Taipei, 1974.

Liu Chih-wan. "The Temple of the Gods of Epidemics in Taiwan". *Bulletin of the Institute of Ethnology* (Academia Sinica, Taipei), No. 22, 1966, pp. 53-95. (Chinese, with English summary, pp. 93-95.

Lü Dzongli and Liu Qun. *Zhongguo minjian zhushen* (*ZMZ*) ["The Popular Deities of China"]. Shijiazhuang (China): People's Press, 1987.

List of Characters

Chang T'ien-shih 張天師
chen-chieh-ma 貞節媽
chen-chün 真君
Chen-wu Ta-ti 真武大帝
Ch'eng-huang 城隍
Chi-kung 濟公
chiang-chün 將軍
chiang-chün wang 將軍王
chiang-yeh 將爺
chiao-chu 教主
chieh 姐
ch'ien-sui 千歲
Chou (dynasty) 周
chu 主
chu-shen 主神
chün 君
ch'uan-chi shen-ming 傳奇神明
en-chu 恩主
en-wang 恩王
erh-kui 餓鬼
fei 妃
Fo 佛
Fo-men sheng-chün 佛門聖君
Fo-shen 佛神
Fo-tsu 佛祖
fu 夫
Fu-hsi 伏羲
fu-jen 夫人
hao hsiung-ti 好兄弟
ho-shang 和尚
hou 侯
hou-kung 侯公
Hou-t'u 后土
Hsi-wang mu 西王母
hsiang-t'u shen-shih 鄉土神祇
hsiao-niang 小娘
hsiao-shen 小神
hsieh-shen 邪神
hsien-ku 仙姑
hsien-sheng 先生
hsien-shih 先師, 仙師
hsien-tsu 仙祖
hsing-chün 星君
hsüan-nü 玄女

Hsüan-t'ien Ta-ti 玄天大帝
Huang-Lao 黃老
Huang-t'ien 皇天
Huang-t'ien Hou-t'u 皇天后土
Huang-ti 黃帝
i-min-yeh 義民爺
jen-ching shen-ming 人境神明
ku-hun 孤魂
K'ung-tzu 孔子
ku-Fo 古佛
Kuan-kung 關公
Kuan-sheng Ti-chün 關聖帝君
Kuan-shih-yin 觀世音
Kuan-ti 關帝
Kuan-yin 觀音
kui 鬼
kui-shen 鬼神
kung 公
kung-chu 公主
kung-tsu 公祖
kung-yeh 公爺
lang-chün 郎君
lao-mu 老母
lao-tsu 老祖
ling 靈
Ling-pao T'ien-tsun 靈寶天尊
lohan 羅漢
Lu-pan 魯班
lung-wang 龍王
ma 媽
Ma-tsu 媽祖
Mi-lo-Fo 彌勒佛
ming-shih 明師
ming-wang 明王
mo (mo-kui) 魔鬼
mu 母
niang 娘
niang-niang 娘娘
nü-hun 女魂
Nü-kua 女禍
P'an-ku 盤古
pai-hsing-kung 百姓公
Pao-kung 包公
Pao-sheng Ta-ti 保生大帝

Pei-chi Ta-ti 北極大帝
P'ei-ou shen 陪偶神
P'eng-tsu 彭祖
po 伯
P'u-hsien 普賢
p'u-sa 菩薩
San-ch'ing 三清
san-chiao 三教
san-fu 三福
San-kuan 三官
Shang (dynasty) 商
Shang-ti 上帝
Shang-ti Kung 上帝公
shen 神
shen-ming 神明
Shen-nung 神農
shen-yeh 神爺
sheng 聖
sheng-che ying-lieh 聖哲英烈
sheng-hou 聖侯
sheng-hsien 聖賢
Sheng-ti 聖帝
sheng-wang 聖王
shih 師
shih yeh 師爺
shih-yeh 使爺
shui-kui 水鬼
Shun 舜
Szu-ming 司命
ta-chiang-chün 大將軍
ta-chung yeh 大衆爺
ta-chung-ma 大衆媽
ta-hsien 大仙
Ta-mo 達摩
ta-sheng 大聖
ta-shih 大使
Ta-ti 大帝
ta-wang 大王
ta-wang-kung 大王公
T'ai-I 太一
tai-k'ao miao-shen 待考廟神
t'ai-shih 太師
t'ai-tzu 太子
Tao-te t'ien-tsun 道德天尊

Ti 帝

ti-chün 帝君

Ti-I 地一

Ti-tsang wang 地藏王

ti-yeh 帝爺

T'ien 天

T'ien Lao-yeh 天老爺

t'ien-chün 天君

T'ien-fei 天妃

T'ien-fu Ti-mu 天父地母

T'ien-I 天一

T'ien-kung 天公

t'ien-nü 天女

T'ien-shang Sheng-mu 天上聖母

T'ien-shen ti-shih 天神地祇

t'ien-shih 天師

T'ien-tsun 天尊

t'ien-wang 天王

Tou-mu 斗母

tsu 祖

tsu-shih 祖師

tsun-hou 尊侯

tsun-wang 尊王

T'u-ti (T'u-ti-kung) 土地公

t'ung-su hsin-yang 通俗信仰

t'ung-tzu 童子

Tung-wang kung 東王公

Tung-yüeh 東嶽

tzu-jan shu-wu 自然庶物

wang 王

wang-ma 王媽

wang-yeh 王爺

wen-kung 文公

Wen-shu 文殊

wu-lao 五老

wu-szu kui-li 無祀鬼厲

Yao 堯

yao-ching 妖精

yao-kuai 妖怪

yeh 爺

Yen-lo wang 閻羅王

you-ying-kung 有應公

you-ying-ma 有應媽

Yü 禹

Yü-huang Ta-ti 玉皇大帝

yüan-shih shen-ming 原始神明

Yüan-shih T'ien-tsun 元始天尊

yüan-shuai 元帥

The Strange Case of the Overdue Book: A Study in the Fortuity of Textual Transmission

Harold D. Roth
Brown University

Introduction

It is all too infrequently that present-day scholars take the time to reflect upon how the texts we analyze and interpret from times long past have traversed the centuries to arrive on our bookshelves. When one takes into account the many generations of human beings who have participated in the transmission of any given ancient text, the vagaries of their lives, the many different social and political upheavals and their impact on the libraries of individuals and governments, it is rather amazing that we possess as many ancient texts as we do. It is not often that we can study in detail the fortuitous series of events associated with the transmission of a particular text because the requisite historical information has simply not survived. Fortunately, this is not the case with one important edition of the Han Dynasty Taoist compendium, the *Huai-nan Tzu.*

In the following article I would like to trace the circuitous route by which the sole extant witness to this edition has reached the twentieth century. Although it may seem rather astonishing, it is perhaps not all that unusual to find that the reason this witness has survived is because one of the greatest textual critics of the Ch'ing Dynasty took his time in returning a borrowed book. In studying the history of this particular edition we will also be able to examine the impact its transmission has had on the quality of its readings, and hence on our ability to understand the text itself. For it is most certainly the case that textual transmission involves textual transformation.[1]

The Northern Sung Edition

The oldest extant complete edition of the *Huai-nan Tzu* is the one known as the "Northern Sung small-character edition," which is available today in the facsimile found in the *Ssu-pu ts'ung-k'an*. As is true of the other eighty-four extant complete editions of this text, it is in the lineage of the composite recension, which is a conflation of thirteen chapters from the original Kao Yu (ca. 160-220) text and commentary, and eight chapters from the original Hsü Shen (58-148) text and commentary.[2] This particular edition preserves evidence of its conflated ancestry: despite bearing the title of the independent Kao Yu recension, *Huai-nan hung-lieh chieh*, and containing Kao's Preface, the title pages of two chapters, 10 and 21, bear the title of the independent Hsü Shen recension, *Huai-nan hung-lieh chien-ku*.

The consistent use of taboo characters throughout the edition from the reign of the Sung Dynasty Emperor Jen-tsung (1023-64) allows us to approximate the date of publication as 1050. The reported presence of one taboo character from the reign of the Southern Sung Emperor Hsiao-tsung (1163-90) on the first page of Chapter 18 does not challenge this conclusion, but rather indicates that this page was probably repaired at the later time.[3] The ancestry of this particular edition remains shrouded in mystery. All that can be safely said is that it comes from a distinctly different lineage of editions than the fragment of the T'ang Dynasty manuscript found in Japan in the 1930's, and seems to represent a later stage in the transmission of the text.[4]

In an era when collectors passionately searched for rapidly disappearing Sung editions, this edition of the *Huai-nan Tzu* was avidly sought after and lavishly praised by those few who were able to examine it. The famous bibliophile Huang P'ei-lieh (1763-1825) wrote of it:

> Recently the Hanlin Junior Compiler Wang Po-shen (Yin-chih) of Kao Yu edited this book (the *Huai-nan Tzu*) and wrote to me saying, 'I have made an exhaustive search (for editions) and could find none better than the Liu Chi edition.' The Liu Chi re-edition of the Taoist Canon edition is inferior to this Sung block-print edition by a distance that cannot be measured. How much more is this so of its superiority over the other editions?[5]

A later owner, Yang I-tseng (1787-1856), called it "the most refined and rare of all editions", and the scholar Ch'en Huan (1786-1863) said it was "the most excellent edition of the *Huai-nan Tzu*."[6]

Despite these highly favourable assessments of the Northern Sung edition, modern scholars have found much to criticize in it, as I will examine below in the final section. The reason for this discrepancy of opinion can be found in the complex history of this edition during the past two centuries, which to this point has not been fully investigated.[7] In order to unravel this history it is necessary to distinguish between the original exemplar owned by Huang P'ei-lieh, and the various copies that were made of this exemplar during the nineteenth century. It is also important to remember that the extant *Ssu-pu ts'ung-k'an* facsimile is based on one of the copies, not on the original exemplar.

Transmission of the Original Exemplar

The original exemplar of the Northern Sung edition was for the most part unknown to the community of scholars and collectors until it was acquired by the famous bibliophile Huang P'ei-lieh[8] from his friend, the Yangchow book-merchant T'ao Wen-hui, (*tzu*: Wu-liu).[9] It was previously included in the collection of the Textile Commissioner of Nanking, Ts'ao Yin (1658-1712) whose family belonged to a company of bond servants of the Manchu Plain White Banner.[10] Due to his great wealth and high official position Ts'ao was able to develop an extensive collection of rare books. The catalogue of this collection, the *Lien-t'ing shu-mu* contains a listing for an edition of the *Huai-nan Tzu* in 12 volumes, contained in one case.[11] These are the same numbers possessed by the exemplar of Huang P'ei-lieh, and so there is no doubt that the one listed in Ts'ao's catalogue is the same as that purchased a century later by Huang.[12] Ts'ao did not realize the value of his possession since he only lists it as an "old edition".

The evidence for the transmission of this exemplar before Ts'ao acquired it is somewhat sparse and has been overlooked by previous scholarship. It consists of a note on the seals imprinted in the original exemplar written by a collector who owned it after Huang, Yang Shao-ho (1828-75).[13] Listing the seals in the order in which they were imprinted, Yang mentions the two seals that precede those of Ts'ao Yin and his family. These seals read "Wang-shih Yen-chao" and "Wang-shih chia," respectively.[14]

An extensive search of bibliographical sources from the Sung through the Ch'ing reveals no men with the surname of "Wang" and personal name "Yen-chao". However there are two men named "Wang" whose courtesy name is "Yen-chao".

The first of these is Wang Han-chih (1054-1123) a native of Ch'ang-shan (in Chekiang Province) who later moved to Tan-t'u, a city in Kiangsu Province near Yanchow.[15] Han-chih, a *chin-shih* of 1073, had a long and successful official career, rising to the post of Vice-Minister of the Ministry of Works. His biographies note that his petition in response to an Imperial proclamation to local officials requesting suggestions on planning the finances for the construction and maintenance of roads was adopted. This had a particularly salutory effect on his official career, moving him from a prefectural posting into the central government administration. No mention is made of any particular literary or philosophical interests. His official career is rather busy and does not suggest that he had the leisure time to build a collection of books.

The second possible owner is Wang K'o-ming (1112-78), a native of the Lo-p'ing district of Jao-chou, Kiangsi Province, who in later life settled in the Wu-ch'eng district of Hu-chou, Chekiang Province.[16] K'o-ming was from an official's family, and is said to have drawn great satisfaction from literary studies. Because he was born with an ailment affecting his spleen and stomach that worsened as he got older, he delved deeply into medical studies. As a result he not only cured his affliction but became a physician as well. His fame spread quickly when he succeeded in controlling an epidemic in the army of Chang Tzu-kai, enabling them to decisively defeat the Chin at Hai-chou. In his official career he rose to a position in the Medical Institute of the Imperial Household.

While there is no totally justifiable reason to prefer one of these men as the earliest known owner of the Northern Sung exemplar, the biographical evidence is somewhat suggestive. Assuming the families of both men continued to live in their home districts, both districts are reasonably close to Nanking and Yangchow, where Ts'ao Yin collected his library. There is nothing in the biographies of Wang Han-chih to suggest that he had either the time or the interest to acquire an exemplar of the *Huai-nan Tzu*. However Wang K'o-ming's interest in literature and medicine, and the fact that *Huai-nan Tzu* is part of the philosophical milieu from which the underlying philosophy of Chinese medicine emerged, makes him the more likely of the two.[17] Furthermore, the evidence that the title page of chapter 18 in the original exemplar contains the taboo character *shen* from the reign of Hsiao-tsung (1163-89) means that it was replaced at this time.[18] Replacement of damaged pages is an activity that often arises from either the sale or acquisition of a book. If this is so, then K'o-ming must have been the owner because only he was alive at this time.

Further evidence to corroborate this conclusion is found in the Mao I-kuei edition of the *Huai-nan Tzu* (1580). Mao's co-editor, Wen Po, was a native of the same district of Wu-ch'eng to which Wang K'o-ming retired. There is also a distinct possibility that one of the editions used by these men was a twenty-one chapter Sung edition.[19] Perhaps Wen Po borrowed this exemplar from the descendants of Wang K'o-ming, or perhaps he bought it but did not place his seal on it. Whatever the case, it must have remained in the Wang family for at least four—if not five—centuries, until it was acquired by Ts 'ao Yin.

After its acquisition by Ts'ao there is little evidence that the Northern Sung exemplar circulated among any of the burgeoning new group of scholars who, during the eighteenth century, were turning their attention to the critical study and reconstruction of Han texts and commentaries.[20] During the entire eighteenth century there is only one scholar who made use of the Northern Sung edition. The scholar is Shen Ta-ch'eng (1700-71), who used it to collate a Ming edition, probably the Mao I-kuei.[21] Because Ts'ao's collection was probably kept in Yangchow, it is likely Shen made use of it at the time that he and his senior, the famous Han Learning scholar Hui Tung (1697-1758), were employed by the Salt Commissioner of Yangchow (1754-57).[22] The fact that Hui Tung's collation notes were recorded in Shen's hand-collated exemplar supports this.

Following Ts'ao Yin's death the family fortunes declined and never again achieved the heights set by Yin himself. Ts'ao's collection was passed on within his family during the eighteenth century. Part of it was sold to a nephew, a certain Ch'ang-ling (*chin-shih*, 1723).[23] During the Chia-ch'ing period (1796-1821) Ch'ang sold off part of the collection to Huang P'ei-lieh. The exemplar of the Northern Sung edition was probably included in Huang's purchase.

The precise date of Huang's acquisition of this exemplar cannot be ascertained. However we can make a reasonable approximation from the testimony of two sources.

The first is a colophon by Huang, dated November 5-6, 1801 and attached to a manuscript exemplar of a 28 *chüan Huai-nan Tzu* edition once owned by the famous art critic Chang Ch'ou (1577-1643).[24] In this Huang tells of his desire to collate this exemplar with the Sung printed edition. Therefore he must have owned the Sung edition by 1801.

The second source is from a collection of bibliographical notes culled from the diary of Niu Shu-yü (1760-1827) entitled *Fei-shih jih-chi ch'ao*.[25] In an entry for the date July 4, 1796, Niu tells of a visit to the house of his friend Huang during which he viewed a number of rare editions. Included among these was a Sung edition of the *Huai-nan Tzu*.

Therefore, based on these two sources, 1796 is the terminal date for Huang's acquisition of the Northern Sung exemplar.[26]

This original exemplar remained within the collection of Huang for more than twenty years. A note dated May 1816 was written when Huang had just finished using it to collate his 28 *chüan Huai-nan Tzu* edition.[27] This is the last known date for Huang's possession of the exemplar. His eyesight was failing; his fortunes were declining; and he was finally forced to sell off a large section of his library to his fellow townsman Wang Shih-chung. By 1820 the original exemplar had passed into the collection of Wang, which was called the I-yün-ching she.[28]

In 1848 Yang I-tseng (1787-1856), a native of Liao-ch'eng in Shantung was appointed Director General of the Southern portion of the Grand Canal.[29] During the subsequent four years Yang purchased a major portion of the collection of Wang Shih-chung. Using the official boats of the Grain Transport he shipped these books north to his library in Shantung, the Hai-yüan ko. Yang remained at his post and organized the defense of the Canal against the Taiping rebels. He died in office in 1856. Among the works he thus saved from destruction was the original exemplar of the Northern Sung *Huai-nan Tzu* edition.

Yang's library became one of the two principal collections of the latter half of the nineteenth century.[30] It passed on to his son Yang Shao-ho (1818-75)[31] who between 1864 and 1869 wrote a catalogue of the entire collection, with special notes on the Sung and Yüan editions. Published in 1871, this catalogue, the *Ying-shu yü-lu* is a valuable source of information on the transmission of the Northern Sung edition.[32]

On the death of Yang Shao-ho the collection passed to his son Yang Pao-i (1854-1910). Being without an heir and fearful of the fate of his great collection, Pao-i wrote a new catalogue, took a handful of the most valuable editions with him to Tientsin, and turned the remainder over to the Shangtung Provincial Government. Though the government retained control, the collection was kept in the Hai-yüan ko.[33] In 1929-30 the army of the warlord Wang Chin-fa occupied Liao-ch'eng and centered its headquarters in this library. Most of the works contained therein were either stolen or destroyed. By some unknown path, the Northern Sung exemplar found its way into the Dairen Library of the Research Department of the Japanese South Manchurian Railway Company.[34]

Diagram 1

THE TRANSMISSION OF THE EXEMPLAR
OF THE NORTHERN SUNG EDITION

Owner		*Date*
Original printing		c.1050
Wang K'o-ming and descendants		c.1160-1695
Ts'ao Yin and descendants		1695-1796
Huang P'ei-lieh		1796-c.1819
Wang Shih-chung		1819-c.1850
Yang I-tseng Yang Shao-ho Yang Pao-i	Hai-yüan ko Library	1850-1911
Hai-yüan ko as administered by the Shantung Provincial Governemnt		1911-1929
Hai-yüan ko occupied by the army of Warlord Wang Chin-fa		1929-1930
Library of the Southern Manchurian Railroad Company, Dairen		c.1930-1945
Russia		1945-present

This was the official scholarly arm of the government of the Japanese occupation state of Manchukuo. At the close of World War II, the library was occupied by the invading Russian Army and its valuable editions, probably including the Northern Sung exemplar, were removed to Russia.[35] The original exemplar of the Northern Sung *Huai-nan Tzu* has not to this point reemerged. It has, for all intents and purposes, been lost. Were it not for the copies made during the nineteenth century, we would no longer have testimony to this valuable edition.

The Copies of the Original Exemplar

The facsimile of the Northern Sung edition published in the *Ssu-pu ts'ung-k'an* owes its existence to historical accident. Were it not for an instance of irresponsible book borrowing, all witnesses to this edition would be lost. The story of its origins begins with Huang P'ei-lieh's acquisition of the original exemplar in 1796. At this time Ku Kuang-ch'i (1776-1835), a brilliant but impoverished scholar who throughout his life earned his living by working in the collections of others, was employed by Huang.[36] Also at this time the most renowned textual scholar of the Ch'ing Dynasty, Wang Nien-sun (1744-1832) and his eldest son Yin-chih (1766-1834), a superb scholar in his own right, were just completing a major work, the *Kuang-ya shu-cheng*, and beginning another, *Tu-shu tsa-chih.*[37] One of the philosophical texts that the two Wangs were emending in this latter work was the *Huai-nan Tzu.*

The fame of Huang's collection did not escape the notice of the two Wangs, who were working some 800 miles away in Peking. In 1796 they had borrowed a Sung edition of the *Kuang-ya* from Huang while completing their study of this text.[38] Sometime between then and 1801, Wang Yin-chih sent a letter to Huang soliciting his assistance in locating rare editions of the *Huai-nan Tzu*.[39] Apparently Huang never replied.

Later, in 1801, when Huang was in Peking, Yin-chih, having failed to get a response to his letter, urged Huang instead to collate his *Huai-nan Tzu* editions and share the results.[40] This prompted Huang to begin work collating his 28 *chüan* manuscript edition with his Northern Sung exemplar. However, as Huang later wrote, various other projects intervened and prevented him from completing this work until 1816. In the end Huang never allowed anyone else to work with his rare Sung *Huai-nan Tzu*. This is certainly unfortunate because it no doubt hindered the research of the two Wangs. However it seems that Huang did have some justification for refusing their request for help.

To begin with, we know that Huang possessed no *fu-pen*, or duplicate working copy, of his Northern Sung *Huai-nan Tzu*.[41] Understandably he was reluctant to permit the original exemplar to be sent over 800 miles away to Peking or to even be used extensively on his own premises for fear of losing or damaging it. Furthermore we also know that Huang had reason to distrust the reliability of Wang Yin-chih as a borrower of books.

It seems that in 1796 when the two Wangs borrowed Huang's rare exemplar of an edition of the *Kuang-ya*, they borrowed it through an intermediary named Sung Ting-chih. Later when their work was published, Huang suspected that it derived primarily from his exemplar, which after five years had still not been returned to him. Apparently one purpose of his visit to Peking in 1801 was to recover his missing book. However Wang Yin-chih did not have it. He claimed to have given it to Sung Ting-chih to return to Huang. It wasn't until over a year after this incident that Huang was able to track down Sung Ting-chih and get back his exemplar.[42] Thus it is easy to understand why Wang Yin-chih didn't press his request to borrow *Huai-nan Tzu* editions from Huang when he saw him in Peking in 1801.

It is undoubtedly due to this incident of the overdue book that today we possess the *Ssu-pu ts'ung-k'an* copy of the original exemplar. The two Wangs, unable to obtain the Northern Sung exemplar from Huang, completed the *Huai-nan Tzu* section of *Tu-shu tsa-chih* without it in 1816.[43] But they still cherished the hope of one day being able to examine it. In the meantime Huang P'ei-lieh was forced by mounting debts to sell off parts of his great collection to his fellow townsman Wang Shih-chung. The original exemplar of the Northern Sung *Huai-nan Tzu* was sold between 1817 and 1819.

In 1819, Wang Yin-chih sent a copy of the *Huai-nan Tzu* section of *Tu-shu tsa-chih* to Ku Kuang-ch'i, requesting the latter's comments and hoping that Ku could provide him notes on the superior readings of the Northern Sung edition.[44] At the time Ku possessed a hand-collated exemplar of the Chuang K'uei-chi *Huai-nan Tzu* edition of 1788 on which he recorded all textual variants from the Taoist Canon edition of 1445, which he borrowed from the collection of Yüan T'ing-t'ao in 1794. Ku added to this hand-collated exemplar reference marks to *Tu-shu tsa-chih*.[45] In August 1820, Ku was able to borrow the original Northern Sung exemplar from Wang Shih-chung and he used it to once again collate his Chuang exemplar.[46] In the process, as a favour to Wang Shih-chung, he reconstructed five missing pages, inserted them in their proper place (see Plate II), repaired out of order sections, and also wrote a colophon that was inserted in the Northern Sung exemplar in which he presented fifty-two examples of its superior readings.[47] In this colophon Ku expressed his admiration for the superb work of Wang Nien-sun, whose emendations are quite often in complete agreement with readings in the Northern Sung exemplar. Furthermore he clearly stated his intention to make a copy of this exemplar and send it to Wang Nien-sun in Peking.[48] While there is evidence that he did make such a copy, he never sent it. As we shall see, he ended up selling it to a man named Hu Yü-t'ang. Instead, Ku sent his collation notes on the superior readings in the Northern Sung exemplar to Wang Yin-chih, who rearranged these and added them as a supplement to the *Huai-nan Tzu* section of *Tu-shu tsa-chih* the following year.[49]

Probably due in no small part to Ku's laudatory comments, Wang Nien-sun finally obtained the permission of Wang Shih-chung to make a copy of the original exemplar. Wang gave the responsibility for this task to his best student, Ch'en Huan, who, like Wang Shih-chung, was a native of Ch'ang-chou in Kiangsu.[50] Ch'en then asked Chin Yu-mei to make a traced facsimile, and he stored it in his own collection, the San-pai shu-she, presumably to do further research on it before sending it to Wang in Peking. He discusses this in an 1824 preface that was attached to his facsimile copy:[51]

> This Northern Sung edition was formerly stored in the Pai-Sung i-ch'an collection of Huang Jao-p'u (P'ei-lieh). Later it went to the collection of Wang Liang-yüan (Shih-chung) of the same city (i.e., Ch'ang-chou). Mr. Wang Huai-tsu (Nien-sun) of Kao-yu entrusted me with the task of borrowing and copying it and sending it to him in Peking. Then I asked Mr. Chin Yu-mei to make a traced facsimile, and I stored it in the San-pai shu-she. The exemplar from which Ku Chien-p'in (Kuang-ch'i) made a traced facsimile copy, and increased its value to 40 silver dollars, is this one. April 1824, written by Ch'en Huan.[52]

Ironically, ten years later it was to this highly-valued facsimile made by Ku Kuang-ch'i that Ch'en had to turn in order to finally complete his textual research on the *Huai-nan Tzu*. He borrowed it from its purchaser, Hu Yü-t'ang to emend the illegible characters in his own facsimile.

> The Northern Sung edition of the *Huai-nan Tzu* in 21 *chüan* is the most rare edition. Formerly it was stored in the Shih-li-chü collection of Huang Chu-cheng (P'ei-lieh) of Soochow. Later it went to Mr. Wang (Shih-chung) of Shang-t'ang. Minister Wang (Nien-sun) had it borrowed and copied, and asked me to collate it. Many of the characters were indecipherable (due to damage). Collation and comparison were rather difficult. I did not get along with Mr. Wang (Shih-chung). Thus I was unable to inspect and copy his books. This was a constant regret for me.

> Ku P'in-weng (Kuang-ch'i) once had a traced facsimile, which he praised as being of high quality. Mr. Hu Yü-t'ang purchased it for 40 silver dollars. It was exactly like the original exemplar that was stored in the Shih-li-chü (of Huang P'ie-lieh). Now I have borrowed this facsimile from Yü-t'ang to use for collating. I once again see how valuable it is. Also, because Mr. Lan-lin (Ch'en Cheng-chih) wrote me with a request to do this, I am using it to collate his Chuang edition for him. ...April 1834.[53]

Thus Ch'en Huan was able to use the high-quality facsimile of Ku Kuang-ch'i to improve the readings in the copy that was made for him by Chin Yu-mei that contained many indecipherable characters. Unfortunately, the valuable facsimile of Ku Kuang-chi and Ch'en's facsimile have both failed to survive. However before Ch'en's copy was lost, Liu Lü-fen (*hao*: Mao-sheng) (1827-79) made his own traced facsimile of it. His brief colophon simply says:

> In 1871 I borrowed this book and the copying was begun. It continued until completion on March 12, 1872.
>
> Written by Liu Lü-fen of Chiang-shan at the Wu-men Publishing Company.[54]

Liu's copy later became part of the Han-fen lou in Shanghai, the library of the Commercial Press. It is now in the Peking Library. In 1920, a photolithographed facsimile copy was made by the Commercial Press and included in the first series of the *Ssu-pu ts'ung-k'an*. This *Ssu-pu ts'ung-k'an* edition was reproduced by I-wen Publishing Company in Taipei in 1974. Through these latter two editions the original Northern Sung exemplar of the *Huai-nan Tzu* is accessible today.

This research contains several new conclusions. Contrary to previous scholarship, Chin Yu-mei and Wang Nien-sun never owned their own facsimiles of the original exemplar.[55] Chin did, in 1824, make a copy for Ch'en Huan, but it remained with Ch'en and was never sent to Wang.[56] In 1834, Ch'en borrowed the superior traced facsimile of Ku Kuang-ch'i in which Ku had replaced the five pages missing from the original exemplar. He used this to improve the readings of his own facsimile. Evidence for this can be seen in the extant *Ssu-pu ts'ung-k'an* edition, which is copied from Liu Lü-fen's tracing of Ch'en's facsimile: there are five pages that have obviously been replaced (compare Plates I and II). Ch'en's facsimile is thus the result of the copying and editing work of three scholars: Chin Yu-mei, Ch'en, and Ku Kuang-ch'i.

The copies of Ku Kuang-ch'i and Ch'en Huan are no longer extant. The original exemplar is probably lost. The sole surviving witness to the Northern Sung *Huai-nan Tzu*, the *Ssu-pu ts'ung-k'an* edition, is a copy, twice-removed, of Ch'en Huan's facsimile. This edition owes its existence to the incident of the overdue book borrowed from Huang P'ei-lieh by Wang Yin-chih. If Wang had been a more responsible borrower it is likely Huang P'ei-lieh would have loaned him the original exemplar in 1801, thus making the later copying work of Chin Yu-mei, on which the *Ssu-pu ts'ung-k'an* edition is ultimately based, unnecessary.

Diagram 2

The Copies of the Original Exemplar

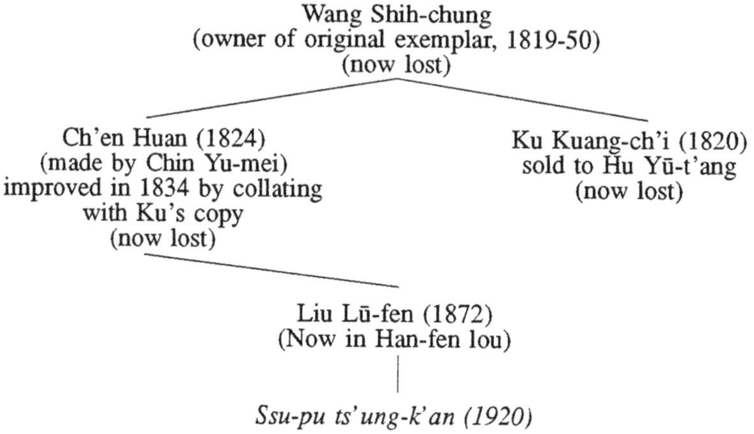

Finally there were four hand-collated exemplars that recorded readings from the Northern Sung edition. They were written by Shen Ta-ch'eng (1757), Huang P'ei-lieh (1816), Ku Kuang-ch'i (1820) and Ch'en Huan (1834). The latter two are still in existence.[57] Ku's hand collated exemplar is discussed in the following section. Ch'en Huan's is the one he completed at the request of Ch'en Cheng-chih, as mentioned in the April 1834 colophon quoted above on page ?.

Textual Errors in the Ssu-pu ts'ung-k'an *Edition*

As we have seen, the greatest textual scholar of his time, Wang Nien-sun, was never able to study the original exemplar of the Northern Sung *Huai-nan Tzu.* However we have the work of four men who did carefully examine it. As we have seen above, two men who actually owned the book, Huang P'ei-lieh and Yang I-tseng, and one scholar who owned a traced facsimile, Ch'en Huan, regarded it as the best edition of the *Huai-nan Tzu.* But of the four only Ku Kuang-ch'i provided textual evidence to support his claims of excellence. In the colophon he wrote in 1820, when he borrowed and repaired the original exemplar for Wang Shih-chung, he lists 52 examples of its superior readings. These have been included in the supplement to *Tu-shu tsa-chih.* In this colophon, Ku says:

> This is truly the best of the extant editions. For example.... From the above items one can see that this edition is far above the Taoist Canon edition to say nothing of the others. As for its commentary, the places where it can correct the mistakes in the other editions cannot be enumerated. Of these I don't even provide a description....[58]

This is high praise indeed, for in *Tu-shu tsa-chih,* Wang Nien-sun calls the Taoist Canon edition the best he was able to examine.[59]

However modern scholars are not as enthusiastic about the Northern Sung edition. Wu Tse-yü acknowledges the excellent readings, but also notices a considerable number of errors.[60] In their praise for this edition, he says, Ku and Yang are guilty of "seeing the gold and ignoring the sand" that is more pervasive. Yü Ta-ch'eng echoes this:

> In looking at this book, there are enough textual errors and common forms of characters to be critical of. To spread out sand and only pick out the gold, this resides in (the eye of) the reader.[61]

Both scholars mention its similarity to the Taoist Canon edition. Yü thinks this Taoist Canon edition either comes directly from the Northern Sung edition, or that both come from the same ancestor.

Wang Shu-min also notes the affinity between these two editions. However he does not share the others' pessimism about the overall quality of the Northern Sung:

> I have completed a detailed comparison of the facsimile copy of the Northern Sung edition in the *Ssu-pu ts'ung-k'an* and the Taoist Canon edition, and from this I understand that the Taoist Canon edition is based on the Northern Sung. From time to time there are excellent readings in the Northern Sung edition that the Taoist Canon does not have. Thus the Northern Sung is superior to the Taoist Canon. It is regrettable that within it there are rather many errors.[62]

Cheng Liang-shu concurs with his teacher Wang Shu-min. He cites several of Ku Kuang-ch'i's examples of superior readings in the Northern Sung edition, then adds more that Ku did not mention. He also praises the condition of the commentary and adds that Wu Ch'eng-shih, the only scholar to write a textualcriticism of the commentary, based some of his emendations on the *Ssu-pu ts'ung-k'an* edition. However, he also takes note of the many simple errors in this edition.[63]

While it is easy to understand how the collectors Huang and Yang would not care to write about the mistaken readings in their prized possession, it is not that easy to understand how a scholar as competent as Ku Kuang-ch'i could have ignored so striking a feature. I think that the disparity in the assessments by Ku and by the modern scholars can be attributed to the fact that Ku worked on the original exemplar, while today only a thrice-removed facsimile exists, the *Ssu-pu ts'ung-k'an* edition.

I have already noted the difficulty that Ch'en Huan had in using the Chin Yu-mei copy for collating purposes. Many of the characters were indecipherable. While it is true that Ch'en improved this copy by collating it with the superior facsimile of Ku Kuang-ch'i, it is also true that the original exemplar of the Northern Sung edition contained many damaged and indecipherable characters. This is noted by Huang P'ei-lieh in a colophon written upon completion of his project of collating the original exemplar with his 28 *chüan* manuscript edition:

> In the Sung block-print edition the characters are small. Also many are damaged. Moreover the printing is indecipherable in some places. Therefore collation was difficult....[64]

However the extant *Ssu-pu ts'ung-k'an* edition, which is based on a copy, twice removed, of the original exemplar, does not have this problem. At some point along the line of copying during the nineteenth century someone had to interpret and clarify these damaged and indecipherable characters. In the process, undoubtedly, some were interpreted erroneously. Therefore the modern copies contain more of these simple errors than did the original.

I do not mean to suggest that the original exemplar studied by Ku was entirely free of errors. One glance at Ku's hand-collated exemplar of the Chuang K'uei-chi edition (facsimile reprint, *CKTCH*), on which he indicated errors in the Northern Sung exemplar, shows this claim to be unfounded. I only mean to say that during the activities of the several men who made copies, the number of errors in the text increased, and thus became a much more striking feature than it was to Ku.

Perhaps a few examples of the kind of errors being discussed will help clarify this. In the collation I did of the *Ching-shen* chapter (no. 7), I found a comparatively high number of very simple copyist's errors. For example, at *Ssu-pu ts'ung-k'an*, 2bl, I found the compound 面氣 , clearly an error for 血氣 which occurs later on the page in its correct form. In the commentary at 2a10 五星 is mistakenly written as 吾工 , because the copyist mistook the top part of 星 for the bottom part of 吾 .

This kind of simple copyist's error occurs rather often. In the recently published mechanical facsimile of the copy of the Ku Kuang-ch'i hand-collated exemplar (see Plate III), all variants between the original Northern Sung exemplar and the Chuang K'uei-chi edition that is being collated are carefully written down. Some of the simple copyist's errors are recorded. Some are not. In the *Ching-shen* chapter, of the twenty variants between the *Ssu-pu ts'ung-k'an* and all other editions, seven are not noted by Ku. All are simple copyists' errors.

Ssu-pu ts'ung-k'an

1b10 坐 : error for 生
2a11 變 : error for 設
2b1 浮 : error for 乎
3b3 揔 : error for 總
4a3 上 : error for 土
6a4 君 : error for 居
8a5 神 : error for 伸

Furthermore there are lacunae totalling six graphs of text, two of commentary on p. 12b in the *Ssu-pu ts'ung-k'an* edition that are also noted by Ku. I can only conclude from this that any errors not written down by Ku must have entered the *Ssu-pu ts'ung-k'an* edition due to the activity of the copyists, Chin Yu-mei and Liu Lü-fen.[65]

Therefore the discrepancy of opinion between the Ch'ing and modern scholars about the overall quality of the Northern Sung edition is, to a considerable extent, the result of the fact that the sole surviving witness to this edition, the *Ssu-pu ts'ung-k'an* facsimile, is a thrice-removed copy into which textual errors that were not in the original exemplar were introduced by nineteenth-century copyists. The modern assessment of the value of the Northern Sung edition is thus not based on the edition itself. Those who wish to prepare a modern critical edition of the *Huai-nan Tzu* must check textual variants in the *Ssu-pu ts'ung-k'an* edition against those recorded in the Ku Kuang-ch'i hand-collated exemplar. Until this is done, scholars who use the *Ssu-pu ts'ung-k'an* edition should take note of this problem.

The story of the original exemplar and copies of the Northern Sung *Huai-nan Tzu* edition demonstrates the extent to which historical accident has played a significant role in textual transmission and the textual transformation which inevitably accompanies it. It reminds us one again that we cannot take for granted either the presence on our bookshelves or the testimony and reliability of any single edition of an ancient text, no matter how old that edition may be.

List of Abbreviations for the Notes

CKTHC *Chung-kuo tzu-hsüeh ming-chu chi-ch'eng* 中國子學名著集成. Taipei, 1977.

ECCP Arthur Hummel (ed.), *Eminent Chinese of the Ch'ing Period.* Washington, D.C.: United States Government Printing Office, 1943.

HFLSL *Han-fen-lou chin-yü shu-lu* 涵芬樓燼餘書錄. Peking, 1951.

HNT *Huai-nan Tzu* 淮南子.

HNTCL Cheng Liang-shu 鄭良樹, *Huai-nan Tzu chiao-li* 淮南子斠理 Taipei: Chia-hsin Cement Company Cultural Foundation, 1969.

HNTSL Wu Tse-yü 武則虞, "*Huai-nan Tzu shu-lu*" 淮南子書錄. *Wen-shih* 文史 2 (1963), 291-314.

HNWSK Yü Ta-ch'eng 于大成, "*Huai-nan Wang shu-k'ao* 淮南王書考." In Yü Ta-ch'eng, *Huai-nan lun-wen san-chung* 淮南論文三種. Taipei: Wen-shih-che ch'u-p'an-she 文史哲出版社, 1975, pp. 1-56.

JPTSTC Huang P'ei-lieh 黃丕烈, *Jao-p'u ts'ang-shu t'i-chih* 蕘圃藏書題識. Compiled by Miao Ch'üan-sun 繆荃孫, Chang Yü 章鈺, and Wu Ch'ang-shou 吳昌綬. Privately printed, 1919. Reprinted in SMTP.

LTMJTP Chiang Liang-fu 姜亮夫, *Li-tai ming-jen nien-li pei-chuan tsung-piao* 歷代名人年里碑傳綜表. Shanghai, 1937. Reprint: Taipei, 1976.

PSICL Huang P'ei-lieh, *Pai Sung i-ch'an lu* 百宋一廛錄. In Chang Chün-heng 張鈞衡, *Shih-yüan ts'ung-shu* 適園叢書. Privately printed, 1914.

SB Wolfgang Franke (ed.), *Sung Biographies*. Munich, 1976. 宋代名人錄

SJCSY *Sung-jen chuan-chi tzu-liao so-yin* 宋人傳記資料索引. Taipei, 1975.

SMTP Wang Tao-jung 王道榮 (compiler), *Shu-mu ts'ung-p'ien* 書目叢編. Taipei: Kuang-wen 廣文, 1967.

SPTK *Ssu-pu ts'ung-k'an* . Shanghai: Commercial Press, 1920.

TSTC Wang Nien-sun 王念孫 and Wang Yin-chih 王引之, *Tu-shu tsa-chih* 讀書雜誌. Privately printed between 1812 and 1832. Reprint of 1870 edition, Taipei: Shih-chieh, 1963.

YSYL Yang Shao-ho 楊紹和 (compiler), *Ying-shu yü-lu* 楹書隅錄. Privately printed, 1871. Reprinted by Yang Pao-i 楊保彝, 1895, and Tung K'ang 董康 in 1911. Reprint of 1911 edition in *SMTP*.

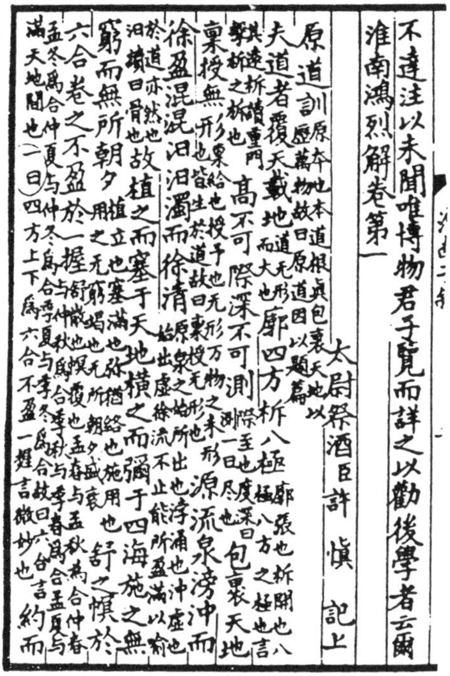

不達注以未聞唯博物君子覽而詳之以勸後學者云爾

淮南鴻烈解卷第一

太尉祭酒臣許慎記上

原道訓 原本也本道根真包裹天地以歷萬物故曰原道因以題篇

夫道者覆天載地 道无形而大也 廓四方柝八極 廓張也柝開也八極八方之極也言其遠也柝讀重門擊柝之柝也 高不可際深不可測 際至也度深曰測 包裹天地稟授無形 稟給也授予也无形万物之未形也皆生於道故曰稟授无形 源流泉浡沖而徐盈 原泉之始所出也浡涌也沖虛也始出虛徐流不止能漸盈滿以喻於道亦然也 混混汩汩濁而徐清 汩讀曰骨也 故植之而塞于天地橫之而彌于四海施之無窮而無所朝夕 植立也塞滿也彌猶絡也施用也无窮竭也无所朝夕盛衰也 舒之幎於六合卷之不盈於一握 孟春與孟秋為合仲春與仲秋為合季春與季秋為合孟夏與孟冬為合仲夏與仲冬為合季夏與季冬為合故曰六合一曰四方上下為六合不盈一握言微妙也 約而

Plate I: The Northern Sung Edition
Liu Lü-fen Traced Facsimile (1872).
Reproduced in the *Ssu-pu ts'ung-k'an*.
chapter 1, folio 2, verso.

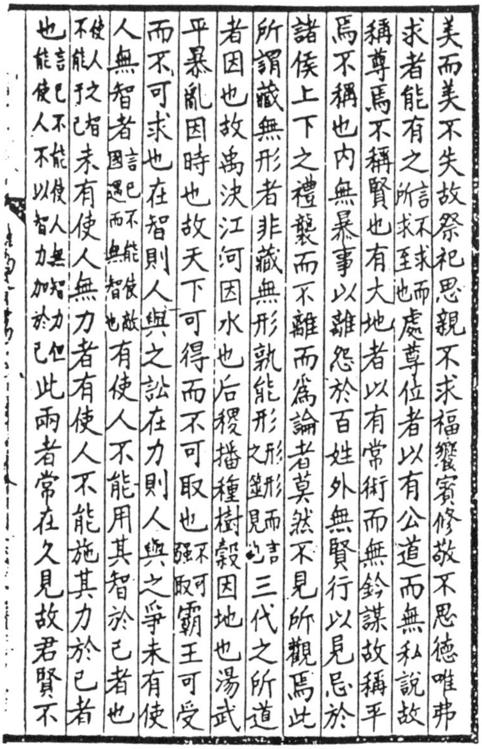

美而美不失故祭祀思親不求福饗賓修敬不思德唯弗求者能有之 言不求而所求至也 處尊位者以有公道而無私說故稱尊焉不稱賢也有大地者以有常術而無鈐謀故稱平焉不稱也內無暴事以離怨於百姓外無賢行以見忌於諸侯上下之禮襲而不離而為論者莫然不見所觀焉此所謂藏無形者非藏無形孰能形 形之形而言跡見也 三代之所道者因也故禹決江河因水也后稷播種樹穀因地也湯武平暴亂因時也故天下可得而不可取也 不可強取 霸王可受而不可求也在智則人與之訟在力則人與之爭未有使人無智者 言己不能使人無智也 有使人不能用其智於己者也未有使人無力者有使人不能施其力於己者也 言己不能使人無智力但能使人不以智力加於己 此兩者常在久見故君賢不

Plate II: The Northern Sung Ed. (SPTK). One of the five pages replaced by Ku Kuang-ch'i. ch. 14, folio 8, recto.

Plate III: The Ku Kuang-ch'i Hand-collated Exemplar (1820) Facsimile of Hsü Tsai-heng (1898). Reproduced in the *Chung-kuo tzu-hsüeh ming-chu chi-ch'eng* (1977). Kao Yu Preface, folio 1, recto.

Notes

1. I would like to define several important terms. A "text" is the unique complex of ideas created by an author. An "edition" is a distinct record of a text, whether it is a handwritten manuscript or it is printed. An "exemplar" is one particular impression of a printed edition or the actual manuscript of a handwritten edition. A "hand-collated exemplar" is an exemplar of a printed edition on which a scholar recorded his annotations, which frequently include both collations with other editions and textual emendations. A "facsimile" is either a traced or mechanically reproduced copy of an exemplar in which the format and arrangement of that exemplar is duplicated.
2. For details on these two commentaries and their merging, see my book, *The Textual History of the Huai-nan Tzu* (Ann Arbor: Association for Asian Studies [forthcoming]), Chapters 2 and 4.
3. The presence of the taboo character *shen* (written without a final stroke) was initially reported by the late Ch'ing bibliophile Yang Shao-ho in the catalogue of his family's collection, *YSYL*, p. 42b. He concludes from this that the page in question was added later. However in the *SPTK* edition this taboo is not observed. As we shall see this is far from the sole discrepancy between the original exemplar of the Northern Sung edition and the *SPTK* facsimile.
4. The T'ang manuscript fragment, which contains about one-half of Chapter 15, was found on the back of a silk scroll containing Heian court poetry. For a detailed analysis of its provenance and value, see Wang Shu-min, *Chu-tzu chiao-cheng* (Taipei: Shih-chieh, 1963), pp. 565-72. It is also discussed in Roth, *op. cit.*, Chapters 3 and 4.
5. Huang P'ei-lieh, *PSICL*, p. 27a.
6. Yang Shao-ho, *YSYL*, p. 41a; *HFLSL*, 3/40a.
7. A number of twentieth-century scholars have investigated certain aspects of the history of this edition, but their conclusions have been incomplete and sometimes inaccurate. Wu Tse-yü, *HNTSL*, pp. 295-6, and Cheng Liang-shu, *HNTCL*, p. 331, state that three scholars owned traced facsimiles, Chin Yu-mei, Wang Nien-sun, and Liu Lü-fen (*qqv.*). As we shall see, Chin and Wang never owned their own copies. They also accurately state that three scholars used the original exemplar for collation with other editions, Shen Ta-ch'eng, Ku Kuang-ch'i, and Ch'en Huan (qqv.), although Ch'en's involvement was considerably greater than this. Yü Ta-ch'eng, *HNWSK*, pp. 21-2, limits his discussion to Liu Lü-fen's copy and its provenance, and ignores the others. The brief discussion by LeBlanc is based on Yü and adds several factual errors, which I will correct below in the notes. See Charles LeBlanc, *Huai-nan Tzu: Philosophical Synthesis in Early Han Thought* (Hong Kong: Hong Kong University Press, 1985), pp. 62-3. Kuraishi Takeshiro, ("*Enanji* no Rekishi", *Shinagaku* 3 (1923): 348-51) presents a perceptive analysis, although my own conclusions differ somewhat from his.
8. *ECCP*, pp. 340-41. Huang was a native of Ch'ang-chou district in the city of Soochow, Kiangsu Province. He was a *chü-jen* of 1788, but failed the higher

exams and bought an official position. He finally retired from the civil service to a life of book collecting, beginning in 1789. He specialized in Sung editions and had a special library, the Pai-Sung i-ch'an, to house them. He himself wrote, or hired others to write, notes on his editions. Huang's notes are very highly respected and studied by collectors and students of bibliography.

9. See Huang's note in the collection of his notes *JPTSTC*, 5/19b.

10. *ECCP*, pp. 740-2. A complete and penetrating analysis of the bondservant and bannerman organizations as exemplified in the life of the family of Ts'ao Yin can be found in Jonathan Spence, *Ts'ao Yin and the K'ang-hsi Emperor: Bondservant and Master* (New Haven: Yale University Press, 1966).

The Plain White Banner was one of the top three divisions of the Manchu Army, each controlled by a Prince. Ts'ao Yin's great grandfather was captured by the Manchus when Shen-yang fell in 1621 and made a bondservant in this Banner. These bondservants and their descendants came to be the first and most trusted Chinese allies of the Manchu rulers, and as such were often favoured in the selection of officials.

Ts'ao Yin's grandfather held the very lucrative position of Salt Commissioner of Chekiang until his death in 1658, and so amassed a considerable fortune.

Ts'ao Yin's father, Ts'ao Hsi, was textile commissioner in Nanking, 1663-84. Ts'ao Yin himself held positions as textile commissioner in Soochow, 1690-92, Nanking, 1692-1712, and Salt Commissioner of Liang-huai in Yangchow. While in these positions, he was the trusted ally of the K'ang-hsi Emperor, performing various tasks, spying on officials, and actually hosting the Emperor on four visits to the South.

In Nanking Ts'ao hosted a group of scholars that included Chu I-tsun (1629-1709, *ECCP*, 182-4). He also established a printing house and published excellent editions of his rare books that are still highly valued. Ts'ao Yin most likely acquired the *HNT* around the turn of the eighteenth century.

The Dream of the Red Chamber was written by Yin's grandson about the lives of this family during its zenith of wealth and power under Ts'ao Yin.

11. The *Lien-t'ing shu-mu* is reprinted from the Ts'ao family manuscript in *Kuo-li Pei-p'ing t'u-shu-kuan kuan-k'an* (1931) vol. 4, no. 6, pp. 81-106; vol. 5, no. 1, pp. 77-102; vol. 5, no. 2, pp. 87-96; vol. 5, no. 3, pp. 91-110. The listing of the *HNT* is found at 5/1, p. 80.

12. Huang clearly states this in a collection of notes on his Sung editions first written in 1803, just after he moved them into the special library built to house them. See *PSICL*, p. 27a.

13. *YSYL* is the catalogue of this collection. It is discussed below in note 32.

14. *YSYL*, p. 41b.

15. For biographies of Han-chih, see *Sung-shih*, 347/5b, *SJCSY*, p. 237.

16. For biographies of K'o-ming see *Sung-shih*, 462/15a, *SJCSY*, p. 293, and *SB*, pp. 1114-5 (written by Manfred Porkert).

SB and *LTMJTP*, p. 277 give K'o-ming's dates as 1069-1135. *SJCSY* says 1112-78. However the general Chang Tzu-kai, whose army K'o-ming cured of the plague, was active between 1140 and 1170. (See *SJCSY*, p. 2342, *Sung-shih, chüan* 369). Thus the latter date must be correct.

The errors in *SB* and *LTMJTP* must be based on the mistake in K'o-ming's biography in the *Sung-shih*. There his death date is given as Shao-hsing 5 (1135), age 67, even though this very same biography says he was active during the Shao-hsing (1131-63) and Ch'ien-tao (1163-74) reign periods. The correct date of death should be Ch'un-hsi 5 (1178).

17. The first Chinese medical treatise, the *Huang-ti nei-ching ssu-wen* is a contemporary of the *HNT*. The two works share a basic philosophical stance and a series of interrelated technical terms. See especially *HNT*, Chapters 1, 2, 3, 7, 20. For further information on this topic see the brilliant pioneering study by Manfred Porkert, *The Theoretical Foundations of Chinese Medicine* (Cambridge: MIT Press, 1974), pp. 18, 20, 191.

18. See above, note 3.

19. Roth, *op. cit.*, Chapter 9.

20. Though not a part of this group of "Han Learning" scholars, the famous scholar and collector Ch'ien Tseng (1629-1701, *ECCP*, 156-8) owned a traced facsimile copy of a twenty-one *chüan* Sung block-print edition of the *HNT* that might have been copied from Ts'ao Yin's Northern Sung exemplar.

In the 1926 Ch'ang-shou edition of the catalogue of Ch'ien's library that was compiled and edited by Chang Yü (1865-1937) and entitled *Ch'ien Tsun-wang tu-shu min-ch'iu-chi chiao-cheng*, the note on this facsimile of a Sung block-print *HNT* is at *chüan* 3A, pp. 20b-21a.

According to *ECCP*, Ch'ien wrote the original catalogue between 1669 and 1684. It was first published in 1726. Chang Yü's edition is a compilation of several earlier editions that contains complete annotations by Chang and earlier editors on each entry. It is principally based on the edition of Kuan T'ing-fen (1797-1880).

Ch'ien Tseng was a good friend of another famous scholar and collector, Chu I-tsun (1629-1709, *ECCP* 182-4), who was in turn an associate of Ts'ao Yin. It is known that Ch'ien and Chu were strong advocates of the new practice of borrowing rare editions and making traced copies for one's own library. Both men hired calligraphers who were well-versed in this practice. Chu greatly improved his own collection by copying rare works from Ch'ien. Furthermore Ts'ao Yin also participated in this practice, borrowing and copying rare works from Chu's library.

Ch'ien's note does not indicate the source of his traced facsimile of the Sung printed *HNT*. However the fact that these men borrowed and copied each other's rare books makes it quite possible that the source of Ch'ien's facsimile was the Northern Sung exemplar of Ts'ao Yin. Unfortunately, without any further evidence we cannot definitely establish that the source of Ch'ien's facsimile was Ts'ao's exemplar. In fact, almost two hundred years ago, Huang P'ei-lieh thought of this possibility but found himself also unable to decide.

Ch'ien's facsimile was used to collate a twenty-eight *chüan HNT* that was later part of the collection of Yang I-tseng (see *YSYL* p. 44a). The note attached to this exemplar is dated May, 1782, but the author's name is lost. Ch'ien's facsimile was purchased by Sung Chih-shan (fl. ca.1820) from the famous Yangchow book merchant T'ao Wu-liu, the very man who sold the Northern Sung exemplar to Huang P'ei-lieh.

It was missing the first volume that contained *chüan* 1-4. In 1819 Kuan T'ing-fen located and purchased the missing volume, intending to give it to Sung. But the person with whom he sent it died en route and the volume was lost. The remainder of Ch'ien's facsimile is also no longer extant.

In addition to *ECCP*, information on the relationships between Ch'ien, Chu and Ts'ao can be found in the following works: Cheuk-Woon Taam, *The Development of Chinese Libraries 1644-1911* (Shanghai, 1935, rep., San Francisco: Chinese Materials Center, 1977), pp. 48-50, 60-61; Ch'en Teng-yüan, *Chung-kuo tien-chi shih* (Taipei, 1971), pp. 322-323, 394-396; and Chu Chia-hua, *Chung-kuo tsang-shu-chia k'ao-lüeh* (Hangchow, 1929), pp. 25a, 88a, 133b.

21. Wu Tse-yü, *HNTSL*, p. 301. The biography of Shen can be found in Ch'ien I-chi, *Kuo-ch'ao Pei-chuan-chi* (Privately printed, 1893), *chüan* 141.

22. *ECCP*, p. 357.

23. *ECCP*, p. 743.

24. L. C. Goodrich and C.Y. Fang (editors), *Dictionary of Ming Biography* (New York, 1976), p. 51.

25. *ECCP*, p. 593. Collected and printed by Yao Wei-tsu of Kuei-an in 1881.

26. Therefore LeBlanc's (p. 62) assertion that Huang obtained the Northern Sung edition in 1815 is incorrect.

27. Huang, *JPTSTC*, 5/20a.

28. *ECCP*, p. 341. *YSYL*, 3/41b contains a colophon by Ku Kuang-ch'i that was written on a separate sheet and included in the original exemplar of the Northern Sung edition. Dated September 1820, it states that Ku borrowed the exemplar from Wang Shih-chung.

29. *ECCP* pp. 888-89, and the introduction to *YSYL*.

30. The other was the library of Ch'ü Yung (fl. a. 1805-60), the T'ieh-ch'in t'ung chien lou, in Ch'ang-shu district, Kiangsu province (*ECCP*, p. 34). The two were referred to by the set phrase "Ch'ü in the South, Yang in the North."

31. *ECCP*, p. 889.

32. The supplement to the *YSYL* also contains copies of all the colophons of books in the Yang collection that had previously been part of the collection of Huang P'ei-lieh and Wang Shih-chung. These copies were made in 1871 by Yang Shao-ho's son, Pao-i, when the *YSYL* was initially published by Shao-ho.

In 1895 Yang Pao-i republished the work. Later, the printing blocks were scattered. Tung K'ang obtained the remaining two-thirds, supplemented the losses, and published a new edition in 1911.

It was republished in 1967 in Taipei as part of the series *Shu-mu ts'ung-p'ien*. Its four volumes are based on the edition of 1911.

33. The catalogue Pao-i compiled in 1909 lists 3,700 works in 208,300 *chüan*, including 464 Sung and Yüan editions in 11,328 *chüan*. It was published in 1931 by the Shantung Provincial Library.

None of the catalogues of this collection records the library at its full height. Unfortunately, 40-50% of its contents were destroyed in March 1861, when the Nien rebels attacked the western region of Fei-ch'eng, Shantung. (c.f. *YSYL, Introduction*)

34. The source for this information is Wu Tse-yü, *HNTSL*, p. 295-6. For details on the Dairen Library see John Young, *The Research Activities of the South Manchurian Railway Company 1907-45* (New York: Columbia University Press, 1966.)

The catalogue of the Japanese Manchukuo Dairen Library does not contain a listing of this exemplar. The catalogue, entitled *Dairen Toshokan Wakan tosho bunrui mokuroku*, was published in Ta-lien by the South Machurian Railway Company in early 1927. Hence the Northern Sung exemplar must have become part of the collection at a later date, probably after the Hai-yüan ko of the Yang family had been occupied in 1929-30.

35. I am indebted to Professor D.C. Lau of the Chinese University of Hong Kong for pointing out to me the meaning of Wu's statement that the Northern Sung exemplar was "taken out of the country." Wu says, "Fifteen years ago I heard it had been taken out of the country."

Wu wrote this in 1962. At this time, as Prof. Lau pointed out, China and Russia were still on friendly terms. Therefore, Wu had to be chary of any phrase that could be interpreted as criticism of Russia. If it had been taken elsewhere Wu would have been able to state it clearly. Young, *op. cit.*, pp. 33-34, mentions that the Russians were particularly interested in the rare Chinese books in the Dairen Library, all of which they confiscated. The rumour that years later they were returned as cultural assets has not been substantiated.

36. *ECCP*, 417-419. Ku lived at Huang's estate from 1794 to 1801, collating works from the latter's collection and helping him to identify genuine Sung editions.

37. *ECCP*, pp. 829-31, 841-2.

38. Huang, *JPTSTC*, *Introduction*, p. 3.

39. Huang, *PSICL*, p. 27a quotes part of the letter. See also Kuraishi, *op. cit.*, pp. 348-9.

40. See Huang's note dated November 5-6, 1801 in *JPTSTC* 5/19a-20a.

41. *PSICL* p. 27a.

42. *JPTSTC*, *Introduction*, p.2.

43. *TSTC*, written by Wang Nien-sun and son Wang Yin-shih, is generally acknowledged to be the greatest work of textual criticism of the nineteenth century. It contains emendations to all major classical texts. Wang Nien-sun's last note in *TSTC* is dated January 19, 1816. See 9/22/29a.

44. See the introduction to the supplement to the *HNT* section of *TSTC*, p. 1. This supplement, written by Wang Yin-chih, is dated January, 1821. It is entitled "Ku-chiao Huai-nan Tzu ko-t'iao."

45. We are fortunate to possess a copy of Ku's hand-collated exemplar in *CKTHC*, vol. 85. For Ku's note see p. 14. Also, in *JPTSTC*, 5/19a, Huang P'ei-lieh says that Ku borrowed the *Tao-tsang* edition to collate the Chuang K'uei-chi edition, and that Huang himself copied Ku's collation notes.
46. See Ku's note about this. *CKTHC*, vol. 85, p. 783.
47. Quoted in the catalogue of the later owner of the original exemplar, Yang I-tseng, *YSYL*, pp. 39a-41b. Colophon is dated September 7-16, 1820.
48. *YSYL*, p. 416.
49. See *TSTC*, ch. 9, supplement pp. 1-14. Yin-chih discusses his correspondence with Ku in a brief preface. Yin-chih's arrangement differs from that in Ku's colophon. Also it includes some passages not noted in the colophon and omits some that are. These changes must have been made by Ku since Yin-chih did not have the original exemplar to use. Small-case comments are by Yin-chih.
50. Ch'en Huan, *tzu*: Shih-fu, studio name: San-pai t'ang, studied with Tuan Yü-tsai (1735-1815, *ECCP*, 782-4) before becoming one of the most advanced pupils of Wang Nien-sun and his son Yin-chih. For his biography, see *Ch'ing-shih lieh-chuan* (Taipei: Chung-hua, 1962), 69/67b-69a.
51. This preface is inserted at the beginning of the *SPTK* edition of the *HNT*.
52. This preface is also quoted in full in the catalogue of the remaining works in the Han-fen lou, the *HFLSL*, p. 3/39b. Ch'en was not friendly with the owner of the original exemplar, Wang Shih-chung. (See the following colophon of 1834.) This must have been one of the reasons he asked another man, Chin Yu-mei to copy it. According to the *Li-tai jen-wu pieh-shu chü-ch'u ming t'ung-chien* (Taipei, 1962), p. 13, Ch'en Huan's studio name was San-pai t'ang. Therefore his library must have been the San-pai shu-she referred to in the preface of 1824.
53. This colophon is attached to a hand-collated exemplar of the Chuang K'uei-chi edition that Ch'en himself prepared on behalf of his friend, the bibliophile Ch'en Cheng-chih (*tzu*: Lan-lin). It is preserved in the *HFLSL*, p. 3/40a. This exemplar was later owned by T'an Hsien (1830-1901), who lent it to three of the most prominent textual scholars of the late Ch'ing: Chao Chih-chien (1829-84), T'ao Fang-ch'i (1845-84) and Sun I-jang (1848-1908).
54. *HFLSL*, 3/39b. The biography of Liu Lü-fen is found in Miao Ch'üan-sun, *Hsü pei-chuan-chi* (Privately printed, 1910), *chüan* 45.
55. See above, note 7.
56. This conclusion is further corroborated by the chronological biography of Wang Nien-sun and his son Yin-chih. Fang Chun-chi, *Kao-yu Wang-shih fu-tzu hsüeh chih yen-chiu* (Taipei, 1974), pp. 1-42, records the topics of correspondence between Ch'en and Yin-chih between 1824-34; no mention is made of the *HNT*. Also there is no record of Wang having received a copy of the *HNT* from anyone during this period.

This should not be at all surprising. Wang Nien-sun completed his research on the *HNT* in 1816. Yin-chih added the supplement to *TSTC*, ch. 9 in 1821. It contained Ku Kuang-ch'i's collation notes of the best readings from the original exemplar. With these notes to supplement the omissions in the earlier research, the two Wangs could justifiably feel that their research on the *HNT* was complete. Indeed, Wang's biography shows both men to have been occupied with other works during this time.

This conclusion, that Ch'en retained this copy, is corroborated by the fact that his most renowned pupil, Kuan Ch'ing-ssu, used a copy of the original Northern Sung exemplar in some research of his own in 1858. This is discussed below in note 65. Kuan must have obtained the copy from Ch'en.

Finally in 1872, Liu Lü-fen made his facsimile at the Wu-men Publishing Co. This is located in Wu-hsien, a neighbouring town to Ch'en's home of Ch'ang-shou in the Soochow area of Kiangsu Province.

57. The above discussion should correct several errors in LeBlanc, pp. 62-3. The first is that Huang P'ei-lieh obtained the Northern Sung exemplar in 1815, and was planning, with a group of friends, to prepare a new edition of the *HNT*. The historical evidence shows that the only person who wanted to prepare a new edition was T'ao Wu-liu (see Huang's note of October 1801 in *JPTSTC*, 5/19b); and of course Huang obtained his Northern Sung exemplar in 1796. Second, LeBlanc states that Ku used his own traced facsimile to collate an exemplar of the Chuang K'uei-chi edition. The truth is that Ku used the original Northern Sung exemplar to do this. Third, the date of the Chuang K'uei-chi edition is 1788, not 1789 (Ch'ien-lung 53). Finally the original Northern Sung exemplar was stored in the Library of the South Manchurian Railway Company in Ta-lien, (Japanese: Dairen) not in the "Dairen University Library". In fact Wu Tse-yü notes that a Japanese scholar, Shimada Yoshimi wrote an essay that must have been based on the colophon of Ku that was inserted in the original Northern Sung exemplar and later recorded in *YSYL*. This essay was printed by the Dairen Library of the South Manchurian Railway Co. See Wu, *HNTSL*, p. 296.

58. *YSYL*, p. 39a-41a.

59. *TSTC*, 9/22, p. 1.

60. Wu Tse-yü, *HNTSL*, p. 296.

61. Yü Ta-ch'eng, *HNWSK*, p. 22.

62. Wang Shu-min, *op. cit.*, p. 565.

63. Cheng Liang-shu, *HNTCL*, pp. 331-2.

64. *JPTSTC*, p. 19b (April 27, 1816).

65. Actually the situation is a bit more complex than I have described. The *CKTHC* reprint of the Ku Kuang-ch'i hand collated exemplar is a facsimile reproduction of a copy made in 1898 by Hsü Tsai-heng. Hsü's copy was, in turn, a facsimile of a copy made in 1858 by Kuan Ch'ing-ssu of the original Ku exemplar. Kuan Ch'ing-ssu was Ch'en Huan's best student (see *Ch'ing-shih lieh-chuan*, 69/67b-69a). After he copied out Ku's full collation notes he then checked them against a copy of the Northern exemplar. I assume that since he was Ch'en's best student, he must have used Ch'en's copy. Whenever he came to a variant between the basic Chuang edition and Ch'en's Northern Sung facsimile copy *that was not* previously noted by Ku Kuang-chi, he wrote

it down. Sometimes (e.g., pp. 33, 42, 47, 52) he added "Chi-yeh chi" ("written by Chi-yeh"). Chi-yeh was his courtesy name.

Now there are many of these notes by Kuan. What they indicate to me is not the carelessness of Ku's scholarship, but the fact that the facsimile Kuan saw (i.e. Ch'en Huan's) already contained differences from the original exemplar that Ku consulted. Often Kuan's notes indicate characters whose form is almost identical to one in the text, but which is written slightly differently. This is a sure sign that the difference was introduced by a copyist who attempted to clarify an illegible or damaged character. Therefore, there must already have been variants between the original exemplar and the copy of Ch'en Huan.

Ch'en Huan's copy was in turn copied by Liu Lü-fen, and is the basis of the extant editions. The seven copyist's errors that I have pointed out in Chapter 7 must have all been made by Liu Lü-fen when he interpreted illegible graphs in Ch'en's facsimile. None of them is recorded by either Ku or Kuan. Therefore these seven were not in either the original or in Ch'en's copy.

From this it can be seen that errors were introduced into modern editions by the copyists who were forced to interpret illegible graphs, first in the original exemplar, and then in the Ch'en copy.

The Strange Case of the Overdue Book

List of Characters

Chang Ch'ou 張丑

Chang Tzu-kai 張子蓋

Chang Yü 張鈺

Chao Chih-chien 趙之謙

Ch'ang-ling 昌齡

Ch'ang-shan 常山

Ch'ang-shou 長洲

Cheng Liang-shu 鄭良樹

Ch'en Cheng-chih 陳徵之

Ch'en Huan 陳奐

Ch'en Teng-yüan 陳登原

Chi-yeh chi 吉也記

Ch'ien Tseng 錢曾

Ch'ien I-chi 錢儀吉

Ch'ien Tsun-wang tu-shu min-ch'iu-chi chiao-cheng
錢遵王讀書敏求記校證

Chin Yu-mei 金友梅

Ch'ing-shih lieh-chuan 清史列傳

Chu Chia-hua 朱家驊

Chu I-tsun 朱彝尊

Chu-tzu chiao-cheng 諸子斠證

Chuang K'uei-chi 莊逵吉

Chung-kuo tien-chi-shih 中國典籍史

Chung-kuo tsang-shu-chia k'ao-lüeh
中國藏書家考略

Ch'ü Yung 瞿鏞

Dairen Toshokan Wakan tosho bunrui mokuroku
大連圖書館和漢圖書分類目錄

Enanji no Rekishi 淮南子の歷史

Fang Chun-chi 方俊吉

Fei-shih jih-chi ch'ao 郋石日記鈔

fu-pen 副本

Hai-chou 海州

Hai-yüan ko 海源閣

Hsü pei-chuan-chi 續碑傳記

Hsü Shen 許慎

Hsü Tsai-heng 許在衡

Hu Yü-t'ang 胡雨塘

Hu-chou 湖州

Huai-nan Tzu 淮南子

Huai-nan hung-lieh chieh
淮南鴻烈解

Huai-nan hung-lieh chien ku 淮南鴻烈閒詁

Huang P'ei-Lieh 黃丕烈

Huang-ti nei-ching ssu-wen 黃帝內經素問

Hui tung 惠棟

I-yün-ching she 藝芸精舍

Jao-chou 饒州

Kao Yu 高誘

Kao-yu Wang-shih fu-tzu hsüeh chih yen-chiu 高郵王氏父子學之研究

Ku Kuang-ch'i 顧廣圻

Ku-chiao Huai-nan Tzu ko-t'iao 顧校淮南子各條

Kuan Ch'ing-ssu 管慶祺

Kuan T'ing-fen 管庭芬

Kuang-ya shu-cheng 廣雅疏證

Kuo-ch'ao Pei-chuan-chi 國朝碑傳集

Kuo-li Pei-p'ing t'u-shu kuan kuan-k'an 國立北平圖書館館刊

Kuraishi Takeshiro 倉石武四郎

Lan-lin 蘭鄰

Li-tai jen-wu pieh-shu chü-ch'u ming t'ung-chien 歷代人物別署居處名通檢

Lien-t'ing shu-mu 楝亭書目

Liu Lü-fen 劉履芬

Lo-p'ing hsien 樂平縣

Mao I-kuei 茅一桂

Mao-sheng 泖生

Miao Ch'üan-sun 繆荃孫

Niu Shu-yü 鈕樹玉

San-pai shu-she 三白書舍

San-pai t'ang 三百堂

shen 愼

Shen Ta-ch'eng 沈大成

Shih-fu 碩甫 or 石甫

Shimada Yoshimi 島田好

Shinagaku 支那學

Sun I-jang 孫詒讓

Sung Chih-shan 宋芝山

Sung Ting-chih 宋定之

Taam, Cheuk-Woon 譚卓垣

Tan-t'u 丹徒

Tu-shu tsa-chih 讀書雜誌

Tuan Yü-tsai 段玉裁
T'an Hsien 譚獻
T'ao Fang-ch'i 陶方琦
T'ao Wen-hui 陶蘊輝
T'ao Wu-liu 陶五柳
T'ieh-ch'in t'ung chien lou 鐵琴銅劍樓
Ts'ao Hsi 曹璽
Ts'ao Yin 曹寅
Tung K'ang 董康
Wang Chin-fa 王金發
Wang Han-chih 王漢之
Wang K'o-ming 王克明
Wang Nien-sun 王念孫
Wang Shih-chung 王士鐘
Wang-shih chia 王氏家
Wang-shih Yen-chao 王氏彥昭
Wang Shu-min 王叔岷
Wang Ying-chih 王引之
Wen Po 温博
Wu-ch'eng hsien 烏程縣
Wu Ch'eng-shih 吳承石
Wu Tse-yü 吳則虞
Wu-hsien 吳縣
Wu-liu 五柳
Yang I-tseng 楊以增
Yang Pao-i 楊保彝
Yang Shao-ho 楊紹和
Yao Wei-tsu 姚慰祖
Ying-shu yü-lu 楹書隅錄
Yü Liang-shu 于大成
Yüan T'ing-t'ao 袁廷檮

Monks and the Relic Cult in the *Mahāparinibbānasutta*: An Old Misunderstanding in Regard to Monastic Buddhism

Gregory Schopen
University of Texas at Austin

It is almost always instructive to look at the actual evidence for what are taken to be "established facts" in the history of Indian Buddhism. If nothing else, such an exercise makes it painfully obvious that most of those "established facts" totter precariously on very fragile foundations. One example only will concern us here.

It is—and has been—constantly asserted that there was in Early Buddhism a fundamental difference between the religious activities of monks and the religious activities of lay persons, especially in regard to worship and participation in cult. Moreover, this fundamental difference is said to distinguish not only the religious lives of monks from the religious lives of lay persons in Early Buddhism, it is also said to distinguish the Mahāyāna monk from his non-Mahāyāna co-religionists. All of this is, of course, asserted as "fact" and far-reaching implications are made to follow from it. But this "fact"—as I have pointed out several times now—stands in jarring contrast to everything we know from Indian epigraphy and archeology.[1] It is, indeed, the accumulating weight of this epigraphical and archeological material which in the first instance forces us to re-examine the evidence on which the "fact" of this asserted difference is founded. That evidence—not surprisingly given the history of Buddhist Studies—turns out to be exclusively literary. But it is not just exclusively literary evidence on which this fact rests: it rests entirely, it seems, on a less than careful reading of a single passage of a single text. The passage in question is, of course, *Mahāparinibbāna-Sutta* V.10:

kathaṃ mayaṃ bhante tathāgatassa sarīre paṭipajjāmāti

avyāvaṭā tumhe ānanda hotha tathāgatassa sarīrapujāya, iṅgha tumhe ānanda sadatthe ghaṭatha, sadattham anuyuñjatha, sadatthe appamattā ātāpino pahitattā viharatha. sant' ānanda khattiya-paṇḍitā pi brāhmaṇa-paṇḍitā pi gahapati-paṇḍitā pi tathāgate abhippasannā te tathāgatassa sarīra-pūjaṃ karissantīti.[2]

This—in Rhys Davids' still standard English translation of the passage—appears as:

"'What are we to do, lord, with the remains of the Tathāgata?'

'Hinder not yourselves, Ānanda, by honouring the remains of the Tathāgata. Be zealous, I beseech you, Ānanda, in your own behalf! Devote yourselves to your own good! Be earnest, be zealous, be intent on your own good! There are wise men, Ānanda, among the nobles, among the brahmins, among the heads of houses, who are firm believers in the Tathāgata; and they will do due honour to the remains of the Tathāgata'."[3]

This single, short passage, probably one of the most frequently quoted passages of Buddhist canonical literature, has been taken to establish, for example, that "śarīrapūjā, the worship of relics, is the concern of the laity and not the bhikṣusaṃgha,"[4] that "advanced monks were not to occupy themselves with such worship of stūpas," and that "the worship of stūpas should be left to the laity alone."[5] But, even if we bracket the distinct possibility raised by Professor Bareau that this passage—and a number of related passages—are 'later' interpolations in the *Mahāparinibbāna-sutta*,[6] the passage *as we have it* simply will not support the conclusions modern scholars have drawn from it.[7] First of all, there is no reference anywhere in the passage to monks. The injunction, if it is an injunction, is addressed to Ānanda, not to all monks. It is true that plural pronominal and verbal forms are used in the Pāli version of this passage. But if the plural forms are used there as inclusive of the category "monk," then they should be used in that same way at, for example, *Mahāparinibbāna* V.7 where the same thing occurs. That, however, as the context makes absolutely clear, is out of the question since the plural *mayaṃ*, "we," is actually used there in such a way as to *exclude* 'monks in different districts'. Likewise at VI.1 where a 1st person plural form of the pronoun is used Rhys Davids himself recognized that it could not be intended to include all monks: he translates *siyā kho pan' ānanda tumhākam evam assa* as "'It may be, Ānanda, that *in some of you* the thought may arise.'" Moreover, when in the *Mahāparinibbāna-sutta* we actually find explicit reference to rules governing the *Saṅgha* as a whole—as we do in the passage dealing with the abolishment of the "lesser and minor precepts" at VI.3—it is explicitly stated to be a matter for the entire *Saṅgha*. But these considerations, though consistently overlooked, may not necessarily be—in the end—the most important ones. The fact would remain that even if it could somehow be argued that the injunction was intended for the entire *Saṅgha* it would still be difficult to establish that that injunction had anything to do with the *stūpa* or relic cult.

There has been more than the usual degree of inconsistency in translating the text of the injunction and virtually no attempt to determine the precise meaning of the term *śarīra-pūjā* as it is used there. Even the great de la Vallée Poussin gives at least four different translations of the injunction, two of them in the same book:

> "Ne vous occupez pas du culte de mes reliques."[8]
> "Ne vous occupez pas des funérailles."[9]
> "Ne vous occupez pas du culte des reliques."[9]
> "Ne vous préoccupez pas d'honorer mon corps."[10]

This kind of inconsistency—which can slip so easily into confusion—is still with us. Recently, for example, Prof. A. Hirakawa said:

> "During the early period of Buddhism offerings to the Buddha's relics (*śarīra-pūjā*) were made by laymen. According to the Mahāparinibbāna Suttanta, the Buddha was asked by Ānanda what type of ceremony should be held for the Buddha's remains. The Buddha replied, 'you should strive for the true goal [*sadattha*] of emancipation [*vimokṣa*].' The Buddha thus prohibited monks from having any connection with his funeral ceremonies and instead called upon wise and pious lay believers to conduct the ceremonies."[11]

Here in four sentences *śarīra-pūjā* is glossed in three different ways: as 'offerings to relics,' as 'ceremony for remains,' and as 'funeral ceremonies.'

The problem, of course, with de la Vallée Poussin's and Prof. Hirakawa's treatment is, as it is with virtually all treatments of the passage, that they make no attempt to establish the precise meaning of *śarīra-pūjā* and, as a consequence, may be inadvertently conflating what are typologically two quite distinct things: *funeral ceremonies and cult activity directed towards relics or reliquaries are fundamentally different forms of religious behavior.* In this instance the texts—*as we have them*—seem clearer than their interpreters.

In arguing for his interpretation of the curious statement at the end of the *Ahraurā* version of Aśoka's first minor rock edict K.R. Norman says "that in Sanskrit *śarīra* in the singular means 'body,' not 'relics,' which is its meaning in the plural."[12] That the same holds for the Pāli *sarīra* in the *Mahāparinibbāna-sutta* is, uncharacteristically, beyond doubt. Before a certain point in the narrative the term is never used in the plural, always in the singular, and can only mean "body": at V.2, for example, the trees burst into bloom out of season and scatter their flowers on *the body* of the dying, but not yet dead, Buddha (*te tathāgatassa sarīraṃ okiranti*); at V.11 the *body* of a *cakkavattin* is said to be wrapped "in a new cloth" (*cakkavattissa sarīraṃ ahatena vatthena veṭhenti*); at VI.13 the Mallas are said to have approached the *body* "with dancing and hymns, and music, and with garlands and perfumes" (*yena bhagavato sarīraṃ ten' upasaṃkamiṃsu, upasaṃkamitvā bhagavato sarīraṃ naccehi gītehi... pūjentā*); at VI.18 the *body* is said to have been wrapped (*bhagavato sarīraṃ veṭhetvā*), placed on the pyre (*bhagavato sarīraṃ citakaṃ āropesuṃ*), etc. Wherever, therefore, the term *sarīra* occurs in the singular in the *Mahāparinibbāna* it unambiguously means *body*, and it occurs in the singular throughout the entire description of the actual funeral. It is in fact only after the funeral proper, only after the cremation, that we find *sarīra* in the plural and it is only here that the text could be speaking about "relics." We can actually watch—at VI.23—the transition in both grammatical number and meaning as it takes place in a single paragraph. The only question that remains, then, is which of the two possible meanings of *sarīra* is in play in the injunction delivered to Ānanda.

Since the text of the injunction uses *sarīra* in compound—*avyāvaṭā tumhe ānanda hotha tathāgatassa sarīra-pujāya*—we have no formal indication of the implied grammatical number and, therefore, of the intended meaning of *sarīra*. But even in the absence of a formal indicator, the contextual indication is virtually certain. The injunction is not an unsolicited declaration. It is a response or answer to a very specific question and the question itself does have the formal indication of grammatical number that we need. The question is put in the following form: *kathaṃ mayaṃ bhante tathāgatassa sarīre paṭipajjāmāti. sarīre* here is almost certainly a locative singular used in the sense of "in regard to" exactly as in the immediately preceding *mātugāme* which is constructed with the same verb: *kathaṃ mayaṃ bhante mātugāme paṭipajjāmāti* (V.9). Rhys Davids translates the latter by "How are we to conduct ourselves, lord, with regard to womankind?" If the construction of the question leading to our injunction is analogous, and if *sarīre* there is in the locative singular, it would accordingly have to be translated: "How are we to conduct ourselves in regard to the body of the Tathāgata?" To argue that *sarīre* is not a locative singular, moreover, would be difficult. The only other thing it could be, as far as I know, is an accusative plural, but there is much against this. A neuter accusative plural in *-e*—though found on occasion elsewhere—would be distinctly out of place in the language of the *Mahāparinibbāna-sutta*;[13] when *sarīra* occurs elsewhere in the *Mahāparinibbāna-sutta* in the accusative plural—and it does so at least five times—it always occurs with the "normal" neuter plural ending *-āni*; in the one other instance where *sarīre* occurs in the final sections of the *Mahāparinibbāna-sutta* it forms a part of a locative absolute so there can be no doubt about its interpretation (*daḍḍhe kho pana bhagavato sarīre*, VI.23).

All of this is only to say that it seems virtually certain that Ānanda, in his question, was not asking about his or anyone else's participation in the relic cult. He was asking about how the *body* of the Buddha should be treated *immediately* after his death, about that which we would call the "funeral arrangements".[14] But if the question is about funeral arrangements, it is at best disingenuous to suggest that the answer and the injunction is about something else. In fact the text of the injunction itself also seems to indicate that *sarīrapūjā*, the activity Ānanda was not to be preoccupied with, was intended only to refer to funeral activities.

The text says at V.11 that the body of the Tathāgata is to be treated in the same way as the body of a Wheel-turning king is treated. It is this that the "wise men… among the nobles, among the brahmins, among the heads of houses" are to do and that Ānanda is not to be overly concerned with. But the treatment accorded to the body of a dead king which is detailed in the Pāli text makes no reference either to relics or to an ongoing cult. The *sarīra-pūja* of a dead king's body described in the text involves the following steps: the body is wrapped elaborately in cloth; the body is then placed in an "oil vessel of iron"; a funeral pyre is built; the body is cremated and a *stūpa* is built. That is all. "This is the way they treat the body of a wheel-turning king, Ānanda," the text says, and then goes on:

> yathā kho ānanda rañño cakkavattissa sarīre paṭipajjanti evaṃ tathāgatassa sarīre paṭipajjitabbaṃ. cātummahāpathe tathāgatassa thūpo kātabbo. tattha ye mālaṃ vā gandhaṃ vā vaṇṇakaṃ vā āropessanti abhivādessanti vā cittaṃ vā pasādessanti tesaṃ taṃ bhavissati dīgharattaṃ hitāya sukhāya.
>
> As indeed, Ānanda, they proceed in regard to the body of a wheel-turning king, so in regard to the body of the Tathāgata the procedure is to be followed. At the main crossroads a stūpa of the Tathāgata is to be made. Who will take a garland or perfume or paint there, or will salute, or will cause their mind to be tranquil, that will be for their benefit and ease for a long time.

It may be of some importance to note the shift in verbal forms that takes place in this passage since that shift would seem to indicate that the final sentence was not intended as a part of the instructions concerning the treatment of the Buddha's body and that, therefore, the activities it describes were not thought to form a part of *sarīra-pūja*. When the text refers to what is to be done in regard to the body of the Buddha it uses future passive participles to indicate what must be done by the wise laymen who will perform the *sarīra-pūjā*: the procedure followed in regard to a deceased king *is to be followed* in regard to the Buddha; a *stūpa is to be made*. These are clear injunctions in both grammar and sense. But the injunctions end here. The final sentence, which contains the only references in the passage to what might be called cult practices, constitutes not an injunction, but a statement about the future. The text shifts from future passive participles with an imperative sense to simple futures; from "it is to be done" to "those who will do." Notice too that the final sentence also introduces a new grammatical subject: context suggests that the injunctions are addressed to the wise laymen who will perform the *sarīra-pūjā*; but the subject of the final sentence is the indefinite *ye* which Rhys Davids renders by "whosoever." All of this, again, would appear to indicate that all those activities which we associate with an ongoing relic cult did not—for the author of our text—form a part of *sarīra-pūjā*, and that *sarīra-pūjā* was used to refer only to funereal activities that began with the wrapping of the body and ended with cremation and constructing a *stūpa* and had—like the injunction as a whole—nothing to do with relics. That this was, indeed, the original meaning of *sarīra-pūjā* is in fact further demonstrated by a number of passages in Hīnayāna literature where we have clear references to monastic funerals.

In an interesting passage from the *Mūlasarvāstivāda-vinaya* we find, for example:

> "Again on that occasion another monk, being sick, died in his cell. Having brought him to the burning ground, having performed *the worship of the body*, that monk was burnt. Then the monks returned to the

> monastery (*...sa bhikṣur ādahanaṃ nītvā śarīra-pūjāṃ kṛtvā dagdhas, tato vihāram āgatā*).[15]

To this passage from the *Mūlasarvāstivāda-vinaya* we might add another from the same source:

> "Again on that occasion another monk died. The monks, having carried out his body, having simply thrown it into the burning grounds (*...tan 'bhinirhṛtya evam eva śmaśāne chorayitvā*), returned to the monastery. The distributor of robes entered the dead monk's cell saying 'I distribute the bowl and robe.' He—the dead monk—having been reborn among non-human beings appeared there wielding a club. He said: 'until you perform *the worship of the body* for me (*yāvan mama śarīra-pūjāṃ kurutha*), do you now distribute (my) bowl and robe?'
>
> The monks ask the Blessed One concerning this matter.
>
> The Blessed One said: 'By the monks *the worship of the body* for the deceased is first to be performed (*bhikṣubhis tasya pūrvaṃ śarīra-pūjā karttavyeti*). After that the bowl and robe are to be distributed.'"[16]

Both of these passages enumerate a sequence of activities involved in the disposal of the body of a monk who has died in his cell. In both it is clear that *śarīra-pūjā*—whatever it involved—took place after the body had been removed and taken to the cremation ground, but before it was cremated, before there could have been anything like what we call relics. It is again fairly certain that *śarīra-pūjā* involved the ritual handling or treatment of the body prior to cremation since the second passage contrasts it with—and insists that it replace—'simply throwing the body into the burning ground.' That it is *the body* and not relics that is the object of this treatment is both clear here and made even more explicit elsewhere.

The forty-eighth *Avadāna* of the *Avadānaśataka* looks very much like a literary elaboration of the much simpler narratives concerning the disposal of the monastic dead found in the *Mūlasarvāstivāda-vinaya*, two examples of which have already been cited. It leaves us in no doubt as to the object toward which *śarīra-pūjā* is directed. It says a certain monk:

> ...kālagataḥ svake layane preteṣūpapannaḥ | tato 'sya sabrahmacāribhir muṇḍikāṃ gaṇḍīṃ parāhatya śarīrābhinirhāraḥ kṛtaṃ | tato 'sya śarīre śarīrapūjāṃ kṛtvā vihāram āgatāḥ |
>
> "...died and was reborn in his own cell as a hungry ghost (*shi nas rang gi gnas khang du yi dags su skyes so*). Then his fellow monks, having struck the *muṇḍikā* gong ("la cloche funèbre"), performed the removal of the body. Then, having performed the worship of the body on his body, they returned to the monastery."[17]

Virtually every element of this passage from the *Avadānaśataka* also occurs in the *Mūlasarvāstivāda-vinaya*. The "*muṇḍikā* gong," or "cloche funèbre,"[18] for example, is referred to in the latter more intelligibly as the *mṛta-gaṇḍī* or "gong for the dead."[19] It is, however, not just the elements of the funeral procedure which are essentially the same in the two works; the sequence in which they are said to occur is also basically the same. It is, therefore, significant that where the *Mūlasarvāstivada-vinaya* has *śarīra-pūjāṃ kṛtvā*, "having performed the worship of the body," the *Avadānaśataka* has corresponding to it the even more explicit *śarīre śarīra-pūjāṃ kṛtvā*, "having performed the worship of the body on his body." This construction leaves no doubt about the object of the *pūjā* involved.[20] Nor is this in doubt in another instance where the construction is used. In the Sanskrit version of the *Mahāparinirvāṇa-sūtra* (48.8) when Mahākāśyapa meets an Ājīvika coming from Kuśinagarī he asks him if he knows his teacher. The Ājīvika answers: *jāne / śramaṇo gautamaḥ / parinirvṛtas te āyuṣmañ chāstā / adya (gate saptāhe va)rtate śarīre śarīra-pūjā*: "I know him. He is the Śramaṇa Gautama. But sir, your teacher is dead. For seven days now the worship of the body on his body is performed."[21] But since the Buddha had not yet been cremated, it is here not just the construction, but the context too that makes it certain that *śarīra-pūjā* was understood to be an activity directed toward the body of the deceased which took place after the individual's death, but before or as a part of his cremation. It could not, therefore, have anything to do with relics for the simple reason that there were none.

All of this is richly confirmed by a variety of other passages as well. In the account of the funeral of Mahāprajāpatī and her companions found in the *Vinaya-kṣudraka-vastu* of the *Mūlasarvāstivāda-vinaya*, for example, in which prominent monks come from afar to undertake the full performance of the worship of her body (*de'i lus la mchod pa lhag par bya ba la brtson par byas*), the text says: "Then, having performed the great worship and having removed the bodies, they set the biers down at an appropriate and isolated spot (*de nas mchod pa chen po byas te khyer nas sa phyogs bar skabs dben par khyogs rnams bzhag go*). Only after the great worship was performed and the bodies removed did the cremation take place (*de nas ... bsregs so*).[22] In the terse account of the end of Aśoka found in the *Divyāvadāna*, the text says that the ministers thought of enthroning the new king only "after having carried out (Aśoka's body) on dark blue and yellow biers, after having performed the worship of the body, and after having cremated him (*yāvad amātyair nīlapītābhiḥ śivikābhir nirharitvā śarīra-pūjāṃ kṛtvā dhmāpayitvā rājānaṃ pratiṣṭhāpayiṣyāma iti*).[23] Here again "worship of the body" precedes cremation; it takes place before in fact there could be any relics. But if these passages make it clear that *śarīra-pūjā* took place before there could have been anything like a relic, still other passages make it clear that it also took place prior to the erection of a *stūpa*. In the *Saṅghabhedavastu* of the *Mūlasarvāstivāda-vinaya*, in a description of events that followed the death of a former Buddha, the text says: "A great crowd of people, after having performed the worship of the body in regard to his body, established a great *stūpa* on an isolated spot" (*tasya mahājanakāyena śarīre śarīra-pūjāṃ kṛtvā viviktāvakāśe pṛthivīpradeśe mahān stūpaḥ pratiṣṭhāpitaḥ*).[24] Similarly, in the description of events that followed the death of a series of former Buddhas found in the *Avadānaśataka*—a description that is repeated at least eleven times—the text says: "The king ..., after having performed the worship of the body in regard to the body of the Blessed One, established a *stūpa* a *yojana* in circumference, etc." (*tato rājñā .... bhagavataḥ śarīre śarīra-pūjāṃ kṛtvā samantayojanastūpaś catūratnamayaḥ pratiṣṭhāpitaḥ krośam uccatvena*).[25] Significantly in several instances this statement is completed with the phrase "and a festival of the *stūpa* was instituted" (*stūpamahaś ca prajñaptaḥ*). In all these cases then, *śarīra-pūjā* could not possibly have been thought to be connected with activity in regard to *stūpa*s since it was only after *śarīra-pūjā* had been completed that a *stūpa* was established. Moreover, in those cases in which it was said that "a festival of the *stūpa* was instituted"—and therefore something like an ongoing cult—this too took place after *śarīra-pūjā* had been performed. *śarīra-pūjā* did not form a part of any ongoing activity.

We might consider here one final and perhaps particularly interesting passage from the Sanskrit text of the *Mahāparinirvāṇa-sūtra* (49.15). When, in this version, Mahākāśyapa approaches the funeral pyre of the Buddha he takes the lid off the oil vessel, removes the cloths wrapped around the body, and "pays reverence to the uncovered body of the Blessed One" (*bhagavataḥ śarīram avigopitaṃ vandate*). Then the following thought occurs to him: *yan nv ahaṃ svayam eva bhagavataḥ śarīra-pūjāyām autsukyam āpadyeya*; "what if I myself, indeed, were to be zealous in regard to the worship of the body of the Blessed One." Having thought this, he brings other cloths, wraps the body with them, puts it back into the vessel, closes the lid, makes a(nother) pyre, and stands to one side. That is all. It is apparently just this sequence of activities which the text intends by the term *śarīra-pūjā*. Although it looks to us like "worship," even what Mahākāśyapa does in regard to the body when he has initially uncovered it is not included; that activity is expressed by a completely different word: *vandate*.

It is also important to note that in the Sanskrit text Mahākāśyapa does precisely what Ānanda is earlier told not to be concerned with, and the two passages use virtually the same words. Ānanda's question is expressed as *kathaṃ vayaṃ... bhagavataḥ śarīra-pūjāyām autsukyam āpadyemahi* (36.2) and the injunction as *alpotsukas tvam ānanda bhava śarīra-pūjāyāḥ...* (36.3), while Kāśyapa's intention appears as *yan nv ahaṃ svayam eva bhagavataḥ śarīra-pūjāyām autsukyam āpadyeya* (49.19). Since we know what Kāśyapa did when he involved himself in *śarīra-pūjā* we also know quite precisely what Ānanda was not to be concerned with and, again, it has nothing to do with the relic cult.[26] But since the Sanskrit text goes to the trouble to point out that Kāśyapa was a monk of the highest standing, one of only four *Mahāsthavira*s alive at the time (49.16), and since it is precisely this *Mahāsthavira* who is said to have engaged in *śarīra-pūjā*, we also know that it is extremely unlikely that the authors of the text understood the earlier injunction addressed to Ānanda to apply to all monks or to forbid monastic involvement in such activity. In fact, if there were any restrictions on participation in *śarīra-pūjā* they appear from the Sanskrit text to have been of a very different order. Since, again, the Sanskrit text takes the trouble to point out that Kāsyapa was not only one of only four *Mahāsthaviras*, but was also—in Buddhist monastic terms—rich and famous,[27] and since he involved himself actively in what Ānanda was counselled not to, the text may be suggesting almost the opposite of what we would expect: it may be suggesting that participation in that part of monastic funerals known as *śarīra-pūjā* was—in at least important funerals—the prerogative of advanced, high status monks.[28] Since Ānanda, at this stage, appears to have been neither, this may only confirm from an unexpected angle that the injunction addressed to him was fundamentally *ad hominem*.

All of the evidence we have, then, would seem to argue for the fact that *śarīra-pūjā* did not originally mean "worship of relics" and did not have anything to do with a relic cult. It would seem to strongly suggest—if not establish—that originally it referred to that part of the funeral ceremony which took place primarily between the time of death and the cremation and construction of a *stūpa*, and involved primarily what we would call preparation of the body. The construction of a *stūpa*—if it is included at all—signalled the end of *śarīra-pūjā*, not its beginnings. But if the available evidence suggests that *śarīra-pūjā* was not connected with an ongoing relic cult, that same evidence suggests that the injunction concerning it that was delivered to Ānanda was not intended to apply to all monks. This last is confirmed from an unexpected source.

The injunction delivered to Ānanda created problems, apparently, for the later Theravāda tradition. It reappears as one lemma of an interesting dilemma in the Fourth Book of the *Milindapañha*. This dilemma is particularly important for our discussion since it allows us to see at least something of how the injunction was understood in Śri Lanka in about the 5th Century C.E.[29] In presenting the dilemma Milinda points out that the Buddha said both "Do not you, Ānanda, be occupied with honouring the Tathāgata's bodily remains," and—in *Vimānavatthu* 82. vs.8—"Venerate that relic of him who is to be venerated (*pūjetha naṃ pūjaniyassa dhātuṃ*); by doing so you will go from here to heaven."[30] It is clear from just this much that by the time this Book was added to the *Milinda* a change in the meaning of *sarīra-pūjā* had occurred; it is clear by the way in which the dilemma is framed that *sarīra-pūjā* was now considered equivalent to 'venerating a relic,' and could now mean that. But it is also clear from Nāgasena's response that even then, and even when taken to refer to relic worship, the injunction addressed to Ānanda had not yet been understood to apply to all monks. If the injunction had already been understood to apply to all monks, or if this interpretation had been widely or fully accepted, Milinda's dilemma could not have arisen and Nāgasena's response would have made no sense.

The response of Nāgasena comes in the following form:

bhāsitam p'etaṃ mahārāja bhagavatā: abyāvaṭā tumhe ānanda hotha tathāgatassa sarīrapūjāyāti. puna ca bhaṇitaṃ:

pūjetha naṃ pūjaniyassa dhātuṃ
evaṃkarā saggam ito gamissathāti

> tañ ca pana na sabbesaṃ. jinaputtānaṃ yeva ārabbha bhaṇitaṃ: abyāvaṭā tumhe ānanda hotha tathāgatassa sarīrapūjāyāti. akammaṃ h'etaṃ mahārāja jinaputtānaṃ yad idaṃ pūjā; sammasanaṃ sankhārānaṃ, yoniso manasikāro, satipaṭṭhānānupassanā, ārammaṇa-sāraggāho, kilesayuddhaṃ sadatthamanuyuñjanā, etaṃ jinaputtānaṃ karaṇīyaṃ; avasesānaṃ devamanussānaṃ pūjā karaṇīyā.

Taking into account the new meaning attributed to *sarīra-pūjā* this can be translated as:

> "Great King, this was indeed spoken by the Blessed One: 'you, Ānanda, should not be concerned with worshipping the relics of the Tathāgata!' And again it was said (by him):
>
> 'Worship the relic of one who is to be worshipped!
> acting thus, you will go from here to heaven.'
>
> But that (which was said) was not (intended) for everyone. Only in reference to the sons of the Conqueror was it said: 'you, Ānanda, should not be concerned with worshipping the relics of the Tathāgata!' For this, Great King, is not an action for the sons of the Conqueror, namely: worship. Thoroughly understanding the conditioned; concentrating the mind; realizing the establishment of mindfulness; taking hold of the most excellent foundations; destroying the impurities; pursuing the highest goal—this is what is to be done by sons of the Conqueror. By the remainder of gods and men worship is to be performed."

The primary purpose of this passage and of the elaborate series of metaphors which follows it is readily apparent. Its primary, if not sole purpose was to establish the meaning of the injunction delivered to Ānanda by establishing to whom that injunction was to apply. The mere fact that this was a "dilemma" can, again, only mean that at the time that this passage was written that had not yet been established, it had not been determined that—as modern scholarship would have it—the injunction was meant for all monks. In fact—and this is the significance of the passage—even this late book of the *Milinda* does not understand the passage in this way. According to the *Milinda* the injunction did not apply to monks, but to what it calls *jinaputtas*, "sons of the Conqueror." But, first of all, this could not have been the intention of the original injunction since the *Dīgha* as a whole is completely ignorant of such a "group." "The compound [*jinaputta*] appears to occur," according to Horner, "three times in Buddv. [=*Buddhavaṃsa*], but nowhere else in the Pāli Canon."[31] Moreover, what little we know about this term comes from a single passage in the *Madhuratthavilāsinī*, a commentary on the *Buddhavaṃsa* which, in Horner's words, "is late."[32] It says simply: *jinaputtā ti dīpaṅkarassa satthuno sāvakā*: "the sons of the Conqueror means the disciples of the Teacher Dīpaṅkara."[33] The equation *jinaputta* = *sāvaka* is, of course, not terribly helpful. It has recently been pointed out that it is not always easy to determine who was understood to be included in the category *sāvaka*, that it certainly included monks—but by no means, perhaps, all monks—and certainly, at times, included some laymen.[34] The group designated *sāvaka* is not therefore certainly coterminous with the group designated *bhikkhu* and—given its vagueness—the group designated *jinaputta* seems even less so. It would as a consequence be difficult to argue even that the author of this Book of the *Milinda* was moving *towards* the modern interpretation which wants to see in the injunction a prohibition of monastic involvement in the relic cult. But even if this argument were to be made, it would have to be conceded that even he is yet a long way from any precision in articulating it. That interpretation, even as late as the Fourth Book of the *Milinda*, simply has not yet been made. Had it been the "dilemma" would not have arisen; had it been the author of Book Four, instead of using a term like *jinaputta*, could have simply used the word *bhikkhu*. The fact that he did not is important; the fact that he used a metaphoric epithet rather than an ecclesiastical title may also be.

bhikkhu and *jinaputta* are fundamentally different kinds of designations. *bhikkhu* is a title conferred on an individual as a result of having undergone a set of formal ecclesiastical procedures for induction into a particular group. It designates his formal membership in that group and that membership is not subject to interpretation or opinion. It is subject to recognized procedure. Anyone who undergoes the procedure is a monk. The same, of course, is not true of an epithet like *jinaputta*, if for no other reason than it obviously cannot be taken literally. An individual so designated cannot literally be "a son of the Conqueror." Moreover, there are no formally recognized procedures that make one such a "son," and no formally recognized criteria for determining membership in this "group." It, in effect, does not designate membership in a particular group but conformity to an ideal notion of what the religiosity of a follower of the Buddha—whether that follower be a layman or a monk—ought to be. This, of course, is decidedly a matter of interpretation and not a matter of ecclesiastical procedure. It may well be, then, that the author of the Fourth Book of the *Milinda* saw in the injunction addressed to Ānanda support for *his* view that *pūjā* was not an activity of what he thought was a *true* monk, but even he could not see in it support for the view that it prohibited all monks from such activity. The contrast for him, in fact, continues to be not that between social groups (laymen and monks), but that between different styles of religiosity (meditative and devotional), and a particular religious style has not yet been identified exclusively with any particular group.

***

It would seem, then, that if the arguments and observations presented here turn out to be even approximately correct we will be required to admit that a good deal of what has been said about early monastic Buddhism is based on a misunderstanding. If *sarīra-pūjā* in the *Mahāparinibbāna-sutta* has nothing to do with relics or an ongoing cult of relics, then the only textual basis for asserting that monks were not allowed to be involved with either disappears. If the "injunction" concerning *sarīra-pūjā*—however the latter be precisely understood—was not addressed to all monks, then once again we are left without any warrant for one of our favorite claims, and we must re-think what we thought we knew about the acultic character of early monastic Buddhism.

Once again, it seems, we have encountered material—this time literary—which appears to suggest that our view of the Indian Buddhist monk is in need of more than a little revision.[35]

Notes

1. See especially G. Schopen, "Two Problems in the History of Indian Buddhism: The Layman/Monk Distinction and the Doctrines of the Transference of Merit," *Studien zur Indologie und Iranistik* 10 (1985) 23ff; Schopen, "The Stūpa Cult and the Extant Pāli Vinaya," *Journal of the Pāli Text Society* 13 (1989) 24ff.
2. T.W. Rhys Davids & J.E. Carpenter, *The Dīgha Nikāya*, Vol. II (London: 1903) 141. All references to the Pāli text are to this edition.
3. T.W. and C.A.F. Rhys Davids, *Dialogues of the Buddha*, Part II (London: 1910) 154.
4. A. Hirakawa, "The Rise of Mahāyāna Buddhism and Its Relationship to the Worship of Stupas," *Memoirs of the Toyo Bunko* 22 (1963) 102.
5. N. Dutt, "Popular Buddhism," *The Indian Historical Quarterly* 21 (1945) 250-51.
6. A. Bareau, "La composition et les étapes de la formation progressive du mahāparinirvāṇa-sūtra ancien," *Bulletin de l'école française d'extrême-orient* 66 (1979) 45-103.
7. As a small sample—and it is only that—of these "conclusions" see H. Oldenberg, *Buddha. Sein Leben, seine Lehre, seine Gemeinde* (Berlin: 1897) 428; N. Dutt, "Place of Laity in Early Buddhism," *The Indian Historical Quarterly* 21 (1945) 164; Ét. Lamotte, "Le bouddhisme des läics," *Studies in Indology and Buddhology. Presented in Honour of Professor Susumi Yamaguchi on the Occasion of his Sixtieth Birthday* (Kyoto: 1955) 80; Lamotte, *Histoire du bouddhisme indien* (Louvain: 1958) 81; D.L. Snellgrove, "Śākyamuni's Final Nirvāṇa," *Bulletin of the School of Oriental and African Studies* 36 (1973) 410; A. Bareau, "Le parinirvāṇa du buddha et la naissance de la religion bouddhique," *Bulletin de l'école française d'extrême-orient* 61 (1974) 283-84; G. Nagao, "The Architectural Tradition in Buddhist Monasticism," in *Studies in History of Buddhism*, ed. A.K. Narain (Delhi: 1980) 193-94; M. Wijayaratna, *Le moine bouddhiste. selon les textes du theravāda* (Paris: 1983) 183; R. Gombrich, *Theravada Buddhism. A Social History from Ancient Benares to Modern Colombo* (London & New York: 1988) 119-24; (see also the works cited in notes 4 & 5 above and notes 8-11 below); etc.
8. L. de La Vallée-Poussin, *Nirvāṇa* (Paris: 1924) 7.
9. L. de La Vallée-Poussin, *Le dogme et la philosophie du bouddhisme* (Paris: 1930) 64; 191.
10. L. de La Vallée-Poussin, *L'inde aux temps des mauryas et des barbares, grecs, scythes, parthes et yue-tchi* (Paris: 1930) 141.
11. A. Hirakawa, "Stupa Worship," in *The Encyclopedia of Religion*, ed. M. Eliade, Vol.14 (New York: 1987) 93.
12. K.R. Norman, "Notes on the Ahraurā Version of Aśoka's First Minor Rock Edict," *Indo-Iranian Journal* 26 (1983) 278.
13. W. Geiger, *Pāli Literature and Language*, trans. by B. Ghosh (Calcutta: 1943) § 78.7; see also *Mahāparinibbāna* V.11 quoted below.

14. This seems clear as well in *Mahāparinibbāna* V.17 where Ānanda tries to dissuade the Buddha from passing away in Kusinārā.
15. R. Vira & L. Chandra, *Gilgit Buddhist Manuscripts (Facsimile Edition)*, Part 6 (New Delhi: 1974) fol.852.8; N. Dutt, *Gilgit Manuscripts*, Vol. III, Part 2 (Srinigar: 1942) 127.13; *The Tibetan Tripiṭaka (Peking Edition)*, ed. D.T. Suzuki, Vol. 41 (Tokyo-Kyoto: 1955) 281-1-1: *de'i tshe dge slong nad pa zhig gnas khang du shi nas de dge slong rnams kyis dur khrod du khyer te ro la mchod pa byas bsregs nas de nas gtsug lag khang du lhags pa dang /*.
16. Vira & Chandra, *Gilgit Buddhist Manuscripts*, Part 6, fol.852.6ff; Dutt, *Gilgit Manuscripts*, Vol. III, Part 2, 127.4ff; *Tibetan Tripiṭaka (Peking)*, Vol. 41, 280-5-6ff: *de'i tshe dge slong zhig shi nas dge slong rnams kyis de phyung ste / dur khrod du de bzhin du bor nas ... re shig kho bo'i ro la mchod pa yang ma byas par ... dge slong rnams kyis sngar de'i ro la mchod pa byas la ...* This and the preceding passage are two of a series of interesting passages dealing with monastic funerals that occur in the *Mūlasarvāstivāda-vinaya*; I am now working on a detailed study of this material.
17. J.S. Speyer (ed.), *Avadānaçataka. A Century of Edifying Tales belonging to the Hīnayāna* (St. Petersburg: 1906-09, repr. The Hague: 1958) i 271.15ff; *Tibetan Tripiṭaka (Peking)*, Vol. 40, 184-1-8ff. On the 'sectarian affiliation of the *Avadānaśataka* see, most recently, J.-U. Hartmann, "Zur Frage der Schulzugehörigkeit des Avadānaśataka," in *Zur Schulzugehörigkeit von Werken der Hīnayāna-Literatur*, hrsg. H. Bechert, Erster Teil (Göttingen: 1985) 219-24.
18. So L. Feer, *Avadāna-Çataka. Cent légendes bouddhiques* (Annales du musée guimet, t. XVIII) (Paris: 1891) 185.
19. Dutt, *Gilgit Manuscripts*, Vol. III, Part 2, 120.6ff.
20. For similar 'cognate' constructions see R. Gnoli, *The Gilgit Manuscript of the Saṅghabhedavastu. Being the 17th and Last Section of the Vinaya of the Mūlasarvāstivādin*, Part I (Serie Orientale Roma XLIX,1) (Roma: 1977) 59.18: *atithīnām atithipūjā kartavyā* (the reading here, however, is not absolutely certain; see 59 n.b); N. Dutt, *Gilgit Manuscripts*, Vol. III, Part IV (Calcutta: 1950) 177.9: *jñātīnāṃ vā jñātipūjā na kriyate*, etc.
21. For the Sanskrit text of the *Mahāparinirvāṇa-sūtra* I refer throughout to the edition in E. Waldschmidt, *Das Mahāparinirvāṇasūtra. Text in Sanskrit und Tibetisch, verglichen mit dem Pāli nebst einer Übersetzung der chinesischen Entsprechung im Vinaya der Mūlasarvāstivādins*, t.I-III (Berlin: 1950-51)—all references are to the paragraph numbers imposed on the text by Waldschmidt.
22. For the Tibetan text of the *Vinaya-kṣudraka-vastu* I have used the 'edition' in *The Sde-Dge Mtshal-par Bka'-'Gyur. A Facsimile Edition of the 18th Century Redaction of Si-Tu Chos-Kyi-'Byuṅ-Gnas Prepared under the Direction of H.H. the 16th Rgyal-Dbaṅ Karma-Pa*, Vol. 10 (Delhi: 1977): the account of the death of Mahāprajāpatī is found at fol.224.6ff.
23. E.B. Cowell & R.A. Neil (eds.), *The Divyāvadāna. A Collection of Early Buddhist Legends* (Cambridge: 1886) 433.13-16; S. Mukhopadhyaya (ed.), *The*

Aśokāvadāna. Sanskrit Text compared with Chinese Versions (New Delhi: 1963) 132.7—the text is cited from the latter; for variants see 132 n.6.
24. Gnoli, *The Gilgit Manuscript of the Saṅghabhedavastu*, Part I, 161.14.
25. Speyer, *Avadānaçataka*, i 349.6, 352.16, 357.3, 361.14, 365.13, 369.18, 373.10, 377.12, 383.2, 387.5; ii 5.17.
26. It is worth noting here that in the Sanskrit text of the "injunction" singular pronominal and verbal forms are used and it is clearly addressed to Ānanda alone.
27. *...āyuṣmān mahākāśyapo jñāto ma(hā)puṇyo lābhī cīvarapiṇḍapāta-śayan(āsana)gl(ā)napratyayabhaiṣajyapariṣkārāṇāṃ*, 49.17.
28. On Mahākāśyapa's place in the text as a whole see Bareau, "La composition et les étapes de la formation progressive du mahāparinirvāṇasūtra ancien," 70ff; Professor Bareau refers to the incidents involving Kāśyapa as "la série des récits inventés par les auteurs de *Vinayapiṭaka* pour glorifier Mahākāśyapa".
29. In dating the section in the *Milinda* in which our passage occurs thus I follow P. Demiéville, "Les versions chinoises du milindapañha," *Bulletin de l'école française d'extrême-orient* 24 (1924) 34-35; Lamotte, *Histoire du bouddhisme indien*, 465; I.B. Horner, *Milinda's Questions*, Vol. I (London: 1963) xxx-xxxi; cf. the discussion in K.R. Norman, *Pāli Literature. Including the Canonical Literature in Prakrit and Sanskrit of All the Hīnayāna Schools of Buddhism* (*A History of Indian Literature*, ed. J. Gonda, Vol. VII, Fasc.2) (Wiesbaden: 1983) 110-13.
30. The text cited here and throughout is from V. Trenckner (ed.), *The Milindapañho. Being Dialogues between King Milinda and the Buddhist Sage Nāgasena* (London: 1880) 177ff; the translation here is from Horner, *Milinda's Questions*, i 249ff.
31. Horner, *Milinda's Questions*, i 250 n.1.
32. I.B. Horner (ed.), *Madhuratthavilāsinī. The Commentary on Buddhavaṃsa of Bhadantācariya Buddhadatta Mahāthera* (London: 1946) vi.
33. Horner, *Madhuratthavilāsinī*, 99; I.B. Horner, *The Clarifier of the Sweet Meaning (Madhuratthavilāsinī). Commentary on the Chronicle of Buddhas (Buddhavaṃsa) by Buddhadatta Thera* (London: 1978) 142.
34. P. Masefield, *Divine Revelation in Pali Buddhism* (London: 1986) 1-36. Masefield's conclusions are not infrequently overstated and problematic but he clearly shows that the Pāli texts will not support a simple equation of *sāvaka* and *bhikkhu*.
35. cf. G. Schopen, "Filial Piety and the Monk in the Practice of Indian Buddhism: A Question of 'Sinicization' Viewed from the Other Side," *T'oung Pao* 70 (1984) 110-26; Schopen, "On Monks, Nuns and 'Vulgar' Practices: The Introduction of the Image Cult into Indian Buddhism," *Artibus Asiae* 49.1/2 (1988/89) 153-68.

THE MAITREYA IMAGE IN SHICHENG AND GUANDING'S BIOGRAPHY OF ZHIYI

Koichi Shinohara
McMaster University

1. Introduction

Guanding's (561-632) biography of Zhiyi (539-598),[1] and other early biographies largely based on Guanding's work, report that Zhiyi ended his life in front of the large Maitreya image at Shicheng.[2] In this paper I would like to examine this account by Guanding and compare it with other stories associated with the Maitreya image at Shicheng preserved elsewhere. Such a comparison might throw some light on the circumstances of Zhiyi's death and the nature of Guanding's account of this event that was to prove particularly influential in later years.[3]

In this investigation I am primarily interested in the nature of Guanding's biography. I am interested in studying traditional biographies of religious figures as religious literature in their own right, and not simply as sources for a critical and historical reconstruction of the lives of these figures. From this point of view I have for some time been studying Chinese biographies of Buddhist monks ("biographies of eminent monks"), paying particular attention to their sources and the manner in which the biographies were "constructed"—for the most part after the death of their subjects. I am particularly interested in the relationship between miracle stories and religious biographies.[4]

A variety of early sources relevant to the study of Zhiyi's biography has been preserved in a collection of historical documents concerning the early history of the Tiantai community called *Guoqing bolu*.[5] Since this work, which Zhiji had begun but was unable to finish before his death, was also completed by Guanding, there is a possibility that Guanding might have adjusted its contents according to his distinctive conception of Zhiyi's life.[6] Nevertheless, these sources are useful for examining the manner in which his important disciple Guanding composed his highly ideological account of Zhiyi's life, relying heavily on a variety of miracle stories woven into the biography itself. Further light can be thrown on the nature of those miracle stories that center around Buddha images and that are found at crucial turning points in Guanding's account by comparing them with other accounts of the miracles associated with the same images that may be found elsewhere. In this paper I focus on the well-established account of Zhiyi's death in front of the Maitreya image in Shicheng and compare it with other stories about this image that have been preserved. One important reason for choosing this focus is the discrepancy between Guanding's account and the underlying theme of the other miracle stories associated with the image: whereas Guanding's stories insist that Zhiyi knew beforehand that he was to die in front of the image, other stories associated with the image indicate that it was often the recipient of fervent pleas for a cure from sickness; these stories suggest that Zhiyi too might have been requesting the image to cure his illness. This discrepancy in turn serves to highlight the ideological and "constructed" character of Guanding's biography.

2. *Guanding's account of Zhiyi's death in front of the Shicheng image*

Guanding devotes a long passage (195c5-196b27) to the description of Zhiyi's death. The first part of this description is devoted to a story of Zhiyi's return to Mt. Tiantai and a miraculous visit of a deity, known to Zhiyi from an earlier encounter, and from whom Zhiyi learned about his approaching death. Let me begin my discussion by briefly summarizing the story about this visit of a deity.

One night, when a bright moon illumined the floor, Zhiyi sat alone and gave a long lecture as if someone had asked a question about a difficult problem. Attendant monk Zhixi (558-629)[7] said to him the next morning, "I don't understand what I saw last night". Zhiyi answered, "I had a dream. First a strong wind suddenly rose and destroyed a treasure *stupa*. Then a foreign monk (*fanseng*) said to me, 'A man's spiritual capacity may be compared to fire wood; the spiritual function of illumination may be compared to the fire; the secondary assistance (*pangzhu*) may be compared to the wind. When these three conditions are met, the path of transformation is in operation ("one's teaching work is successful"?). During the night (many years ago when we met) on top of the Huading peak, we agreed on (my always being with you at your side) like a shadow or an echo. The capacity and function are about to be exhausted; the secondary assistance has also ceased (i.e., the three conditions mentioned above are about to be lost). Therefore, I came to tell you about this.' I also saw the Master of the Nanyue and Meditation Master Xi[8] who asked me to lecture on the teaching. So, I said to myself, 'All other teachings are clear and one can study them by oneself. Only the teaching of the Three Contemplations and Three Wisdoms must first be taught face to face'. After I finished lecturing on the teaching, they said to me, 'The other realm is decorated and put in order (to welcome you). We have been waiting for you for a long time. The karmic condition dictates that you must go. We shall send you over there.' I paid respect to them and accepted their judgement. The sign of death has now been given. I remember the dream I had as a young man in which it was said that I should end my life here.[9] This is the reason why I was always happy to return to this mountain. I have now been miraculously informed (of my approaching death). My death will occur in the near future. After I die, place my corpse in the place I have specified on the south-western peak.[10] Place stones around the corpse and plant pine trees to cover the grave pit. Build two white *stupas*, so that those who see them may give rise to the aspiration for enlightenment."[11]

The ruler[12] had returned in the tenth month and sent Gao Xiaoxin into the mountain to bring Zhiyi back. Zhiyi distributed his possessions to be given to the poor; he marked the location of temple buildings with sticks, and drew a diagram of the manner in which the temple was to be built; he instructed the monks, saying, "The temple will be built according to these instructions. I can see its staircases rising awe-inspiringly right in front of my eyes, but the building will be completed after my death. I will not see it, but you will see it. Later, you shall build the temple, following these instructions." Disciples doubted the veracity of this prediction and said, "This mountain is very steep. How could a temple be built on this mountain?" Zhiyi answered, "It's not a small project. It will be managed by the prince's family (*wang jia*, which could also be read as Wang family)." Monks present heard these words together, but speculated differently about their meaning. Some said that the word *wang* is a surname; others said that the word means the king of gods; still others said that it refers to the king of the state. Many views were debated loudly, but no consensus emerged. Now (when Guanding is writing this biography), the matter has been settled by what actually happened; we all know what the Master meant earlier. It meant the "king" in the sense of the imperial ruler of the state.[13]

In the first half of this long passage the "foreign monk" (*fanseng*) mentions the incident on the Huading peak. The incident on the Huading peak is described in detail in an earlier passage in Guanding's biography describing Zhiyi's first visit to Mt. Tiantai (193b1-16). There the same figure is described as the "supernatural monk" (*shenseng*) who appeared to Zhiyi after his conquest of the monsters on the Huading peak, taught him the teaching of One Real Truth (*yi shi di*) and promised to be with him all the time after that incident. The meaning of these stories seems clear: Zhiyi's teaching attained its distinctive identity and uniqueness while he was on Mt. Tiantai for the first time, and came to an end when he returned to the same mountain for the second time at the end of his life; when he went back to Tiantai, Zhiyi became fully aware that he was soon to die.

The second half of this passage focuses on the close relationship between Zhiyi's life and the building of the Guoqing temple on Mount Tiantai shortly after his death. I have spelled out in greater detail elsewhere what I would regard as the basic framework of Guanding's biography of Zhiyi: the life of Zhiyi was constructed very carefully as the story of the emergence of the Tiantai community with the support of the Sui ruler Yangdi.[14] The emergence of the community and the ruler's support were said to have been predicted a long time before they occurred; the implication is that these events were predetermined and inevitable. Zhiyi's experience on the Huading peak that occurred shortly after his first entry into Mt. Tiantai and the building of the Guoqingsi there shortly after Zhiyi's death were both crucial elements in this general framework. Here the story of Zhiyi's death is tightly incorporated into this basic framework through references to these events; it also shares their character of being predetermined. Zhiyi's death needed to occur at the time it did, during his last visit to Mt. Tiantai and before the construction of the Guoqing temple, and Zhiyi was himself fully aware of the inevitability of his death at this time.

In the subsequent section in Guanding's biography which describes the immediate circumstances of Zhiyi's death a Maitreya image appears and plays an important role.

Zhiyi followed Gao Xiaoxin, whom Prince Guang, Zhiyi's secular patron, had sent, and started on the journey to Jiangdu, the city where Prince Guang, who rose meteorically in power after Zhiyi's death and became the second Sui-emperor Yangdi, lived. When they arrived at Shicheng in Shanxian, Zhiyi said that he was ill. Zhiyi said to his disciple Zhiyue (544-611)[15], "The great prince wanted me to come. I could not disobey his words, and so I came. I know that my life is to end here. Therefore, we should not proceed any further. Shicheng is at the Western gate of the Tiantai mountains. The great Buddha (located there) is the miraculous image of the future Buddha (Maitreya). It is a good location to attend to last things mindfully. Divide my robes, bowls, and other implements into two sets and offer one to Maitreya (ie., the stone image) and use the other to meet the needs of the monastic community."[16] After saying these words, Zhiyi lay down on his right side, facing West, and recited the names of Amitabha, Prajna, and Avalokitesvara.

After rejecting medicine and food, Zhiyi dictated his will, wrote 46 characters with his own hands, and left his incense burner with the pattern of lotus flowers and the *ruyi* made of rhinoceros horn to the great king. Zhiyi asked his one bowl and three robes to be cleaned and to have two scriptures (*erbu jing*) recited so that these scriptures would be the last sounds that he heard and reflected upon in this life. These scriptures were the Lotus and *Wuliang shou* scriptures, and Zhiyi then listened to them as they were recited, uttering certain phrases. When the scriptures were being recited, an official of Wu Region, Zhang Da and others, accompanied by five people, saw the vision of a great Buddha, twice as large as the stone image. Its light filled the mountain and entered into the hall. Some monks had an auspicious dream and others saw extraordinary manifestations. Even though they had these experiences in different places, the experiences occurred at this same time.

Zhiyi's final instructions included an exchange with his disciple Zhilang, in which he comments, answering one of Zhilang's questions, that his teachers and friends were coming to him in the company of Avalokitesvara. After these instructions, Zhiyi said to the monastic officer, "When a man's life ends, you hear the sound of the bell. He increases his concentration, and his breathing becomes slow and extended. When he stops breathing, that is his end. Why should we wait until the body cools down and then sound the bell? As for the worldly practice of uttering the loud sound of crying and wearing funeral dresses, you should not adopt these practices." After saying these words, Zhiyi uttered the names of the three treasures; he looked as if he was entering a meditative state. At the *wei* hour (2:00 am) on the 24th day of the 11th month of the 17th year of the Kaihuang period, sixty year cycle designation *dingsi* (598), he passed away. He was in his 60th year, and in his 40th year as a monk.

According to this account by Guanding, Zhiyi who had known from earlier miraculous conversations with the foreign monk, his teacher Nanyue, and his former disciple Faxi, that he was going to end his life shortly, chose the site of the great Buddha image in Shicheng as the location of his death. The Shicheng image was a Maitreya image, and Zhiyi appears to have presented to it half of his remaining possessions at the time of his death. Later when the *Wuliangshou jing* was recited in front of Zhiyi, miracles occurred around the image and elsewhere.

3. The text of Zhiyi's vow (Guoqing bolu, no. 64)

The *Guoqing bolu* contains a very important document composed by Zhiyi himself that concerns the Shicheng image. It is a letter to Prince Guang dated the 21st day of the 11th month of the 17th year of Kaihuang (598), namely, three days before his death, in which Zhiyi requests the prince to repair important objects of worship located in three places: to bring together the images of Vipasyin and Kasyapa in the Wu Commandary and restore them to their original form (these images were originally found together), to repair the Asoka *stupa* at Mao District, and to redecorate the ten *zhang* tall Maitreya image at Shan District with gold leaves.[17] This letter, designated as *Fayuan shuwen* and preserved as the 64th item in the *Guoqing bolu*, is referred to as the "the text of a vow" (*Fayuan shu*) in another very important letter by Zhiyi to Prince Guang.[18]

The document begins as a letter in which Zhiyi requests Prince Guang to repair these objects of worship located in the three diffrent places.[19] But this short paragraph is then followed by a statement that "Zhiyi respectfully speaks". Zhiyi begins the long section following this phrase by commenting on the importance of the images and the shortcomings of his own life, and then makes the following statement: "Happily I encountered an illustrious age when the rulers (of the Sui dynasty) became the pillar of the Buddhist world which spread the blessing of the Teaching everywhere like the sun. Relying on the imperial virtue, and receiving the support of the power of the multitude, and in order to encourage those who enjoy right karmic conditions, I vow to repair the objects in the three places—first, to promote and glorify the Teaching of the Three Buddhas, second, to protect the land of the Great Sui, and third, looking downward, for the sake of all sentient beings in the world." The passage continues describing the benefit of repairing the *stupa* and images in terms of the three categories mentioned, that of benefits to the Buddhas, the emperor, and the people.

A new theme is then introduced: Zhiyi says that he had entertained this thought of repairing the *stupa* and the images for a long time, but had never had the opportunity to realize his desire. Now, his illness has become more grave and he is approaching his death ("journey to the West"); he certainly does not hold any attachment to his physical body that was to be compared with a jar of poison[20] or a fragile earthen ware; his life had already been given to the Three Treasures earlier. After this comment, Zhiyi then puts a question or a request to "a deity" (*weishen*): "If my life is to survive this illness, and if I am capable of good deeds and will not stain the Buddha's Teaching, then please remove this sickness soon and let me fulfil my vow quickly and completely. If my life, though not completely ended, is full of obstructions posed by Mara, and I am to do a great deal of damage to those endowed with good capacities, and stain and disturb the Buddha's Teaching, then there is no reason that I should remain in this world; please (*yuan*) let my life end, and after my life ends, pass my various vows (concerning the repair of the *stupa* and images) on to someone who remains behind (*houren*; probably a reference to Prince Guang),[21] and let him carry out the work of repair in an orderly fashion. I beg that the restoration of the Three Treasures (here probably referring to the *stupa* and images in question) be completed quickly."

Zhiyi then states that he had made this vow earlier at the Jinguangming daozhang hall at Folong, and that he was making the vow for the second time in front of the stone image of Shicheng.

The letter that began with a request to Prince Guang to repair the sacred objects in three locations appears to end with Zhiyi's fervent request to the stone image. The vow described in this document has a complex structure: on one level, the vow is a vow to repair the objects of worship in the three locations of Wu Commandary, Mao District, and Shan District. This may have been the vow that he had made earlier at Folong and is repeating here. On a different level, however, Zhiyi is making a related but slightly different vow. Having stopped in front of the stone image at Shicheng and realizing the graveness of his illness, Zhiyi is making a twofold request to the stone image: if he is to live, let him complete the task set forth in the previous vow quickly himself; if he is not to live, let someone else, that is, Prince Guang carry out the task quickly and successfully.

Focusing on the fact that the vow is made in front of the Shicheng image, I interpret the meaning of this second level of the vow as follows. Realizing the gravity of his illness, Zhiyi wanted to live and made the vow in front of the large image, promising that if he could live he would repair the image. This might have been the immediate context of the vow. References to the other two places where Zhiyi promised to repair the sacred objects associated with King Asoka would in this interpretation have been secondary. Zhiyi may possibly have been trying to enhance the importance of the Shicheng image by placing it in the company of a very well-known Asoka *stupa* and image. If we read the immediate context of Zhiyi's vow in this way, then the meaning of the second part of his request may be interpreted as follows. Zhiyi is here speaking both to the stone image and to Prince Guang: he promised the stone image that even if he died, the repair would be completed (this weakens the force of his first vow, but makes it less of a matter of crude *do ut des*); he at the same time emphasizes the importance of the request to Prince Guang by saying that it was a promise he had personally made to the stone image.

Why did Zhiyi write a special letter to Prince Guang only three days before his death concerning the repair of one Asoka *stupa* and two images? Repairing *stupas* and images was indeed a meritorious act and one may answer the question by saying that this letter simply confirms Zhiyi's eagerness to perform meritorious deeds. But why did Zhiyi repeat the vow at this crucial point in time? There may well have been a more immediate and urgent reason. By reading this complex document in the manner proposed above, we can answer these questions more coherently: Zhiyi was not ready to die, and realizing the gravity of his illness, he was trying steadfastedly, even three days before his death, to obtain a miraculous cure from an image. It is thus natural that the vow was made so close to his death; the more serious the situation, the more likely Zhiyi must have been to resort to this dramatic measure.

Guanding's biography noted that Zhiyi presented his possessions to Maitreya. Later, Guanding records a series of miracles involving this image: Zhang Da and others had a vision of a large Buddha, twice the size of this image; its light filled the mountain.[22] These stories may have been related to the making of the vow mentioned in the *Guoqing bolu*, document no. 64. Zhiyi made the vow and presented his possessions to the image; later, the miracle may have been believed to have occurred in response to Zhiyi's request.

We have noted above that in his *Biezhuan* biography, Guanding describes Zhiyi's death as an event that Zhiyi himself knew was about to take place. Even before he travelled to Shicheng, Zhiyi is said to have made necessary preparations for his death, choosing the site of the later Guoqingsi temple, and predicting how it was to be built later; he then chose Shicheng as the site of his death. In contrast, the *Fayuan shuwen* projects a different picture of Zhiyi in front of the image. Zhiyi here does not seem to have been fully prepared to die at that time; rather, he describes the image in very favorable terms by grouping it with other well-known Asoka images, and suggests that if he recovers from the illness, he will repair the image.

We have noted earlier that we can no longer assume that all documents in the *Guoqing bolu* are historically reliable and free from editorial distortions. Yet, the fact that the description in the *Fayuan shuwen* diverges from that in Guanding's description of the same events in the *Biezhuan* appears to indicate that the *Fayuan shuwen* account is at least free of an editorical revision in Guanding's hand. A brief review of the tradition associated with the Shicheng image also suggests that the *Fayuan shuwen* account may be closer to the actual historical circumstances, and it was Guanding who revised this existing account rather extensively in his description of Zhiyi's life in the *Biezhuan*.

4. Stories about the Shicheng image

Let us now turn to a brief survey of the stories concerning the Shicheng image that are found in other sources; indeed their content lends support to the analysis of Zhiyi's vow that I have just offered. The image at Shan District is described as "a stone image of Maitreya, ten *zhang* tall" in the *Guoqing bolu*, document no. 64 (line 2,3). In the official inscription for Zhiyi compiled by Liu Guyan (*Guoqing bolu*, document no. 93), the compiler of the inscription, Liu Guyan, describes the image as a stone image, one hundred *zhi* tall and covered with gold leaf, and says that the image was created by Prince Yuanxiang of Nanping, *taizai* of Liang (1.108). This title refers to Xiao Wei, the eighth son of Wendi of the Liang dynasty and a brother of Wudi; he first bore the title of Prince of Jian'an.[23] The location is given here in greater detail: "in the Shicheng temple to the east of Shan" (l. 107).

a. The Gaoseng zhuan story

The *Gaoseng zhuan* biography of Senghu (412ab) is for the most part a story of the stone image of Maitreya, ten *zhang* tall, at the Yinyuesi temple of Shicheng mountain. Senghu was originally a man of Shan[24] in Kuaiji. He later lived at the Yinyuesi temple in the Shicheng mountain. There was a cliff of rock, undisturbed by worldly visitors, to the north of the temple. The cliff went straight up to a height of more than ten *zhang* (about 25 meters). In the middle of the cliff was a pattern that looked like the representation of flames and light on Buddhist images. There were bushes and trees on top of the cliff, and their twisting trunks cast shadows over the cliff. Senghu frequently went to the wall, and then saw bright light illumininating it and heard instrumental music and songs of praise. Because of this he held an incense burner and made the vow to carve the mountain cliff and make a stone image ten *zhang* in height there. This image was respectfully to copy the appearance of Maitreya 1,000 *zhi* (about 240 meters) tall; it would enable all those sentient beings whose karmic conditions were suitable to see what it would be like when Maitreya Buddha appeared as predicted in the scriptures on three future occasions to preach and bring salvation to them.[25] During the Jianwu period of the Southern Qi dynasty (494-497),[26] Senghu gathered monks and laymen (to form the community in support of this project) and began carving the image. After several years, when only the rough outline of the face of the image had been carved, Senghu became ill and died. Just before his death, he made the vow saying that his project was not something that anyone could finish in one life time, and that he would complete the project in his second incarnation.

Later, a monk Sengshu resumed the project, but for lack of resources, he was unable to bring it to completion. In the sixth year of the Tianjian period (of the Liang dynasty; 502-519) Lu Xian of the Wu Commandary, who had the position of the Director of Shifeng, had left the city to which he had been assigned and was returning to the capital. He was spending the night at Shanji (same as Shan District?). The wind began to blow and it started to rain; it became very dark. Lu Xian was frightened, and only half asleep (*jiamei*). Suddenly, three monks (*daoren*, "men of the Way") appeared in a dream and said to him, "Your knowledge and trustworthiness are correct and firmly established, and you are naturally safe and at peace. The honourable one of Jian'an (referring to Xiao Wei) is suffering from illness and he is not yet cured. If you can arrange to have the stone image started by Senghu brought to completion, the prince will regain his health. Miraculous communication is not unreal. You ought to get the work started." Xian returned to the capital, but after a year, he forgot about this earlier dream. Later, when he was going out of the city gate, he saw a monk and said to him, "Will you let us hear you give a lecture at my place and stay overnight?" The monk replied by saying, "Do you still remember the matter about the Prince of Jian'an I entrusted to you last year at Shanji?" Xian was then frightened, and said, "I don't remember". The man of the Way said laughing, "You should think about it carefully", and took his leave. Xian realized that this monk was not an ordinary monk and went after him quickly, but after 100 steps, the monk suddenly disappeared. Xian suddenly understood the meaning of the monk's statements, and remembered the earlier dream. The monk was the third monk among those whom he saw in Shanji. Xian then ran to the Prince of Jian'an. The prince reported the story to the emperor. The emperor then ordered the Vinaya master Sengyou to take charge of the matter of the image.[27] The faith of the Prince was increased, and overjoyed he made offerings and vowed to complete the work of building the image.

The day before Sengyou arrived, a monk at the (Yinyue?) temple had a dream in which a great deity wearing a black robe followed by an army of powerful soldiers stood at the site of the cave in which the image was being carved, and they discussed numbers (?). The next day the Vinaya master You appeared. Such was the miraculous nature of this event. The cave for the image that Senghu had carved was too shallow. It had to be carved further for a length of five *zhang* (about 12 meters). Then the head dress was carved. After that the torso was carved and the polishing of the torso was about to be completed. In the middle of the night the place of the character *wan* changed its colour to red and became raised. On the chest of the present image, the place of the character *wan* is still not covered with gold leaf, and the red colour remains. The work on the image began in the 12th year of Tianjian (513) and ended in the spring of the 15th year of Tianjian (516). In the sitting position the image is five *zhang* tall; standing up it is ten *zhang* tall.[28] In front of the image cave, a three story platform was built; a temple gate and other buildings were also constructed, and a community of monks was established for the purpose for serving the image... After the image was completed, Prince of Jian'an's sickness slowly disappeared.

We have noted above that in Liu Guyan's inscription the Shicheng image is said to have been built by Prince Yuanxiang of Nanping, *taizai* of Liang, and that this prince had the title of Prince of Jian'an. The stone image in Senghu's biography is also said to be that of Maitreya (a14), ten *zhang* tall (a13), located in the Shicheng mountain (a9) or in Shan District (a23). There is little doubt that the Shicheng image that is mentioned in Guanding's biography and in Zhiyi's letter to Prince Guang is identical with the image in Senghu's biography. Two major themes in the story about this image in Senghu's biography are of particular interest to us here. First, the relationship between this image and Prince Jian'an is described here as a story of a cure. Liu Guyan's reference to the same prince as the person who originally built the image indicates that this image was known widely as the image closely associated with this prince, and thus, the reputation of this image as an image of miraculous cure may also have been well-established. If this were the case, then our interpretation suggested above that Zhiyi may have appealed to this image for a cure from his own illness becomes more plausible.

The second theme that bears on our discussion is that of the long history behind this image. According to the *Gaoseng zhuan*, the construction of this image was started earlier by monk Senghu, and Prince Jian'an only helped to bring the task to completion many years after the monk's death by arranging to have the famous monk Sengyou placed in change of the project. In his complex statement about the vow discussed in some detail above, Zhiyi appeared to realize that he might not be able to fulfil his promise to repair the image and is instructing his patron Prince Guang to bring the task to completion. If Zhiyi was familiar with the long story about this image now preserved in the *Gaoseng zhuan*, he might have understood his own situation of having promised to repair the image but being prevented from fulfilling the promise because of his illness as a situation similar to that which obtained when the image was first constructed. In both cases illness was to be cured when the work on the image was completed; in both cases, however, it was going to be secular princes who were to bring the tasks to completion, and the monks who started the task were not going to be able to complete them.

b. Daoxuan's story in the Xu gaoseng zhuan *biography of Sengming*

Daoxuan's various collections of image miracle stories contain passages on this image at Shicheng in the Shan District. Thus we can examine the later developments of the stories about the stone image of Senghu by consulting these passages. In the list of image miracle stories attached at the end of the biography of Sengming, Daoxuan tells the story of Senghu's stone image (693c15-28).

More recently under the Northern Qi dynasty of the Gao family, monk Senghu was single-minded in following the Way, but rather than cultivating the path of wisdom, he made the vow to build a stone image of the height of eight *zhang*. Everybody wondered how such a massive project could be carried out. Later in a valley to the north of his temple he found a large rock which was eight *zhang* long. He then hired a rock carver and began the work of carving the image. The carver worked around the rock and roughly finished carving the front of the torso, but the back was still uncarved and facing the ground. The carver used six implements[29] and tried to lift the rock, but he could not move it. Then overnight the rock had turned itself over. Thus, the carver finished the work and moved the image to the image hall.

On the day when Jinzhou[30] was to fall (in the year 576)[31], the image sweated and the sweat flowed on the ground. When the (Northern) Zhou soldiers entered (Northern Qi) and burnt down many Buddhist temples, this image alone did not change its appearance (or, did not show fear?). The soldiers wanted to tear it down. Over sixty people and oxen pulled it, but it would not move. Suddenly a strange monk appeared and hitting the ground with bricks and wood, built a fort around it. The work was completed in a very short period of time, and then the monk disappeared. The image later appeared in a dream of a pious layman and said, "I have pains in my fingers". After waking up, the man looked at the image. Seeing that two of its fingers were damaged, he repaired them. In the tenth year of Kaihuang (590), a thief stole the flag and parasol decorating the image. Then, the thief dreamt that a man, eight *zhang* tall (about 20 meters) came into his room and accused him. The thief was frightened and apologized for his crime. The image still exists, and the story is found in the *Jingyiji* and various records of monks.

The location of the image is not explicitly stated, but it must have been Jinzhou, since the story about the soldiers trying to tear it down is told in connection with the fall of Jinzhou and the invasion of Zhou soldiers into Qi. Since Jinzhou here is clearly a different location from the Shicheng in the Shan District in which the image in Zhiyi's biography and that in the *Gaoseng zhuan* story of Senghu's image was situated, the story about Senghu's image reported in this *Xu Gaoseng zhuan* passage is about a different image from the one we have examining here. Yet, there are obvious parallels: both are tall stone images, though the height of the two images is given slightly differently; the name of the monk who originally worked on the images is given as Senghu. Perhaps a separate story about Senghu's image developed in a different location under the influence of the *Gaoseng zhuan* story, and Daoxuan picked up that story and recorded it in this collection of miracle stories. Earlier in a discussion of miracle stories associated with Huida, I noted that the geographical setting of Huida's story expanded with Daoxuan from a narrow area in Southern China to a much wider circle including North West China.[32] The shift in the location in the story of Senghu's image have resulted from the same tendency in Daoxuan's work concerning miracle stories. One other notable feature about this version of the Senghu image story is the similarity between this story and other stories associated with Asoka images: stories about the extraordinary weight and its miraculous capacity to escape plundering in a conquered city are most notable.[33]

c. The Ji shenzhou sanbao gantong lu *story*

Daoxuan records the story of the stone image in the Shan District in the *Ji shenzhou sanbao gantong lu* as an appendix to the story about the eight *zhang* tall golden image at the Guangzhai temple (419c-420a).[34]

The image was originally produced by King Asoka at the beginning of Chinese history (*song qu*). Earlier Meditation Master Tanguang arrived from the north. He travelled along mountains and rivers and made nature the dwelling place of his spiritual life. Seeing the beauty of this mountain, he built a grass hut at the top of the peak. He heard heavenly music in the sky and a voice which said, "This is a land of the Buddha. How come you are making a vegetable garden here?" Hearing this Guang moved southward to the Tiantai mountain. Later, he built a Buddha image. He worked over many years but could not complete the work. (And Tanguang died?)

When Prince Jian'an of the Liang dynasty was ill, it was communicated through a dream that if one could build a stone image at Shan District, then his illness would be cured. Consequently, the Vinaya master Sengyou was invited to come to the mountain. Sengyou disliked the shape and construction of the earlier image that Tanguang had worked on, considering it as too provincial and vulgar. While he was still thinking about it incessantly, in the middle of the night, the mountain collapsed, and an image appeared inside. Only the head was showing, and the body below the neck was still buried in the rock. As they carved the rock, the stone pieces flew away, and the image at the base appeared. This perfectly shaped image was hidden in the rock all the time. Liu Xie wrote an inscription, and it is placed at the site of the image.[35]

There is little doubt that the image in this story is identical with the Shicheng image we have been studying here. It was the image in Shan District that was completed by Sengyou and its completion cured Prince Jian'an's illness. In this story the image is for the first time said explicitly to have been originally produced by King Asoka. Interestingly, the name of the monk who began the work on this image is given as Tanguang, and not as Senghu as in the *Gaoseng zhuan* biography. Thus, if we follow Daoxuan's account alone, Senghu who is associated with a different image in a different location has nothing to do with the Asoka image in Shan District. What was one story in the *Gaoseng zhuan* appears to have split into two in Daoxuan's collections.

Tanguang was closely associated with the Tiantai mountain. We have seen earlier that the name Tanguang was mentioned in connection with the story of Zhiyi's first visit to the Tiantai mountain in Guanding's *Biezhuan*. The *Gaoseng zhuan* biography of Jin Sengguang (395c) states that the latter was also known as Tanguang and says that this monk went to the Shicheng mountain in Shan (District) during the Yonghe period of the Jin dynasty (345-356). He first stayed in a rock cave in the southern part of the mountain, but later was told by a mountain deity in a dream to move to the Hanshishan mountain in Zhang'an District. Others built thatched huts next to his residence and the community expanded. These buildings evolved into a temple, which was later called Yinyue.[36] He lived in the mountain for 53 years and died at the end of the Taiyuan period of the Jin dynasty (376-396) at the age of 110.[37]

In Daoxuan's *Ji shenzhou sanbao gantong lu*, the connection between the Shicheng image and the Tiantai mountain received even greater emphasis by its new connection with Tanguang. One theme that remained constant was the story that connects the completion of the massive project of building this image with the cure of Prince Jian'an's illness. Daoxuan compiled this collection over 50 years after Zhiyi's death and Guanding's compilation of Zhiyi's biography. If this theme remained closely associated with the Shicheng image at that time, even though the earlier stories associated with this image had gone through a number of changes, it seems quite plausible that both Zhiyi and Guanding were quite familiar with this story about the image as an image known for its power of miraculous cure.[38]

5. Concluding comments

In an earlier paper I suggested that the death of Zhiyi must have been a profoundly "liminal" incident for the Tiantai community.[39] The effort of the community to adjust itself to the new situation was furthermore affected profoundly by the meteoric rise of its principal lay sponsor Prince Guang. Zhiyi died on the 24th day of the 11th month of the 17th year of the Kaihuang period of the Sui dynasty (*Biezhuan*, 196b26,27). This date translates into January 7, 598 in the solar calendar. Prince Guang became the crown prince in the year 600 and then rose to the throne in the 604 as Emperor Yangdi. The temple which had been built in Zhiyi's honour[40] was give the name "Guoqingsi" by an imperial edict issued on the 29th day of the tenth month of the first year of Daye (606).[41] Ikeda suggests the date of Liu Guyan's inscription for Zhiyi, titled the "the inscription for the Guoqingsi temple issued by an imperial edict" (*Guoqing bolu*, no. 93) as the third year of the Daye period (607). These dates suggests that the fortunes of the Tiantai community must have risen dramatically after Zhiyi's death, and these years must have been a rather heady time for this community.

A large number of miracle stories are recorded from this period. I pointed out in my earlier article that the basic framework of Guanding's biography, which appears to have been compiled between the years 601 and 605, was constructed by several stories of miraculous events that were said to have occurred at important turning points in Zhiyi's life.[42] A comparison of the miracle stories reported in earlier sources and the stories used to construct the basic framework in Guanding's biography indicates that Guanding must have chosen several stories that were widely known and suitable to his purposes and used these stories as crucial reference points in constructing the framework of his biography. A complex and subtle process of choice must have been made in this context to choose stories that were suitable for Guanding's purposes from the larger pool of available stories and reject others that were not suitable.

The brief review above of the stories associated with the stone image of Maitreya at Shicheng in the Shan District indicates that this image was known as an image capable of miraculous cure. The discussion of the text of the vow that Zhiyi made in front of this image suggested that three days before his death Zhiyi might indeed have been requesting a miraculous cure from this image. As we noted earlier, this theme of Zhiyi (and probably others accompanying him) requesting a miraculous cure of his illness from this stone image is entirely absent in Guanding's biography. According to the account in this biography Zhiyi had received a message from his protective deity that he was to die shortly and himself chose the site of this image as the place where he was to end his life. Would it be entirely inappropriate to speculate that in writing the story about Zhiyi's death, Guanding was confronted with the inconvenient fact that Zhiyi's attempt to secure a miraculous cure from a Maitreya image at Shicheng, known widely for its capacity confer such cure, had failed, and that Guanding had to develop a different set of miraculous stories to explain the timing of Zhiyi's death?

In his discussion of Zhiyi's death Sato Tetsuei commented briefly on the fact that the *Biezhuan*'s description was characterized by dual emphases on the faith in the Lotus sutra and the faith in Amitabha Buddha and that early sources often mention that Amitabha, Avalokitesvara, and Mahasthamaprapta appeared to Zhiyi to welcome him into the other world.[43] Since these figures are more closely associated with the theme of death and rebirth in the Pure Land, it is tempting to speculate that the connection between Zhiyi's death and the Maitreya image in Shicheng, known for its association with the theme of miraculous cure was deemphasized in the stories that developed about Zhiyi's death in the Tiantai community and these stories replaced that theme with an emphasis on stories about Zhiyi's rebirth.

(The research for this paper was carried out with the assistance of a grant from the Social Sciences and Humanities Council of Canada.)

Notes

1. Zhiyi's dates are given in most modern works as 538-597. These dates appear to have been calculated as follows: Guanding's biography gives date of Zhiyi's death as the 24th day of the 11th month of the 17th year of the Kaihuang period (*Taisho daizokyo*, vol. 50, p. 196b26, 27). Zhiyi was said to have been sixty years old at the time of his death. Though the Taisho edition of the *Xu gaoseng zhuan*, based on the Korean edition, gives the date of Zhiyi's death slightly differently, as the 22nd day, the variant reading in the majority of other editions consulted by the editors of the Taisho edition, gives the same date as Guanding's biography, ie., the 24th day. Daoxuan's *Xu gaoseng zhuan* biography states that Zhiyi was sixty-seven years old at the time of his death (567b25). If we adopt the solar calendar date for the 17th year of the Kaihuang period as 597 and, taking account of the traditional Chinese way of counting age, subtract 59 from 597, we can arrive at Zhiyi's dates as 538 to 597, the dates generally given in modern sources. Strictly speaking, however, the lunar and solar years do not correspond with each other perfectly and, most importantly for our purposes, the 24th day of the 11th month of the 17th year of the Kaihuang period happens to correspond to January 8th of the solar year 598 (See Xie Zhongsan and Ouyang Yi, *A Sino-Western Calendar for Two Thousand Years 1-2000 A.D.*, Taipei, 1966, p. 120.) If we follow the same procedure as above, following Guanding's view that Zhiyi was sixty years old at the time of his death, we can propose the year 539 as the date of Zhiyi's birth.

2. *Sui tiantai zhizhe dashi biezhuan* by Guanding, *Taisho daizokyo*, vol. 50, pp. 194a9-b26; *Tiantai guoqingsi zhizhe chanshi beiwen* by Liu Guyan, Ikeda Rosan, *Kokusei hyakuroku no kenkyu* (Tokyo, 1982), p. 467-468, ll. 107-118; *Xu gaoseng zhuan, zhuan* 17, *Taisho daizokyo*, vol. 50, pp. 567a25-b24. Shicheng is located in the Shan District and the image is sometimes identified as the great stone image in Shan district (*shanxian dashifo*, *Ji shenzhou sanbao gantong lu*, *Taisho daizokyo* vol. 52, 419c17.)

3. Zhiyi's biography was discussed in detail in Leon Hurvitz, *Chih-i (538-597): An Introduction to the Life and Ideas of a Chinese Buddhist Monk*, *Mélanges chinois e bouddhiques*, publié par L'Institut Belge des hautes Etudes Chinoises, Douzième volume: 1960-1962 (Bruxelles, Juillet 1962). The emphasis in this discussion is on the critical reconstruction of Zhiyi's life. Guanding's biography, while recognized as indispensable for this reconstruction, is treated with caution "because of Kuan-ting's *Tendenz*" (p. 100). Sato Tetsuei's biography of Zhiyi in the beginning section of his monumental *Tendai daishi no kenkyu* (Kyoto, 1961), pp. 28-73 shares the same basic orientation: it is also an attempt to reconstruct Zhiyi's biography based on a critical examination of sources. I have completed a preliminary study of Guanding's biography of Zhiyi and presented its summary at the annual meeting of the Canadian Society for the Study of Religion in Quebec City in June, 1989 ("Guanding's Biography of Zhiyi: Its Framework and the three Miraculous Images"). The present paper is based on one section of this larger study.

4. I have published a preliminary study of Chinese Buddhist biographies in an article entitled "Two Sources of Chinese Buddhist Biographies: *Stupa* Inscriptions and Miracle Stories", in Phyllis Granoff and Koichi Shinohara, *Monks and Magicians: Religious Biographies in Asia*, (Oakville, Ontario, 1988), pp. 119-228.
5. *Taisho daizokyo*, vol. 46, pp. 793-823. A detailed study of this work with an annotated Japanese translation was recently published by Ikeda Rosan: *Kokusei hyakuroku no kenkyu, ibid.*
6. Hirai Shun'ei, in *Hokke mongu no seiritsu nikansuru kenkyu* (Tokyo, 1985), recently suggested that the comments on Zhiyi's commentaries on the Vimalakirti sutra that are found in the *Guoqing bolu* might have been inserted in historical records in order to strengthen the view that Guanding and later the Tiantai community wished to maintain; in this manner they may have been trying connect the version of these commentaries they produced directly to Zhiyi himself. Hirai's arguments, found in pp. 45-52 in his important work, are summarized in detail in Ikeda Rosan's riview in *Komazawa daigaku bukkyogakubu ronshu*, 16 (1985), pp. 414-434. The comment on the reliablity of the *Guoqing bolu* appears in p. 49 in Hirai's work and p. 419a in Ikeda's summary. Although certain parts of the records in the *Guoqing bolu*, particularly those related to the compilation of Zhiyi's works recorded and edited by Guanding, might have been manipulated by Guanding, we might nevertheless be justified in taking other parts of the records, especially those directly related to Zhiyi's biography and yet not in harmony with Guanding's biography, as faithful reproductions of earlier historical records. It is also possible that these records might reflect the divergent, and possibly earlier, views of the Tiantai community. The information that the collection of documents originally started by Zhiji was later completed as *Guoqing bolu* by Guanding is given in Guanding's preface, *Kosei hyakuroku no kenkyu*, p. 129. See also Ikeda's comment in pp. 13-14 in the same work.
7. His biography is found in the *Xu gaoseng zhuan*, *zhuan* 19, *Taisho daizokyo*, vol. 50, p. 582a-583a.
8. The *Issaikyo (shidenbu)*, vol. 10, p. 609, n. 98 identifies this figure as Faxi who became Zhiyi's disciple at age 60. His short biography is found in *Fozu tongji*, 197. The monk was already dead at the time the incident at the Tiantai mountain described in the present passage took place, and that may have been the reason why his name was mentioned in this context.
9. Ref., 191b26.
10. Later in the biography (196c6) Guanding notes that Zhiyi was buried at the place specified by Zhiyi, presumably referring to the same location as the place mentioned here.
11. 195c12-25. For a translation of the last section of this passage, see Hurvitz, *ibid.*, p. 169.
12. The term *huangshang* ("emperor") is used here to refer to Prince Guang of Jin. The prince became the emperor in the year 604. So, if the term is meant to

mean the emperor here, this would indicate that the passage in its present form was written after that date.

13. 195c28-18. *Guoqing bolu*, no. 69, line. 5,6 also refers to the story about the construction of the temple building. This document in the *Guoqing bolu* bears the date of the 15th day of the second month of the 18th year of Kaihuang [598], showing that the idea of this story existed by that time, ie., only two and a half months after Zhiyi's death.

14. "Guanding's biography of Zhiyi: Its Framework and the Three Miraculous Images", *ibid.*

15. Zhiyue's biography is found in the *Xu gaoseng zhuan*, *zhuan* 17, *Taisho daizokyo*, p. 570c-571a.

16. Uemura Shincho, in his translation of the *Biezhuan* in the *Kokuyaku issaikyo* (Tokyo, 1967, p. 611, n. 9), explains that the latter refers to the expenses for the funeral.

17. In an earlier article I discussed in some detail the traditions associated with the Asoka *stupa* in the Mao District and the stone images in the Wu Commandary, also believed to have been related to King Asoka. See "Two Sources of Chinese Buddhist Biographies", *ibid.*, p.163-167.

18. This letter preserved in the *Guoqing bolu*, document no. 65 is Zhiyi's testament written in the form of a letter to Prince Guang. It contains a long autobiographical passage that describes Zhiyi's life in a very different tone from that of existing biographies. I plan to discuss this letter in greater detail on a different occasion, in order to comment on different dynamics of biographies and autobiographies and further to highlight the constructed character of both types of writings. The reference to the *Fayuan shu* is found in l. 64.

19. Ikeda Rosan recently published a study of the *Guoqing bolu* entitled *Kokusei hyakuroku no kenkyu* (Tokyo, 1892). Ikeda presents in this volume a critical and punctuated edition of the text, principally based on the Taisho edition, together with detailed notes and the translation of the text. My discussion of the materials from the *Guoqing bolu* here, particularly the summary of the document no. 64 given below, is heavily indebted to Ikeda's work.

20. The expression *duqi*, translated here as "jar of poison" also appears in Guanding's *Biezhuan* biography (196a20): Zhiyi is said to have used this expression in his oral reply turning down a meal; he then dictated his will, which probably refers to the document preserved as the 66th document in the *Guoqing bolu*. Guanding may have taken the expression "*duqi*" from the *Fayuan shuwen*, and used it in composing his description of Zhiyi's state just before he dictated his will to Prince Guang.

21. As we noted above, the document that contains the text of the vow, namely, *Guoqing bolu*, no. 64, is written as a letter to Prince Guang and begins with a request to the Prince to repair the three sites in question. Another document, Zhiyi's testament written in the form of a letter to Prince Guang (*Guoqing bolu*, document no. 65, pp. 363-379), mentions the text of the vow under examination here in the list of requests that he had left for the prince (line 64). Prince Guang's reply to this latter letter, now written in the form of a letter he

wrote to the Tiantai community upon receiving the news about Zhiyi's death (*Guoqing bolu*, document no. 66, pp. 379-389), refers to the list of requests that Zhiyi had made in his testament and promises to carry out the projects Zhiyi had requested. The sites where repair work (*zhuangshi*) is required are given here as the Mao District *stupa*, stone images in Wu Commandary, the Maitreya image in Shan District (ie., the Shicheng image), and the location where Zhiyi died (p. 380, ll. 40-42). It seems appropriate, in view of the fact that Zhiyi had left the text of the vow to the prince himself in a letter that begins with a request to repair these sites, and that the prince later promised to carry out the repair work, that Zhiyi was referring to Prince Guang by the expression *houren* ("someone left behind") in this passage of the text of the vow.

22. 196b1,2.

23. His biography is found in the *Liangshu*, *zhuan* 22 (pp. 346-48).

24. Written with the same character as Shanxian (Shan District) above and probably refers to the same location.

25. Maitreya's preaching on three future occasions is mentioned in the *Fo shuo mile xiasheng jing* (Taisho n. 453), *Taisho daizokyo*, vol. 14, p. 422bc, *Fo shuo mile xiasheng chengfo jing* (Taisho, n. 454), *ibid*., 425b, and *Fo shuo mile xiasheng jing* (Taisho, n. 455), *ibid*., 427c.

26. Taisho edition, which reproduces the text of the *Gaoseng zhuan* found in the Korean edition, gives the name of the dynasty as "Northern Qi", but lists the variant reading "Qi dynasty" found in Song, Yuan, Ming and Kunaicho editions. The Northern Qi dynasty lasted between 550 and 577, but never used the era name Jianwu. Since the story later gives the date of the sixth year of the Tianjian period (507-508) as the date on which a crucial event possibly many years after Senghu's death occurs, the dynasty in question could not have been the Northern Qi, but rather must have been the Qi or Southern Qi dynasty which lasted 479-502. There was a Jianwu period under the Southern Qi dynasty; the period lasted 494-497.

27. Sengyou's biography mentions Shanxian's stone image along with the great images of Guangzhai and of Sheshan as images the Sengyou built (402c19). The story of the great image in the Guangzhai temple is told in Fayue's biography (412c-413a). The imperial order placing Sengyou in change of this image is mentioned in 412c28,19. See also 413b7,9 for further comments on the Guangzhai temple image.

28. The meaning of this sentence is unclear. Were there two images?

29. The meaning of the expression *liu ju* in 693c19 is not clear. I am here tentatively assuming that it means "six implements", assuming these implements to be a variety of common tools for moving heavy objects.

30. Northern Qi used this name for a city, earlier called Pingyangfu under the Northern Wei dynasty, in the Shanxi province. The city was also called Jinzhou under the Tang dynasty. See Morohashi, 5, 863, 4.

31. Jinzhou under the rule of Northern Qi was conquered by Northern Zhou forces in the tenth month of the fifth year of the Jiande period according to the Northern Zhou calendar (the seventh year of the Wuping period according to the

Northern Qi calendar; the tenth month of this year was in the year 576 according to the Western calendar). The description of this incident is found in the second part of the chronicle of the rule of the emperor Wu in the sixth fascicle of the dynastic history of Northern Zhou (*Zhou shu*, p. 95); the event is also mentioned briefly in the chronicle of the last ruler of the Northern Qi dynasty in the eighth fascicle of the dynastic history (*Beiqi shu*, p. 109).

32. "Two Sources...", *Ibid.*, p. 179.

33. For example a story about the unusual weight of images is told about the two stone images in Wu Commandary ("Two Sources...", *ibid.*, 165; *Ji shenzhou sanbao gantong lu*, *Taisho daizokyo*, vol. 52, 414a and *Fayuan zhulin*, *Taisho daizokyo*, vol. 53, 383a) and the story about the Asoka image of Manjusri in Mt. Lu discovered by Tao Kan (*Ji shenzhou sanbao gantong lu*, 417b and *Fayuan zhulin*, 386b). The Tao Kan image stories in the *Ji shenzhou sanbao gantong lu* include a story about an old monk to whom the image spoke miraculously, ordering him to stay in the temple after others had left because of rampant bandit activities: when rebel soldiers entered the city and attempted to decapitate the monk, the image miraculously protected him. We might note that the Manjusri image in Mt. Lu is also mentioned in Guanding's biography of Zhiyi, *Sui tiantai zhizhe dashi biezhuan*, 194c5-8. Here the mountain in which the image was housed was spared of disturbance and burning when rebellion occurred in a neighbouring city. The story about the image's weight is also told in Guanding's biography of the Asoka image in the Changsha temple (*Gaoseng zhuan*, 356a: the biography of Tanyi; see also the earlier *Mingseng zhuan* biography of Tanyi, preserved in the *Meisodensho*, *Zokuzokyo* / *Xu zang jing*, vol. 134, p. 7Ba). The *Xu gaoseng zhuan* story about this image includes a story about a fire which miraculously did not burn the building that housed this image (692c).

34. This same passage is also found in the *Fayuan zhulin*, 389b. I have recently completed three articles on the sources of the *Ji shenzhou sanbao gantong lu*: "The *Ji shenzhou sanbao gantong lu* ("Collected Records of Three Treasure Miracles in China"): Some Exploratory Notes", *Kalyana-Mitta: Professor Hajime Nakamura Felicitation Volume* (Delhi: Indian Books Centre, 1991); "Dao-xuan's Collection of Miracle Stories about 'Supernatural Monks' (*Shen-seng gan-dong lu*): An Analysis of its Sources", *Chung-hwa Buddhist Journal* Vol. 3 (April, 1990), pp. 319-380; "A Source Analysis of the *Ruijing lu* ("Records of Miraculous Scriptures"), *The Journal of the International Association of Buddhist Studies* (forthcoming).

35. The text of Liu Xie's inscription is preserved in the *Yiwen leiju*, *juan* 76, Shanghai guji qubanshe edition (n.d.), pp. 1302-1303. Liu Xie's inscription is also mentioned in Zhipan's comment on this image in the *Fozu tongji*, 347a.

36. Yinyuesi at the Shicheng mountain was the name of the temple in which Senghu lived according to the *Gaoseng zhuan*, 412a9.

37. Guanding's *Biezhuan* also mentions the name Bai Daoyou in connection with the story of Zhiyi's first visit to the Tiantai mountain (193a8). This name

must refer to the monk called Zhu Tanyou whose biography is given in the *Gaoseng zhuan*, 395c-396a. His biography is rather similar to that of Tanguang briefly summarized above. Daoxuan's work *Shijia fangzhi* contains a story of Zhu Tanyou which mentions a supernatural temple in the Tiantai mountain (972c22-973a1). This same story is found as a story of Jin Taoyou or Zhu Daoyou in the *Ji shenzhou sanbao gantong lu*, 423b-c17. We might at this point note the earlier connection between Shicheng and Zhidun. A brief comment on this connection is found in Hayashi Denho, *Chugoku bokkyo shiseki yosetsu*, vol. 1 (Kyoto, 1979), p. 53.

38. The stone image at Shicheng is mentioned in three passages (347a, 389c and 467c) in Zhipan's comment on this image in the *Fozu tongji*, compiled in the course of the 12 years between the sixth year of Baoyou (1258) and the sixth year of Xianchun (1269)(the information concerning these dates is found in 129c). Thus the image and the stories about it appear to have been well-known during the Song period. The passage in 347a, after summarizing the stories about this image in the *Gaoseng zhuan* and the *Xu gaoseng zhuan* with some additional details, notes that the Vinaya Master Daoxuan of the Tang period met a heavenly deity (*tianshen*) who said to him "The Master (referring to Daoxuan?) is a later incarnation (*houshen*) of Senghu, Sengshu, and Sengyou". For this reason, the passage continues, the image was called "*sansheng shifo*", which may be translated as the "stone Buddha of three lives" or the "stone Buddha which has been born three times". The point of this story is not entirely clear. The phraseology in this passage suggests that the "Master" (*shi*) who is said to be the later incarnation is indeed Daoxuan himself, and reminds us of the story in Daoxuan's biography in the *Song gaoseng zhuan* in which Daoxuan's mother after conceiving him miraculously was told by a foreign monk who appeared in a dream that the child she conceived was the Vinaya Master Sengyou of the Liang period (790b). We might also recall Senghu's statement in the *Gaoseng zhuan* biography that he would complete his project of carving the image in question in his next incarnation (412a17,18). In the *Gaoseng zhuan* biography this statement is immediately followed by a statement which says that Sengshu later continued Senghu's project, but could not complete it again. There may an implicit suggestion here that Sengshu was a later incarnation of Senghu. Since the project was eventually completed by Sengyou, some might have believed that Sengyou also was a reincarnation of Senghu, and the image might have been called by the name given in this passage in the sense that it was completed in the course of three lives, those of Senghu, Sengshu, and Sengyou. The deity's words to Daoxuan might simply have been connecting the two stories which were originally entirely independent of each other: one story was about the Shicheng image which established that Sengyou was a reincarnation of Senghu and Sengshu, and the other story was a biographical story about Daoxuan, which indicated that Daoxuan was the reincarnation of Sengyou. If this was the case, there may not have been any logical connection between the words of the heavenly deity to Daoxuan, explaining that he was the fourth reincarnation of Senghu and the fact that the image was called the "stone

Buddha of three lives", even though 347a passage in the *Fozu tongji* uses the conjunction "therefore" (*gu*) in this context. It is also possible that the heavenly deity's words to Daoxuan were spoken on an occasion when the Shicheng image was not the topic of conversation. It may have been Zhipan who introduced this story in the context of a discussion of the Shicheng image.

The story of the statement that a heavenly deity made to Daoxuan about this image is also told in another passage in the *Fozu tongji* located in 467b in an abbreviated form. Here the words of the deity are given without the reference to the "Master", and the words may be read as saying that the stone image itself is the later incarnation (or bodily representation) of Senghu, Sengshu, and Sengyou. It is a little easier to harmonize this reading of the deity's statement with the information given immediately after it, which states that the image was called the "stone Buddha of three lives" or the "stone Buddha which has been born three times". The designation then might refer to the fact that the three monks produced the same stone image on three different occasions.

The passage in 389c reports that the Wuyue ruler Qian Liu established the Ruixiang temple at the Shicheng mountain and offered it to the "stone image of three lives" or the "stone image that had been born three times" (*sansheng shixiang*). This reference might indicate that the image was in fact known later as an image of "three lives".

The note following this passage mentions several sources including a work called,"*Tianren gantong zhuan* (Stories of Miraculous Communications between Gods and Men?)". This latter work may have been a record of widely known incidents of Daoxuan's miraculous conversations with deities. Although the best known record of this conversation in a work called "*Daoxuan lushi gantong lu*" (T. 2107) or the "*Luxiang gantong zhuan* (T. 1898) does not include a story about this image, references to Daoxuan's exchanges with deities in the *Fayuan zhulin* indicates that a larger body of records of these incidents might have existed earlier. I am currently preparing a study of the stories about Daoxuan's exchanges with deities.

39. "Guanding's Biography of Zhiyi: Its Framework and the Three Miraculous Images", *ibid.*

40. *Guoqing bolu*, no. 87, line 1 (Ikeda, *ibid.*, p. 450).

41. *Guoqing bolu*, no. 89, lines 10, 11, 14, and 15 (Ikeda, *ibid.*, p. 453). See also *Guoqing bolu*, no. 90, lines 2 and 3 (Ikeda, *ibid.*, 458.

42. Guanding's colophon (197c18,19) indicates that his work on the *Biezhuan* biography began with a conversation with Liu Guyan which took place in the 21st year of the Kaihuang period (which is identical with the first year of the Renshou period, the year 601). An informal biography of Zhiyi (*Xingzhuang*, an "account of conducts") compiled by Guanding is mentioned in one document preserved in the *Guoqing bolu* (no. 86). This *Guoqing bolu* document records the conversations between the messenger from the Tiantai community and court officials; the conversation in which the *Xingzhuang* is mentioned is said to have taken place on the 20th day of the 10th month of the first year of Daye (605)(Ikeda, *Kokusei hyakuroku no kenkyu*, *ibid.*, 14, p. 443, line 7 and p. 444

line 30). Since the *Xingzhuang* appears to be identical with the *Biezhuan*, the latter had been completed by the year 605.

43. Sato Tetsuei, *ibid.*, pp. 64-66. The references to Amitabha, Avalokitesvara, and Mahasthamaprapta appear in *Biezhuan*, 196b5, *Guoqing bolu*, 66 (lines 9, 10; Ikeda, p. 379), 67 (lines 12, Ikeda, p. 390), 68 (line 10, Ikeda, p. 68).

List of Characters

Bai Daoyou 白道猷

Beiqi shu 北齊書

Biezhuan 別傳

Baoyou 寶祐

Changsha 長沙

daoren 道人

Daoxuan 道宣

Daoxuan lushi gantong lu
道宣律師感通錄

Daye 大業

dingsi 丁巳

erbu jing 二部經

Fayuan shuwen 發願疏文

Fayuan shu 發願疏

fanseng 梵僧

Faxi 法喜

Fayuan zhulin 法苑珠林

Fayue 法悅

Folong 佛龍

Fo shuo mile xiasheng jing
佛說彌勒下生經

Fo shuo mile xiasheng chengfo jing
佛說彌勒下生成佛經

Fozu tongji 佛祖統紀

Gao 高

Gao Xiaoxin 高孝信

Gaoseng zhuan 高僧傳

gu 故

Guang 廣

Guangzhai 光宅

Guanding 灌頂

Guoqing 國清

Guoqing bolu 國清百錄

Hanshishan 寒石山

houren 後人

Huading 華頂

Ikeda Rosan 池田魯參

Issaikyo (shidenbu) 一切經

Ji shenzhou sanbao gantong lu
集神州三寶感通錄

Jiangdu 江都

Jian'an 建安

Jiande 建德

Jianwu 建武

jiamei 假寐

Jin 晉

Jin Sengguang 帛僧光

Jingyi ji 旌異記

Jinguangming daozhang 金光明道場

Jinzhou 晉州

Kai-huang 開皇

Kokusei hyakuroku no kenkyu 國清百録の研究

Kokuyaku issaikyo 國訳一切経

Kuaiji 會稽

Liang 梁

Liang shu 梁書

Liu Guyan 柳顧言

Liu Xie 劉勰

Lu 廬

Lu Xian 陸咸

Luxiang gantong zhuan 律相感通傳

Mao 鄮

Meisodensho 名僧傳抄

Mingseng zhuan 名僧傳

Nanping 南平

Nanyue 南嶽

pang zhu 傍助

Qi 齊

Qian Liu 錢鏐

Renshou 仁壽

rui 如意

Ruijing lu 瑞經錄

Ruixiang 瑞相

sansheng shifo 三生石佛

sansheng shixiang 三生石像

Sato Tetsuei 佐藤哲英

Senghu 僧護

Sengming 僧明

Sengshu 僧淑

Sengyou 僧祐

Shan 剡

Shanji 剡溪

Shanxian 剡縣

shanxian dashifo 剡縣大石佛

shen seng 神僧

Sheshan 攝山

shi 師

Shicheng 石城

Shifeng 始豐
Shijia fangzhi 釋迦方志
Song gaoseng zhuan 宋高僧傳
song qu 宋初
Sui 隋
Sui tiantai zhizhe dashi biezhuan
隋天台智者大師別傳
Taisho daizokyo 大正大藏経
Taiyuan 太元
taizai 太宰
Tang 唐
Tanguang 曇光
Tanyi 曇翼
Tao Kan 陶侃
Tendai daishi no kenkyu
天台大師の研究
Tianjian 天監
Tianren gantong zhuan 天人感通傳
tianshen 天神
Tiantai 天台
Tiantai guoqingsi zhizhe cha*n*shi beiwen
天台國清寺智者禪師別傳
Uemura Shincho 上村真肇
wan 萬
Wang 王
wang jia 王家
wei 未
weishen 威神
Wendi 文帝
Wu 吳
Wu* 武
Wudi 武帝
Wuliangshou jing 無量壽経
Wuliang shou 無量壽
Wuping 武平
Wuyue 吳越
Xi 喜
Xian 咸
Xianchun 咸淳
Xiao Wei 蕭偉
Xing zhuang 行狀
Xu gaoseng zhuan 續高僧傳
Yangdi 楊帝
yi shi di 一實諦

Yinyue 隱嶽

Yinyuesi 隱嶽寺

You 祐

yuan 願

Yuanxiang 元襄

Zhang Da 張達

zhang 丈

Zhang'an 章安

Zhilang 智朗

Zhipan 志磐

Zhixi 智晞

Zhiyi 智顗

Zhou 周

Zhou shu 周書

Zhu Tanyou 竺曇猷

zhuan 卷

zhuang shi 裝飾

Zokuzokyo / Xu zang jing 續藏經

RECENT DEVELOPMENTS IN THE TEXT CRITICAL STUDY OF THE PLATFORM SCRIPTURE

Ryosho Tanaka
Komazawa University

1. Introduction

According to the Tun-huang text S 5475, Hui-neng of Ts'ao-ch'i, the sixth patriarch of Chinese *ch'an* Buddhism, conferred precepts and preached to monks and laymen at the Precept Platform of the Ta-fan-ssu temple of Shao-chou. The record (*ching*, *sutra*) of this sermon compiled by his disciple Fa-hai is generally called "the Platform Scripture of the Sixth Patriarch" (*liu-tzu t'an-ching*).[1] Scholars of *ch'an* Buddhism have been greatly interested in this record and there exist a large number of studies on this subject.[2] We can glimpse the scale of existing scholarship on this topic by the fact that 41 books, 57 philological articles, and 28 articles with a variety of emphases are listed as studies of the Platform Scripture in Appendix II in *Eno Kenkyu* (A Study of Hui-neng), the recent work that was the result of the joint efforts of the Zenshushi Kenkyukai (*Ch'an* history research team) of Komazawa University.[3] In this paper I would like to review some of the recent examples of this large body of scholarly literature.

The history of the study of the Platform Scripture has been discussed by other scholars on several occasions in the past. One recent and important example is Yanagida Seizan's comprehensive discussion in 32 pages in a volume that appeared in 1980, *Tonko Butten to Zen* (Buddhist literature from Tunhuang and *ch'an*).[4] In this paper I will concentrate on more recent developments in the study of the text of the Platform Scripture.

The text of the Platform Scripture exists in more than ten variant versions, including the oldest existing version that is found in the Tunhuang text S 5475. These variant versions are systematically ordered into three groups: the Tunhuang text, Hui-hsin text, and Ch'i-sung text. There is a general consensus that this basic threefold classification may be further developed into a fivefold list by adding two derivative texts: (1) the Te-yi text that appears to have been compiled using an old manuscript from the Tunhuang text group and the Ch'i-sung text as its basis, and (2) the Tsung-pao text that was primarily based on the Ch'i-sung text.[5] Recently, previously unknown texts belonging to earlier layers in this fivefold classification of the texts of the Platform Scripture have been discovered, and important studies of these texts have been published. My review of recent developments in the textual study of the Platform Scripture will focus on these new discoveries.

2. *Kinzan Tenneiji Text*

This text was mentioned first in the *Wakanjo becchibon mokuroku* (*Catalogue of Special Collections [Chinese and Japanese Works]*), published in 1936 by Tohoku Imperial University, and then again apparently on the basis of the information given in that catalogue, in the *Shinsan zenseki mokuroku (Newly Compiled Catalogue of Zen Buddhist Literature)*, published in 1962 by the Library of Komazawa University. The existence of this text has, therefore, been known for some time, but no serious scholarly attention has been paid to it. The manuscript in question is kept in a special collection called Kano Library and is designated as a rare book by the Tohoku University Library. Shiina Koyu had an opportunity to examine and photocopy this manuscript, and published a report of his bibliographical study.[6] A photographic reproduction of this text may be found in Yanagida Seizan's *Rokuso Dangyo shohon shusei (Variant Versions of the Platform Scripture)* to be discussed below. Here I will comment on the general character of this text on the basis of Shiina's report.

This text is divided into two parts (*jo* and *ge*) and said to be a manuscript produced during the Kamakura period. Its title is given as "*Shao-chou Ts'ao-ch'i-shan Liu-tsu-shih t'an-ching*" in a form that is identical with the title of the Daijoji text. Its relationship with the Daijoji text is made clearer in the following collophon found at the bottom of the cover (*zhih*) of the manuscript.[7] The second part of this colophon contains a statement entrusting this text to a disciple (the disciple may have been Sokyo). This paragraph may be summarized as follows:

> This text of the Platform Scripture consists of two fascicles and was discovered in a secret treasure box that was kept in the storage building of Kinzan Tenneiji Temple. The versions of the Platform Scripture that are read widely at the present time vary from each other extensively, and diverge from the original text. Students can not help but be puzzled by these divergences. The only exception is the text that has been kept secretly in the temple of the Soto sect, Daijoji in Kaga (present Ishikawa Prefecture). This Daijoji text is believed to preserve the original text of the Platform Scripture. When I compared the two fascicle version of the Kinzan Tenneiji Temple with it, the two versions matched perfectly character for character. The only regret was that a few sheets were missing in this two fascicle version. I copied these pages from the Daijoji text and made this two fascicle version complete by

adding them to it. Please make sure that this text will not ever be lost. I entrust this to your safe keeping.

The first part of the collophon informs us that this task of supplementing missing sentences was performed by the monk Hakuei Egyoku who resided at the Kinzan Tenneiji during the first ten days in the seventh month of the fourth year of Enkyo period (1747).[8]

Shiina reports that this Kinzan Tenneiji temple is an old temple of the Myoshinji School of the Rinzai sect that is located in Fukuchiyama city in Kyoto district. The temple was first established by Guchu Shukyu (-1409) in the fourth year of the Teiji period (1365), and Hakuei Egyoku was the eighth patriarch of this temple. An examination of the calligraphy indicates that sections supplemented by Egyoku are probably found in the second fascicle: from the second sheet to the second line in the fifth sheet and from the seventh to the ninth sheets. The text orginally consisted of 25 sheets in the first fascicle including the preface and the 38 sheets in the second fascicle. Shiina suggested that the first fascicle consisted of 21 sheets including the preface, that the section supplemented by Egyoku was found in the second and third sheets in the second fascicle, and that eleven sheets from the fourth to fourteenth sheets in the second fascicle were now missing.[9] This analysis needs to be corrected.

As we noted above, the content of this text matches that of the Daijoji text for the most part. One important issue pointed out by Shiina is the lineage of the "transmission of the lamp" among patriarchs in the West that is found in the section called "*shih yi, chiao-shih shih-seng ch'uan-fa*". The list in the Daijoji text is identical with the list that was first established in the *Pao-lin chuan* (801), ie., the theory of 28 Western patriarchs of the Vasumitra tradition. This list was then adopted in subsequent histories of the "transmission of the lamp", and thus became the standard paradigm of the "transmission of the lamp" in *ch'an*/Zen Buddhism. By contrast, the Kinzan Tenneiji text gives a distinct list that stands closer to the list in the Tunhuang text. The five older texts of the Platform Scripture, including the Shinpukuji text to be discussed below, list the following patriachs in the section of the transmission under consideration here.

Tunhuang text	Shinpukuji t.	Tenneiji t.	Koshoji t.	Daijoji t.
Ananda	Ananda	Ananda	Ananda	Ananda
Madhyantika	Madhyantika		Madhyantika	
Sanavasa	Sanavasa	Sanavasa	Sanavasa	Sanavasa
Upagupta	Upagupta	Upagupta	Upagupta	Upagupta
Dhrtaka	Dhrtaka	Dhrtaka	Dhrtaka	Dhrtaka
				Miccaka
				Vasumitra
Buddhanandi	Buddhanandi	Buddhanandi	Buddhanandi	Buddhanandi
Simha bhiksu	Simha bhiksu	Simha bhiksu	Simha biksu	Simha biksu
Sanavasa	Sanavasa	Sanavasa*	Basiasita	Basiasita
Upagupta*	Upagupta**	Upagupta**	Upagupta**	Punyamitra
Sangharaksa	Vasumitra*	Vasumitra*	Vasumitra*	Prajnatara

Subhamitra	Sangharaksa*	Sangharaksa*	Sangharaksa*	
Bodhidharma	Bodhidharma	Bodhidharma	Bodhidharma	Bodhidharma

(* and ** indicate alternate forms in which the names are given in Chinese characters.)

The list in the Kinzan Tenneiji text is similar to the list in the Daijoji text in only one respect: both fail to mention Madhayantika. The list in the Kinzan Tenneiji text is otherwise closer to the list in the Tunhuang text: both the list in the Tunhuang text and that in the Tenneiji text fail to mention Miccaka and Vasumitra mentioned in the list in the Daijoji text; in the second half of the list after Simha biksu, the Daijoji text diverges from the others and follows the *Pao-lin chuan* tradition, while the others follow the list in the Tunhuang text more closely. Both the list in the Tenneiji text and that in the Shinpukuji text reverse the order between Sangharaksa and Vasumitra (Subhamitra) from that given in the Tunhuang text. Since both the list in the Shinpukuji text and that in the Tunhuang text mention Madhyantika, who is not mentioned in the list in the Tenneiji text, we may conclude that the Shinpukuji text is closer to the Tunhuang text. The first half of the list in the Koshoji text follows the corresponding part of the list in the Tunhuang text, but the second half of the list in the Koshoji text, ie., the section after Simha biksu, reveals its transitional character—Sanavasa is here confused with Basiasita as in the list in the Daijoji text.

Shiina reports that the transmission verses of the six partriarchs in China cannot be discussed comparatively since the sheets that recorded the relevant section in the Kinzan Tenneiji text are missing.[10] In fact no such sheets existed to begin with. Though the Tunhuang text records transmission verses for all six patriarchs in China, all the other texts only record the transmission verses of Bodhidharma and Hui-neng, and fail to give the transmission verses for any of the other patriarchs.

The appearance of the Kinzan Tenneiji text makes it possible to go behind the Daijoji text: the comparison between the two texts enables us to reconstruct and restore in more perfect form the text dated to the sixth year of Cheng-he (1116) that lay behind these two existing texts. In this sense the Kinzan Tenneiji text is extremely valuable as a new source in the study of the Platform Scripture.

3. The Publication of the Rokuso dangyo shohon shusei *and the* Eno kenkyu

We have noted above that the Kinzan Tenneiji text is kept as a rare book in the special collection called Kano Library in the Library of Tohoku University. It is therefore not easily accessible to a general readership. The original copies of other important texts of the Platform Scripture, such as the Tunhuang text S 5475 located in the British Library, are similarly inaccessible. Recent technological developments in photographically based printing have changed this situation: we are now able to examine the photographic copies of these manuscripts published in book form. Important texts of the Platform Scripture were collected and published in 1976 under the title *Rokuso dangyo shohon shusei (Manuscripts and Printed Editions of the Platform Scripture of the Sixth Patriarch)* edited by Yanagida Seizan.[11] This work contains the following items:

Complete texts:

(1) the Tunhuang text, one fascicle (manuscript; S 5475 in the British Library)

(2) the Koshoji text, two fascicles (printed edition; located in the Koshoji temple in Horikawa, Kyoto; reproduced by Suzuki Teitaro)

(3) the Kinzan Tenneiji text, two fascicles (manuscript copied during the Kamakura period; located in the Kano Library, Tohoku University Library)

(4) the Daijoji text, two fascicles (*jo/t'ieh*) (manuscript copied during the Kamakura period, property of the Daijoji temple in Kanazawa and located at the Prefectural Art Museum of Ishikawa Prefecture)

(5) the Kao-li text, one fascicle (printed in the ninth year of the Kuang-hsü period [1883] and published by the Chia-yeh-shan Hai-yin-ssu temple in Korea; the copy in possession of Anayama Sumiko, Fukuoka)

(6) the southern collection text, Ming edition, one fascicle (printed at the Kaiyuji temple in Kikugawa-cho, Yamaguchi Prefecture)

(7) the Cheng-t'ung text, Ming edition, one fascicle (manuscript based on the Cheng-t'ung text printed in the fourth year of Cheng-t'ung [1439] during the Ming period, in possession of Yanagida Seizan)

(8) the Chen-p'u reprint edition text, Ch'ing period, one fascicle (printed in the *ping-chen* year (1676?) during the Ch'ing period, in possession of Yanagida Seizan)

(9) the Ts'ao-ch'i original text, one fascicle (printed in the third year of Hoei [1706] in Japan, in possession of Yanagida Seizan)

(10) the popular text, one fascicle (manuscript copied during the Edo period in Japan, in possession of Yanagida Seizan)

(11) the Chin-ling k'e-ching-ch'u text, one fascicle (printed in the 18th year of the Chung-hua min-kuo [1929], in possession of Yanagida Seizan)

Appendices:

A. Fragments

(1) the Kanazawa Bunko text, fragment (manuscript copied during the Kamakura period, located in the Kanazawa Bunko library)

(2) the Hsi-hsia translation (1), fragment (manuscript, located in the Peking National Library)

(3) the Hsi-hsia translation (2), fragment (manuscript, located in Ryukoku University Library)

(4) the Ts'ao-ch'i ta-shih chuan, one fascicle (manuscript, property of the Hieizan Enryakuji temple in Otsu, located in the Nara National Museum, reproduced by Kokeiso)

B. Articles

Yanagida Seizan, "Bibliographical explanation"

Kawakami Tenzan, "On the Platform Scripture in Hsi-hsia translation" (In Japanese), originally published in the *Shina bukkyo shigaku*, vol. 2, no. 3 (September, 1938).

Yanagida Seizan, "The Platform Scripture of the Sixth Patriarch as a Scripture of Mahayana Precepts", originally published in the *Indogaku bukkyogaku kenkyu*, vol. 12, no. 1 (January, 1964).
The *Rokuso dangyo shohon shusei* is thus an extremely valuable publication. It provides photographic reproductions of important texts of the Platform Scripture; it brings together other relevant materials for the study of the Platform Scripture and also includes some major scholarly discussion of this subject.

In March, 1978, roughly two years after the publication of the *Rokuso dangyo shohon shusei*, the Zen History Seminar ("*zenshushi kenkyukai*") at Komazawa University collected the results of our joint research project that had been underway for about eight years and published the large volume mentioned at the start of this paper that is entitled, the *Eno kenkyu* (A Study of Hui-neng).[12] As its subtitle "Preliminary studies on the biography and the sources on Hui-neng" makes clear, its content consists of two sections: the first section entitled "Studies" consists of studies of the biography of Hui-neng and the second section entitled "Sources" is a study of the sources for the study of Hui-neng and is broader in scope. The "Study" section consists of two chapters. The first chapter is devoted to presenting the critical edition accompanied by an annotated translation of a basic source for the study of Hui-neng's biography, "*Ts'ao-ch'i ta-shih chuan*". The second chapter is devoted to an analysis of eighteen works that enable us to trace how Hui-neng's biography changed during the 600 years beginning with the *I-fa t'a-chi* (676) and the *Yüan-ch'i wai-chi* (1291) that was appended to the *Tsung-pao* text of the Platform scripture. These sources are examined in terms of their contents; the examination focuses on some 53 items. The "Sources" section consists of three chapters. The first chapter contains a synoptic edition of the five texts of the Platform scripture, and the second chapter a critical edition of the *Chin-kang ching chieh-yi* based on six texts. The third chapter is titled "A compilation of sources for the study of Hui-neng" and reproduces relevant passages from 116 works. Finally, a chronological table of historical events relevant for the study of Hui-neng and a bibliography of secondry literature are appended. We decided to exclude from the book materials that relate exclusively to the study of Hui-neng's thought, but it does contain materials that are relevant to virtually all other subjects that touch upon the study of Hui-neng. Yet, it is still a "preliminary study", and the "study of Hui-neng" based on the materials prepared in this volume remains to be written.

The *Eno kenkyu* makes two contributions to the study of the text of the Platform scripture. The first chapter of its "Sources" section, as I noted above, contains a synoptic edition of the five texts of the Platform scripture. It also contains a bibliographical introduction entitled "General Remarks on the Platform Scripture of the Sixth Patriarch". The five texts chosen for synoptic comparison are (1) the Tunhuang text, ie., the oldest existing text of the Platform scripture that is kept at the British Library, (2) the Daijoji text, which is believed to have been copied during the Kamakura period and is ultimately based on the Hui-hsin text group, (3) the Koshoji text, which represents the

Gozan edition text, (4) the Te-yi text that was published by Chia-yeh-shan Hai-yin-ssu in the 9th year of the Kuang-hsü period of Kao-li (1883) and is believed to be ultimately based on the Ch'i-sung text, and (5) the Tsung-pao text that is found in the *fu* box of the Northern collection of the Ming edition of the Tripitaka, published in the 37th year of Wan-li period (1609). These texts are placed side by side using the breakdown of the Platform scripture into 92 sections that D.T. Suzuki used earlier in editing the Tunhuang text of this work. The *Rokuso dangyo shohon shusei* edited by Yanagida Seizan enables us to examine the original manuscripts and printed editions paying attention to the caligraphy and the appearance of the original documents; the synoptic edition of the Platform scripture ("*Rokuso dangyo gohon taisho*") in the *Eno kenkyu* highlights the differences in the contents of the highly variant versions represented in the five texts. Virtually all relevant information concerning the sources for studying the text of the Platform scripture are thus now available in an easily accessible form in these two works.

4. The Discovery of the Shinpukuji text.

Earlier in the section on the Kinzan Tenneiji text I presented a list comparing the names of Indian patriarchs mentioned in different textual traditions, and included in this list the relevant information from the Shinpukuji text. The discovery of this text was made public in October, 1978. The text was discovered by Ito Takatoshi of Komazawa University and through the arrangements made by Ito, Ishii Shudo of Komazawa University conducted a thorough investigation of this text and published the results.[13] Ishii reproduced the Shinpukuji text in his article and discussed it in detail commenting on its form, lineage, and other notable features. My comments on the Shinpukuji text here are based on Ishii's report.

The Shinpukuji temple is a major temple that belongs to the Chizan School of the Shingon Sect located in the Naka-ku District of Nagoya city. The Shinpukuji Library in which the new text of the Platform Scripture was discovered is housed in the Hoshoin of the Shinpukuji temple. Two catalogues of the works preserved in the Shinpukuji Library have been published: the "*Shinpukuji zenpon mokuroku*", edited by Kuroita Katsumi in October, 1935 lists 241 works; the "*Shinpukuji zenpon mokuroku zokushu*" published in May, 1936 mentions 580 items. However, the text of the Platform scripture discovered recently is not mentioned in either of these catalogues, and Ito who specializes in the study of the San-lun school discovered it accidentally in the course of his search for materials related to the San-lun school preserved in the Library.

The Shinpukuji text is a hand copied manuscript bound into two booklets. Ishii believes that the manuscript was probably copied during the Nanbokucho period (1337-1392) but possibly even earlier during the last years of the Kamakura period (1192-1333). The outside covers of both booklets bear the title "*Liu-tzu t'an-ching (The Platform Scritpure of the Sixth Patriarch)*"; inside the booklet the title is given in the second fascicle as "*Liu-tzu t'an-ching, chüan hsia (Platform Scripture of the Sixth Patriarch, Part II)*", but no corresponding title is found in the booklet containing the first fascicle; at the end of each fascicle the appropriate title is given as "*Liu-tsu t'an-ching, chüan shang (The Platform Scripture of the Sixth Patriarch, Part I*" and "*Liu-tsu t'an-ching, chüan hsia*" respectively and the preface by Hui-hsin and the postscript by Chou Hsi-ku are appended. Hui-hsin's preface is also found in the Koshoji text, which also carries the preface by Ch'ao Tzu-chien. Both the Daijoji text and the Kinzan Tenneiji text are based on the Hui-hsin text, but Hui-hsin's preface are missing in these texts, and the preface by Ts'un-chung is found in its place.

The postscript by Chou Hsi-ku which was originally attached to a printed edition and gives its date as the eighth day of the tenth year of the fifth year of the Ta-chung-hsiang-fu period (1012) is unique to this text and is particularly noteworthy.[14] Isshi clarifies the significance of this postscript by refering to Hu Shih's discussion in "*T'an-ching k'ao chih erh—Pa nihon kyoto horikawa koshoji ts'ang pei-sung hui-hsin pen t'an-ching ying-yin pen*".[15] There Hu Shih first mentions the passage on the Platform Scripture in the 16th fascicle of the Chü-chou text of the *Chün-chai tu-shu chih* prepared by Ch'ao Kung-wu. Ch'ao Kung-wu copied this work and wrote a preface in the twenty-first year of the Shao-hsing period (1151). Two years later in the twenty-third year of the Shao-hsing period (1153) Ch'ao Tzu-chien printed the Ch'i-chou text. This Ch'i-chou text is the original on which the Koshoji text was based. Both Ch'ao Kung-wu and Ch'ao Tzu-chien were seventh generation descendants of Ch'ao Chiung; Cha'ao Kung-wu was the paternal cousin ("*tang-ti*") of Ch'ao Tzu-chien. This passage mentions the Platform Scripture in three fascicles compiled by Hui-hsin which contained 16 sections and carried a preface by Chou Hsi-fu.[16] On the basis of this information Hu Shih suggested that the Hui-hsin text accompanied with a preface by Chou Hsi-ku, namely the tradition of the text to which the Shinpukuji text belongs, existed in three fascicles and with 16 sections at one time. Furthermore, sometime during the 120 year period between the ninth year of the T'ien-sheng period (1031) when Ch'ao Chiung copied the manuscript and the twenty-first year of the Shao-hsiang period (1151), someone must have reorganized Hui-hsin's text of the Platform Scripture in two fascicles and containing 11 sections into a text in three fascicles and containing 16 sections. Hu Shih speculated that the three fascicle text might have been the Ch'i-sung text that the monk Ch'i-sung produced in the third year of the Chih-he period (1056) of the Northern Sung dynasty.

Ishii notes that the discovery of the Shinpukuji text enables us to reject this speculation by Hu Shih. The Shinpukuji text accompanied by Chou Hsi-ku's postscript is obviously related closely to the Hui-hsin text mentioned in Ch'ao Kung-wu's *Chün-chai tu-shu chih* and in other sources based on it mentioned by Hu Shih, for example, the bibliography in the *Wen-hsien t'ung-k'ao* by Ma Tuan-lin. Hu Shih appears to have been misled by some scribal errors: the text mentioned in the sources quoted by Hu Shih must have been in two fascicles; the "sixteen sections" must have been a mistake for "eleven sections". The "preface by Chou Hsi-fu" must refer to the "postscript" composed by Chou Hsi-ku. Chou Hsi-ku's postscript informs us that the Shinpukuji text was based on the Hui-hsin text printed in the tenth month of the fifth year of the Ta-chung-hsiang-fu period (1012).

Ishii examined the prefaces to other texts belonging to the Hui-hsin text group and established the transmission of the Hui-hsin text as follows:

1) Hui-hsin learned that students were discouraged by the cumbersomeness of the old text of the Platform Scripture and established the original Hui-hsin text consisting of two fascicles and divided into eleven sections on the *hsin-hai* or the 23rd day of the *juei-pin* month in the *t'ai-sui ting-mao* year, *ie.*, the 23rd day of the fifth month of the fifth year of the Ch'ien-te period (967).

2) Scholars have noted that there are some differences between the names given to the eleven sections in the Daijoji text and those in the Koshoji text and that the Daijoji text preserves the older names. The Shinpukuji text uses the same old names that the Daijoji text uses, but adds the word "*mon/men* (gate)" to each of the eleven names. These names found in the Shinpukuji text provide us with additional evidence for reconstructing the titles and the contents of the 11 sections of the original Hui-hsin text.

3) Accoring to Ch'ao Tzu-chien's preface to the Koshoji text, he learned the existence of the manuscript of the Hui-hsin text which Ch'ao Chiung (951-1034), his ancestor going back seven generations, had seen on sixteen separate occasions in the ninth year of the T'ien-sheng period (1031) when he was 81 years old; His seventh generation descendant, Ch'ao Tzu-chien became a Deputy Governor in the Ch'i-chou Commandary, and met the governor Kao-kung shih-yü. In the course of their conversation the topic of the manuscript of the Platform Scripture that Ch'ao Chiung saw came up. Since Ch'i-chou was the memorable place where the Sixth Patriarch had received the robe of transmission, Kao-kung said that a copy of the Platform Scripture ought to be available there. And so it was that Ch'ao Tzu-chien punctuated the text and printed it on the 20th day of the sixth month of the 23rd year of the Shao-hsing period (1153). Thus, as Hu Shih pointed out earlier, the two prefaces to the Koshoji text, one by Hui-hsin and the other by Ch'ao Tzu-chien, enable us to reconstruct the lineage of the Koshoji text as follows:

Hui-hsin text (the fifth year of the Ch'ien-te period [967]) → Ch'ao Chiung's manuscript (the nineth year of the T'ien-sheng period [1031]) → the text printed by Ch'ao Tzu-chien in Ch'i-chou (the 23rd year of the Shao-hsing period [1153]) → Gozan reprint text → Koshoji text.

4) The original version of the Shinpukuji text came into being in the fifth year of the Ta-chung-hsiang-fu period (1012). It is important to note that this text thus appeared earlier than Ch'ao Chiung's manuscript (the nineth year of the T'ien-sheng period [1031]), or the Ch'i-sung text in three fascicles (the third year of the Chih-he period [1056]), which was said to have been based on an old text in Ts'ao-ch'i and transmitted later through the Te-yi text and the Tsung-pao text. The *Ts'ao ch'i liu-tsu ta-shih t'an-ching ("The Platform Scripture of the Great Master, the Sixth Patriarch of Ts'ao-ch'i")*, mentioned in Chou Hsi-ku's postscript, was a hand-copied manuscript. The Shinpukuji text group may have been the oldest printed version of the Hui-hsin text.

5) Both the Daijoji text and the Kinzan Tenneiji text were based on Ts'un-chung's reprint edition dated the sixth year of the Chih-he period (1116). The Kinzan Tenneiji text, which preserves the old colophon, appears to represent the old form of the text more closely. The analysis of the patriarchal lineage presented above showed that the Daijoji text had gone through further editorial changes. Furthermore, Chou Hsi-ku's text was printed earlier in the fifth year of the Ta-chung-hsiang-fu period (1012) than Ts'un-chung's reprint text (dated 1116). We may assume that the former must have preserved the original Hui-hsin text more faithfully. Chou Hsi-ku's text is the original on which the Shinpukuji text is based.

Taking these considerations into account, a diagram describing the transmission of the variant versions of the Platform Scripture may be drawn (Appendix II).

Certain distinctive features of the content of the Shinpukuji text show that this text stands much closer to the Kinzan Tenneiji text and the Daijoji text than to the Koshoji text. Relevant evidence for this analysis includes the reference to Hui-neng as "*mou-chia*", the treatment of the exchange over wind and banner, the exchange with Hui-ming, and the reference to the posthumous title of "Zen master Ta-chien". The comparison of the patriarchal lineage given in the Shinpukuji text with those in other texts, on the other hand, shows that it is closest to that given in the Kinzan Tenneiji text. The difference between the list in the Shinpukuji text and the list in the Koshoji text is greater, and the difference between the list in the Shinpukuji text and the list in the Daijoji text is the greatest.

At the end of Ishii's article, the text of the Shinpukuji text is reproduced using the framework proposed in the *Eno kenkyu (A Study of Hui-neng)*.

5. Reconstruction of the Hui-hsin text and the hypothesis concerning the Ch'i-sung text

Important advances were made in the study of the Hui-hsin text group thanks to the discovery of the Shinpukuji text which appears to preserve the original form of the Hui-hsin text more faithfully. Following his article announcing the discovery of the Shinpukuji text and publishing the text, Ishii Shudo continued his work on this subject and attempted to reconstruct the original Hui-hsin text of the Platform Scripture. The newly discovered Shinpukuji edition was used as the basis for this reconstruction, and four other texts that belong to the Hui-hsin text group were consulted; these four texts were the Kinzan Tenneiji text, the Daijoji text, the Koshoji text, and the text printed by Nakano Inchiuemon in the eighth year of the Kan'ei period (1631). The reconstructed text was then compared to the Tunhuang text.[17]

A five text synoptic edition of the Platform Scripture that reproduced the Tunhuang text, the Daijoji text, the Koshoji text, Te-yi text, and Tsung-pao text side by side had been included in the *Eno Kenyu (A Study of Hui-neng)* published earlier. Ishii's new contribution carried the work that lay behind this synoptic edition one step further. Two of the five texts included in the synoptic text in the *Eno Kenkyu (A Study of Hui-neng)* edition are derived from a common ancestry, ie., the original Hui-hsin text. This original Hui-hsin text is reconstructed in Ishii's new contribution on the basis of the Shinpukuji text and compared with the Tunhuang text. Following the basic framework used in the synoptic edition in the *Eno Kenkyu (A Study of Hui-neng)*, the Tunhuang edition and the reconstructed Hui-hsin text are given synoptically: the former in the top half of the page and the latter in the bottom half of the page; variant readings of the Hui-hsin group texts are noted and the Japanese reading of the texts given in the top and bottom halves of the page are given independently. The editorial note mentions the works consulted in editing the texts and producing their Japanese reading: Philip B. Yampolski, *The Platform Sutra of the Sixth Patriarch*[18] and Yanagida Seizan, *Zen Goroku*[19] and for the Koshoji edition, Nakagawa Taka, *Rokuso dankyo*.[20] Thus, Ishii's article reproduces the oldest existent text of the Platform Scripture that is accessible to us, ie., the Tunhuang text dated around 790 and the second oldest Hui-hsin text dated 967 and gives their Japanese reading in a convenient synoptic format, facilitating detailed comparative discussion of the text of the Platform Scripture.

No copy of the Hui-hsin text itself is known to us. The text reconstructed in the manner described above is no more than a scholar's hypothetical reconstruction. The other important early text of the Platform Scripture, ie., the Ch'i-sung text which constitutes the origin of the later expanded "popular" text of the Platform Scripture, also has been lost to us. Having thrown considerable light on the original form of the Hui-hsin text, Ishii moved on to an investigation that resulted in a hypothesis concerning the origin of the Ch'i-sung text.[21]

As Hu Shih pointed out, the existence of the three fascicle text of the Plaform Scripture edited by Fo-jih Ch'i-sung (1007-1072) of the Yün-men School is known from the "*Liu-tsu fa-pao chi hsü*" compiled in the third year of the Chih-he period by Lang Chien. This preface is found in the eleventh fascicle of Ch'i-sung's *Hsin-chin wen-chi*. Hu Shih discussed the Ch'i-sung text in two articles: "*T'an-ching k'ao chih yi: Pa ts'ao-chi ta-shih pieh-chuan*" (January, 1930) and "*T'an-ching k'ao chih erh: Pa nihon kyoto horikawa koshoji ts'ang pei-sung hui-hsin-pen t'an-ching ying-yin*" (April, 1934). Hu Shih's views are examined in Ishii's article in the light of the newly discovered materials from the Hui-hsin text group.

The last half of Lang Ch'ien's preface records that Ch'i-sung obtained an old Ts'ao-ch'i text in the third year of the Chih-he period (1056) and by editing this text produced the Ch'i-sung text of the Platform Scripture that consisted of three fascicles. We may assume therefore that if we can determine the identity of this "old Ts'ao-ch'i text", we will be able to learn a good deal of concrete information about the nature of the Ch'i-sung text. The Ming edition of the Platform Scripture mentions a prediction concerning the bodhisattvas who were to come from the east seventy years after the death of Hui-neng.[22] Hu Shih suggested that this prediction comes from the "*Ts'ao-ch'i ta-shih chuan*" that appeared around the year 781, and argued that this "*Ts'ao-*

ch'i ta-shih chuan" was the "old Ts'ao-ch'i text" in question. Ishii lists relevant quotations from the "*Ts'ao-ch'i ta-shih chuan*", "*Tsu-t'ang chi*", "*Ching-te ch'uan-teng lu*", "*Ch'uan-fa cheng-tsung chi*", and the Tsung-pao text of the Platform Scripture and draws the following conclusion: the prediction concerning the activities of the two bodhisattvas who appear 70 years after the death of Hui-neng does indeed first appear in the "*Ts'ao-ch'i ta-shih chuan*", but the Tsung-pao text of the Platform Scripture is based not on the "*Ts'ao-ch'i ta-shih chuan*" but on the Transmission of the Lamp literature, particularly on the *Ching-teng ch'uan-teng lu* on which the text relies most closely. Furthermore, all four examples that Hu Shih mentioned in order to prove its reliance on the "*Ts'ao-ch'i ta-shih chuan*" are drawn from the Transmission of the Lamp literature, such as the *Ching-te chuan-teng lu*. Thus, it is possible that the "*Ts'ao-ch'i ta-shih chuan*" may have been quoted indirectly in the Ch'i-sung text. But the "old Ts'ao-ch'i text" must doubtlessly have been a version of the Platform Scripture and not the "*Ts'ao-ch'i ta-shih chuan*". Ishii suggests that the version of the Platform Scripture in question might have been a manuscript of the Hui-hsin text.[23]

Concerning the content of the Ch'i-sung text in three fascicles Hu shih first suggested that this text was based on the old text of the Platform Scripture (represented in the Tunhuang manuscript) and the "*Ts'ao-ch'i ta-shih pieh chuan*". Later, after learning the existence of the Koshoji text, he came to believe that Ch'i-sung text in three fascicles was based on the Hui-hsin text (represented in the Koshoji text) in two fascicles and the "*Ts'ao-ch'i ta-shih chuan*" in one fascicle. As we noted earlier, Hu Shih also speculated that the Hui-hsin text mentioned in the *Chün-chai tu-shu chih* that consisted of three fascicles, divided into 16 sections, and containing a preface by Chou Hsi-ku (the original *Chün-chai tu-shu chih* text gives the name as Hsi-fu) might have been the Ch'i-sung text. But the discovery of the Shinpukuji text containing Hui-hsin's preface and Chou Hsi-ku's postscript dated the fifth year of the Ta-chung-hsiang-fu period (1012) showed that the Hui-hsin text in three fascicles and divided into 16 sections did not exist at all. The "three fascicles" and "sixteen sections" mentioned in the *Chün-chai tu-shu chih* are scribal errors for "two fascicles" and "eleven sections" respectively. Hui-hsin's preface speaks of "dividing the text into two fascicles and unfolding it into eleven sections". Thus, the editorial organization into two fascicles and eleven subsections was Hui-hsin's contribution and the distinctiveness of this text was found in this organization.

As for the content of the Ch'i-sung text in three fascicles, Ishii suggested the following: Ch'i-sung used the Hui-hsin text in two fascicles and eleven sections as his basis; he then added to this basic text the words of instruction associated with such figures as Liu Chih-lüeh, Fa-hai, Chih-ch'e, Chih-t'ung, Chih-tao, Hsing-ssu, Huai-jang, Hsüan-chüeh, Chih-huang, and Wo-lun taken from the *Ching-te ch'uan-teng lu* and other related sources; the Tsung-pao text shows how these materials were added. The Tun-huang and Hui-hsin texts presuppose a situation in which Ch'an Buddhism was dominated by the descendants of the ten great disciples of Hui-neng, ie., Fa-hai, Chih-ch'eng, Fa-ta, Shen-hui, Chih-ch'ang, Chih*-t'ung, Chih-ch'e, Chih-tao, Fa-chen, and Fa-ju. Ch'an Buddhism at the time of Ch'i-sung was by contrast dominated by different leaders, ie., those who belonged to the Nan-yüeh and Ch'ing-yüan groups. Ch'i-sung therefore found it necessary to include words of instruction attributed to Huai-jang of Nan-yüeh and Hsing-ssu of Ch'ing-yüan, and since these words were not found in the "*Ts'ao-ch'i ta-shih chuan*", he must have supplied them from the Transmission of the Lamp literature. This supplementary material filled one fascicle, and therefore the length of the entire text was expanded to three fascicles.

Ishii further suggested that the lineage of transmission among Indian patriarchs presented in the Ch'i-sung text must have been the Vasumitra lineage based on the *Pao-lin chuan.* Ch'i-sung advocated this list in his *Ch'uan-fa cheng-tsung chi (Record of the Correct Transmission of the Buddha's Teaching)* and elsewhere. Hu Shih suggested that the shift from the Sunavasa lineage to the Vasumitra lineage must have occurred with the Ch'i-sung text. Ishii evaluated Hu Shih's view on this point positively, and argued that the introduction of this shift must have been the most important motive that led Ch'i-sung to edit the two fascicle Platform Scripture into the three fascicle version. Ch'i-sung wrote extensively in defending the "correctness" of the "transmission of the Buddha's teaching" in the Ch'an tradition and answering the criticisms that scholastic circles directed against the Ch'an theory of partriarchal transmission. Ch'i-sung, however, also found the Hui-hsin text unsatisfactory. Ishii believed that this was the context in which the Ch'i-sung text first emerged. Ishii further highlighted the uniqueness of the Ch'i-sung text by noting the following points. Shen-hui's influence had disappeared in this text. The Platform Scripture lost its character as a text of transmission: the work which originally had the character of a sermon preaching the Precept of Formlessness was transformed into a more general collection of a variety of sermons.

The discovery of the Shinpukuji text that preserved the original form of the Hui-hsin text threw considerable light on the history of the Platform Scripture. We are now able to trace more concretely how the history of the emergence and later transformations of the Platform Scripture reflect the different stages in the development of Ch'an Buddhism and its thought.

6. The Discovery of the new Tunhuang text

When we speak about the Tunhuang text of the Platform Scripture, we generally take it for granted that we are refering to the text in the Tunhuang manuscript S 5475, a text identified by Yabuki Keiki while he was inspecting the Tunhuang materials in the British Library for the second time between 1922 and 1923. This text is often treated as the only copy of the Platform Scripture that was found in the Tunhuang library, and its importance is emphasized in the light of this situation. However, the existance of other Tunhuang texts of the

Platform Scripture has been known and references have been made to them from time to time.

The *Tun-huang yi-shu tsung-mu so-yin* published in May, 1962 by the Shang-wu yin-shu-kuan in Beijing contains a section called "4. *Tun-huang yi-shu san-lu*". The second item in this section is designated as "*Lü-shun po-wu-kuan so-ts'un tun-huang chih fo-chiao ching-tien (Buddhist scriptures from Tunhuang in possession of the Lü-shun museum)*". This list was based on the periodical *T'u-shu-kuan-hsüeh chi-k'an*, Vol. 1, no. 4. The item 0179 in this section is described as "*Nan-tsung ting-chiao (tsui-shang ta-ch'eng mo-ho-pan-jo po-lo-mi-to ching*".[24] This text probably refers to a version of the Platform Scripture. The character "*ting*" ("top") in the phrase "*nan-tsung ting-chiao*" is probably a mistake for "*tun*" ("sudden"), and the title "*tsui-shang ta-ch'eng mo-ho-pan-jo po-lo-mi-to ching*" matches perfectly with the first part of the title of the existing Tunhuang text of the Platform Scripture, ie., S 5475. We can infer that this text was identified and taken out of Tunhuang by the Otani expeditionary party and was later kept at the Lü-hsun museum. Nothing is known, however, about the later circumstances of the Lü-shun museum, and the present location of the Buddhist scriptures from Tunhuang in its possession. Thus, it is not possible to pursue the investigation of this text any further.

The existence of another Tunhuang text of the Platform Scripture had been reported even earlier. The Hsiang Ta's "*Hsi-cheng hsiao-chi*" published in the *Kuo-hsüeh chi-k'an*, Vol. 7, no. 1 (July, 1970) mentions a text in possession of Jen Tzu-yi. The "*Hsi-cheng hsiao-chi*" is the record of the investigation of old manuscripts that Hsiang Ta, then a professor of Beijing University, conducted on several occasions in Tunhuang. Yanagida discusses this work in his article in the *Tonko butten to Zen* mentioned earlier. The relevant section of this discussion may be summaried as follows.[25] Hsiang Ta's comments:

> Jen Tzu-yi owned some manuscripts of sutras found in the Tunhuang caves. Hsiang Ta was shown these manuscripts: six *chüan* of hand copied scriptures and three books of fragments. In addition, there was a booklet consisting of 93 sheets. This booklet contained four works: the "*P'u-t'i-ta-mo nan-tsung ting shih-fei lun*", the "*Nan-yang ho-shang tun-chiao chieh-t'o ch'an-men chih-liao-hsing t'an-yü*", the "*Nan-tsung tun-chiao tsui-shang ta-ch'eng t'an-ching*" as well as the commentary on the "*Ching-kang pan-jo po-lo-mi-to hsin-ching*" by Shen-hsiu's disciple Ching-chüeh. Except for the 12 lines in one sheet at the beginning of the "*Ting shih-fei lun*", all works were complete and at the very end there was a collophon by monk Kuang-fan which lacked one sheet... This material in possession of Jen Tzu-yi is undoubtedly a manuscript copied during the Five Dynasties or early Sung period, and the format that copies six lines in a half page follows the format of the Sung edition. The "*Nan-tsung ting shih-fei lun*" in this collection enables us to supplement the missing parts of the texts of the same work in British and French collections. The "*Nan-yang ho-shang t'an-yü*" in this collection is a complete text; there is a fragment of this work in Beijing

Library. The text of the Platform Scripture here can be compared with the manuscripts in England and France. The Heart Sutra (*hsin ching*) with a commentary by Ching-chüeh has a preface by Li Chih-fei, indicating that this commentary was composed in the 15th year of the K'ai-yüan period. Ching-chüeh was a disciple of Shen-hsiu. Since this work has been missing in the tripitaka for a long time, this will enable us to throw some light on the doctrines of the Northern school of gradual teaching. All four works included in this collection are important sources for the study of Ch'an Buddhism.

The "British and French collections" mentioned in connection with the "*P'u-t'i-ta-mo nan-tsung ting shih-fei lun*" here ought to be corrected as "French" and the "England and France" mentioned in connection with the "Platform Scriptrue" ought to be changed to "England". Yet, Hsiang Ta's concluding remark that these four works constitute extremely valuable source materials is certainly appropriate. Hsiang Ta included this record of his investigations in the *T'ang-tai Ch'ang-an yü Hsi-yü wen-ming* that he published in April, 1957 from the Hsin-hua shu-tien, but did not comment on what happened to this booklet later.

During his visit to Beijing Yanagida enquired about this material at Beijing Library and the Chinese Academy of Social Sciences. Later, Ch'ang Shu-hung, the Director of the Tunhuang Institute (*tun-huang wen-wu yen-chiu so*) who visited Japan in November, 1979, responded to Yanagida's question about this material as follows: the location of the original material is unknown; but he had seen the same material in possession of Jen Tzu-yi that Hsiang Ta saw earlier, and he owns a photographic copy of the material. He thus indicated that textual critical work based on photographic copies of relevant works may become possible in the near future.

The present location of this text became known through a recent publication, *Tun-huang t'u-lu-fan wen-hsien yen-chiu lun-chi (Essays in the Study of Literary Findings from Tunhuang and Turfan)*, volume 3 (Beijing-ta-hsüeh ch'u-pan-she, February, 1986). In a section entitled, "*Tun-huang hsien po-wu-kuan ts'ang tun-huang yi-shu mu lu (Catalogy of Tunhuang Manuscripts in Tunhuang Prefectural Museum)*" in this volume the Tunhuang Museum listed and described the 78 items of Tunhuang manuscripts in its possession. A work with the title "*Nan-tsung tun-chiao tsui-shang ta-ch'eng po-jo po-lo-mi ching*" appears at the seventy-seventh item in this list and a short description of this work is provided.

Yang Tseng-wen, professor in charge of Buddhist studies, Institute for the Study of World Religions, Chinese Academy of Social Sciences, learned about this manuscript in the same year, and, after examining this manuscript on the basis of a photographic copy provided by the Tunhuang Museum, reported on his findings at the Second Japan-China Conference on the Study of Buddhism in October, 1987.[26] The report begins with a brief description of the manuscript containing four kinds of *ch'an* works that is in possession of the Tunhuang Museum (to be called Tunhuang Museum manuscript below) and the circumstances that led Yang to investigate this manuscript. A survey of the study on Tunhuang *ch'an* manuscripts conducted by Japanese and Chinese scholars in the past sixty years follows. A subsection entitled "The Discovery and Study of the Tunhuang text of the Platform Scripture" provides a summary history of the scholarship on the widely known Tunhuang manuscript of the Platform Scripture. The following section entitled, "The Academic Value of the Tunhuang Museum manuscript (Jen Tzu-yi manuscript) of the Plaform Scripture, *Nan-tusng ting shih-fei lun*, and other works" gives the summary of Yang's findings. Important items in this summary include the following points.

1) The Tunhuang Museum manuscript no. 077 was originally discovered by Jen Tzu-yi in 1935 in the temple at the top of the Ch'ien-fo-shan mountain in Tunhuang. In addition to the four *ch'an* works mentioned earlier by Hsiang Ta, the manuscript also contains the *Nan-tsung ting hsieh-cheng wu-keng-chuan*, probably composed by Shen-hui, and one five-character poem appended to it.

2) The Tunhuang Museum text of the Platform Scripture consists of 42 sheets (84 pages). Each half-sheet contains six lines, and each line 25 characters. Altogether the text contains around 12,000 characters. Its title and content are identical with those of the well-known Tunhuang manuscript (S 5475). This text belongs to the same group of the texts of the Platform Scripture as the manuscript S 5475.

3) Yang reports that the well-known Tunhuang text S 5475 lacks three lines, altogether 68 characters, and the meaning of the passages where these characters are missing is unclear. These three lines are preserved in the Tunhuang Museum text, and thus the latter enables us to restore the original form of these passages.

Example 1.

In a passage in which Hui-neng is lecturing on meditation, the Tunhuang text S 5475 gives, "*shan-chih-shih, yü wu chi ch'eng chih*". However, *yü* ("to meet") is a mistake for "*yü**" ("ignorant"), and 18 characters are missing in the S 5475 following this character. The Tunhuang Museum text gives the passage as "*shan-chih-shih, yü*-jen chih-jen, fo-hsing pen yi wu ch'a-pieh, chih yü mi-wu, mi chi whe wu, wu chi ch'eng chih*".

Example 2.

In a passage where Hung-jen orders his disciples to write a verse, the Tunhuang S 5475 text gives an unintelligible phrase "*huo chi chi*". The Tunhuang Museum text gives the phrase as "*huo chi tso*", and the meaning is clear here ("Make the verse quickly").

Example 3.

The meaning of the expression "*fo-hsin chung-sheng*" in one passage in the Tunhuang S 5475 text is obscure. This passage that reads: "*tan shih fo-hsin chung-sheng, chi neng shih fo*" (translated as "they have only to know that the Buddha mind is within sentient beings; then they will be able to know the Buddha" by P. Yampolski[27]) in S 5475 is given as "*tan shih chung-sheng, chi neng shih fo* (Only if they know sentient beings, do they immediately know the Buddha)" in the Tunhuang Museum text. This suggests that the two extra characters "*fo-hsin*" in S 5475 were added by mistake.

4) The Tunhuang text S 5475 and the Tunhuang Museum text were copied from manuscripts that belong to the same group. This group of manuscripts represents what may be designated as the original Tunhuang text. This original Tunhuang text was transmitted from Fa-hai through Tao-chi to Wu-chen. The text contains the story about "determining which was the correct Buddhist teaching and which not" twenty years after Hui-neng's death and also gives the names of the twenty-eight patriarchs in detail. On the basis of this evidence, Yang concludes that this original Tunhuang text was a revised version of the Platform Scripture produced by a disciple of Shen-hui or someone who had been under Shen-hui's influence; this revised version came into existence after the original text compiled by Fa-hai had circulated for some time. Yang suggests that the original Tunhuang text came into being during the period between the twentieth year of K'ai-yüan (732) and the appearance of the *Pao-lin chuan* in the 17th year of Chen-yüan (801).

Yang gives the transmission of the early text that lies behind the Hui-hsin text of the early Sung ("Hui-hsin's original text" in the sense of the text used by Hui-hsin) as Fa-hai through Chih-tao through Pi-an through Wu-chen to Yüan-hui. Hui-hsin's preface states that this text contained more sentences ("cumbersome"). This text thus contained materials added later to the original Tunhuang text. Yang hypothetically gives the date of this text as early or middle ninth century. The text that circulated widely at the time when Ch'i-sung (1007-1072) revised the text of the Platform Scripture was characterized as "vulgar, cumbersome, and disparate in writing" (Lang Chien's preface). Yang believes that this text must have been "Hui-hsin's original text", ie., the text that Hui-hsin used in producing his own text, and not the Hui-hsin text itself which resulted from editing this "Hui-hsin's original text" into the text in two fascicles and divided into eleven sections. Yang then notes that the text that Ch'i-sung produced through his revision does not exists any more, but that the Te-yi text and the Tsung-pao text from the Yüan period as well as the "original Ts'ao-ch'i text" from the Ming period belong to the group of texts that trace their origin to Ch'i-sung's text.

The Tunhuang text S 5475 is notorious for its poor quality. The newly discovered Tunhuang Museum text enables us to conduct new critical discussions of the early Tunhuang text. Furthermore, what we have seen above indicates that the benefit of the new text will not be confined to this contribution: it will also enrich immeasurably our discussion of broader issues in the study of the Platform Scripture. Yang reports that the Tunhuang Museum text will be published from the Wen-wu ch'u-pan-she under the title, *Tun-huang hsien po-wu-kuan so-ts'ang t'ang-mo wu-tai hsieh-pen "t'an-ching", "nan-tsung ting shih-fei lun" teng ch'an-tsung wen-hsien yen-chiu* in a near future. We look forward eagerly to the appearance of this work.

7. Conclusion

We have reviewed the remarkable developments in the text critical study of the Platform Scripture. We have confined our attention to the discussion of newly discovered texts. There remain a number of major questions that await elucidation in the study of the Platform Scripture. These questions include, for example, the question of the origin of the Platform Scriptrue on which Yaganida proposed a daring hypothesis in the past,[28] and the questions closely related to this issue concerning Hui-neng's biography and his thought.

APPENDIX I

1. The colophons of the Tenninji Text: 延享四丁卯七月上澣，再修表帙而備足闕文蝕字。
   金山天寧常住，現白英惠玉記焉。
   此壇經全部二卷，出于金山寶藏秘函之中矣。今流布于世叢林壇經，舊刊新削不一，或多或省，分門字數皆失。本經之正者間有之，末流之學者，不能無疑於其間也。特秘賀北洞宗大乘禪寺寫本壇經，目為正本傳焉。今次此二冊考合之，不違一字，只有闕紙數枚為恨而已。幸得賀北正本寫書，而書加而備足之，永莫廢失。至囑。

2. Chou Hsi-ku's postscript:
   後敘
   余資公暇，信覽曹溪六祖大師壇經，導化迷愚之人，令識本心，見本性，自悟成佛，莫向外求。言直理玄，法法非法，不可思議。乃勸諸善，諦印經受持，獲大功德，無上菩提者也。
   大中祥符五年歲次壬子十月八日，傳教弟子宣德郎守尚書屯田員外郎騎都尉賜緋魚袋周希古敘。都勸緣廣教院主僧保昌。金花山人嚴放外書。滝西阜海 刊字。

3. The passage from the *Chün-chai tu-shu-chih* quoted by Hu Shih:
   六祖壇經三卷 右唐僧惠昕撰。記僧盧慧能學佛本末。慧能号六祖。
   凡十六門。周希復有序。

4. The prediction passage in the Ming edition of the Platform Scripture:
   吾去七十年，有二菩薩從東方來，一出家，一在家，同時興化，建立吾宗，締緝伽藍，昌隆法嗣。

APPENDIX II

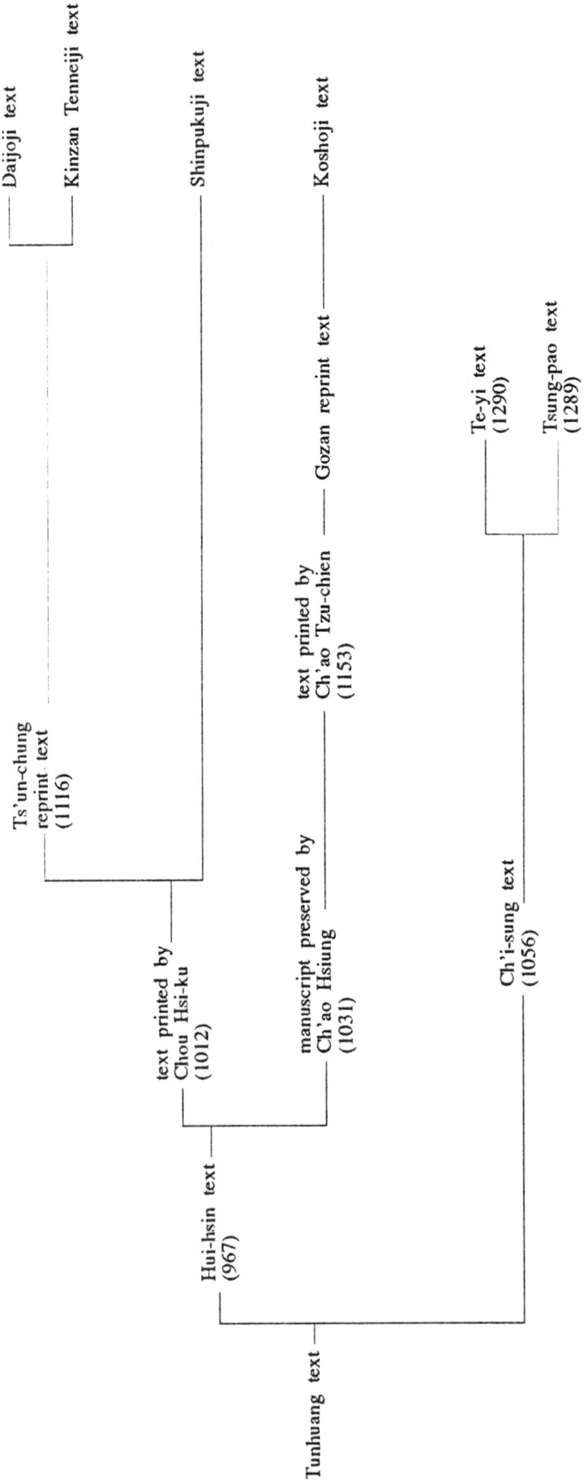
Tunhuang text
Hui-hsin text (967)
Ch'i-sung text (1056)
text printed by Chou Hsi-ku (1012)
manuscript preserved by Ch'ao Hsiung (1031)
Te-yi text (1290)
Tsung-pao text (1289)
Ts'un-chung reprint text (1116)
Shinpukuji text
text printed by Ch'ao Tzu-chien (1153)
Gozan reprint text
Koshoji text
Daijoji text
Kinzan Tenneiji text

NOTES

1. Here I am calling this work "*t'an-ching*" (Platform Scripture) following Ui Hakuju's usage. Ui called his study of this text in his work "*Dankyo ko*", ie., "Reflections on Platform Scripture" refering to the text as *dangyo/t'an-ching*. See Ui, *Daini Zenshushi kenkyu* (Tokyo: Iwanami, 1941), Chapter 1. p. 1.
2. This text has often been treated as a topic that every scholar must study. Ui, for example, stated in his preface to the study of this text that "Students of the history of *ch'an* Buddhism must *without fail* investigate this Platform Scripture at least at one point in their work..." (emphasis by Tanaka). Ui, Hakuju, *ibid.*, p. 1.
3. Komazawa Daigaku Zenshushi Kenkyukai, *Eno kenkyu*, Tokyo: Taishukan, 1978.
4. Yanagida Seizan, "Issues Surrounding the Tunhuang Text of the Platform Scripture" (in Japanese), Shinohara Hisao and Tanaka Ryosho (eds.), *Tonko butten to zen*, Koza Tonko series, no. 8, Tokyo: Daito shuppansha, 1980, pp. 19-50.
5. Ref., *Eno kenkyu*, *Ibid.*, p. 398. A diagram represening the relationship among variant versions ("*Ihon keitozu*") is found in p. 399.
6. Shiina Koyu, "On the Kinzan Tenneiji Text of the Platform Scripture" (in Japanese), *Indogaku Bukkyogaku Kenkyu*, Vol. 23, no. 2, pp. 291-295.
7. Yanagida Seizan (ed.), *Rokuso Dangyo shohon shusei*, Kyoto: Chubun shuppansha, 1976, p. 67.
8. The original text of these colophons are found in Appendix I.
9. Shiina, *ibid.*, p. 292.
10. *Ibid.* p. 293.
11. *Rokuso dangyo shohon shusei*, *ibid.* This work was published as the seventh volume of the ten volume series entitled *Zengaku sosho* under the general editorship of Yanagida Seizan.
12. See footnote 3 above for facts of publication.
13. Ishii Shudo, "A New Manuscript of the Liu-tsu t'an-ching discovered by Ito Taketoshi in the Shinpukuji Temple: Its Relationship to the Hui-hsin Text" (in Japanese), *Komazawa daigaku bukkyogakubu ronshu (Journal of Buddhist Studies)*, no. 10, November, 1979, pp. 74-111.
14. The original text of this postscript is found in Appendix I.
15. Yanagida Seizan, ed., *Koseki zengakuan* (Chubun shuppansha, June, 1975), pp. 79-80.
16. The relevant passage is reproduced in Chinese in Appendix I.
17. The result of this attempt was published as "A Study of Hui-hsin's text of the Platform Scripture: its text reconstructed and compared with the Tunhuang text" (in Japanese) in two issues of the *Komazawa daigaku bukkyogakubu ronshu*, no. 11 (November, 1980), pp. 96-138, and no. 12 (October, 1981), pp. 68-132.
18. Columbia University Press, 1967

19. *Sekai no meicho series: zoku 3* (Chuokoronsha, October, 1974), pp. 93-179.
20. *Zen no Goroku* series (Chikuma shobo, February, 1976), pp. 1-201.
21. The outcome of this investigation was published in his article entitled, "A Hypothesis concerning the Ch'i-sung text of the Platform Scripture" (in Japanese), *Shugaku kenkyu*, no. 23 (March, 1981), pp. 202-208. This article appeared in March, 1981 after the first part of his study of the Hui-hsin text, "A Study of Hui-hsin's text of the Platform Scripture: its text reconstructed and compared with the Tunhuang text" had appeared in the *Komazawa daigaku bukkyogakubu ronshu*, no. 11 (November, 1980) but before the publication of the second part of this same article in no. 12 (October, 1981) issue of the same periodical. Prof. Ishii, however, first completed his study of the Hui-hsin text and then investigated the Ch'i-sung text.
22. The original text is found in the Appendix I.
23. In Contrast Prof. Lou Yü-lieh of Beijing University agrees with Hu Shih's view that identifies the "old Ts'ao-ch'i text" that Ch'i-sung obtained with the *Ts'ao-ch'i ta-shih chuan* and develops his argument from the viewpoint that "the Ch'i-sung text was a composite version based on Hui-hsin text (or possibly the Tunhuang text) and the *Ts'ao-ch'i ta-shih chuan*". See his article, "On the Tunhuang text of the Platform Scripture, the *Ts'ao-ch'i ta-shih chuan*, and the Early Ch'an Thought" (in Japanese), *Matsugaoka bunko kenkyu nenpo*, no. 2, February, 1988, p. 2.
24. p. 317.
25. *ibid.*, p. 35-36.
26. Yang's paper was entitled "On Chinese and Japanese Studies of Tunhuang Ch'an Buddhist Literature with Some Comments on the Academic Value of the Manuscripts of the Platform Scripture, the *Nan-tsung ting shih-fei lun*, and other works in the Tunhuang Museum". A Japanese translation prepared by Mugiya Kunio of this paper is found in the October 23rd, 1987 issue (no. 23706, pp. 10-12) of the *Chugai nippo*, published by the Chugainipposha that sponsored this conference from the Japanese side.
27. *Ibid.*, 180.
28. Yanagida Seizan, *Shoki zenshu shisho no kenkyu* (Kyoto, 1967), pp. 148-212, 253-278.

(Translated by Koichi Shinohara).

List of Characters

Anayama Sumiko 穴山寿美子

Beijing-ta-hsüeh ch'u-pan-she 北京大學出版社

ch'an 禪

Ch'ang Shu-hung 常書鴻

Ch'ao Chiung 晁迥

Ch'ao Kung-wu 晁公武

Ch'ao Tzu-chien 晁子健

Chen-p'u 真樸

Cheng-he 政和

Cheng-t'ung 正统

Chen-yüan 貞元

Ch'i-chou 蘄州

Ch'i-sung 契嵩

Chia-yeh-shan Hai-yin-ssu 伽耶山海印寺

Ch'ien-te 乾德

Chih-ch'ang 知常

Chih-ch'e 志徹

Chih-ch'eng 志誠

Chih-he 至和

Chih-huang 智隍

Chih-t'ung 智通

Chih*-t'ung 知通

Chih-tao 志道

Chikuma shobo 筑摩書房

Chin-kang ching chieh-yi 金剛經解義

Chin-ling k'e-ching-ch'u 金陵刻經處

ching 經

Ching-chüeh 淨覺

Ching-kang pan-jo po-lo-mi-to hsin-ching 金剛般若波羅密多心經

Ching-te ch'uan-teng lu 景德傳燈錄

Ch'ing 清

Ch'ing-yüan 青原

Chizan 智山

Chou Hsi-fu 周希復

Chou Hsi-ku 周希古

Chü-chou 衢州

chüan hsia 卷下

chüan shang 卷上

Ch'uan-fa cheng-tsung chi 傳法正统記

Chubun shuppansha 中文出版社

Chugai nippo 中外日報
Chugainipposha 中外日報社
Chün-chai tu-shu chih 群齋讀書志
Chung-hua min-kuo 中華民國
Chuokoronsha 中央公論社
Daijoji 大乘寺
Daini Zenshushi kenkyu 第二禪宗史研究
Daito shuppansha 大東出版社
Dankyo ko 壇經考
Edo 江戸
Enkyo 延享
Eno kenkyu 慧能研究
Fa-chen 法珍
Fa-hai 法海
Fa-ju 法如
Fa-ta 法達
fo-hsin 佛心
fo-hsin chung-sheng 佛心衆生
Fo-jih Ch'i-sung 佛日契嵩
fu 扶
Fukuchiyama 福知山
Fukuoka 福岡
ge 下
gozan 五山
Guchu Shukyu 愚中周及
Hakuei Egyoku 白英慧玉
Hieizan Enryakuji 比叡山延曆寺
Hoei 寶永
Horikawa 堀川
Hoshoin 寶生院
Hsi-cheng hsiao-chi 西征小記
Hsi-hsia 西夏
Hsiang Ta 向達
hsin ching 心經
Hsin-chin wen-chi 鐔津文集
hsin-hai 辛亥
Hsin-hua shu-tien 新華書店
Hsing-ssu 行思
Hsüan-chüeh 玄覺
Hu Shih 胡適
Huai-jang 懷讓
Hui-Hsin 惠昕
Hui-ming 慧明

Hui-neng 慧能

huo chi tso 火急作

huo chi chi 火急急

I-fa t'a-chi 瘞髮塔記

Ihon keitozu 異本系統圖

Indogaku bukkyogaku kenkyu 印度學仏教學研究

Ishii Shudo 石井修道

Ishikawa 石川

Ito Takatoshi shi hakken no shinpukuji bunko shozo no rokusodangyo no shokai--ekinbon rokusodangyo 伊藤隆寿氏發現の真福寺所藏の「六祖壇經」の紹介ー 惠昕本「六祖壇經」の祖本との関連 tono kanren

Ito Takatoshi 伊藤隆寿

Jen Tzu-yi 任子宜

jo/*t'ieh* 帖

jo 上

juei-pin 蕤賓

K'ai-yüan 開元

Kaga 加賀

Kaiyuji 快友寺

Kamakura 鎌倉

Kanazawa 金沢

Kan'ei 寬永

Kanazawa Bunko 金沢文庫

Kano 狩野

Kao-kung shih-yü 高公世史

Kao-li 高麗

Kawakami Tenzan 川上天山

Kikugawa-cho 菊川町

Kinzan Tenneiji 金山天寧寺

Kinzan tenneiji kyuzo rokusodangyo nitsuite 金山天寧舊藏「六祖壇經」について

Kokeiso 古徑莊

Komazawa 駒沢

Komazawa daigaku bukkyogakubu ronshu 駒沢大學佛教學部論集

Komazawa Daigaku Zenshushi Kenkyukai 駒沢大學禪宗史研究會

Koseki zengakuan 胡適禪學案

Koshoji 興聖寺

Koza Tonko 講座「敦煌」

Kuang-fan 光範

Kuang-hsü 光緒

Kuo-hsüeh chi-k'an 國學季刊

Kuroita Katsumi 黑板勝美

Lang Chien 郎簡

Li Chih-fei 李知非

Liu Chih-lüeh 劉志略

Liu-tsu fa-pao chi hsü 六祖法寶記敘

liu-tzu t'an-ching 六祖壇經

Lou Yü-lieh 樓宇烈

Lü-hsun 旅順

Lü-shun po-wu-kuan so-ts'un tun-huang chih fo-chiao ching-tien 旅順博物館所存敦煌之佛教經典

Ma Tuan-lin 馬端臨

Matsugaoka bunko kenkyu nenpo 松ケ岡文庫研究年報

Ming 明

mon/men 門

mou-chia 某甲

Mugiya Kunio 麥谷邦夫

Myoshinji 妙心寺

Nagoya 名古屋

Naka-ku 中區

Nakagawa Taka 中川孝

Nakano Inchiuemon 中野市右衛門

Nan-tsung ting shih-fei lun 南宗定是非論

nan-tsung ting-chiao 南宗頓教

Nan-tsung tun-chiao tsui-shang ta-ch'eng po-jo po-lo-mi ching
南宗頓教最上大乘摩訶般若波羅蜜多經

Nan-tsung ting hsieh-cheng wu-keng-chuan 南宗定邪正五更轉

Nan-tsung tun-chiao tsui-shang ta-ch'eng t'an-ching 南宗頓教最上大乘壇經

Nan-yang ho-shang tun-chiao chieh-t'o ch'an-men chih-liao-hsing t'an-yü
南陽和上頓教解脫禪門直了性壇語

Nan-yang ho-shang t'an-yü 南陽和上壇語

Nan-yüeh 南嶽

Nanbokucho 南北朝

Nara 奈良

Otani 大谷

Otsu 大津

P'u-t'i-ta-mo nan-tsung ting shih-fei lun 菩提達摩南宗定是非論

Pao-lin chuan 寶林傳

Pi-an 彼岸

ping-chen 丙辰

Rinzai 臨濟

Rokuso dankyo 六祖壇經

Rokuso Dangyo shohon shusei 六祖壇經諸本集成

Rokuso dangyo gohon taisho 六祖壇經五本對照

Ryukoku 竜谷

San-lun 三論

Sekai no meicho 世界の名著

shan-chih-shih, yü*-jen chih-jen, fo-hsing pen yi wu ch'a-pieh, chih yü mi-wu,
mi chi whe wu, wu chi ch'eng chih
善知識, 愚人智人, 佛性本亦無差別, 只緣迷悟, 迷即為悟, 悟即成智.

shan-chih-shih, yü wu chi ch'eng chih 善知識, 遇悟即成智

Shang-wu yin-shu-kuan 商務印書館

Shao-chou 韶州

Shao-chou Ts'ao-ch'i-shan Liu-tsu-shih t'an-ching 韶州曹溪六祖師壇經

Shao-hsing 紹興

Shen-hsiu 神秀

Shen-hui 神會

shih yi, chiao-shih shih-seng ch'uan-fa 十一, 教六十僧傳法

Shiina Koyu 椎名宏雄

Shina bukkyo shigaku 支那佛教史學

Shingon 真言

Shinohara Hisao 篠原壽雄

Shinpukuji zenpon mokuroku zokushu 真福寺善本目錄續輯

Shinpukuji zenpon mokuroku 真福寺善本目錄

Shinpukuji 真福寺

Shinsan zenseki mokuroku 新纂禪籍目錄

Shugaku kenkyu 宗學研究

Sokyo 祖鏡

Soto 曹洞

Sung 宋

Suzuki Teitaro 鈴木貞太郎

Ta-chien 大鑑

Ta-chung-hsiang-fu 大中祥符

Ta-fan-ssu 大梵寺

Taishukan 大修館

t'ai-sui ting-mao 太歲丁卯

tan shih chung-sheng, chi neng shih fo 但識衆生 即能識佛

tan shih fo-hsin chung-sheng, chi neng shih fo 但識佛心即能識佛

T'an-ching k'ao chih erh--Pa nihon kyoto horikawa koshoji ts'ang pei-sung hui-hsin pen t'an-ching ying-yin pen
壇經考之二—跋日本京都堀川興聖寺藏北宋惠昕本
壇經影印本

t'an-ching 壇經

T'an-ching k'ao chih yi: Pa ts'ao-chi ta-shih pieh-chuan
壇經考之一：跋曹溪大師別傳

Tanaka Ryosho 田中良昭

tang-ti 堂弟

T'ang-tai Ch'ang-an yü Hsi-yü wen-ming 唐代長安與西域文明

Tao-chi 道際

Te-yi 德異

Teiji 貞治

T'ien-sheng 天聖

ting 頂

Ting shih-fei lun 定是非論

Tonko Butten to Zen 敦煌佛典と禪

Tonkobon Rokuso Dangyo no shomondai 敦煌本六祖壇經の諸問題

Ts'ao-ch'i 曹溪

Ts'ao ch'i liu-tsu ta-shih t'an-ching 曹溪六祖大師壇經

Ts'ao-ch'i ta-shih chuan 曹溪大師傳

Tsu-t'ang chi 祖堂集

tsui-shang ta-ch'eng mo-ho-pan-jo po-lo-mi-to ching 最上大乘摩訶般若波羅密經

Ts'un-chung 存中

Tsung-pao 宗寶

T'u-shu-kuan-hsüeh chi-k'an 圖書館學季刊

tun 頓

Tun-huang 敦煌

Tun-huang yi-shu tsung-mu so-yin 敦煌遺書總目索引

Tun-huang hsien po-wu-kuan so-ts'ang t'ang-mo wu-tai hsieh-pen "t'an-ching", 敦煌縣博物館所藏唐末五代寫本「壇經」 "nan-tsung ting shih-fei lun" teng ch'an-tsung wen-hsien yen-chiu 「南宗定是非論」等禪宗文獻研究

tun-huang wen-wu yen-chiu so 敦煌文物研究所

Tun-huang t'u-lu-fan wen-hsien yen-chiu lun-chi 敦煌吐魯番文獻研究論集

Tun-huang hsien po-wu-kuan ts'ang tun-huang yi-shu mu lu 敦煌縣博文館藏敦煌遺書目錄

Tun-huang yi-shu san-lu 敦煌遺書散錄

Ui Hakuju 宇井伯壽

Wakanjo becchibon mokuroku 和漢書別置本目錄

Wan-li 萬曆

Wen-hsien t'ung-k'ao 文獻通考

Wen-wu ch'u-pan-she 文物出版社

Wo-lun 臥輪

Wu-chen 悟真

Yabuki Keiki 矢吹慶輝

Yamaguchi 山口

Yanagida Seizan 柳田聖山

Yang Tseng-wen 楊曾文

yü 遇

yü* 愚

Yüan 元

Yüan-ch'i wai-chi 緣起外記

Yüan-hui 圓會

Yün-men 雲門

Zengoroku 禪語錄

Zen no Goroku 禪の語錄

Zengaku sosho 禪學叢書

zenshushi kenkyukai 禪宗史研究會

zhih 帙

The Development of Chinese Culture: Some Comments in Light of the Study of the Introduction of Indian Buddhism into China

Tang Yijie
Beijing University

In the *Historical Records* (*Shiji*) there is a saying: "Those who, living today, are interested in the ancient Way as the mirror in which they see themselves reflected are different (from ordinary people)". Jia Yi, in "On the Past of the Qin Dynasty" (*Guoqin lun*), quoted a proverb: "Remembrance of the past is the teacher of the future". Past things cannot be taken in their entirety as models of future things; however, is it not possible to analyze and examine the course of past history, find some regularity behind certain phenomena, and let that regularity serve a frame of reference in terms of which to think about the present? If the answer to this question were simply negative, then there would be no point in studying history and reflecting upon it. Therefore, I think there is some truth in the saying: "Remembrance of the past is the teacher of the future".

In the course of the development of Chinese history, there were three major occasions when a foreign culture was introduced into China. 1) The introduction of Indian culture after the first century, A.D. The Indian culture that was introduced consisted principally of Indian Buddhism and influenced Chinese culture profoundly. 2) The introduction of Western civilization that began in the seventeenth century (the middle of the Ming dynasty period). This consisted principally of the efforts of Western missionaries such as Matteo Ricci to introduce Western civilization. 3) The introduction of Marxism after the May Fourth Movement.

The historical conditions of these three events were different. These introductions of a foreign culture occurred in different periods in Chinese history; the nature of the cultures introduced and the manner in which they were introduced were also different. Consequently, these three events had different effects on Chinese culture. It is a major enterprise to investigate this matter comprehensively, and such an enterprise is beyond the limits of my ability. In this paper I would like only to discuss the historical example of the introduction of Buddhism, and examine certain phenomena that appear after the foreign culture that has been introduced comes into contact with the native culture. I would also like to see whether an examination of these phenomena can provide us with some meaningful insights regarding the more general issue of the introduction of a foreign culture.

Generally speaking, the introduction of Indian Buddhism involved the following stages: first, Buddhism attached itself to the native culture so that it could spread; secondly, certain contradictions and conflicts arose between Buddhism and traditional Chinese culture; finally, Buddhism was assimilated by Chinese culture and contributed on a large scale to the further development of Chinese culture. I would like to comment briefly on each of these stages.

I

When Indian culture was first introduced into China, it attached itself to the native Chinese culture so that it could spread and exert its influence. When Buddhism was introduced into China in the Han Dynasty period (206, B.C.-220), it was attached to the native Chinese "techniques of the Way" or "Taoist techniques" (*daoshu* or *fangshu*). During the Wei and Jin Dynasties (220-419), when the metaphysical speculation of the "profound learning" (*xuanxue*) was popular, "Buddha" and "Emperor Huang and Lao Zi" were treated as similar entities. The Prince of Chu "read the sayings of Emperor Huang and Lao Zi and honored the Buddha's temple (*rensi*)." (*Houhan shu*, chapter 42). Emperor Huan (reign years: 147-167) also built shrines for Emperor Huang and Lao Zi as well as for the Buddha in his palace (*Houhan shu*, chapter 30B, *Xiang Kai zhuan*).

At that time even Buddhists themselves called their teaching "techniques of the Way (*daoshu*)." In the essay, "On the Resolution of Puzzles" (*Lihuo lun*), Mou Zi treats Buddhism as one of the ninety-six types of techniques of the Way: "There are ninety-six different kinds of spiritual Ways (*dao*). If you look for the august and great, none surpasses the Way of the Buddha (*fodao*)." In the *Scripture in Forty-Two Chapters* (*Sishi'erzhangjing*), Buddhism is also called "the Way of Buddha (*fodao*)" by its Buddhist author.

The content of Buddhist teaching at that time was mainly summarized by such theses as "the imperishability of the soul" and "moral retribution of causes and consequences". There does not seem to have been any understanding of the teaching of "no self" in Indian Buddhism. The idea of "the imperishability of the soul" had existed indigenously in Chinese philosophy, where it took the various forms of "theories about ghosts" (*yougui lun*). In the *Book of Poetry* there is a saying that the human spirit goes to heaven after passing away (*Sanhou zaitian, Daya, Fuwang*). In the *Huainan Zi* it is said that "body can die, but the spirit cannot die" (*Jingshen xun*). In opposition to these thoughts, during the Han Dynasty period Huan Tan developed a theory that "when the body is dead the spirit is also dead." Wang Chong (27-90?) also said, "A person who is dead does not become a ghost." Nevertheless, the theory that "the imperishability of the soul" can be achieved by certain physical and spiritual cultivation was native to Chinese philosophy.

As for "moral retribution of causes and consequences," though there are differences between the discussions in Buddhism and native Chinese philosophy, the Buddhist idea which was popular in the Han Dynasty was consistent with the native Chinese idea of "good deeds produce happiness and licentiousness, misfortune" (*Fushan, huoyin*). The *Book of Changes* (*Yijing*) says, "A family which accumulates good deeds is bound to have a lot of happiness; a family which fails to accumulate good deeds is bound to have misfortunes."

Toward the end of the Han Dynasty period and around the beginning of the Wei Dynasty period (220-265) numerous new translations of Buddhist scriptures appeared. Buddhism spread in China in two major streams: one was the school of An Shigao, which taught Hinayana Buddhism and emphasized the method of meditation; another was the school of Zhi Loujiachen (Skt., Lokakṣema?), which taught Mahayana Buddhism and lectured on the Perfection of Wisdom philosophy. An Shigao translated many Buddhist scriptures. His most influential translations were the *Ānāpāna Sūtra* (*Anban shouyi jing*) and the *Yinchiru jing* (*skandha-dhātu-āyatana-sūtra*?). The *Ānāpāna sūtra* discussed the techniques of breath control, which was similar to the breath control techniques of Chinese Taoists and those who followed the cult of immortals (*shenxian*). The *Yinchiru jing* explained Buddhist terms and concepts and was similar to the commentarial scholarship of scriptures that flourished during the Han Dynasty period.

The *Yinchiru jing* took the concept of "original breath (*yuan qi*)" as its basic category and developed a theory of the universe and human life; *yuan qi* was said to be the same as the "five elements" (*wuxing*). It also discussed the Buddhist theory of "five accumulations" (*wuyin*, an earlier term used to translate *skandha*, which was later translated as *wuyun*), treating the five categories of form (*se*, or *rūpa*), feeling (*shou*, or *vedanā*), perception (*xiang*, or *samjñāna*), volition (*xing*, or *saṃskāra*), and consciousness (*shi*, or *vijñāna*) as the effects of the Five Elements. From these examples we can detect that An Shigao advocated the Hinayana method of meditation; it is also clear that he attached Buddhism to the teachings of the "techniques of the Way" (*daoshu*) that were prevalent in China and explained Buddhism using as his model these teachings about the technique of the Way.

The school of Zhi Loujiachen taught the Mahayana learning of the Perfection of Wisdom; it believed that the basic principle of life is "the mind (or spirit, *shen*) reverting to the original truth (*benzhen*)" and becoming one with the "Way". Here we can see the influence of the Taoist thought of the *Lao Zi* and the *Zhuang Zi*. The second generation disciple of Zhi Loujiachen, Zhi Qian, translated the *Prajñāpāramitā sūtra* ("Perfection of Wisdom scripture") into Chinese, giving its title as the "Scripture of Salvation into the Infinite Through Great Brightness" (*Daming du wuji jing*). The word "*prajñā*" in the title was here translated as "great brightness (*daming*)". The word "brightness (*ming*)" must have been taken in the sense of the statement "Knowledge of the constant is known as discernment (or brightness, *ming*)" in the *Lao Zi* (chapter 16). The word "*pāramitā*" was translated as "salvation into the infinite (*du wuji*)". This expression must similarly refer to the state of union with the "Way" ("Return to the Infinite", *Lao Zi*, chapter 28).

During the Wei and the Jin Dynasties, the ontology of the "profound learning" metaphysics based on the Taoist thought in the *Lao Zi* and the *Zhuang Zi* was very popular. The central issue of "profound learning" metaphysics was the question of the relationship between the Root (*ben*) and the Branches (*mo*) and between Being (*you*) and Nonbeing (*wu*). The central issue of the Buddhist teaching of the Perfection of Wisdom (*prajñā*) was the question of Emptiness (*kong*) and Existence (*you*, "Being"). Thus the Buddhist discussion was somewhat similar to that of the "profound learning" metaphysics. It was for this reason that many Buddhists of that time used the "profound learning" metaphysics to interpret Buddhist philosophy, even going so far as to use the so-called methods of "matching concepts (*ge yi*)" and "linking similar things (*lian lei*)."

Dao'an once said: "Among the twelve categories of Buddhist scriptures that of the *pimuluo* (meaning *pifuluo*, ie., *vaipulya* which probably meant Mahayana) scriptures is most popular; this was because the *Vaipulya* scripture's teaching of 'forgetting both existence and nonexistence' was similar the thought taught in the land in the *Lao Zi* and the *Zhuang Zi*." Here we can see that this famous teacher of that time already recognized that the popularity of Buddhism depended on its being understood in light of the thought of the *Lao Zi* and the *Zhuang Zi*.

There is a passage in the "Letters and Scholarship" section of the *New Account of Tales of the World* (*Shishuo xinyu*): "During the Zhengshi era (240-249), Wang Bi (226-249) and He Yan (ca. 190-249) had favored profound and transcendent (*xuansheng*) conversations about the *Lao Zi* and the *Zhuang Zi*, and after that the world set great store by them. But at the time of the crossing of the Yangze River (307-312) Buddhist doctrines became especially popular." (quoted in Liu Xiaobiao's commentary).

In the beginning of the Eastern Jin Dynasty (317-419), the study of "*prajñā*" became extremely popular and the so-called "six schools and seven sects" (*liujia qizong*) developed. The issue that they were interested in was essentially the question of the relationship between the Root (*ben*) and the Branches (*mo*) and between Being (*you*) and Nonbeing (*wu*). What is called the "teaching of the Original Nonbeing" (*benwu yi*) inherited and developed further the teaching that "valued Nonbeing" (*guiwu*) taught by Wang Bi and He Yan; the "teaching of Annihilating Mind" (*xinwu yi*) was similar to Ji Kang and Ruan Ji's idea of "No Mind" (*wuxin*); the "teaching of Matter As Such" (*jise yi*) is related to Guo Xiang's thought of "Exalting Being" (*chongyou*)

Why did all of this occur? I think any culture has its conservative elements, which gives that culture a resistance to foreign cultures. Thus, foreign cultures must first adjust themselves to the native culture and attach themselves to it. Those parts which are similar to the native culture will then spread easily; those parts which are alien to the native culture will then be slowly assimilated by the native culture and thereby influence the native culture.

II

As it spread broadly after the Eastern Jin Dynasty, Indian Buddhism gave rise to contradictions and conflicts between the traditional Chinese culture and the imported Indian culture. Yet in the midst of these contradictions and conflicts Indian Buddhism contributed to the further development of Chinese culture.

In the early years of the Eastern Jin Dynasty, the Buddhist teaching of Perfection of Wisdom (*prajñā*) attached itself to the "profound learning" metaphysics based on the *Lao Zi* and the *Zhuang Zi*; this position may be called the "Buddhist profound learning metaphysics (*foxuan*)". By the end of the Eastern Jin Dynasty and the beginning of the Liu Song Dynasty, other schools of Buddhism, both Hinayana and Mahayana, started to be introduced; they offered a variety of interpretations of the Buddhist scriptures, and exegetical scholarship on scriptures developed.

In the final analysis, Indian culture and native Chinese culture represent two distinct and different types of cultural traditions. Indian culture could not remain permanently attached to Chinese culture.

By the end of the Eastern Jin Dynasty period and later, numerous translations of Buddhist scriptures appeared, and these translations became more and more systematic. At the same time the superiority of some aspects of Indian culture over traditional Chinese culture became evident. Contradictions and conflicts inevitably arose between the two different cultural traditions.

The translation of Buddhist scriptures into Chinese began in the Han Dynasty period. According to the Kaiyuan catalogue of Buddhist scriptures, about 1420 volumes of Buddhist scriptures were translated during the roughly 250 years between the Han Dynasty and the Western Jin Dynasty. But during the Eastern Jin Dynasty (if we include the activities in the northern dynasties of Later Qin, Western Qin, Former Liang, and Norther Liang), about 1716 volumes of Buddhist scriptures were translated. More scriptures were translated during these 100 years than during the 250 years that preceded them. Particularly noteworthy in this context are Kumārajīva's precise translations of Mahayana and Hinayana scriptures, monastic rules, and doctrinal treatises; these translations enabled readers to understand the original meaning of the teachings that were representative of Indian Buddhist culture. By that time, not only foreign monks, but also Chinese monks had attained a relatively correct understanding of Buddhism which tallied with the original Indian meaning of its teachings. As they achieved a relatively correct understanding of Buddhism, new problems confronted these Buddhists: should they continue to understand Buddhism in terms of Chinese culture, or should they teach Buddhism in China according to the original meaning of its teaching? Thus began the inevitable conflicts between these two different types of cultures.

During the Southern and Northern Dynasties period (420-589), the conflicts between Buddhism and native Chinese culture occurred in many fields. These conflicts surfaced as problems of political and economic interests; they also appeared as problems in the fields of philosophy, religion, and ethics.

An important historical work has been preserved for us, and this work provides us with the broad outline of the contradictions and conflicts between Indian Buddhism and traditional Chinese culture during this period. This work is the *Hongming ji*. Through this work we can glimpse the issues that arose at that time: the controversy over the immortality or mortality of the spirit (or soul, *shen*); the controversy over karmic retribution, which involved the philosophical issue of moral causality (*yinguo*, "causes and consequences") vs. preordained fate (*ziran*; "our preordained nature [*xingming*] is self-so"); the relation between Emptiness and Existence; the controversy over the question whether monks should pay respect to the ruler, which involved the issue of this-worldly or other-worldly ethics (*chushi*; *rushi*); the relationship between human beings and other "sentient beings" (*sattva*). He Chengtian, basing himself on the *Book of Changes*, maintained that human beings, Heaven and Earth are three distinct entities, and criticized Buddhists for failing to make these distinctions, treating human beings and other sentient beings on the same level. This issue was related to the defence of the Confucian tradition.

There was also a controversy about Chinese culture and foreign cultures. He Chengtian, in "Reply to Zong Bin", wrote: "Chinese people and foreigners are naturally different, and this difference is rooted in their different natures (*xing**). Chinese people are endowed with a clear and harmonious nature, and are capable of humane sentiments and upholding correct morality; therefore Duke of Zhou and Confucius taught them the teaching of human nature and learning; foreigners are endowed with a violent nature and are greedy and full of anger; therefore Śākyamunī imposed on them the discipline of the five precepts." Gu Huan, in his "On Chinese and Foreigners" (*Yixia lun*), also claimed that China is the country of "rites and morality" (*liyi*) and that therefore we should not abandon the Chinese ways and imitate foreign countries. The principle on which he based his argument was roughly the same as that of He Chengtian.

During this period Emperor Wu in the North Chou Dynasty ordered the persecution of Buddhism, not only for political and economic reasons, but also for cultural reasons. In this period the contradictions and conflicts between Buddhism and Taoism, which was the traditional religion of the Chinese people, also became acute. First, there was the controversy about the theory that Lao Zi transformed himself into a foreign teacher (the Buddha); this was then followed by the controversies over death and rebirth, body and mind (*shen*, "spirit"), as well as the controversy about the relationship between Chinese and foreign cultures.

All these controversies were expressions of the contradictions and conflicts between two different types of cultures. Some of these controversies continued right into the Sui and Tang Dynasties (581-617; 618-907). I will not comment on them further here.

It is clear from the situation described above that after two different types of cultures come into contact with each other, contradictions and conflicts inevitably arise. One important question is how to deal with these contradictions and conflicts: either to repel foreign cultures using political power, or to remain amidst these contradictions and conflicts and absorb and assimilate what is good in the foreign culture. This is a large question. From the Southern and Northern Dynasties (420-589) to the Sui and Tang Dynasties there were contradictions and conflicts between Indian culture and the native Chinese culture. In my opinion Chinese people did not reject the foreign culture, but rather absorbed and digested the foreign culture as much as possible. This attitude showed the confidence of the nation as well the values of its own culture.

The experience of these contradictions and conflicts and the continued assimilation of Indian culture into traditional Chinese culture that resulted from it contributed forcefully to the development of Chinese culture. During this period, Chinese culture flourished in philosophy, literature, architecture, technology and even medicine. There is no doubt that all these accomplishments were related to the way in which Indian culture was treated in China at that time.

III

Indian Buddhism was gradually assimilated by Chinese culture after the Sui and Tang Dynasties. First Sinified Buddhist schools were established. By the Song Dynasty (960-1279) Buddhism had become a part of traditional Chinese culture and was completely blended into it—Buddhism evolved into the Neo-Confucian Philosophy of Principle (*lixue*) of the Song and Ming Dynasties.

Among the several schools of Buddhism that appeared during the Sui and Tang Dynasties, the Tiantai School, Huayan School, and Chan School were in fact Sinified schools of Buddhism. The central issues that these three schools concentrated on were the problem of the relationship between mind (*xin*) and human nature (or essence)(*xing**) and the problem of the relationship between principle (*li*) and fact (*shi*). The problem of the relationship between mind and human nature had always been an important issue in traditional Chinese philosophy, in which the discussion of this issue can be traced back to Confucius and especially to Mencius. When Mencius talked about "giving full realization to his mind" (*jinxin*), "understanding his own nature" (*zhixing*), and "knowing heaven" (*zhitian*) side by side in one sentence, he was clearly touching upon the issue of nature and mind.

The above-mentioned three schools of Buddhism all discussed the issues of Buddha nature (*foxing*) and the original mind (*benxin*). The Chan School was specially interested in the issue of mind and human nature. According to the Chan School the Buddha nature is identical with the original mind; the Chan School in fact had developed the indigenous Chinese discussion of mind and human nature in a new context from one particular perspective.

As for the problem of principle and fact, the Hua-yen School talked about the "free and harmonious interpenetration between principle (*li*) and fact (*shi*)(*lishi wu'ai*)" and the "free and harmonious interpenetration among facts (*shishi wu'ai*)." This discussion was not unrelated to the "profound learning" metaphysics of the Wei and Jin Dynasties, since the idea of "the identity of the substance (*ti*) and function (*yong*)" had already existed in the "profound learning" metaphysics of that time. For example, Wang Bi once claimed that "Nonbeing is the cause of Being." He also said, "Although [Heaven and Earth] are engaged in great undertakings and have great wealth in possessing the myriad things, each thing still has its own character. Although it is valuable to have Nonbeing as its function, nevertheless there cannot be substance without Nonbeing."(Commentary on the *Lao Zi*, chapter 38). Both these statements explain the relationship between Being and Nonbeing on the basis of "the identity of substance and function". The idea of the "free and harmonious interpenetration between principle (*li*) and fact (*shi*)" is thus related to Wang Bi's thought. On the other hand, the idea of the "free and harmonious interpenetration among facts (*shishi wu'ai*)" was influenced by Guo Xiang's theory of "self-transformation of things" (*duhualun*).

In China, the Huayan school and Chan school have had the most influence on Chinese philosophy. This was because they represented Sinified Buddhism. By contrast, the Faxiang school only lasted about thirty years, in spite of the fact that it was promoted by the famous Xuanzang. This was because the Faxiang school was purely Indian Buddhism.

In the Song Dynasty the Neo-Confucian Philosophy of Principle (*lixue*) opposed Buddhism, and from the longer perspective of the development of Chinese philosophy, this Neo-Confucian Philosophy of Principle took over the place that Buddhism had occupied earlier. This development was not a matter of accident, either. We can understand the reasons behind this development in a coherent way. From the beginning traditional Chinese thought has been "this-worldly" (*rushi*); in other words it has focussed on the realization of "ordering the state and pacifying the entire world (*zhiguo ping tianxia*)". This basic orientation differed fundamentally from that of "other-worldly" (*chushi*) Buddhist thought. However, even in traditional Chinese thought questions such as "What is the basis for the establishment of a perfect society?", and "How are we to realize the ideal of the 'ordering of the state and pacifying the entire world'?" became very important.

In this connection the concept of "Heavenly principle (*tianli*)" was introduced. Cheng Hao said, "There are many things in my learning that I have received from others, but the two character phrase *tianli* ("heavenly principle") is derived from my own experience." The *tianli* ("heavenly principle") is not *kongli* ("empty principle" or "principle of emptiness") but rather *shili* ("substantial principle" or "principle of the real"); it is the "virtue that expresses perfection." As for the relation between "Heaven (*tian*)" and "Man (*ren*)" (or *renxing*, ie., the nature of human being), Neo-Confucianists either claim that "The nature is the principle (*Xing ji li*)," or state that "The mind is the principle (*Xin ji li*)". Both these statements refer to the issue of the relation of the mind and the human nature. Thus this issue was a basic question in Neo-Confucianism.

In both the Neo-Confucian positions expressed in these theses (" Nature is the principle" and "The mind is the principle"), the question of the relationship between Heaven and human beings arises. Consequently, the Neo-Confucian thinkers established in their ontology "the unity of Heaven and human beings". The Cheng brothers described the relation between Heaven and human beings by the statement "The substance (*ti*) and the function (*yong*) share the same source; what is manifest (*xian*) and what is subtle (*wei*) are not separated from each other". Zhu Xi described this relationship of Heaven and human beings using the thesis "Every human being has his Great Ultimate (*taiji*), and every object has its Great Ultimate". Lu Jiuyuan says "the Universe is my mind and my mind is the Universe". And Wang Shouren spoke about the identity of Heaven and human beings (*tianren yiti*) when he stated, "The mind is the principle. When we say mind, we are at the same time referring to all of Heaven, Earth, and myriad things."

When the ideal that "the Heaven and human beings become one being" is perfectly realized, the project of "ordering the state and pacifying the entire world" is also realized; from the perspective of perfecting an individual human being, what is required is to manifest the "Heavenly principle" in himself. In order to manifest the "Heavenly principle" in himself, a person must raise the standard of his morality to the point where the unity of knowledge and action is achieved, and he must engage in the spiritual cultivation of his own mind. An important linkage developed in this sphere of mind cultivation between the Neo-Confucian Philosophy of Principle during the Song (960-1279) and Ming (1368-1661) periods and the spiritual cultivation and practice of Chan Buddhism that had flourished earlier. However, the goal of the moral practice of Neo-Confucianism was not to enable the individual to achieve Buddhahood, but to realize their ideal of a harmonious society. Neo-Confucianism criticized Buddhism on the one hand, and absorbed and assimilated Buddhism on the other, and in this way developed for Chinese philosophy a system that was even closer to perfection; this system contained an ontology, a theory of value and a philosophy of life.

In the period starting from the Han Dynasty (206 B.C.-220) and ending with the Song and Ming Dynasties, Chinese philosophy experienced the impact of a foreign culture, and completed a course of development that may be described by the formula of thesis, antithesis, and synthesis. The three developments we have examined above may be understood as expressions of this threefold formula of historical development. The encounter and assimilation of Indian Buddhism was the first example of this kind in the history of Chinese philosophy.

What can we learn from this process? I believe that there are at least four lessons.

1) The process of the absorption of Indian culture into Chinese culture lasted several hundred years. This shows that the absorption and assimilation of one culture into another cannot be accomplished overnight, but that it requires a certain duration of time and certain conditions. We can say the following on the

basis of the example of the introduction of Indian culture: although Indian Buddhism was very popular between the first and the tenth century, traditional Chinese culture also revealed its great vitality; each of the three stages of thesis, antithesis, and synthesis pointed to the places where the vitality of traditional Chinese culture lay and showed in what sense it was valuable; each of these stages showed how traditional Chinese culture dared to welcome a foreign culture into its midst, and how effective it was in absorbing and assimilating it. From this example, we can conclude that the attitude of "openness" towards foreign cultures is a sign of the vitality of the national culture. The capacity of a culture to assimilate a foreign culture is an important condition for the more rapid growth of that culture. Foreign cultures act as stimuli for the development of the native culture. When a vigorous culture faces the challenges of a foreign culture, not only does it not reject outright that culture, but it assimilates the foreign culture, in order to foster its own healthy development. Such viewpoints as "cultural relativism" (*benwei wenhua*) and "nativism" (or "national essence ideology", *guocui zhuyi*) not only stifle the development of Chinese national culture; they are themselves expressions of the decline of that culture.

2) This analysis of the phenomena which appeared after the encounter of native Chinese culture with Indian culture is a product of our current understanding. At the time this process of historical development occurred, people who were directly involved in this development were not aware of what we know today with hindsight, namely that the development went through a series of distinctive stages. When we study these stages of development today, we can recognize the following phenomena: at one stage in the introduction of a foreign culture, the foreign culture frequently spontaneously adjusts itself to the needs of the native culture in a variety of ways and searches for points of integration with the native culture. For example, during the Han Dynasty period, Buddhism emphasized such slogans as "the imperishability of the soul" and "moral retribution of causes and consequences"; later, it also adjusted itself to the "profound learning" metaphysics of the Wei and Jin Dynasties and advocated the "Buddhist metaphysics of profound learning (*foxuan*)". It was by no means simply a matter of accident that these developments occurred at that time.

Can we then say that this kind of development constitutes a certain universal law? I believe we can. If a foreign culture takes the place of the native culture (or a certain part of that culture) instead of adjusting itself to the native culture, it will then have negated everything about the native culture (or the corresponding part of that culture.) This will result for the host country in cutting off its own history and in abandoning the spirit upon which the existence of its own nationality has depended over a very long period. In this case, the foreign culture becomes something imposed by force on the people or the nation to which the foreign culture was introduced. Consequently, that foreign culture remains a rootless culture and could hardly survive over a long period of time there.

If, after a foreign culture has been introduced, a native culture is able self-consciously and deliberately to seek out the points of integration between itself and the foreign culture, and to let that foreign culture adjust quickly and smoothly to the needs of the development of the people and the nation to which it has been introduced, the situation will be different. Not only will the development of the native culture be enriched, but the native culture will also be able to generate under the impact of the foreign culture new possibilities for reorienting some of the areas of its development.

3) Every culture has its own distinctive characteristics which distinguish it from other cultures. If it is to exist as an unique culture its fundamental characteristics must be protected; otherwise it will become a thing of the past and not continue as a real culture that functions in real life. Compared with Indian Buddhism, the most evident characteristic of traditional Chinese culture is that it teaches us how to realize the ideal of "ordering the state and pacifying the entire world." Such a "this-worldly" spirit differs completely from the "other-worldly" spirit of Indian Buddhism. After being introduced to China, Indian Buddhism exerted profound influences on the social life of Chinese people; it changed many aspects of the social life of Chinese people. But the basic "this-worldy" spirit of Chinese culture has never been changed by the imported Indian culture. Hence, Chinese culture as an independent cultural system continued to exist and be developed.

Whether traditional Chinese culture can be further developed in the future thus depends on two factors: first, it must be able to keep its own distinctive characteristics; secondly, it must also be brave in assimilating foreign cultures in order to meet the developmental needs of actual social life. The first of these two conditions allows for the expression of the unique and distinctive value of a particular traditional culture. If a culture is unable to keep its own characteristics, it will vanish from the stage of history. The second condition gives expression to the fact that if a vigorous culture preserves its distinctive characteristics, and at the same time is also able to follow contemporary developments and assimilate new things, it is then bound to be able to develop further. If a culture loses its capacity for assimilating new things, it can no longer continue to exist as a culture which keeps its own characteristics. The history of the development of traditional Chinese culture illustrates that Chinese culture fulfilled these two conditions in the course of its history.

4) After the introduction of Indian culture into China, there was a period in which the influence of Buddhism in daily life was greater than that of the native Chinese culture. The bibliographical chapter in the *History of the Sui Dynasty* (*Suishu, Jingjizhi*) says that since Emperors promoted Buddhism, it developed so greatly that "everyone admired Buddhism. The copies of Buddhist scriptures that circulated among ordinary people were a hundred times more numerous than those of the Six Classics." Thus, many of the new developments in Chinese culture during the Sui and the Tang Dynasties were connected with Buddhism. Many famous thinkers during that time were monks and some of the Buddhist schools contributed to the development of Chinese philosophy. This situation may represent phenomena that necessarily occur at one stage after two different

traditions of culture have remained in contact with each other over a long period.

However, Chinese Buddhist schools and sects did not develop in the direction of forcefully adapting the spirit of social life in China to the demands of Indian culture; on the contrary, Buddhism developed in the direction of Sinification. It is particularly important to note in this context that the distinctively "religious" characteristic of Buddhism was destroyed by the emergence of Chan Buddhism. Chan taught that you not only do not have to recite scriptures and pray to the Buddha; you may also swear at the Buddha and patriarchs. Furthermore, according to Chan, the ideal of becoming the Buddha can be realized in daily life. In this sense, the place of Buddhism is taken by traditional Chinese culture: "Carrying water and chopping fire wood—without exception these are all spiritual paths." It will require only one more step beyond this in order to reach the position that "serving the father and serving the ruler" is the way of becoming a sage and a wise man. Once this step is taken, traditional Chinese culture has replaced Buddhism completely.

At present, the development of history demands that we place the question "how should Chinese culture develop?" again on the agenda for our discussion of contemporary issues. Our nation is again placed under the impact of various intellectual trends of Western culture: how are we to reflect upon the value of traditional Chinese culture, how are we to reform and develop it further so that it will adapt to the currently unfolding trends of modernization? In order to do justice to these questions, we must continuously explore and meet new challenges. We have discussed the introduction of Buddhism to China, and described the variety of phenomena that appeared after our native culture experienced the impact of a foreign culture. This exploration ought to serve as a very important reference point for studying the future development of Chinese culture.

(Translated by Koichi Shinohara)

List of Characters

An Shigao 安世高

Anban shouyi jing 安般守意經

ben 本

benwei wenhua 本位文化

benwu yi 本無意

benxin 本心

benzhen 本真

Chan 禪

Cheng 程

Cheng Hao 程顥

chongyou 崇有

Chu 楚

chushi 出世

daming 大明

Daming du wuji jing 大明度無極經

dao 道

daoshu 道術

Daya 大雅

du wuji 度無極

duhualun 獨化論

fangshu 方術

Faxiang 法相

fodao 佛道

foxing 佛性

foxuan 佛玄

Fushan, huoyin 福善禍淫

Fuwang 父王

ge yi 格義

Gu Huan 顧歡

guiwu 貴無

Guoqin lun 過秦論

Guo Xiang 郭象

guocui zhuyi 國粹主義

He Yan 何晏

He Chengtian 何承天

Hongming ji 弘明集

Houhan shu 後漢書

Huainan Zi 淮南子

Huan Tan 桓譚

Huan 桓

Huang 黃

Huayan 華嚴

Ji Kang 嵇康

Jia Yi 賈誼

Jingjizhi 經籍志

Jingshen xun 精神訓

jinxin 盡心

jise yi 即色義

Kaiyuan 開元

kong 空

kongli 空理

Lao Zi 老子

li 理

lian lei 連類

Lihuo lun 理惑論

lishi wu'ai 理事無碍

Liu Xiaobiao 劉孝標

liujia qizong 六家七宗

lixue 理學

liyi 禮義

Lu Jiuyuan 陸九淵

ming 明

mo 末

Mou Zi 牟子

Pinaye xu 毗奈耶序

ren 人

rensi 仁祠

renxing 人性

Ruan Ji 阮籍

rushi 入世

Sanhou zaitian 三后在天

se 色

shen 神

shenxian 神仙

shi 事

Shiji 史記

shili 實理

shishi wu'ai 事事無礙

Shishuo xinyu 世說新語

shou 受

sishi'erzhangjing 四十二章經

Suishu 隋書

taiji 太極

ti 體

tian 天

tianli 天理

tianren yiti 天人一體

Tiantai 天台

Wang Bi 王弼

Wang Shouren 王守仁

Wang Chong 王充

wei 微

wu 無

wuxin 無心

wuxing 五行

wuyin 五陰

wuyun 五蘊

xian 顯

Xiang Kai zhuan 襄楷傳

xiang 想

Xin ji li 心即理

xin 心

xing 行

xing* 性

Xing ji li 性即理

xingming 性命

xinwu yi 心無義

Xuanzang 玄奘

xuansheng 玄勝

xuanxue 玄學

Yijing 易經

Yinchiru jing 陰持入經

yinguo 因果

Yixia lun 夷夏論

yong 用

you 有

yougui lun 有鬼論

yuan qi 元氣

Zhengshi 正始

Zhi Qian 支謙

Zhi Loujiachen 支婁迦讖

zhiguo ping tianxia 治國平天下

zhitian 知天

zhixing 知性

Zhu Xi 朱熹

Zhuang Zi 莊子

ziran 自然

Zong Bin 宗炳

A New Look at the Earliest Chinese Buddhist Texts

E. Zürcher
Rijksuniversiteit te Leiden

1. Introductory remarks

The Chinese Buddhist texts that on the basis of internal and external evidence may be ascribed to the "embryonic phase" of Chinese Buddhism—the second and early third century AD—constitute a corpus of writing materials roughly equal to one-third of the *Hou Han shu*. If we compare this large body of archaic Chinese Buddhist scriptures with the few bits of available information on the historical aspects of Han Buddhism, or with the pitiful amount of original source materials on Han Taoism (or, indeed,on any other aspect of religious life of that period), it is obvious that, at least as far as the scriptural evidence is concerned, we might be tempted to conclude that Buddhism is by far the most richly documented sector of Later Han spiritual life. At first sight it would seem possible to analyse the doctrinal *contents* of these texts in order to fill in the empty contours of Han Buddhism: what the first generations of Chinese devotees believed is to be found in the scriptures.

This, of course, is a methodological error. In spite of all the changes and adaptations which the scriptures may have undergone in the course of translation, they basically remained intrusions from another civilization, containing an enormous range of concepts, rules, literary images and religious lore which, once introduced into China, lost their original degree of cohesion and integration. Some elements in a scripture could—for a variety of reasons—"catch on" and become productive factors in Chinese Buddhism, whereas other notions figuring in the same text would remain alien and undigested.[1] The argument that the fact that certain scripture was selected for translation implies a conscious choice of the translator and therefore to some extent reflects the predilections of the Chinese public does not hold good either, for that choice may have depended on other factors as well: the foreign masters produced the texts that they happened to have memorized before their arrival in China, or that were available as manuscripts. In general, as far as actual impact and productivity are concerned, we have to use other criteria, such as the occurrence of certain notions in the earliest commentaries, prefaces and colophons and in certain passages that, as far as we can judge, did not figure in the original text and were added for the benefit of a Chinese audience. Some of the ideas we find there also play a central role in the scriptural texts, such as the concepts of impermanence and causation, the elimination of desire, the elusive and dangerous nature of uncontrolled thought and the need to control it by means of psychic exercises. Such ideas may indeed be recognized as central concepts in Han Buddhism. But the mere fact that a certain theme figures in a translated Han scripture may certainly not be taken to mean that it was part of the Chinese religious experience.

There is, however, another possible approach that may yield some new, if indirect, clues: an analysis of the formal aspects of these texts, and an attempt to define their linguistic, terminological and stylistic features. Since I have presented a survey of the linguistic peculiarities of the earliest Buddhist translations elsewhere,[2] I shall in this article confine myself to a very brief summary of the purely linguistic features, and concentrate on matters of terminology and style. In doing so, I shall not go into the complicated textual relations between earlier and later Chinese versions, nor shall I make any detailed comparisons between these ancient translations and their extant Pāli and Sanskrit parallels. The question will be to what extent, and in what ways, these archaic translations can be made to yield information about the intellectual and social context of the very first stage of Chinese Buddhism, when it still was an obscure subcultural religion in extramural Luoyang.

In order to do so, we must first clearly define the corpus of texts that can be accepted as genuine. This is a sad necessity, for Chinese Buddhist bibliographers through the ages have been ever more generous in their attributions—in the successive bibliographies the number of works attributed to An Shigao has grown from 34 to 179, and those "by Lokakṣema" from 7 to 23!

The criteria for selection are the following:

(1) In general, no attention has been paid to attributions made later than the fourth century AD. This means that in most cases I have relied on what is considered the best authority regarding archaic translations: the *Zongli zhongjing mulu*, completed by the scholar-monk and eminent bibliographer Dao'an in 374 AD.[3] To some extent I have also been guided by information drawn from the early fourth century bibliographer Zhi Mindu.

(2) Wherever possible, corroborating evidence has been drawn from textual glosses, from contemporary or very early colophons and prefaces, and from the fact that certain scriptures are quoted or referred to in the earliest Chinese Buddhist commentaries,[4] or have been the basis of secondary, "polished" recensions that were produced shortly after the end of the Han.

(3) On the basis of (1) and (2), some "landmarks"—unquestionably authentic products of certain translators—could be established, e.g. T 224 *Daoxing jing* attributed by Dao'an to Lokakṣema; mentioned as Lokakṣema's work in Dao'an's preface to the same scripture; confirmed by a contemporary

colophon dated October 26, 179 AD supplying details about place and circumstances of translation, names of collaborators, etc.), or T 602 *Anban shouyi jing* (attributed by Dao'an to An Shigao; often quoted in the earliest [first half 3rd century] Chinese commentaries; preface by Kang Senghui ca. 250 AD mentioning An Shigao as the translator, and supplying names of Chinese devotees from the school of An Shigao who transmitted the scripture).

(4) These "landmarks" were subjected to terminological and stylistic analysis in order to define a number of distinctive lexical and stylistic features peculiar to certain translators' teams.

(5) The other extant scriptures attributed by Dao'an and Zhi Mindu to Han translators were re-examined in the light of (4); as a result, two of these had to be eliminated.

This critical selection has yielded a body of 29 texts that may be considered genuine Han translations, made at Luoyang by five different translators' teams between 150 and 220 AC. Their titles are listed in the Appendix to this article; for reasons of space the detailed bibliographical data concerning each text have been omitted.

2. *The 'scriptural idiom'*

Anybody who even casually has looked into an early Chinese Buddhist text must have been struck by the very peculiar kind of language used in it—a literary medium that differs as much from standard classical Chinese as it does, rather surprisingly, from the fairly regular classical language of the earliest Taoist documents.[5] In some scriptures this particular idiom prevails throughout; in other cases we find various degrees of *wenyan* admixtures: classical stylistic features such as a regular four-syllable prosodic pattern, the use of Chinese-type parallelism, and archaisms such as *si* for "this" and *jue* as a third person possessive pronoun. It is obvious that we have to do with a "scriptural idiom" serving as the vehicle of a marginal literature written for a special type of readership.

It cannot be doubted that this idiom largely reflects the vernacular language of the period, the more so since many features that are characteristic of our texts agree with the findings of scholars in the field of Chinese historical linguistics.[6] However, it should be pointed out that the source materials used by such scholars (such as Zhao Qi's second-century Mencius commentary; selected passages from early dynastic histories, and *Shishuo xinyu*) fully belong to the sphere of the cultured elite and therefore are written in a standard *wenyan* that only occasionally contains some vernacular elements, especially in direct speech. The Buddhist materials exhibit those features to a much greater extent, and in this respect by far surpass any secular text. The elements of living speech, which in secular literature are no more than vernacular intrusions embedded in a mass of classical idiom, here play a dominating role.

Yet it would be a gross simplification to regard this early Buddhist scriptural idiom as a completely faithful reflection of Late Han vernacular. We have to consider the influence of various distorting factors.

In the first place, with one or possibly two exceptions[7] we are dealing with translations, and sometimes we find distortions, especially at the syntactic level, that must be due to the non-Chinese (Indian) original. One interesting case is the frequent use of the vocative. In native Chinese literary prose, where it is rather uncommon, it invariably is placed in isolation at the beginning of the sentence. In Buddhist texts it is often inserted awkwardly somewhere in the first part of the sentence, thereby giving rise to such monstrosities as *Rushi, Shelifu, zhufo* ..."And so, Śāriputra, all Buddhas ...". Another curious case may be the use of the particle *yi* meaning "and" in enumerations, possibly under the influence of Indian *ca* or *athavā*. In general, however, this type of distorting influence is only rarely found. The archaic translations are very free and seldom aim at word-for-word rendering, as clearly can be observed in the translation of stereotyped formulas of which the Indian original can be defined with certainty.

In the second place, we often find distortions due to prosodic patterns, especially in the somewhat more "sophisticated" scriptures. It is well-known that Chinese literary prose of the second and third century shows a marked preference for the four-syllable line. To take one example from contemporary secular literature: the *Shenjian* by Xun Yue (ca. 200 AD) shows a distribution in which 52% is made up of four-syllable clauses, against 17.3% three-syllable, and 15.5% five-syllable groups. In some Buddhist texts the four-syllable pattern reaches the same proportions, and the habit is clearly growing with the development, in the course of several decades, of a conventionalized Chinese "scriptural style". The phenomenon has been described by Yoshikawa (1958) and Hrdličková (1958). It is obvious that in such texts the translator may tend to reduce binomes to monosyllables, to expand monosyllabic forms into uncommon or even artificial binomes, to drop verbal complements, or to insert meaningless particles, all this in order to make the narrative fit into the Procrustes bed of the four-syllable pattern.

And, finally, we can assume that the vernacular character of the scriptural idiom was weakened by the very fact of its being written down in a script which had become fully adapted to a largely artificial monosyllabic literary language. Its distorting effects, such as cases of artificial "mono-syllabization", can occasionally be observed in our texts.

Some characteristic features of an archaic, largely vernacular text—Lokakṣema's translation of the *Prajñāpāramitā in 8000 stanzas* (*Aṣṭasāhasrikā-prajñāpāramitā*) of 179 AD[8]—can be shown by comparing it with parallel passages as they occur in a much more polished mid-third century version ascribed to Zhi Qian.[9] A single example may suffice. The loud wailings of the Bodhisattva Sadāprarudita ("Always Weeping") are compared with the laments of a poor victim of injustice.

	Lokakṣema:
亦無有菩薩所行法則,	"And also there was no norm-and-rule practised by the Bodhisattvas,
用是故甚大愁憂,啼哭而行	and because of that reason he was very much grieved, and he wept and wailed as he went.
譬如人有過於大王所 其財產悉入縣官.	It sounded like a man who has committed a transgression at the great king's residence—his property is all confiscated by the authorities,[10]
父母及身皆閉在牢獄	and his parents and he himself are locked up in prison—
其人啼哭愁憂不可言	that man will weep and wail and be grieved in such a way as cannot be told:
薩陀波倫菩薩愁憂 啼哭如是	in the same way the Bodhisattva Sadāprarudita was grieved, and wept and wailed."
	Zhi Qian:
國無開士 所行淨法	"Nor was there in (that) land the pure norm practised by the Revealers.
是故哀慟	Therefore he grieved,
如人有過 於國王所 財產悉沒	like a man who has committed a transgression at the king's residence—his property is all confiscated,
父母及身 閉於牢獄	and his parents and he himself are locked in prison."

Here we see the "polisher" at work in various ways: proper names have been translated rather than transcribed (*kaishi* instead of *pusa*), or even left out (as in the case of the cumbrous *Satuobolun*) if the context is clear enough. Binominal forms are often replaced by monosyllables (*wu* for *wuyou*; *fa* for *faze*; *mo* for *moru*; the bisyllable *laoyue* is maintained *metri causa!*); "vulgar" expressions have been replaced by more regular forms (*shigu* for *yongshigu*); the narrative has been concentrated by leaving out irrelevant words and phrases (including the Homeric elaboration of the simile: "that man will weep …") and finally the whole passage, which in the Han version does not show any metric regularity, is forced into a rigid four-syllable pattern.

Zhi Qian's polished version of the *Aṣṭasāhasrikā* is an invaluable yardstick by which "vulgar" (hence probably vernacular) elements can be set apart, and the ways and degrees of stylistic adaptation can be defined in the products of various translators' teams.

3. Linguistic features

As I said above, a number of linguistic traits of the archaic Chinese translations have been described by me elsewhere. Here I shall only mention a number of salient features without textual examples, for which the reader may be referred to the article mentioned in note 2. Some of the most salient features are

- An abundant use of binomes (even in an adverbial position, like *huanfu* "again");
- verbal compositions with direction complement (*songchu* "to send out"; *shequ* "to reject");
- a very strong reduction of forms in the pronominal system (e.g. personal pronouns virtually being reduced to *wo* and *ru*);
- the very frequent use of plural suffixes, both simple (*-deng*, *-bei*, *-cao*) and composite (*-caodeng*, once even *-caodenbei*);
- the obsolescence of the nominal sentence AB *ye* and the development of copula *shi*.

We can conclude that the language of the earliest Buddhist translations is based on a substrate that in a somewhat formalized way reflects the second century spoken language of the metropolitan area. This substrate forms a clearly recognizable system that deviates from the literary language in a very consistent way.

4. Terminological and stylistic features

The distinctive features of the vernacular substrate figure in every text on our list, but they do not do so to the same extent. In some cases it really forms the substance of the text, without any clearly recognizable classical admixtures; on the other end of the scale we find some texts in which it merely "filters through", being distorted by classical fossilized forms, rhythmical patterns (both in prose and in unrhymed verse), Chinese-type parallelism and other stylistic embellishments. There are, moreover, considerable differences in the ways in which various translators rendered foreign proper names and Buddhist technical expressions: very different Chinese equivalents have been coined (or borrowed from other sources) to render the same foreign name or concept, and some translators obviously tried to find Chinese terms for everything, whereas others prefer to make frequent use of transcription.

A closer look at those differences in style and terminology will allow us to define certain "schools" of translators; and on the basis of bibliographical and historical evidence these can be arranged in a chronological order. This in turn may enable us to trace the steps of a gradual process of sinization, eventually resulting in the formation of a distinctly Chinese Buddhist "scriptural style".

(a) *Terminology and style: schools and stages of development.*

Chinese Buddhism starts with a mysterious embryonic phase about which very little is known. There is a gap of about eight decades between the first unquestionable sign of Buddhism in China (65 AD) and the arrival of An Shigao in Luoyang (148 AD) that marks the beginning of regular translation activities. We do not know any literary product of that primeval period; the traditions concerning the so-called *Sūtra in Forty-two Chapters* (*Sishierzhang jing*) supposedly translated under Emperor Ming, are utterly unreliable, and even the most archaic of the many extant versions is probably of post-Han date.[11] Secular sources supply a few bits of very early terminology which are vastly different from anything we know. Terms like *futu* for *buddha*, *sangmen* for *śramaṇa*, *yipusai* for *upāsaka*[12] are nowhere found in extant Buddhist translations. There is no evidence of any connection between this embryonic Buddhism, with its quaint terminology and its puzzling relations with court and courtiers, and the activities initiated by An Shigao.

The oldest and most primitive nucleus in our materials is formed by the sixteen short scriptures which may be regarded as genuine products of An Shigao and his collaborators. It is a very homogeneous group of texts, clearly recognizable by their linguistic and stylistic features. The language is erratic, crude, full of vulgarisms, often chaotic to the point of unintelligibility. There is a marked preference for translation of technical terms (making free use of non-Buddhist Chinese pseudo-equivalents such as *dao dizi* for *bhikṣu* and *dushi wuwei* for *nirvāṇa*), whereas foreign proper names are mostly transcribed. The style is strikingly "un-Chinese". There is no trace of any concession to Chinese literary taste (or of any familiarity with it): no tendency to impose prosodic patterns on the narrative; no syntactic parallelism; no use of typical fossilized *wenyan* elements. Versified passages are rendered in prose, even when introduced by the words "The following is said in *gāthās*".[13] The works of this type were produced roughly between 150 and 170 AD.

In the next phase (ca. 170-190 AD), the Indo-Scythian Lokakṣema and his collaborators produced a number of translations, seven of which have been preserved. These again form a distinct and very homogeneous type, very different from the products of An Shigao and his school. The language is more natural and intelligible than that of An Shigao; in certain narrative passages it may reach a high level of fluency and liveliness, with abundant use of vernacular elements. On the other hand, Lokakṣema's versions are characterized by a preference for transcriptions of both proper names and technical terms that frequently overburden the narrative with phonetic renderings of up to twelve syllables. There is no sign of Chinese-type literary embellishment. However, we observe the first beginnings of Chinese unrhymed Buddhist verse, made, as it were, with some hesitation: in the same text some originally metrical portions are rendered in prose, whereas other versified passages have been translated into Chinese *gāthās* of 5, 6 or 7 syllables.[14]

Somewhat later, in the 'eighties of the second century, and apparently working in isolation from Lokakṣema's team, the Parthian An Xuan and his Chinese collaborator Yan Foutiao produced the "mirror of the Dharma", *Fajing jing* (T 322). This scripture again represents a very distinct type of translation technique. The terminology is very original and differs completely from that of An Shigao and Lokakṣema. Virtually all proper names and technical terms have been translated (sometimes in somewhat bizarre ways: *gougang* for *srota-āpanna*; *dadao* for *mahāyāna*; *shujin* for *bhikṣu*; *miao* for *vihāra*) and there is some admixture of typical *wenyan* elements. The prose is sometimes prosodic.

A third generation of translators was active near the end of the second and in the early third century AD. The first of these was the Indo-Scythian Zhi Yao whose *Chengju guangming dingyi jing* (T 630) again appears to be a highly individual creation. All proper names and technical terms are rendered by Chinese equivalents which do not occur in the works of earlier translators. Most striking is the literary style of this work. The language is more classical than that of any other Han Buddhist text; the prosodical four-syllable pattern is carried to extremes (comprising more than 60% of the prose narrative), and there are many examples of the purest Chinese-type parallelism;[15] *gāthās* are rendered in unrhymed verse.

In the early years of the third century, two or possibly three translators, the Sogdian Kang Mengxiang and the Indians Zhu Dali and Zhu Tanguo (Mahābala and Dharmaphala?) made a Chinese version of a *Life of the Buddha*, the two parts of which were produced as two distinct scriptures (T 184: *Xiuxing benqi jing*, and T 196: *Zhong benqi jing*). In these works, the literary influence is very marked: frequent use of *wenyan* elements and stylistic embellishment, Chinese-type parallelism, and a very regular prosodic pattern. The *gāthās* are rendered in unrhymed verse of varying lengths, often with great sophistication. The new element is terminological syncretism. Foreign names and Buddhist expressions are rendered by means of a mixed vocabulary borrowed from various earlier translators, resulting in a great variety of forms that serves a double purpose: to avoid monotony, and to enable the translator to conform to the four-syllable pattern by choosing a prosodically suitable rendering. From a literary point of view these two Buddha biographies are no doubt the most sophisticated products of Han buddhism. Shortly after the fall of the Han (in the period 220-250 AD) the whole of T 184 and the first part of T 196, together with some passages drawn from two other sources, were combined and re-edited by Zhi Qian under the title *Taizi ruiying benqi jing* (T 185). As incorporated into this composite narrative, the Han account of the Buddha's life was for centuries to remain one of the most popular texts of early Chinese Buddhism.

(b) *Early buddhist scriptural style: the process of sinization*

The pattern that emerges from this chronological survey is very clear. Even in this very early period of Chinese Buddhism, we observe a process of gradual digestion of the literary "alien bodies" that were introduced from outside into the world of Chinese civilization. A common semi-literary idiom, deeply influenced by the vernacular, became increasingly conventionalized by the formation of a whole set of typically Chinese stylistic and terminological features. As early as the third century AD a distinctly Chinese Buddhist "scriptural style" had developed, as different from Chinese secular literature as from its Indian prototypes; in its turn it became frozen into a kind of canonical language and divorced from the living language.

Several forces were at work in shaping the terminological and stylistic conventions of this vast literature: the persisting influence of the Indian original; the influence of classical Chinese; the role of the translator's personal inventivity in creating new forms and ways of expression or in borrowing them from other sources.

At the level of terminology, it is quite clear that the translators, faced with the problem of faithfully rendering non-Chinese names and terms, in the Later Han period oscillated between two extremes: maximum adherence to the Indian original (hence maximal transliteration, of which Lokakṣema's *Daoxing jing*, T 224, with its monstrosities like *pusa-mohesa-moheyan-sengnie*: *bodhisattva-mahāsattva-mahāyāna-saṃnāha-saṃnaddha* is the most glaring example), or maximum intelligibility (hence total translation, even avoiding such well-known borrowings as *biqiu* (*bhikṣu*) and *nihuan* (*nirvāṇa*), and replacing them with Chinese "equivalents" like *chujin* and *miedu*). But in the end both extremes disappeared. In the late third century a mixed vocabulary had crystallized, in which both transcriptions and translation played their part, in a rather consistent way.

As far as translating names and terms is concerned, independent invention and borrowing both played important roles. In many cases we recognize the fruits of personal inventiveness. Expressions like *shanlai* "welcome" (= *svāgata*), *rulai* "thus-come" (*tathāgata*) and *zuxingzi* "son of good family" (*kulaputra*) obviously are neologisms; so are also some curious mixed translations like *hengsha*, "sand of the Ganges" (*gaṇgānadīvālukā*) and *chatu*, "field, region" (*kṣetra*). In some cases we have to do with misguided creativity, probably based on wrong information supplied by the foreign master: *du*, "crossing" for *pāramitā* is based on a false etymology (*param* + *ita*, "gone beyond"), and *weicengyou*, for "marvellous" (*adbhuta*) is derived from a misinterpretation of a Prākrit form (*abbuta*, mistaken for *abhūta* "not become").

The use of Chinese native terminology in rendering Buddhist ideas will be discussed more extensively in the next section. Here it will suffice to say that, in general, terminological borrowings clearly derived from the Confucian tradition are rare; that some basic terms have obviously been taken over from popular Taoism, and in a number of interesting and puzzling cases the Chinese redactors appear to have drawn their inspiration from obscure local cults and beliefs with which they were somehow associated—a fact that in one case is supported by epigraphical evidence.

But here again the extremes have been obliterated in the course of the process we are describing. The most glaring Taoist borrowings eventually disappeared from the scriptural idiom. For *nirvāṇa* the older Chinese "equivalents" were supplanted by a transcription, and *pusa* took the place of *mingshi* and *kaishi*. Lokakṣema's remarkable *trouvaille benwu* for *tathatā* ("suchness", indicating the metaphysical Emptiness underlying all phenomenal existence) was rejected in favour of the neologism *zhenru*. Thus, Buddhist terminology gradually gained its own identity, and the wild experiments of the founding fathers never were repeated.

At the level of style and composition we see that analogous forces at work in shaping a fairly uniform scriptural style, and here the pattern is even more clear.

As far as the influence of the Indian original is concerned, it is obvious that the first translators' teams were, so to speak, helplessly and passively undergoing the impact of these literary intrusions from another world. *Wenyan* conventions and stylistic features may have been unknown to them, but even if they had had some classical training, they may have been unable to apply it to a body of texts so completely alien to Chinese literary tradition.

Gradually, however, some features of Chinese literary style and composition were introduced by the successive generations of translators. The most striking example is the increasing use of the prosodic four-syllable pattern in prose, a stylistic convention that played a dominating role in secular classical literature of the period. The stages are very clear: total absence in the works of An Shigao and Lokakṣema, occasional appearance in the 'eighties of the second century (An Xuan, T 322); universal application in the latest Han translations. It was to remain dominant in all later Chinese Buddhist scriptures.

The same holds good for one of the most characteristic features of Chinese classical composition: the rigid pattern of paired sentences showing semantic and syntactic parallelism. It can nowhere be found in the earliest translations, not even in the *Fajing jing* by An Xuan which otherwise contains quite a number of *wenyan* elements. It only appears at the end of the second and in the early third century in the texts that also in other respects are deeply influenced by Chinese literary conventions.

The case of what may be considered as the most characteristic feature of Chinese scriptural idiom, the so-called "prosimetric form",[16] is somewhat different: here we have to do not with a one-way intrusion of Chinese stylistic conventions into an emerging scriptural idiom, but with the formation of a *new* stylistic device, developed under the stimulus of the Indian example, and, as far as we know, not inspired by any pre-existing Chinese literary pattern. Alternation of prose and versified passages (*gāthās*, sometimes translated as *song*, sometimes transcribed as *jie* or *jue**) formed an integral part of the Indian literary tradition. Sometimes they are placed at the end of a sermon, summarizing its essential content; in other cases (particularly in scholastic treatises) they introduce the work as a whole (laudatory stanzas addressed to the Buddha, the Dharma and the Saṅgha), or they precede the individual sections of the work in the form of extremely concentrated mnemonic verses (*kārikā*). Mostly, however, they are embedded in a continuous narrative. In a prose context, the versified portions often render direct speech, being introduced by such formulas as "and then, speaking in *gāthās*, he said ...". But direct speech may also end somewhere in the middle of the hymn, which then goes on to describe other happenings in verse, or, on the contrary, only a part of the *oratio recta* may have *gāthā* form, the prose monologue or prose dialogue suddenly turning into verse, and from verse into prose again.

All these were elements of a great foreign literary tradition which, once transplanted into China, had to find its own means of expression. The complicated patterns of Indian metre could not be expressed in Chinese, and it was equally impossible to retain the original palmodic melodies to which the *gāthās* had to be sung. Both the metric form of the text and the musical form of the recitative had to be adapted to the nature of the Chinese language and the conventions of Chinese musical art.

This process started early, and our Han materials allow us to observe its various stages. In the very first phase (An Shigao and his collaborators) the translators evidently were at a loss what to do with the *gāthās*. The introductory stanzas of the *Daodi jing* (T 607) are rendered in clumsy prose, and in several other texts of this school the words "the following is said in *gāthās*" are followed, somewhat paradoxically, by passages in prose.

One generation later, Lokakṣema occasionally attempts to introduce Chinese unrhymed stanzas, whereas in other passages—even in the same scripture—verse is turned into prose. Anyhow, by this occasional use of unrhymed Chinese verse Lokakṣema introduced a literary device that would for centuries remain characteristic of Chinese "scriptural style". As such it was a step of momentous importance, for the prosimetric style to which he (or rather his Chinese collaborators) had given the start was to find its way, via Buddhist *bianwen* and their secular counterparts, into later Chinese popular literature, where it would survive till modern times.

It is unknown whether this Chinese response to the Indian *gāthās* tradition was a free invention or a borrowing from an unknown native source. Two of Lokakṣema's collaborators are known to have been patrons of some obscure local cult, and it would be tantalizing to suppose that through them some kind of popular incantation may have been introduced into the translation work in which they themselves were engaged. But this is pure speculation. For all we know, earlier and contemporary Chinese lyrics were universally characterized by the use of rhyme (it is true that a number of Odes of the *Song* section of the *Book of Songs* are rhymeless, but even granting the fact that *gāthās* are often called *song*, it would be too far-fetched to regard this as more than coincidental; *song*, for *gāthā*, obviously just means "laudatory hymn"). Taoist hymns and other versified texts cannot have been a source of inspiration (even if we suppose that such texts existed as early as the second century AD), for in early Taoist scriptures the stanzas invariably are rhyming, even in texts that are deeply influenced by the Buddhist scriptural style.

The Chinese device thus created was very simple. Han scriptures contain stanzas of four, five or seven syllables. Cases of *enjambement* are very rare: in general, each verse forms either a full independent sentence (e.g., *xin qi xiang ze chi*) or at least a well-defined clause forming part of a more complex sentence (e.g. *Song shi sanmei shi/sile zuo shamen*). The short (3, 4 or 5 syllable) lines just consist of so many syllables without any further internal prosodical pattern. In 7-syllable *gāthās*, however, we observe an interesting phenomenon, no doubt inspired by secular poetry: there is a distinct attempt to put a caesura after the fourth syllable, even in the earliest examples.[17]

After the first attempts by Lokakṣema's team, we see how the prosimetric form becomes more sophisticated. It culminates, as far as Han scriptures are concerned, in the Buddha biographies of the early third century (T 184 and T

196), which contain several dozens of versified passages. Whereas in the earlies specimens (Lokakṣema, Zhi Yao) the *gāthā* passages are mere "blocks" of direct speech, we find here all patterns of alternation (direct speech turning into description, and the reverse, within a single poetic passage) which lend a special flavour to the narrative. It would not be an exaggeration to say that the epic description of the Buddha's struggle with Māra in T 184 in liveliness and dramatic power far surpasses anything written in Chinese secular literature of the period.

A third area of invention and experiment was created by the necessity to render the numerous stereotyped formulas and standard passages found in every Buddhist text. In their original form the Indian *clichés* are completely stereotyped elements, a kind of literary modules that may range from one sentence or short paragraph (e.g. the well-known opening and closing sentences of any *sūtra* or the formula describing how a person politely inquires after the Buddha's health) to whole passages (such as the elaborate description of the happy reign of a Universal King, or the long sequence beginning with the Buddha emitting a radiance that pervades the whole universe and then smiling, and finally uttering the prophecy of someone's future Buddhahood).

In trying to coin suitable Chinese equivalents, the earliest translators show two tendencies, both of which bear the stamp of "Chinese taste": condensation and variation. In rendering the literary *clichés* the translators (or rather the Chinese redactors) time and again appear to have made concessions to the Chinese predilection for terse and concentrated description by leaving out stages, cutting out unessential elements, and thus reducing the Indian luxuriant verbosity of the original. In the same way, there is a strong tendency to avoid the monotonous effect of another characteristic feature of the Indian scriptural style: the verbatim repetition of whole passages, by introducing a certain amount of diversification and irregularity. The Chinese eventually did create a number of formulas (thus the opening words *Evaṃ maya śrūtam* "So I have heard" soon became *wen rushi*, since the late fourth century—probably for metric reasons—supplanted by *rushi wo wen*), but in the early period such formulas never were as rigidly stereotyped as their Indian prototypes, and in the same translated scripture we often find various alternative forms and longer or shorter versions of the same *cliché*.

The process of sinization which we have traced in terminology, style and composition thus resulted in the formation of a distinctly Chinese form of literary expression; in its essential features this scriptural style had already become conventionalized in the early third century—barely seventy years after An Shigao's first primitive attempts. In this respect, as in so many others, the Han experience has been decisive.

5. The Chinese audience

We may start from two self-evident facts: we are dealing with products of translation, and those translated *sūtras* were written down. Both facts have a whole range of implications which cannot be elaborated here. For our present subject it is important to note that, in the first place, the translation effort, which appears to have started soon after An Shigao's arrival at Luoyang around 148 AD and which was quite productive (yielding, according to Dao'an, some seventy *juan* of Chinese versions in the first forty years), implies that there must have been a Chinese *clientèle* large enough to warrant such an undertaking. And, secondly, the production of such a considerable body of written texts is highly significant. We do not know to what extent oral propagation played a role as well, but the very existence of our texts proves that Buddhism primarily addressed itself to an educated minority.

On the other hand, the linguistic and stylistic features make clear that when dealing with these archaic scriptures we are very far removed from the literary culture of the true elite. In most texts the language is rather primitive and clumsy; the vocabulary is limited and repetitive, and seen in the more "sophisticated" scriptures we hardly find any conventional expressions borrowed from the Chinese high-class literary tradition.

We may conclude that these texts circulated among a public of Chinese lay devotees with rudimentary schooling, standing outside the elite of scholar-officials, but sufficiently literate to read these texts with their limited vocabulary and their unadorned style. In the context of the urban society of Later Han times, one may think of a sub-elite of clerks and copyists, the lowest fringe of the bureaucracy, and traders and artisans. The propagation of Buddhism at the intermediate level would also explain why the official historical records do not contain a single reference to this "Church of Luoyang", and why there is no evidence of any connection between the hybrid court Buddhism mentioned in secular historiography and the activities of the Buddhist missionaries at Luoyang.

There probably were no fully ordained Chinese monks before the third century AD.[18] However, this does not mean that the scriptures offered to the Chinese devotees were limited to the kind of "edifying texts" that were primarily destined to be read by the lay public. On the contrary: most Han scriptures are highly technical and scholastic, and they treat subjects that normally belong to the practice of monastic Buddhism, such as *dhyāna* exercises, respiratory techniques, numerical categories, themes of contemplation, and the constituent elements of the pseudo-personality. Lay believers apparently took part in such exercises—in fact, around the middle of the third century a certain Chen Hui, no doubt a layman, is known to have expounded the highly scholastic *Yin chi ru jing* and the treatise on "Respiratory Concentration", *Anban shouyi jing*, both translated by An Shigao.[19]

It therefore seems that the fundamental distinction between monastic and lay Buddhism had not yet taken shape, as far as the Chinese believers were concerned. There are, however, some signs indicating that among the laity itself there was a certain diversity of interests, some believers being attracted by the simple and easily digestible teachings of lay Buddhism, and other by the *arcana* of Buddhist scholasticism and contemplation.

6. The believers and the experts

If we inventorize the stylistic and terminological features of the extant Han scriptures, there are four texts that form a distinctive category of their own.

(1) T 322 "The *sūtra* of the Mirror of the Doctrine", *Fajing jing*, translated by An Xuan, ca. 180 AD;

(2) T 630, "The *sūtra* on the Mental Fixation of Integral Illumination", *Chengju guangming dingyi jing*, attributed to the late second century translator Zhi Yao.

Both texts are characterized by a considerable number of classical admixtures, a very idiosyncratic terminology (e.g. *chujin* and *chue* for *bhikṣu*), and, above all, the fact that the translators have done their utmost to translate everything into Chinese, even including proper names such as *Wenwu guo* for Śrāvastī. This peculiarity—which by itself would already suggest an attempt to cater to the taste of a fairly cultured "non-professional" public—becomes even more relevant if we look at the contents of T322 and T680: they are the only Han scriptures in which a detailed description is given of the moral duties and devotional practices of the lay believer, or, as T 322 calls him, "the Bodhisattva who practices the Way while staying in the household".

(3) T 184, "The *sūtra* on the Origin of (Religious) Practice", *Xiuxing benqi jing*, and

(4) T196, "The Middle (Part) of the *sūtra* on the Origin (of Religious Practice)", *Zhong benqi jing*, both translated by the Sogdian Kang Mengxiang, with the assistance of the Indian monks Zhu Dali and Zhu Tanguo, around 200 AD.[20]

The two texts, which contain an account of the Buddha's career from the prophecy of his future Buddhahood under Dīpaṃkara to the middle part of his ministration, actually form one continuous narrative. The style is rather literary, with many *wenyan* elements and a regular rhythmic four-syllable pattern. The quality of Kang Mengxiang's style, its "grace and fluency"[21] is quite conspicuous; the combined text of T184/T196 no doubt forms the most readable, and even enjoyable, part of archaic Chinese Buddhist literature. The religious message of the narrative is simple and direct: feats of supernatural power, moral rules, edifying anecdotes, and stories about the retribution of sins. Purely doctrinal matters play a minor role.

We can conclude that these scriptures constitute the "popularizing sector" in Han Buddhist literature—elementary texts written in a semi-classical style, preaching a rather simple kind of morality: the Three Refuges; the Five Rules of lay Buddhism; devotion; love towards all creatures; the impermanence of all things, and the inevitability of karmic retribution. The texts sharply contrast with the other prevailing type of Han scriptures: the much more vernacular and generally abstruse scriptures of a more specialized nature, which emphasize mental discipline and *dhyāna* practices, respiratory techniques, the ecstatic "visualization" of Buddhas, the contemplation of the impure, the eradication of all desire (*chu yu*) and of all uncontrolled mental activity (*xinyi*).

It may well be that the latter type of scriptures reflects the interests of another group of devotees within the same subculture: not the simple *upāsakas* looking for moral guidelines and a new type of religious piety, but the active practicants attracted by a master like An Shigao, who already in his life-time appears to have been regarded as a powerful magician.[22]

7. *Buddhism and indigenous Chinese traditions: the exotic alternative*

In spite of occasional (and surprisingly rare) terminological borrowings from Confucian and Taoist lore, the most striking aspect of Han Buddhism is its novelty. The view that Buddhism was accepted because it, in certain ways, accorded with indigenous traditions must be rejected; Buddhism was attractive not because it sounded familiar, but because it was something basically new. Certain concepts and practices bore a superficial resemblance to Taoist notions, but the basic difference in orientation and application must have been obvious right from the start. In Taoism, breath control serves to accumulate the vital essence inside the body; in Buddhism, *ānāpāna* is practised as a mental tranquilizer before entering meditation. In Taoism, sexual techniques are used as a means to achieve salvation; in Buddhism, all desire—and sexual desire in particular—is a negative force; rebirth as a woman is the result of karmic sin, and the female body is an instrument of moral destruction.[23] And, most important of all, the Taoist belief in the possibility of bodily immortality is incompatible with the Buddhist idea that *all* bodily existence—even that of the gods—is transitory and doomed to decay. And here, again, the opposition appears to be reflected by the written language, for the hybrid, semi-vernacular idiom of the Buddhist texts completely differs from the simple but regular *wenyan* of the earliest Taoist scriptures and commentaries.

If Han Buddhism, in its most essential aspects, was not a variant from but rather a distinct alternative to Taoism, the same must be said of its relation to Confucian ethics. It is true that lay morality includes a number of rules that basically accord with Confucian norms of social behaviour: observing ones' duties towards relatives and other dependents; temperance; sincerity in social relations, and indifference to worldly praise or blame. But even in the two scriptures which exclusively deal with the moral and religious duties of the Buddhist layman, the essential message is hardly compatible with Confucian ethics. In all his actions, the lay devotee should consider the transitoriness of all things and the inanity of all worldly relations.[24] Even when serving his parents and showing love to his children he should regard the household as a prison and his relatives as dangerous enemies.[25] He should train himself to feel no special attachment to his nearest kin, for his love should go to all creatures: and, after all, why love your son more than all those fellow-creatures in the world, who may have been your sons and daughters in innumerable former lives?[26] Far from accommodating with the rules of Confucian social ethics, Han Buddhism preached a detached attitude towards even the nearest relatives, coupled with an ideal of "universal love" far more radical and comprehensive than anything that could be found in traditional Chinese thought.

The same universalistic and non-familial kind of morality is found time and again in T 630. In the fifty-five moral rules for lay devotees (fifteen for high officials, ten for commoners, twenty-five for noble ladies, and ten for common women) the specific virtues of family life (filial piety, brotherly love, etc.) which form the very heart of Confucian ethics, are hardly touched upon. Only in the rules for "noble ladies" the theme of her obligations towards husband and near relatives are mentioned in passing. For the rest the full emphasis is on ethical behaviour towards the world at large, or towards specific groups of people beyond the family (the poor and destitute; servants and slaves; the people under one's jurisdiction; even sinners who should be kindly treated and converted).

Here, again, we may find a most un-Confucian position of Buddhist lay ethics reflected in the terminology of our scriptures, in which clear Confucian borrowings are extremely rare.

But are we not, after all, on a wrong track by trying to define the ideological position of Han Buddhism in terms of the easy dichotomy "Confucian/Taoist"? Chinese society of the second century AD—and for centuries afterwards—was not a "Confucian society" as we know it from late imperial times. Confucianism was represented by an extremely small elite—a very thin top layer, under which there was an immense variety of local beliefs, cults and religious practices.

In many cases these may have been variations within a common fund of religious and magical lore without any special affinity either to Confucianism or to Taoism. In fact, the terminology of Buddhist texts contains a number of quaint Chinese "equivalents" that look like borrowings from unknown sources of Chinese religious lore. What is the background of the very common archaic term *yin*, "dark(ening) element"(?), as used for *skandha*, the constituent parts of the human person? Why is the universal ruler (*cakravartin*) referred to as a "flying emperor", *feixing huangdi*? Why are the gods (*deva*) called *tian*? Is the term "subterranean prison", *diyu*, a Buddhist neologism, or does it reflect some popular belief concerning the fate of sinners after death? It may well be that further analysis of archaic Buddhist terminology will teach us more about this unexplored zone of Han popular religion.

If one would try to indicate, in most general terms, what may have been the special appeal of a doctrine that so clearly rejected some of the most firmly established ideas of the age, the answer probably would lie in the Buddhist preoccupation with Impermanence, its (sometimes almost morbid) insistence on the transitoriness of all pleasure, on death and decay, and mental purification as the only way to escape from it.

As Yoshikawa Kōjirō has shown,[27] the awareness of impermanence, the "fleeting life" with its sorrows and sad partings, had become a dominant theme in the Late Han period. Buddhism showed how this *vanitas* forms the very substance of all existence, and, at the same time, offered a way out which was comparatively simple: eternity could be gained by the radical destruction of all desire.

It did so, in this very early phase, without any tendency to compromise. It was not the semi-Taoist mongrel which it is sometimes held to be: on the contrary, it was not yet domesticated. It may therefore have recruited its first followers not from the many who expected familiar answers, but rather from marginal elements who were prepared to break with tradition. Therefore it was, in spite of its almost microscopic scale, a ferment in Late Han society. As a radically alternative way to individual salvation it reminds one of those alien and obscure cults which at the other end of the Euro-Asiatic continent, and roughly in the same period, became popular all over the Roman empire, and even of the "orientalizing" sub-cultures of our own age. The universality of the phenomenon may, after all, justify the attention we have given to the very first stage of Chinese Buddhism—that tiny exotic plant flowering on the ruins of the Han empire.

Notes

1. To give only one example: the ideal of supporting oneself by food-begging never became popular in China, in spite of the fact that it is very often referred to in the scriptures as an essential part of the monastic life.

2. "Late Han Vernacular Elements in the Earliest Buddhist Translation", *Journal of the Chinese Language Teacher's Association* 12.2 (October, 1977),. pp. 177-203.

3. Cf. my *Buddhist Conquest of China*, Leiden, 1959, pp. 30-31.

4. The first commentaries that quote or refer to Chinese Buddhist scriptures are T1694 *Yin chi ru jing zhu* (glosses on An Shigao's *Yin chi ru jing*, T 603, by a certain Chen Hui), and the anonymous glosses in the first chapter of T225, *Da mingdu jing*, wrongly attributed to Zhi Qian (cf. Lewis R. Lancaster, "The Chinese Translation of the *Aṣṭasāhasrikā-prajñāpāramitā-sūtra* attributed to Chih Ch'ien", *Monumenta Serica* 28 (1969), pp. 246-257).

5. The "Inscription of Laozi" (*Laozi ming*) of 165/166 AD by Bian Shao (incorporated in the *Lishi* by Hong Gua, ed., *Sibu congkan* p. 3.1a) is obviously a product of court literature, written in the over-ornate rhetoric style that was commonly used for such commenorative inscriptions. The *Liexian zhuan*, certainly not by Liu Xiang, but probably a Han work (as it is quoted twice by Ying Shao in his *Hanshu* commentary, second half second century AD), is written in regular *wenyan* without any trace of "vulgar" language. But even the three texts that at least by some scholars are associated with late Han popular Taoism: the *Taiping jing* and the *Xiang'er* and *Heshang Gong* commentaries on *Laozi*, are all written in a simple and artless but rather regular *wenyan*, and do not show any feature characteristic of the language of archaic Buddhist scriptures.

6. Cf. W.A.C.H. Dobson, *Late Han Chinese*, Toronto, 1964; Ushijima Tokuji, *Kango bumpō ron: chūko-hen*; Yoshikawa Kōjirō, "*Sesetsu-shingo* no bunsho", *Tōhōgaku* (Kyoto 10.2, 1939, pp. 86-110 (English translation by Glen Baxter, "The *Shih-shuo hsin-yü* and Six Dynasties Prose Style", *HJAS* 18, 1955, pp. 124-242); *id.*, "Rikuchō joji shōki", in Yoshikawa's Collected Works, *Yoshikawa Kōjirō zenshū*, vol. 7, Tokyo 1968, pp. 473-598; *id.*, *Bussetsu Muryōjugyō no bunshō*; Hong Cheng, "Lun Nanbeichao yiqian Hanyu de xici", *Yuyan yanjiu* 2, 1957, pp. 1-22; Liu Shiru, "Lüe lun Wei Jin Nanbeichao zidongci 'shi'-zi de yongfa", *Zhongguo yuyan* 66.12 (1957), p. 19-24.

7. T 1508 *Ahan koujie shi'er yinyuan jing*, which, as indicated by the title, appears to be an "oral explanation" of the Chain of Causation and some other related scholastic subjects, and T 602 *Da anban shouyi jing*, which partly consists of an early commentary on a text translated by An Shigao.

8. T224 *Daoxing jing*.

9. The work no doubt dates from the mid-third century, but it shows certain terminological peculiarities that plead against the attribution to Zhi Qian. Cf. the article by L.R. Lancaster referred to in note 4.

10. The term *xianguan* is used many times in Buddhist texts, and there invariably refers to the administrative officers, "the authorities", quite distinct from the supreme power of the sovereign (*wang*, *dawang*). This is even quite explicit in T 630 (*Chengju guangming dingyi jing*), p. 457.1: "If there is a worthy born into a noble family, who (later) is charged with general supervision over the (local) administrators ..." (*ruo you xianshi, sheng yu zhongxing zhi jia, tongling xianguan...*), and, *ib.*: "If a worthy has by his birth a (karmic) affinity with the administration .. ." (i.c. is destined to become a high official): (*xianshi sheng you xianguan zhi yinyuan...*). It is nowhere used for the person of the emperor, as is occasionally done in secular Han texts.

11. The text as we find it in the Korean recension of the Taishō canon (T 784) possibly is a redaction made by Zhi Qian in the period 220-250 AD; cf. Tang Yongtong, *Han Wei liang Jin nanbeichao fojiao shi*, Shanghai, 1938, pp. 38-39.

12. **b'jiəu-d'uo; *sang-muə*n; **i-p'uo-sə*k.

13. *Conghou shuojue* (**dz'iwät* apparently is a transcription of *gāthā*; the initial remains puzzling) in T150; cf. in T 607 the curious formula *Conghou fushushuo*, "The following is said in a bound (=metrical?) way". The common *jie* (**g'iät*) for *gāthā* occurs for the first time in Lokakṣema's *Banzhou sanmei jing* (T 418).

14. The Korean recension of T 418 is the only one in which the *prose* parts which render the *gāthās* of the original have been preserved (T 418, p. 906.1-2 and 907.2-3); in the other redactions they have been transposed into Chinese *gāthās* as well.

15. E.g. T 630, p. 453.2, a passage which reads like a Chinese essay:

"whilst dwelling in the house of instability/
his mind thinks of the protection (afforded by) Expediency"
"whilst staying in the pit of snakes/
his mind contemplates on the path of Abandonment ...

猗不固之屋，心思方便之護；
坐蛇蚖之地，心念捨遠之徑。

"

and so on, through a series of nine couples of paired phrases, interrupted, in true parallel style, by the words *Shigu kaishi*, "Therefore the Revealer ...", after which the 5-6 metre is resumed. 是故開士

16. For this term see V. Hrdličková, "The first translations of Buddhist sūtras in Chinese literature and their place in the development of story-telling", *Archiv Orientální* 26, 1958, pp. 114-144.

17. Clearly observable in the seven-syllable *gāthās* in Lokakṣema's *Banzhou sanmei jing* (T 418) of 179 AD, e.g. (p. 611.2),

般舟三昧經，佛語阿難，汝見不；五百人等在〃立；其心歡然歌頌曰：我等亦當逮得法

etc.

18. According to *Gaoseng zhuan* (T 2059, p. 324.3) An Xuan's collaborator Yan Foutiao was *śramaṇa*, a fully ordained monk. However, in the corresponding passage in *Chu sanzang ji ji* (T 2145, p. 96.1) it is only said that he had

"left the household", *chujia*, an expression that is also used for one who has joined the Order as a novice. In fact, the only work which he has produced independently was a treatise on the "Ten Rules for the Novice", cf. *Buddhist Conquest*, pp. 55-56.

19. Cf. note 4 above, and *Buddhist Conquest*, pp. 53-54.

20. The *Xiuxing benqi jing* is not mentioned by Sengyou in his *Chu sanzang ji ji*, but the authenticity of the text as a late Han translation is beyond all doubt. In the first place it forms a continuous whole with T 196 (the last paragraph of T 184 actually is repeated *verbatim* at the beginning of T 196); in the second place, its early date is proved by the fact that many passages from it have been incorporated into Zhi Qian's "polished" version of the Buddha's life (T 185, *Taizi ruiying benqi jing*), and, thirdly, the text contains a number of glosses introduced by the words *Han yan...*, which points to a date before 220 AD. T 196 is explicitly attributed to Kang Mengxiang and Zhu Tanguo in *Gaoseng zhuan* I, p. 324.3, probably on the basis of an early colophon.

21. Remark made by Dao'an, *yiyi liubian*, reported in *Chu sanzang ji ji* XIII, p. 96.1

22. An Shigao's biography in *CSDJJ* and *GSZ* is a mosaic of miraculous stories, some of which are extremely interesting. But some of An Shigao's supernatural powers (such as telling the future and understanding the language of the birds) are already described in Kang Senghui's preface to the *Anban shouyi jing* (*CSDJJ* VI 43.2), and this information was no doubt supplied by the three devotees from An Shigao's school who transmitted the scripture to him. And in an anonymous preface (the author only refers to himself as Mi—apparently his personal name) to Chen Hui's early third century commentary on the *Yin chi ru jing* (T 1694 p. 9.2), again from the same school, An Shigao is referred to as "a bodhisattva of universal manifestations" (*An hou Shigao zhe puxian pusa ye*). This may be mere rhetoric—but it could also be related to the curious stories about An Shigao's miraculous adventures in North, Central, and South China, in successive lives, such as we find in his GSZ "biography".

23. The female lay devotee should perform her religious observance three times a day, and each time "she should devoutly implore (the Buddha), always wishing to get rid of her female body" (致心懇惻，常願離於女人之身 TT 630, p. 457.2).

24. T 322, p. 16.2-3.

25. T 322, p. 17.2-28.1.

26. T 322, p. 18.1-3.

27. Notably in his brilliant analysis of the *Nineteen Old Poems* and their persistent theme of "sorrow at the passing of time": "*Suii no hiai (Koshi jūkyūshu no shudai)*", *Chūgoku bungakuhō*, 14, 1961, pp. 1-21.

Appendix
Buddhist Texts of the Later Han Period

I. Translations made by An Shigao (active ca. 150-170 AD)

I.1 T 13 *(Chang ahan) shi baofa jing*, 1 ch.
Classification of terms in groups of ten, with short explanation.

I.2 T 14 *Ren ben yu sheng jing*, 1 ch.
Explanation of the twelve members of the Chain of Causation.

I.3 T 31 *Yiqie liu she shou yin jing*, 1 ch.
Very short text explaining the way to extirpate the Impurities (*āsrava*).

I.4 T 32 *Si di jing*, 1 ch.
Exposition of the Four Noble Truths.

I.5 T 36 *Ben xiang yi zhi jing*, 1 ch.
Causal series leading from "bad company", via "unbelief", "wrong thoughts" ... to "desire", and the opposite series, leading from "good company" to "emancipation".

I.6 T 48 *Shi fa fei fa jing*, 1 ch.
Examples showing how the viruous monk will never boast of his religious attainments, and how he who is lacking in virtue will become arrogant, to his own detriment.

I.7 T 57 *Lou fenbu jing*, 1 ch.
Scholastic enumeration of the Impurities, Sense-desires, Feelings, Perceptions, etc., together with their causal factors and their bad consequences.

I.8 T 98 *Pu fayi jing*, 1 ch.
Various series of 12, 20, 16... etc. factors, every series being either conducive or obstructive to Emancipation.

I.9 T 112 *Ba zheng dao jing*, 1 ch.
The eight bad ways of action and the eight good ways of action that constitute the Eightfold Path.

I.10 T 150 *Qi chu san guan jing*, 2 ch.
A collection of 47 very short *sūtras*, 30 or which have their Pāli counterparts in the *Aṅguttara-nikāya*. Various numerical series of phenomena, actions, attitudes, and human types.

I.11 T 602 *Da anban shouyi jing*, 2 ch.
Treatise describing the practice of "Respiratory Concentration" (*ānāpāna-smṛti*), together with a commentary that has become inextricably mixed up with the text.

I.12 T 603 *Yin chi ru jing*, 1 ch.
Scholastic compendium dealing with sense-perception, the four bases of supernatural power, the five powers, etc.

I.13 T605 *Chanxing faxiang jing*, 1 ch.
Very short text containing a list of themes for contemplation.

I.14 T 607 *Daodi jing*, 1 ch.
Primitive translation of Saṅgharakṣa's *Yogācārabhūmi*, a treatise on *dhyāna*.

I.15 T 792 *(Fo shuo) fa shou chen jing*, 1 ch.
Very short text explaining how sexual desire obstructs the way to insight and true happiness.

I.16 T 1508 *Ahan koujie shi'er yinyuan jing*, 1 ch.
Commonly, but no doubt wrongly, attributed to An Xuan; the attribution to An Shigao made by Dao'an is substantiated by the terminology. An exegetical work explaining, *inter alia*, the Chain of Causation, the composition and functions of the body, the elements as the causes of diseases, etc.

II. Translations by Zhi Loujiachen (? Lokakṣema) (active ca. 170-190 AD)

II.1 T 224 *Daoxing (banruo) jing*, 10 ch.
The earliest translation of the "Perfection of wisdom in Eight Thousand Stanzas", *Aṣṭasāhasrikā-prajñāpāramitā*; the title is borrowed from the heading of the first chapter (*Daoxing pin*).

II.2 T 280 *(Fo shuo) dousha jing*, 1 ch.
Short *sūtra* containing a description of the miraculous apparition of Buddhas and Bodhisattvas from all directions of space and an enumeration of their names. The title is unexplained.

II.3 T 313 *Achu fo guo jing*, 1 ch.
"Pure Land"-type *sūtra* devoted to the glorification of Akṣobhya, the Buddha of the Eastern Paradise.

II.4 T 418 *Banzhou sanmei jing*, 3 ch.
The earliest version of the *Bhadrapāla-sūtra* (the title is a transcription of *Pratyutpanna-samādhi-sūtra*), dealing with the power of this *samādhi* that enables the devotee to visualize the Buddha Amitābha. Only the Korean recension of T 418 represents Lokakṣema's original translation; the other recensions contain a great number of interpolations and variants that probably were borrowed from a late third century version by Dharmarakṣa. In the Taishō canon this text is preceded by a shorter version (T 417, 1 ch.) with the same title and also bearing the name of Lokakṣema. Internal evidence proves that it actually is a later "polished" extract based upon T 418. A detailed study of the complicated textual problems is found in Paul Harrison, *The Pratyutpanna-buddha-saṃmukhāvasthita-samādhi-sūtra, an annotated English translation of the Tibetan version* (PhD. dissertation, A.N.U.), Canberra, 1979, Appendix A, esp. pp.200-235. Harrison concludes that chapters 1-6 of the Korean recension go back to Lokakṣema's original translation; that the prose of chapters 7-26 of all recensions may with some hesitation also be attributed to Lokakṣema, but that the *gāthās* are the work of a somewhat later hand. The text, with

which chapters 1-6 have been conflated is another early version; its attribution to Dharmarakṣa is rejected by Harrison on stylistic grounds.

II.5 T 458 *Wenshushili wen pusa shu jing*, 1 ch.
Exposition of the stages of the Bodhisattva career, explained in terms of the doctrine of universal Emptiness. The *sūtra* shows an interesting affinity with the *Vimalakīrti-nirdeśa*.

II.6 T 350 *Yi ri moni bao jing*, 1 ch.
Archaic translation of the *Kāśyapaparivarta*, about the Bodhisattva career and the doctrine of Emptiness.

II.7 T 626 *Azheshi wang jing*, 2 ch.
Mahāyāna treatment of the theme of King Ajātaśatru of Magadha being tortured by remorse after having killed his father; he is converted by the Bodhisattva Mañjuśrī.

II.8 T 807 *(Fo shuo) neizang bai bao jing*, 1 ch.
A mahāyānistic interpretation of the Buddha's life as a series of "magical performances" intended to lead all beings to salvation.

III. Translation by An Xuan and Yan Foutiao (active ca. 180 AD)

III.1 T 322*Fajing jing*, 1 ch.
Earliest translation of the *Ugra(datta)-paripṛcchā*, in which the Buddha explains the duties of the lay believer to the householder Ugra(datta), in Mahāyānistic terms.

IV. Translations by Kang Mengziang, Zhu Dali (? Mahābala) and Zhu Tanguo (? Dharmapala) (active ca. 200 AD)

IV.1 T 184*Xiuxing benqi jing*, 2 ch.
Account of the early part of the Buddha's career, from the prophecy of his future Buddhahood under Dīpaṃkara to the happenings in the first days after his Enlightenment.

IV.2 TT 196*Zhong benqi jing*, 2 ch.
Actually the second half of a continuous "life of the Buddha", of which T 184 is the first part. Account of the middle part of the Buddha's career, and some later episodes.

V. Translation attributed to Zhi Yao (late second century)

V.1 T 630 *Chengju guangming dingyi jing*, 1 ch.
Mahāyāna scripture treating two different subjects. The first part is devoted to the Six Perfections (*pāramitā*) and the "Mental Concentration of Integral Illumination". The second part contains a description of the moral and religious duties of various classes of lay devotees.

VI. Three archaic texts with doubtful attributions.

VI.1 T 105*Wu yin piyu jing*, 1 ch.
Very short text containing a number of stereotyped similes illustrating the unreality of the five constituent elements (*skandha*) of the pseudo-person. Attributed by Dao'an to An Shigao. The text is no doubt archaic, but style and terminology are definitly not those of An Shigao and his team.

VI.2 T 109*Zhuan falun jing*, 1 ch.
Archaic translation of the Buddha's first sermon held at Benares, with an introductory passage that does not appear in any other known version. Attributed by Dao'an to An Shigao, but the text contains stylistic features and *wenyan* admixtures that do not normally appear in An Shigao's translations.

VI.3 T 624*Dunzhentuoluo suo wen rulai sanmei jing*, 3 ch.
Archaic translation of the *Druma-kiṃnararāja-paripṛcchā*. Very elaborate text, largely consisting of numerical series, in which both the Buddha and King Druma (the ruler of the semi-human beings called *kiṃnara*) explain and glorify the Bodhisattva career and the Mahāyāna doctrine of universal Emptiness. The scripture culminates in the prophecy of King Druma's future Buddahood. Listed as "lost" by Sengyou (CSTJJ II, p. 6.2); in the *Kaiyuan shijiao lu* of 730 AD and later catalogues it is again mentioned as an existing text attributed to Lokakṣema. In view of the style and terminology it may certainly be regarded as a Han scripture, albeit with some hesitation as regards its attribution to Lokakṣema.

List of Characters

Achu fo guo jing 阿閦佛國經

Ahan koujie shi'er yinyauan jing 阿含口解十二因緣經

An Xuan 安玄

An Shigao 安世高

Anban shouyi jing 安般守意經

Azheshi wang jing 阿闍世王經

Ba zheng dao jing 八正道經

Banzhou sanmei jing 般舟三昧經

-bei 輩

Ben xiang yi zhi jing 本相猗(v. 倚)致經

benwu 本無

Bian Shao 邊韶

biqiu 比丘

Bussetsu Muryōjugyō no bunshō 佛說無量壽經の文章

-cao 曹

Chanxing faxiang jing 禪行法想經

(Chang ahan) shi baofa jing (長阿含)十報法經

chatu 刹土

Chen Hui 陳慧

Chengju guangming dingyi jing 成具光明定意經

chu yu 除欲

chue 除惡

chujia 出家

chujin 除饉

conghou shuojue 從後說絕

conghou fushushuo 從後縛束說

Da anban shouyi jing 大安般守意經

Da mingdu jing 大明度經

da-dao 大道

dao dizi 道弟子

Dao'an 道安

Daodi jing 道地經

Daoxing (banruo) jing 道行(般若)經

Daoxing jing 道行經

Daoxing pin 道行品

dawang 大王

-deng 等

di 帝

diyu 地獄

du 度

Dunzhentuoluo suo wen rulai sanmei jing
伅真陀羅所問如來三昧經

dushi wuwei 度世無為

*dz'iwät 絕

fa 法

Fajing jing 法鏡經

faze 法則

feixing huangdi 飛行皇帝

(Fo shuo) dousha jing
(佛說)兜沙經

(Fo shuo) fa shou chen jing
(佛說)法受塵經

(Fo shuo) neizang bai bao jing
(佛說)內藏百寶經

futu 浮屠

gougang 溝港

Han Wei liang Jin nanbeichao fojiao shi
漢魏兩晉南北朝佛教史

Han yan... 漢言

hengsha 恒沙

Hesang Gong 河上公

Hong Cheng 洪誠

Hong Gua 洪适

huanfu 還復

jie 偈

jie (*g'iät) 偈

jue 厥

jue* 絕

kaishi 開士

Kang Mengxiang 康孟詳

Kango bumpō ron: chūko-hen
漢語文法論：中古編

laoyue 牢獄

Laozi ming 老子銘

Liexian zhuan 列仙傳

Lishi 隸釋

Liu Shiru 劉世儒

Lou fenbu jing 漏分布經

Lüe lun Wei Jin Nanbeichao zidongci 'shi'-zi de yongfa
略論魏晉南北朝繫動詞「是」字的用法

Lun Nanbeichao yiqian Hanyu de xici
論南北朝以前漢語的繫詞

Mi 密

miao 廟

miedu 滅度

mingshi 明士

mo 沒

moru 沒入

nihuan 泥洹

Pu fayi jing 普法義經

pusa 菩薩

pusa-mohesa-moheyan-sengnie
菩薩摩訶薩摩訶衍僧那僧涅

Qi chu san guan jing 七出三觀經

Ren ben yu sheng jing 人本欲生經

Rikuchō joji shōki 六朝助字小記

ru 汝

rulai 如來

Rushi, shelifu, zhufo
如是,舍利弗,諸佛

rushi wo wen 如是我聞

Satuobolun 薩陀波倫

sangmen 桑門

Sengyou 僧祐

Sesetsu-shingo no bunsho
世說新語の文章

shanlai 善來

Shenjian 申鑒

shequ 捨去

shi 是

Shi fa fei fa jing 是法非法經

shigu 是故

Shigu kaishi 是故開士

Shishuo xinyu 世說新語

Shou yi 守意

Si di jing 四地經

si 斯

Sishierzhang jing 四十二章經

song 頌

songchu 送出

Suii no hiai (Koshi jukyushu no shudai)
推移の悲哀(古詩十九首の主題)

Taiping jing 太平經

Taizi ruiying benqi jing
太子瑞應本起經

Tang Yongtong 湯用彤

tian 天

Ushijima Tokuji 牛島德次

wang 王

weicengyou 未曾有

wen rushi 聞如是

Wenshushili wen pusa shu jing
文殊師利問菩薩署經

Wenwu guo 聞物國

wo 我

wu 無

Wu yin piyu jing 五陰譬喻經

wuyou 無有

Xiang'er 想爾

xianguan 縣官

xin qi xiang ze chi 心起想則癡

xinyi 心意

Xiuxing benqi jing 修行本起經

Xun Yue 荀悅

Yan Foutiao 嚴浮調

ye 也

yi 亦

yin 陰

Yi ri moni bao jing 遺日摩尼寶經

Yin chi ru jing 陰持入經

Yin chi ru jing zhu 陰持入經注

Ying Shao 應劭

yipusai 伊蒲塞

Yiqie liu she shou yin jing
一切流攝守因經

yiyi liubian 奕奕流便

yongshigu 用是故

Yoshikawa Kōjirō 吉川幸次郎

Yoshikawa Kōjirō zenshu 吉川幸次郎全集

Zhao Qi 趙岐

zhenru 真如

Zhi Loujiachen 支婁迦讖

Zhi Mindu 支敏度

Zhi Qian 支謙

Zhi Yao 支曜

Zhong benqi jing 中本起經

Zhu Dali 竺大力

Zhu Tanguo 竺曇果

Zhuan falun jing 轉法輪經

Zongli zhongjing mulu 總理眾經目錄

zuxingzi 族姓子